THE INTERIOR CASTLE

The Interior Castle

THE ART AND LIFE OF

Jean Stafford

ANN

HULBERT

1 9 9 2

ALFRED A. KNOPF   NEW YORK

FOR STEVE

Contents

Introduction

"I AM SO SICK of ... feeling that nothing I can possibly say ever can convey what it's like to be inside this particular skull," Jean Stafford once wrote to a close friend. She was sighing over the futility of psychiatry, to which she had had plenty of exposure, but her skepticism about the power of confession is also a warning about the difficulty of biography. Stafford's "interior castle," the image she borrowed from St. Teresa of Avila to symbolize the secret recesses within the skull, was a well-barricaded place.

What to make of her sense of isolation was perhaps the centrally painful, and inspiring, question that Stafford faced in her life, which began in 1915 and ended in 1979. Her characteristic stance was to be intensely protective of her privacy and solitude. That didn't mean she was quiet and retiring. On the contrary, she was readily distracted by friends, of whom she had many, and by larger social gatherings, at which she was renowned for telling long stories in her low, gravelly voice. But she saw to it that sociability was not the same thing as easy intimacy. Stafford had a "predilection for masks and disguises," as her close friend Howard Moss was far from the only one to notice. He was speaking literally, remembering one occasion when she had come to the door in a mask with a big red nose, and another when she appeared wearing a cocktail waitress's outfit, but he also meant it metaphorically. Stafford devoted a great deal of energy, some of it anxious but much of it comical and high-spirited, to playing out different personas.

Her "Lowell-to-Liebling-to-dowager mask," as another friend, Wilfrid Sheed, summed up her long-running public performance, mostly took the form of variations on the innocent child and the ironic spinster.

When Stafford looked back on her first marriage in 1940 to the poet and New England scion Robert Lowell, she generally cast herself as the provincial girl from Colorado. But after her divorce from Lowell in 1948 she also mastered the arch Bostonian lady, the well-pedigreed, imperious Puritan grande dame she never really had a chance to be. During her marriage to A. J. Liebling, the *New Yorker* writer, she was the innocent-savvy "reporter's moll, a kid you could take anywhere," as Sheed put it. And then when her husband died in 1963, she jokingly called herself "the Widow Liebling" and set about cultivating the pose of the eccentric rural recluse in East Hampton, where she lived out her life in a house that he had left to her.

Well practiced at maintaining a certain detachment in her personal life, at making intimacy an intricate and entertaining game, Stafford was even more vigilant about independence and self-protection in her literary life. It was again a somewhat paradoxical mission, since she certainly made no effort to avoid literary company. But whenever she faced an occasion to present some public statement about writing (which, though she disliked it, she intermittently did), she ended up delivering a lecture on the dangers of exhibitionism, the virtues of reticence, the snares of the literary world. She announced that she was against the fashion of being "forthrightly autobiographical," and that the most important lesson she had ever learned, from Ford Madox Ford, was that portraiture drawn too directly from life was "impolite and it's not fiction." In yet another talk, she attacked "the private-made-public life" of authors on the promotion circuit. And indirectly invoking St. Teresa's metaphor of the many-chambered inner castle, she offered her own vision of the quintessentially solitary act of creativity: "Writing is a private, an almost secret enterprise carried on within the heart and mind in a room whose doors are closed."

In a commemorative tribute given at the American Academy and Institute of Arts and Letters after Stafford's death, her longtime friend Peter Taylor perhaps best summed up her often perplexing determination to remain aloof. "Although it often may have seemed otherwise to those who didn't know her well," he said, "Jean set little store by the literary world. . . . It was only her work, not herself, that she wanted to deliver into the narrow ways of the literary world. . . . *She* remained a 'private person' (her phrase)." And as if that were not caution enough to a literary biographer, he went on to confess his suspicion that finally Stafford's private person remained a mystery. "Actually, what she was like when she sat down to write her wondrous novels and stories may be something beyond the comprehension of any of us," Taylor suggested as he looked back over her career. "In a sense, her literary personality remains her best kept secret. Perhaps it was in that role that she was the most private of private persons, and perhaps, in order to preserve that role, it was necessary for her to have the privacy she was always seeking."

My aim is to pursue the mystery of Stafford's literary personality, which means confronting just how complicated her creative identity was. Without claiming to penetrate that best kept secret, I hope the search casts some clarifying light into the rooms of her imagination. The route I have taken is through her writing, which suggests again and again that isolation is a state as much to be feared as sought after, and through her writing life, in which, despite her professed desire for distance from the literary world, she in fact energetically courted close literary connections. Stafford struggled outwardly to defend the quiet chambers of her castle, but she also struggled inwardly against a terror of loneliness and a destructive urge to succumb to the peace of isolation.

Charged by this tension, her life, though not publicly dramatic, and her work, though not prolific, continually strain against their ostensibly circumscribed boundaries. Beneath the carefully crafted surfaces, there are chasms; and the neat dichotomies—inner and outer, self and other—keep threatening to dissolve. Stafford resolutely refused to follow literary vogues, with the result that she wrote fiction that is anachronistic in the best sense. At the same time, both the independent course of her literary career and the idiosyncratic life of which it was a part offer a revealing perspective on an American literary generation in the middle of the century. In probing the problems of subjectivity, she avoided the confessional route favored by many of her much-read poetic contemporaries, which may have made her work seem dated then but has subsequently had the opposite effect. She couldn't help being wary of the notion of the declaratory self; she wasn't ready, however, simply to embrace the now-fashionable notion of the fragmented self. In her explorations of the mysteries of identity, Stafford managed to maintain a sense of their complexity, to resist facile confidence or skepticism about the power of the imagination. She was obsessed by the idea of an autonomous self at war with the outer world, but she also dared to admit the potentially illusory nature of that idea.

To understand the sense of marginality, personal and creative, that was at once a source of strength and a cause of deep insecurity for Stafford in her life as well as her art, it helps to situate her career in a wider literary milieu. The assertively maverick Stafford, whose provincial origins in the American West played such a large part in her self-definition, also saw to it that she found a place among writers who were shaping literary and critical debate and expectations in America. At twenty-four she married the promising poet Robert Lowell, and like him came of literary age with the New Critics as mentors and with a circle of intense young writers as friends. While their older guides—Allen Tate, Robert Penn Warren, John Crowe Ransom—were transforming the study of literature in American universities, Lowell and his contemporaries— Delmore Schwartz, John Berryman, Randall Jarrell—were embarked on feverishly creative but ill-fated courses, paths that hauntingly converged, earning the group the status of a tragic generation. Later Lowell wrote of himself and his fellow poets, "Yet really we had the same life, / the generic one / our generation offered."

Stafford's place in the circle, biographically and creatively, was an uneasy one. In a sense her life was not so different from that generic one of exhilarating heights and troubled depths. Like the poets, she stumbled early into fame. At twenty-nine she published *Boston Adventure* (1944) to great success, just before the start of Lowell's spectacular rise. By the time she left Lowell, her life looked as tragic as the rest of the poets' would soon look. Having smashed her skull in a car accident with Lowell a year before they married, she was in Payne Whitney with a mental breakdown two months after they separated. The insomnia, suicidal urges, emotional and physical illness, marital trouble, and alcoholism that in different ways plagued Lowell, Berryman, Schwartz, and even Jarrell never ceased to afflict her. Like them, she didn't hide her suffering; she could and did disrupt lives around her with her difficulties.

Yet her art, and her subsequent creative life, took a different direction. For Lowell and Berryman, suffering and writing became inextricably connected, the one unimaginable without the other, the turmoil fueling and fueled by the writing in an exhausting cycle. Stafford instinctively resisted any conflation of her life and her art or, just as important, of her identities as a woman and as a writer, as she made clear in a despairing letter to Lowell in 1947. "What do I care if Randall [Jarrell] likes my book?" she wrote to him:

> Or anyone? Why should it console me to be praised as a good writer? These stripped bones are not enough to feed a starving woman. I know this, Cal, and the knowledge eats me like an inward animal: there is no thing worse for a woman than to be deprived of her womanliness. For me, there is nothing worse than the knowledge that life holds nothing for me but being a writer.

After a brief unsuccessful marriage to Oliver Jensen, an editor at *Life* and then *American Heritage,* Stafford found a third husband in a literary enclave worlds away from the one in which she had begun. When she married A. J. Liebling in 1959, she was a happy woman for the first time, she said—and she all but ceased being a writer.

Clearly the divisions in her life were not actually as stark as she made out. Though she resisted conceiving of herself as a "woman writer" and made little effort to cement ties with other women writers or with anything that might be described as a feminine literary tradition (and though she was acerbic about the feminist movement late in her life), Stafford was intimately conscious of the pressures that male influence and expectation exerted on her. Her response was far from straightforward, which is just one reason to avoid schematically reducing her plight to the paradigm of victim and victimizer. She knew full well the allure of victimhood, as both her life and her fiction show. Yet for her, oppression raised questions first of all about the often perverse ways of the individual will, and only then about the peculiar susceptibility of women to domination.

Stafford's ambivalence about the power and the vulnerability of the isolated imagination is the presiding theme of her three novels, *Boston Adventure* (1944), *The Mountain Lion* (1947), and *The Catherine Wheel* (1952), which were highly acclaimed when they appeared. It was also an underlying preoccupation of the short stories that she published regularly during the 1940s and 1950s, mostly in *The New Yorker* and then in several collections, *The Interior Castle* (1953), *Children Are Bored on Sunday* (1953), *Bad Characters* (1964), and finally *The Collected Stories of Jean Stafford* (1969), which was awarded the Pulitzer Prize in 1970. Close to home though that theme was, Stafford consistently resisted the urge to frame it in confessional form. The work that she produced before she faced troubles with her fiction in the 1960s was worlds away from the increasingly autobiographical, less formally structured writing to which Lowell turned.

Perhaps the most disturbing and memorable quality of Stafford's art, which has won growing attention since her death, is the stylistic composure with which she unfolded a vision of profound psychic disequilibrium. "The esthetic distance she keeps between us and the untouchable otherness of her characters," Guy Davenport observed, is the source of great power in her evocations of disenchantment; "she does not allow us to violate their essential privacy with sentimentality or an easy understanding."

Insisting on impeccable formal control of her material, she probed the depths of private consciousness with psychological acuity, spiritual rigor, metaphorical inventiveness, and well-aimed wit. She also ventured onto social terrain, where again no detail escaped her scrutiny. There great temptations and even greater entrapments awaited her characters, who could hardly have been further from the image of the *poète maudit* made famous by her poetic contemporaries. Her protagonists—many of them female, all of them precariously poised, hungry for hope and a sense of belonging, and almost always disappointed in both—stand out for their ironic innocence, or more accurately for their innocent irony. With a childlike calm and clarity, Stafford looked into the abyss—and then wrote terrifying, tragicomic stories with titles like "Life Is No Abyss" and "Children Are Bored on Sunday."

And yet to emphasize only that concerted, accomplished effort at detachment is to simplify Stafford's effort to find both privacy and inspiration in her interior castle. All the while that she proclaimed loyalty to an impersonal aesthetic, learned from the New Critics among whom she began her career, she also waged an unceasing struggle to find fictional shape for some of her most troubling personal experiences—a struggle that helps explain why she all but stopped publishing fiction during the last two decades of her life. Though she knew her own imagination was threatened by her efforts to draw immediately from life, and though she disapproved of others' readiness to do just that, she couldn't resist trying again and again to convey more directly what it was like to be inside her "particular skull." For years she worked intermittently on a novel she called *The Parliament of Women,* which she described as her most autobiographical fictional endeavor, one that she promised would (among other things) cut up "the poets to a fare-thee-well." Gleefully she reported that "A well-known American poet, with whom I was once closely associated, is petrified. And well he should be!"

As it happened, that comically scathing account of her marriage to Lowell and its collapse was the only part of the stalled manuscript that was published during Stafford's life. Her longtime editor and friend Robert Giroux helped her excerpt it for publication as a story, "An Influx of Poets," in *The New Yorker* in 1978. By then Lowell was dead, so he never had a chance to read her version, which bore little resemblance to the assorted memories of their life together that he himself had committed to poetry over the years. The merciful nostalgia that often moved Lowell in memorializing his past was not a mood that came easily to Stafford.

But neither was "An Influx of Poets" simply a vehicle of revenge, as she had humorously hinted it might be. The struggle to free her imagination from bitterness, to find a liberating aesthetic distance, was all-consuming, and the last story that appeared in her lifetime was proof of the dauntingly high standards she had always set for herself. She ventured closer than ever before to intimate, painful facts of her life; and amid ruthless satire, of her young self and of the young poets, she found a way to cast a light of comic forgiveness on the scene. She wasn't after factual veracity, and she wasn't after agonized self-dramatization, and yet because she wasn't, she found both truth and tragedy.

Stafford's words, in her fiction and in her eloquent streams of talk, were rarely transparent windows onto anything so simple as the facts, which is one of the triumphs of her art and one of the frustrations and fascinations of her life. Those words are well worth listening to carefully, as Lowell himself, not long before he died, urged in a late poem, "Jean Stafford, a Letter":

> You have spoken so many words and well,
> being a woman and you . . . someone must still hear
> whatever I have forgotten
> or never heard, being a man.

PART I

Cowboys and Indians and Magic Mountains
1915–1936

CHAPTER I

California and Colorado

Toward the end of her life Jean Stafford claimed that she had a terrible dream eight nights in a row. In it she was coming downstairs to join her family for breakfast. The Colorado day was bright, and all the faces at the table were smiling at her. "If I have that dream again," she told her friend Wilfrid Sheed, "I'll go ab-so-lutely crazy." It was an ironic nightmare, perfect grist for the wry anecdotes at which Stafford excelled. But it was also truly a nightmare. Her exclamation was a rare confessional moment on a subject—the family she had left behind out West—that she usually did her best to skirt, either quietly or comically. It was hardly the whole story, of course, but the simple breakfast tableau summoned up Stafford's long, complicated past and her bitter ambivalence about her family. She couldn't forgive them for a hapless optimism that she felt had ruined all of their lives: those smiles masked disappointments that she, at least, had never gotten over. And yet there was also a hint of wistfulness about her exclusion from the circle in the kitchen. She stood apart, impatient to disown her past but lonely in her rootless pessimism.

Stafford told a little more of the story, in a similarly oblique but more literary way, in the author's note to her *Collected Stories* in 1969, which turned out to be a more definitive autobiographical statement than she perhaps expected. The collection was her last book and a Pulitzer Prize winner. There she implied that a deep homesickness propelled her writing, yet her nostalgia was anything but straightforward. Beneath her breezy salute to the West, where she had been born and raised, there was real disenchantment about her family, especially about her father, which she clearly felt had flavored both her life and her art.

She opened the author's note with a double-edged tribute to him: "By the time I knew him, my father was writing Western stories under the *nom de plume* Jack Wonder or, occasionally, Ben Delight," she wrote. "But before that, before I was born, he wrote under his own name and he published a novel called *When Cattle Kingdom Fell.*" In case anyone might mistake this for a loyal bow to her literary heritage, Stafford emphasized that it was only her father's title, not his text (which "to [her] regret" she never actually read), that inspired her, and then only in her youth, when she too wrote about Colt .45s and men with steely blue eyes.

Stafford's page-long note slyly undercut the conventional author's dedication. Perhaps she even had her father's inscription to *When Cattle Kingdom Fell* (1910) in mind. (She had surely gotten that far in the novel.) John Stafford had dutifully dedicated his only book to his father, Richard Stafford, "whose life-long interest and success in the cattle business, whose ideals and purposes in the world of men, furnished me with the materials from which this tale is drawn." Her own father's legacy was radically different: he had furnished droll, unworldly pen names and odd titles (she was fond of citing a work of his called "The Transmogrified Calf").

Stafford liked to suggest that her father's fanciful creations entranced her as a child and amused her in 1969, but the rest of the author's note revealed that the transition from discipleship to detachment was not so smooth. After a brisk sketch of her career—"as soon as I could," she wrote, "I hotfooted it across the Rocky Mountains and across the Atlantic Ocean"—Stafford's preface wound down on a more uneasy note: she had hurried away from home after college hoping to discover her identity, only to lose it. She rejected the romanticized Old West her father wrote about and also the more recent "tamed-down" West of her youth. Yet she never completely escaped. "My roots," she wrote, "remain in the semi-fictitious town of Adams, Colorado," a less than idyllic place that played an important role in her fiction. And she wasn't sure where her whole self belonged: "The rest of me may abide in the South or the Midwest or New England or New York." The truth was, she didn't "abide" anywhere. Invoking Mark Twain and Henry Adams as incongruous literary kin, she confessed to a sense of "dislocation" that had no cure. She was like her characters, who "are away from home, too, and while they are probably homesick, they won't go back." Stafford made sure that she returned home rarely: between her graduation from college and her parents' deaths, she saw her father four times, briefly, over thirty years and her mother twice in ten years.

In private, Stafford exposed the real animus behind the backhanded acknowledgment of paternal influence in her preface. In a letter to her oldest sister written in the same year as the author's note, 1969 (three years after John Stafford's death at the age of ninety-one), she was outright belligerent on the subject of her father, as she often was with her two older sisters, Mary Lee and Marjorie, who had stayed out West and been steady daughters to the end. "*When Cattle Kingdom Fell* is back from the binder," Stafford reported to Mary Lee, who lived with her husband, Harry Frichtel, on a cattle ranch in Hayden, Colorado. "I am still unable to read that book and I'm not going to try again. What a waste! Obviously he was gifted but he was completely undisciplined and completely lazy and completely self-indulgent and I can't forgive him." Stafford could hardly have been less eager to praise his "ideals and purposes in the world of men."

John Stafford's literary legacy was only half of the burdensome inheritance he bequeathed his daughter. His eccentric writing career had gone hand in hand with financial disaster, which had radically unsettled his family's life. The other part of the story, which Stafford left out of her preface and to which she silently alluded in her letter to her sister, was that her father had squandered his inheritance from his father, a prosperous cattleman who died in 1899—and it had been considerable. (In 1920, her father's stocks, bonds, and real estate, she later estimated, were worth almost three hundred thousand dollars.)

In 1910, when he wrote his grateful dedication to Richard Stafford in *When Cattle Kingdom Fell,* John Stafford was still in clover. He was, as he said, well furnished with the materials from which his tale was drawn. He had plenty of Wild West lore to propel his plots. And thanks also to the exploits of his father, an Irishman who had emigrated at eighteen and amassed cattle land in the Texas Panhandle, in Arizona, and in Missouri, John Stafford had money and land to support a leisurely writing career—as well as a family. Three years earlier he had married Ethel McKillop. He had met her in Tarkio, Missouri, while she was taking summer courses and he was living there in a rented house with his mother, Phoebe Ann Wilson Stafford, a severe woman committed to the temperance movement, women's suffrage, and later Christian Science. Their marriage took place in nearby Rock Port, where Ethel had grown up and where her father, Malcolm McKillop, had been a prominent lawyer and served as mayor and a member of the Missouri legislature.

Born in Canada, the son of Scottish Presbyterians who had left the Isle of Arran around 1830, Malcolm McKillop had abandoned the farming life of his father. With his wife, Carrie Lee Thurber McKillop, he had raised four daughters in a Victorian house called Maple Lawn, in surroundings as genteel as John Stafford's youth had been rugged. (John liked to claim that one day when he was a boy Jesse James had arrived in the Staffords' dusty yard asking for a place to sleep.) The marriage of thirty-one-year-old Ethel and thirty-two-year-old John, as Jean Stafford later portrayed it, was a union of paleface and redskin clans—of prim pillars of the community and independent-minded adventurers. Like his daughter, John Stafford was inclined to be condescending about the tame McKillops. But as he settled down to family life and the pursuit of fiction in 1907, the provincial gentility of his new circumstances must have been appealing. He had every reason to think that a lifelong interest and success (to echo his tribute to his father) awaited him in his business, which would be writing rather than ranching.

It seemed that he was at last on his way, after a somewhat meandering start. John Stafford had majored in classics at Amity College in College Springs, Iowa, and then spent some time as a cowpuncher in the Texas Panhandle. Following a stint as a reporter for the *Chicago Sun* and a New York City newspaper, he had returned to Missouri in 1899 when his father died, and had worked briefly for the telephone company in Tarkio. A fellow journalist and friend urged him to come back to the big city and "get down to what he called business," John Stafford remembered later, but he "couldn't see it." Instead, blessed with land and money from his father, he stayed on with his mother and tried his hand at writing in a more imaginative vein. He managed to sell some stories, which marked his debut in the genre of frontier adventure and humor. John Stafford clearly enjoyed his pen names; it's not hard to detect an ironic streak in the cowboy fiction of this erstwhile classicist who took evident pride in avoiding ordinary "business" for a more eccentric career path. Eleven years later he had a novel, full of quick-on-the-draw drama and a dash of comedy, to show for his pleasant labors, and he had a very solicitous, proper wife and a family.

Ethel McKillop, who after two years of college had begun teaching school, first in Rock Port, Missouri, and then in Salida, Colorado, had been more than ready to embark on married life. The Staffords settled in Tarkio and began having children almost immediately, first Mary Lee in 1908, then Marjorie in 1909. John Stafford continued his agrarian existence, scribbling away and supervising the family lands from a distance, while his wife tended an immaculate house, cooked energetically, and kept in close touch with her relatives. A son, Dick, was born in 1911, and soon after that John Stafford left Tarkio with his family and headed for California, part of the more general migration westward at that time. The Staffords evidently had in mind a fresh start that nonetheless didn't mean abandoning kin altogether. John's mother and sister had already moved to Los Angeles, and an uncle and two aunts of Ethel's (Malcolm McKillop's siblings) lived in San Diego. With some of his inheritance, John Stafford bought ten acres of land in Covina, not far from Los Angeles, on which he planned to start a walnut farm.

At the Covina ranch he set about custom designing an agrarian idyll. He ordered a large house built, installed solar collectors on it, put prismed glass in the big front door, and planted a line of midget palm trees along the front of the land. There was a Japanese servant to help with the walnuts, the wash, and the housework, about which Ethel Stafford was fanatical. Inside, rough-hewn native trophies—Indian baskets and an old Indian tomahawk, Mexican serapes, a pair of sabers, John Stafford's cowboy spurs and wide cartridge belt—were displayed next to shelves of Dante, Dickens, Shakespeare, Balzac, Voltaire, Mark Twain, Robert Louis Stevenson, lots of children's books, and the *Encyclopaedia Britannica*. While his wife dedicated herself to the domestic order, John Stafford continued to write, not only stories but also short diatribes on assorted political, social, and economic issues, which editors routinely rejected. He read his work aloud as he went along (to himself or to any listener he could corral), undistracted by the hens that sometimes flew in the window of his room. In that house, on July 1, 1915, Jean Wilson Stafford was born and lived for the next five years.

"Our days on the ranch were idyllic," is the way her sister Marjorie Stafford Pinkham remembered Covina in an account of their youth, the fullest record of those early years. Her memoir conjured up a portrait of childhood bliss, siblings at play in a natural paradise presided over by a dreamy but not impractical father and a nurturing mother. The older sisters doted on their pretty baby sister, lavishing attention on her and only occasionally teasing her. Dick was quickly fond of her, though he was famous in the family for having greeted Jean's arrival into the world with "She's all right, I guess, but I wish she'd been a dog." (As family

lore had it, all the children, unaware that their plump mother was pregnant, were told that a surprise awaited them; a dog was Dick's hope, and
Mary Lee and Marjorie had a long list of treats in mind.) The two
younger children shared a room in the big house and became devoted
companions.

Jean's version was different. Though late in life she too described a
scene of "pastoral serenity" in a draft of a speech she never gave, a hint of
family disharmony and personal estrangement cast its shadow. The Staffords were in California because her father had "uprooted himself and
my mother and my sisters and my brother," and she, though the coddled
baby, was also disappointed:

> On the lippia lawn there grew an umbrella tree under which I
> could stand in the afternoon waiting for Dick and Margie and
> Mary Lee to come home on the bus from the one-room school-
> house, bringing me presents of stolen paper-clips and rubber bands.
> I collected the paper-clips like the pampered daughters of doting
> daddies in the fatuous books my sappy sisters read; these little prin-
> cesses, on birthdays and at Christmas, were given a pearl; eventu-
> ally, if they lived long enough, they had an Add-a-Pearl necklace.
> By the time I was three, going on four, I had two and a half full-
> length Add-a-Paper-Clip necklaces.

The slightly mocking tone of the portrait indicated Stafford's retrospective sense of the inadequacy of the idyll. The small girl she described
made do with mere paper clips and had no hope of pearls. In much
darker memories, Stafford's most remote past was haunted by a lurking
fear that perhaps everyone in the family had been wanting something
very different from a new baby.

Her real fall from innocence, she suggested in a short story she wrote
as an older child, came after Covina. "There is a drama in the life of
every child, and tragedy that grownups can never know," she wrote
grandly in one of her youthful, autobiographical efforts at fiction. "He
who has not felt the sharp edge of drama cutting clean through his body
between the ages of three and eight has never had the right to call himself experienced." For Stafford the decisive drama of loss began when she
was five. In 1920 John Stafford sold the walnut ranch. Convinced he
could make a killing in the stock market, he moved his family to a house

in San Diego so that he could be near the exchange there. Within a year, he had lost all of his money. In 1921 the Staffords packed up and headed for Colorado in a heavily laden car. The trip was billed as adventure and a quest for a healthier climate, but it looked more like flight from the scene of catastrophe. And as Stafford remembered it later in an essay, the new physical setting struck her as anything but bracing: "The Rocky Mountains were too big to take in, too high to understand, too domineering to love; the very spaciousness of the range and of the limitless prairies to the east turned me claustrophobic."

After a brief pause in Pueblo and four years in Colorado Springs, the family moved to Boulder in 1925 so that Mary Lee—and then Marjorie and, in 1932, Jean—could afford to go to the University of Colorado there. (Dick went to Colorado A & M in Fort Collins.) Granted scholarships, they lived at home—in a full house. To help make ends meet during hard times made harder by the Depression (and by Grandmother Stafford's growing disinclination to help out her son), Ethel Stafford at first thought of running a tearoom, then began taking in students as boarders. What her mother undertook in a spirit of mostly cheerful resourcefulness, well practiced over the years since they had left California, Jean Stafford suffered with deep embarrassment. Much of her mortification was social: renting out rooms to condescending sorority girls was hard for an acutely status-conscious adolescent to bear.

But what Stafford saw as the undermining of her home also roused a deeper sense of humiliation. She blamed her parents, though she was hardly consistent in her condemnations. She was full of resentment toward her unintellectual, supremely domestic mother, who seemed too reconciled to a lot that her daughter deemed beneath them. At the same time, she herself knew the allure of fastidious domesticity; years later she wrote of a character, drawn from her own experience, that "in truth [she] would have liked to pause here in this female precinct where the winter sunlight discovered her [mother's] impeccable housekeeping." However philistine, Ethel Stafford's carefully tended domain of order stood in striking contrast to John Stafford's increasingly disheveled life and futile literary labors. He sold less and less of his work, and in Boulder he became more bitter and reclusive. As Stafford later described it, he was always holed up in the basement venting his spleen or spinning out some fantasy while the rest of the family coped:

My father . . . cursed the stock exchange . . . and cursed the editors
who would not buy his stories. My father believed . . . that his failure could be attributed to the degeneracy of the modern world. . . .
My father, a small poor friendless man, believed he cut quite a figure in the world.

For fifteen years he sat before the typewriter, filling page after
page. . . . We bought our father postage and paper; my mother
spared his feelings; we believed he was an artist.

Stafford started out as an admirer of her father. That didn't preclude
ambivalence, as it rarely does for complicated children, and certainly
John Stafford was a complicated father. He was the artist in the family,
and he was its betrayer. He was the high-minded scholar-in-residence
("his mind was an orderly and vast storehouse of information on almost
any subject," Marjorie wrote in her memoir), and he was the increasingly
moody, irascible character in the basement. He had been a man with a
mission—an agrarian ideal of life—who had been reduced to a man
haunted by visions of persecution. And yet he himself seemed unmoved
by the disparities: he just kept on typing, as though at some point deliv-
erance would come and he would be discovered. "She was nearly always
furious with him or afraid of him and nearly always admired him, but
she did not associate these feelings with hate or love," Stafford wrote later
of her autobiographical persona in a draft of *In the Snowfall,* the novel
about her life that she began in the mid-1940s. She never finished it,
largely because she failed to establish imaginative or emotional distance
from her material—which makes it a particularly revealing biographical
source. The raw novel, though hardly a repository of reliable facts about
her youth, is one record of her struggle for perspective on her family,
especially her father. "It was not a question of loving or not loving him
(what that meant precisely she didn't know); he was a fact, or rather a set
of contradictory facts as permanent a feature in her life as the trees in the
backyard."

It was, however, a question of imitating him: "It never occurs to her
that she will not be a writer and only occasionally does it occur to her,
depressingly, that she is going to grow into a woman, not a man." According to Stafford's usual version of the family alignments, there was a
battle of the sexes, and of sensibilities, and she sided with the men. For
the most part, her mother—whom she cast as the genial, prosaic house-

wife in the novel—was a model of what Stafford strove to avoid, down-playing any inclinations in that direction (though she clearly had them: she zealously tended her bedroom, which shifted depending on the number of boarders in residence, re-creating a corner of cozy domesticity every time). She was the family's "problem feeder," the alienated last child who resisted maternal nurturing and sisterly bonding. Instead, she struggled for the affections of her brother and the approval of her literary father.

But the struggle was far from straightforward, her allegiance far from steady. Later, in her moments of most Olympian bitterness, she claimed that she didn't side at all. She watched them all from a withering distance. "The Stafford-McKillop predilection for complaint, for perpetually blaming others for their misfortunes and even for the *accidents* that befall them," she raged in a letter to Marjorie in the 1960s, "is one of the many reasons that for all practical purposes I left home when I was 7." At the same time, she herself was known for complaining about exactly the opposite: she blamed them for their infuriating habit of hoping for the best, her father forever pounding away at his typewriter, her mother forever cleaning and looking at the bright side of things.

Marjorie's own cheerier view of the Boulder years provides a useful contrast to Stafford's agonized reflections. In her distinctly more nostalgic version, the household was not divided but gathered in solidarity around an admittedly strange but also engaging character. Her chatty memoir and subsequent reminiscences leave the impression that John Stafford's high intellectual expectations and verbal energy set the tone in the family, and that his subsequent troubles were a source of pity more than outrage. It seems that relations with his much more conventional wife were, not surprisingly, strained at times. His high-minded refusal to assume any practical responsibility for their situation imposed an enormous burden on her. But her resentment at the patronizing treatment and the hardship seems to have been leavened by more than mere tolerance of her maverick husband's expectations. She too, a practiced storyteller from a well-read family, was eager in her own genteel way not simply to feed but to cultivate her children. When Grandmother Stafford impatiently urged that her grandchildren be sent to work after high school, her son refused, and Ethel Stafford gamely managed: her boardinghouse made possible their college educations.

Marjorie's account suggests that her youngest sister's plight was per-

haps not as distinctive as Jean liked to imply, which makes the quality
and intensity of her response to it all the more notable. As Marjorie
portrayed the family, all three daughters, not just the last, were under
their father's sway—especially Mary Lee, who was his first disciple in
the family, an avid reader and budding writer as a child and later an
excellent college student. Marjorie's foray into print stands as her own
proof of the family's literary self-conception (though she had started out
wanting to be an artist); in her prose, with its slightly mannered blend of
provincial conventionality and idiosyncratic quaintness, McKillop and
Stafford styles seem to mix. As for Dick, his response to the paternal
presence emerges as a quietly graceful escape: he pursued the time-
honored Stafford path, away from words and into the wilderness. But
unlike his more aggressive forebears, he cultivated a naturalist's detachment, leaving the family house on the Boulder hillside whenever he
could to hike and explore in the surrounding mountains. To his father's
disappointment, Dick wouldn't take a gun.

That perhaps the youngest Stafford was more aloof, somehow more
troubled early on by the family's trials, emerges even from Marjorie's
genial account. "Jean was a quiet child who did not whine, yell, or have
tantrums like the rest of us. She usually waited to voice protests until she
had thought of something incisive and withering to say." As Stafford
herself told it, words were her recourse very early on. They were evidently at once a refuge in her loneliness and a way of encountering her
father on his own ground. Stafford later said that she "pledged allegiance
to the English language," which was the guiding light of John Stafford's
life, and her verbal precociousness was a source of pride within the family. It seems to have counted for less in her relations with her brother,
Dick, though she rarely offered more than abstract testimonials of her
youthful devotion to him. Perhaps the most vivid image of their friendship, captured in a photograph that became very important to her, was of
happily united action, rather than combative speech: Jean, small and
smiling blissfully, riding on the back of her brother's bicycle, confidently
holding on to him. "Sometimes when my eye falls on it," she wrote later,
"I go rather funny in the head at the spectacle of such joy."

But her most reliable source of pleasure, and of self-confidence, was
language. In retrospect Stafford emphasized how physical her early engagement with words had been. She liked to claim that she had learned
Braille in kindergarten (though her family told her she must have been

remembering an abacus), and her first novel, a thriller written in seventh grade and set in the British Museum, was memorable for its form not its substance: "I typed it all out in upper case letters on the biggest and oldest and loudest typewriter ever seen. . . . I filled in the punctuation by hand with colored pencils." Under her father's influence, she developed the taste for the incongruous textures of language that became a hallmark of her virtuosic style. She learned some Latin, read his favorite highbrow and lowbrow authors, and pored over the dictionary, cultivating a vocabulary as exotic and as colloquial as his.

By high school she had also cultivated a tone of arch irony and a prose of strident individualism rather like her father's. (Even in elementary school, she apparently took pains to stand out, and John Stafford was the inspiration: a friend, Howard Higman, remembered her walking from school, slowly and awkwardly, dragging her father's saber with her.) At Boulder State Preparatory School, which she attended from 1929 to 1932, Stafford was a good student (except in math) and above all a conspicuous nonconformist—though you wouldn't guess it from a demure photograph, probably a school portrait, of sixteen-year-old Jean, her face looking innocently pretty above the ruffled collar of her dress. She was a member of a small group of self-styled literati who favored exotic reading (O'Neill, Boccaccio's *Decameron,* Voltaire's *Candide,* as Higman recalled) and conducted "Voltaire dinners," which they did their best to make decadent affairs (held at midnight, mothers' permission required). As part of her antiphilistine style, she disdained physical fitness and made resistance to gym a vigorous cause. Her chief extracurricular activity, predictably, turned out to be the school newspaper, the *Prep Owl,* which she joined at the urging of the editor, who was impressed by several pieces she submitted.

Those signs of confident independence, though, were far from the whole story. The sense of unbridgeable loneliness and insecurity that she later traced all the way back to her babyhood was clearly a burden particularly during adolescence. At home, Stafford could now claim more of the solitude she wanted, since her siblings were leaving one by one (Mary Lee to teach school in Hayden, where she promptly got married; Marjorie to teach on an Indian reservation in Oklahoma; Dick to college), but she was evidently more, rather than less, unhappy. With her friends from school—she had some, not many—she tended to be reserved, skirting real intimacy. She apparently felt more comfortable when conversation was impersonal, and although she had a ring that she reportedly bestowed on whatever male classmate was currently in favor (Higman had it for a while; so did the editor of the school paper), she was interested in intellectual companionship, not romantic involvement. Her suitors didn't challenge her desires. Behind Stafford's detachment seems to have lurked a defensive secretiveness about her life at home, above all about the man in the basement. Almost none of her friends ever saw the inside of her house. Anyone who walked with her from school was firmly discouraged from accompanying her all the way home.

But if scrawny, tobacco-chewing John Stafford in the flesh was a secret she did her best to keep hidden away, in spirit her father was still a dominant force for her, especially in her writing. In an editorial in the *Prep Owl* in 1931, her junior year, Stafford displayed a maverick style that was clearly modeled on his and aired the kind of aggressively unconventional views of which he would have approved. Her denunciation of the philistine aspirations of the social elite of the school, which she presented under the pseudonym Vox Populi, created a stir, and everyone at Boulder Prep guessed who had written it. Stafford was brutal about the rest of her schoolmates, especially the girls, whom she called

> a race of social-climbing sniggering hypocrites. . . . [T]hey fear individuality. . . . [If I were a mother] I would dress my daughter in sack cloth and ashes and compel her to read Pilgrim's Progress. . . . I'm strong for university education for women but not for women like these because they don't want education. They're going to make sorority, to probably flunk out of school to give their lives a collegiate air and to return fine and polished young Americans.

Stafford was taking on not only her classmates (given that she still had a year to go, it was proof of her willingness to be unpopular), but also her conformist mother and sisters, who saw nothing wrong with sororities. In fact, her struggle with her family had been the implicit, and sometimes very explicit, theme of much of her writing ever since she had begun producing stories (probably in junior high school, though few are dated). She specialized in melodramatic declarations of pained isolation from a conventional world, which usually meant the female side of her family. Yet very early on, she also seemed to appreciate the disproportion of her estrangement and to see the juxtaposition of her histrionic alienation and her perfectly friendly family as an occasion for irony at her own expense. Even as the self-important Vox Populi, she used exaggerated rhetoric to make herself sound slightly ridiculous—just the kind of nut she knew her classmates would dismiss. In her youthful stories about a family named Smith, which closely resembled her own, she routinely deflated her characters' flamboyant declarations of martyrdom. "It wasn't everyone who had suffered so. And she so young!" exulted a character called Sarah, who had just announced that "her family was her barrier to happiness." Polly, Sarah's younger sister, promptly undermined that self-dramatizing despair, commenting on all her relatives, including her sister: "They were asses. They were so stupidly serious." In other stories about the Smiths, Stafford portrayed Ursula, the baby (her counterpart), as a forlorn creature—but also made fun of her often theatrical unhappiness.

Above all, Stafford's exaggerated irony was a way to emulate her father's peculiar literary enterprise, even as she mocked it. When she was about fifteen she poked fun at their common, undisciplined approach to their literary occupation in a humorous portrait called "Fame Is Sweet to the Foolish Man," about a summer trip she and her father had taken to a cabin in the mountains. They intended to spend the vacation writing, promising their family that "before August was over we would have gained national recognition for our outstanding work in the literary field. . . ." Instead they were seduced from thoughts about "the philosophy of the short story and the movement of the drama to the extraordinarily inviting snow-capped peaks and cool shaded lakes." In another story, she described Mr. Smith huddled in the basement "pounding out 'shorts' and 'squibs' on an ancient Remington. . . . Mr. Smith was always surprised and flattered when he received a check. He would chew a match thoughtfully and say, 'May Plutus be praised.' He was never quite sure about his classical references but since the rest didn't know the difference he could consult Bullfinch [*sic*] before he said anything else. . . ."

Stafford sometimes focused her wit not on her father himself, but on his incongruous fixations—Latin and bizarre tall tales. In "Our Latin Teacher," she facetiously celebrated an implausible romance between two Latin teachers, who fall in love "with only the true passion that a hysteron proteron can inspire, happy mortals that they were in comparison to us who had never felt our heartstrings pulled by the sight or the sound of Latin rhetoric." At thirteen, in "Miss Lucy," she produced a curious narrative in colloquial dialect, which was a specialty of her father's and which continued to fascinate her throughout her writing career. Told from the perspective of an innocent boy, it featured his extremely odd relative Lucy, who was "the most imaginative of all our family. She always is or has a new character and she keeps us in gales of laughter from dawn to night. She is far from insane but to one who does not know her peculiar manners, she gives that impression." Outlandish Lucy sounds like a not-so-distant relative of Stafford's father, or an imagined version of Stafford herself grown up.

Flattering her father by imitation, Stafford's humor at his expense seems to have amused him—which was at least in part what she intended. The spirit of their curious literary alliance (and an augury of its evolution) was captured by a photograph that John Stafford made a point of showing, roughly thirty years after it was taken, to Stafford's second husband, Oliver Jensen, with whom he carried on a brief correspondence:

> I am sending you just as soon as I can locate it my favorite picture of her. She knows what it is. She was about 12 or 13 when I took it. She had come into my basement yarn factory dressed up as a young man sporting my own blackthorn stick and by the Powers she did such a whale of a good job of impersonating, I didn't know who the Devil [*sic*] that for a fleeting instant it was given to me to believe or at least to hope that I was being honored by the very personable agent of some hopeful editor who had heard of me but who had never seen any of my stuff. When I came out of my trance I took the picture of her and we were both hilariously proud of it for a long time. But in time her enthusiasm for it weakened while mine increased.

It was an odd scene, re-created in John Stafford's self-consciously colloquial style. In part it was evidently wish-fulfilling fantasy, as Stafford played up to her father's literary hopes and he eagerly succumbed. The picture, to judge by his fondness of it, evoked the closeness of their relationship, perhaps shortly before it began to erode; though his daughter was on the brink of adolescence, her childhood devotion was still in evidence. Yet the photograph also conveyed a joke. Certainly in retrospect John Stafford was making fun of himself; with his "yarn factory" and his "trance," he was acknowledging his delusions of literary grandeur. Stafford, too, surely had had mockery in mind, of herself as well as of her father, when she came down to the basement all dressed up for a charade based on the ludicrous expectations they both cultivated.

Just how far she could go mocking him by his own lights she showed in her first published writing a few years later, in 1930, when she was fifteen. "Disenchantment" is an ironic tale of her family's disillusioning trip from California to Colorado. The essay, which won the annual state high school contest, was published in the Boulder *Daily Camera* and prefaced by the announcement that "her father is a noted author." Whether or not Stafford appreciated the implication of direct paternal influence, her father was the unspoken subject of the essay and one of his favorite authors, Mark Twain, was the implicit model. *Roughing It* (one of the books at Stafford's bedside when she died) lurked as the evident inspiration for the anticlimactic adventure story.

In her prize-winning essay, Stafford had not picked an easy subject. The trip, which was the turning point of her childhood, marked her father's fall. She was oblique about it: John Stafford didn't figure in the essay, and there was no clue as to why the family in her story was on the move. But her theme—ridicule of a romanticized vision of the West—was an implicit comment on his failed dreams of writing frontier fiction in golden California. Her young narrator, like Twain's, was bursting with expectations of adventure in the Wild West, which she knew only (and erroneously) from books. Twain's naïvely eager narrator started out envying his brother's expedition to establish himself as secretary of the Nevada Territory: "Pretty soon he would be hundreds and hundreds of miles away on the great plains and deserts, and among the mountains of the far West, and would see buffaloes and Indians, and prairie dogs and antelopes, and have all kinds of adventures, and maybe get hanged or scalped and have ever such a fine time." Stafford opened on a similar note:

The Reo was packed to bursting. Its generous bosom was swelling with camp cots and army blankets and us, dismally resplendent in sickish looking khaki and tennis shoes which, unasked, turned up at the toes. Despite our funeral [*sic*] externalities, we were jubilant, rollicking, noisily happy. Our family was leaving San Diego for that land of adventure, that storied country where life and death hung in the balance, where college professors wore chaps, and where barbers were unnecessary because of the abundance of Indians who scalped you gratis, namely, Colorado.

Like Twain's, her style relied on exuberant overstatement and an incongruous vocabulary, and her device was episodic deflation of fantasy— and then deflation of disillusionment: "How we suffered, suffered, suffered!" Twain's narrator exclaimed, and Stafford's echoed the theatrical disappointment when the West proved drab. She and her siblings were devastated in a very grand manner: "Our beautiful dreams were shattered. . . . A tragedy was this scarcely less than Shakespearean. Ah, yes, what pain we have suffered."

Stafford allowed the satire of her father to get quite sharp. Unlike Twain's narrator, who was leaving behind "years of tiresome city life" in Missouri and who ultimately reached a shining San Francisco, Stafford's had come to Colorado from that coast and wasn't going back. "We were dismayed to think that we had left the place where we might rise before our neighbor and steal oranges from his grove with wicked satisfaction, where one might stare enchanted and terrorized at jelly-fish. . . . That we had left all these joys for something far more stupid and dusty was a thing incredible." The blame was laid very close to home: "It was monstrous that we had been tricked by Tom Mix and Zane Grey and all the others whose bloated fancies have produced such glamorous exaggerations." Jack Wonder and Ben Delight were implicitly indicted along with Grey, the classic Western yarn spinner.

Yet with Twain as an intermediary and model, Stafford could suggest a kind of camaraderie of irony: she was drawing on an approved tradition of mockery, to which her father himself subscribed. And she closed the essay with a lesson that suggested solidarity with her nonconformist father. She refused to let the disillusioning world convert her to censorious realism or genteel hypocrisy. She too could cultivate rebellious distance. Here she was, after all, winning the state essay contest with a piece that slandered the state. "Sighing, we accepted the conventionalities of the lied-about state, sealed the wounds of our disenchantment. . . ." The self-proclaimed tragic members of this family had learned to minimize their material disappointment and to be "celestial spirited"—a lesson her unconventional, head-in-the-clouds father himself might have taught.

THROUGHOUT HER LIFE, Stafford's invocations of Twain, explicit and implicit, were an important part of her attempt to make some sense of the legacy of literary eccentricity and provincial poverty bequeathed by her father. Twain's spirit and his satiric, colloquial American voice preside over her juvenilia, the short stories about Adams, Colorado, of her middle career, and some of the journalism of her last years.

She went so far as to suggest, directly and indirectly, affinities between her cowpuncher-newspaperman-writer father born in Missouri, and the steamboat pilot–newspaperman–writer from the same state who had become famous while John Stafford was a boy. In an outline of the "people of the narrative" for *In the Snowfall,* she described the character modeled on her father this way:

> After his schooling (and it must be observed that despite his cantankerous and disobedient nature, he is an excellently educated man, and if only he had been wise as well as intellectual, he might have been someone one would be ambitious to know) he went to New York and spent his heyday working on newspapers. . . . His real aspiration was to write short stories—he had met Rex Reach at a champagne party and had seen Mark Twain in the lobby of a hotel in Boston.

The kinship with Twain, sketchy as it was, could help clarify and dignify her father's dilemma and thus her own heritage. Stafford continually emphasized the incongruous mix of redskin and paleface in her inheritance—vigorous Stafford and tame McKillop—and Twain showed the way to one appealing resolution: a kind of literary hickness. His career demonstrated that the tradition of frontier humor to which John Stafford turned could be fertile ground for something other than mere hack fiction. Twain, the champion of the vernacular, had faced the disapproval of his wife (to say nothing of such genteel mentors as his friend Mary Fairbanks, who at one point got Twain to swear, "I will rigidly eschew slang and vulgarity in the future"). John Stafford could similarly be cast as the victim of the prim McKillops. It was a tension Stafford suggested in the author's note to her *Collected Stories,* juxtaposing *When Cattle Kingdom Fell* with another element of her family literary legacy, memory books from her mother's more decorous side of the family. She elaborated on the McKillop literary style in an article for *Vogue,* in which she excerpted a little meditation on slang from her mother's memory book. It sounded like Mary Fairbanks's censoriousness—and like the sappy girls in Tom Sawyer's class:

> Some persons may ask what is the harm in using "slang," but there is a great deal of harm in it; for if a person would use it long enough, it might lead to swearing and from swearing to drinking and gambling and all from the use of a few harmless words as "Rats" or "Chestnuts." Some young ladies think it gives them an air of smartness to use slang just as some boys think it is smart to chew tobacco.

This, as Stafford tended to see it in her moods of solidarity with her father, was the sensibility that the two of them were up against. They were in Twain's camp.

Suggesting a parallel between her father and Twain helped justify the man who sat in the basement talking to himself as he typed. Her father could be hailed as an admirable original who scorned material comforts and laughed at prevailing pieties, who had decided simply to write straight from his own quirky soul. But the parallel also inspired a less generous judgment. Was her father simply a thwarted man who had betrayed his vigorous inheritance and then been beaten down by a genteel world, reduced to a bitter, clowning caricature of an artist? Throughout her life, Stafford took sides, switched sides, was filled with gall, then with guilt.

In fact, Twain's own reputation, whether Stafford knew it or not, was also the subject of a debate that heated up in the 1930s during her adolescence, when she felt most intensely ambivalent about her father. In 1932 Bernard De Voto published *Mark Twain's America,* largely a response to a book that had roused controversy a decade earlier, Van Wyck Brooks's *The Ordeal of Mark Twain* (which had appeared in 1920 and was then reissued, slightly revised, in 1933). A salvo in the attack on the genteel tradition, Brooks's analysis debunked the prevailing hagiographic view of Twain. Far from America's heroic writer, Twain was a "frustrated spirit, a victim of arrested development," a mere humorist who had been diverted from fulfilling his true satiric promise by stifling social and psychological pressures. Thanks to his Calvinist mother, his crude western surroundings, and his genteel wife, among other influences, "the poet, the artist in him . . . had withered into the cynic and the whole man had become a spiritual valetudinarian." De Voto countered with an attack on Brooks's crude psychologizing and a defense of Twain as a brilliant humorist whose devastating send-up of the Gilded Age was built on a tradition of frontier comic writing that blended ballads, tall tales, and folktales.

IN STAFFORD's last published work, "Woden's Day," which appeared in 1979, after her death, she again tackled the subject of her father in fiction, but she had switched sides. Mocking tolerance, even admiration, had given way to much sterner treatment. The story was excised from the manuscript of the unfinished autobiographical novel she worked on at the end of her life, *The Parliament of Women,* but it drew on earlier fictional efforts as well: Stafford's long silence about her father over the years was not for lack of trying to turn him into a workable character. Like "Disenchantment," "Woden's Day" addressed his downfall in Twainian style, but her youthful exuberance had turned into more high-strung, almost surreal satire. Certainly the old innocent irony had long since faded from her father's style. John Stafford had hung on, not dying until 1966, and his always dubious literary career had been derailed for decades. "Of course there's no market for the Thud and Blunder which in palmier days once brought me enough checks to pay about half the rent while that faithful saint, your mother, made our living," he wrote to Jean in 1963. Instead, he had devoted himself to pamphleteering against the stupidity of humanity. He had plans for peace, for deficit reduction—and even for a deadly weapon he called a Hell Ray that would make all such meliorative schemes unnecessary.

But there was also an ever-present note of bitter self-irony in his presentation of his obsessions. In his letters—which his daughter dreaded getting—he frequently acknowledged his own errors along with the rest of mankind's: "Only a few people have brains enough to get down to brass tacks on fully desirable and practicable enterprises. The overwhelming majority please themselves with daydreams of a helluva big something for nothing and generally return from their expeditions sadder, but instead of wiser more determined than ever to continue in the practice of their congenital imbecility."

In "Woden's Day" Stafford delineated a lurid "ordeal" of Dan Savage, her name for the character inspired by her father, and his "arrested development." Whether or not she had Brooks's portrait of Twain in mind when she started, it's clear that when she ended Twain wasn't far from her thoughts, for the figure based on her father evokes Huck Finn's pap, as she herself observed in *In the Snowfall.* Again, her fiction was far from factually accurate: Stafford omitted the California chapter of their lives, staging the whole story in Missouri. There she conjured up an unhappy valley, called Graymoor, where Dan Savage began to go wrong.

The account was full of colloquialisms and caricature and bustle, as crowds of Savage (Stafford) and McKinnon (McKillop) relatives of her grandparents' generation made unexpected entrances and dramatic departures, all in period dress and mode of transport. But Stafford paused over two portraits of Dan, which together anchor the busy story. The first was a picture of Dan the cosseted writer son, who was funded by his dead father and fussed over by his mother. She had summoned a photographer to commemorate the sale of his first story:

> There was a photograph of him sitting at his writing table beside an open and uncurtained window: some flowering tree is in bloom just outside and through its white, enclouded branches, the sun lies full upon a huge dictionary held closed by flanges on a stand.... The table is strewn with papers, on one of which Dan is writing with a long-stemmed pen; his other hand is relaxed, the fingers (how filled with ease they seem!) touching another sheet. He is in profile and because his sharply aquiline nose is in shadow, his face looks delicate and young. How young, how unlined, how cleanly his high forehead reaches up to meet the dense curls of his dark hair. He has taken off his collar ... and the sleeves of his shirt look uncommonly full, they look as full as bishop sleeves, and the starched cuffs are closed with oval links; his galluses are wide. In the foreground, on the floor or perhaps on some low stool, there is a jardinier of branches bearing flowers. It is a portrait of youth in the youth of a year. You read his mortal vulnerability in his lowered eyes (he does not yet wear thick glasses) and in his bent, clean-shaven neck.

This was the Victorian gentleman writer, overeager to pose for conventional praise, vulnerable in his false vanity. The "good" son, Dan had been granted his inheritance in capital, not in trust, and he had in mind a suitably dignified agrarian existence, disdaining exertion in more worldly enterprises. But Dan couldn't resist the shine of the Gilded Age altogether, especially if the glow came from gold without sweat: he proceeded to lose all his money in the stock market.

The second portrait was of Dan after his downfall, and it calls to mind one of E. W. Kemble's illustrations of Huckleberry Finn's pap, the frighteningly disheveled disgrace of the town of Hannibal, Missouri, for the first edition of *Huckleberry Finn:*

> Dan's bilious moods came oftener, his "spells" were terrifying: one time he went into Hubbard's Dry, where both Aunt Jane and Aunt Amy clerked, and inveighed against his father-in-law with such blood-curdling invective, such heart-splitting blasphemy that Mr. Hubbard himself ushered him out of the store like a hobo. And he looked like a hobo: barefoot, his long underdrawers showing beneath his unlaced cavalry britches; his hair was as long as William Jennings Bryan's and he hadn't shaved in a week; tobacco juice oozed down his chin from the quid he held in his cheek. . . . The town was appalled and off its head with delight; the schoolchildren imitated Dan's limp and spat imaginary tobacco juice at the Savages' feet and made up tirades with nonsense words to scream at them until Abigail, with mysterious and quietly theatrical power, one day at recess stood on the top step on the stairs leading to the main door and commanded silence. "My father is a genius," she said. "My father is poetically licensed by President Wilson to do anything he likes. Hark to my words and from now on cease and desist this persiflage." It worked.

This man, whose "laughter strangled him; his eyes screwed up like a bawling baby's and the veins on his forehead swelled and pulsed, a dreadful blue," had betrayed his father, been abandoned by his mother, and was then trapped by his wife's father, a blistering Scottish Presbyterian who tyrannized his kinsmen. It was only at the close of the story, when Grandfather McKinnon died after a stroke brought on by an apoplectic rage, that Dan could escape to Adams, Colorado, with his family. It was hardly a triumphant journey westward.

Between "Disenchantment" and "Woden's Day," Stafford struggled to find a satisfactory portrait for a character based on her father, trying to reconcile the man she described in *In the Snowfall* as this "figure, this replica (save that he was not a drunk) of Huck Finn's pap, with the figure I had never seen but heard about"—the man whom "someone once in my hearing had called ... a genius," who had cut a civilized profile in Missouri. These two pieces of writing were as close as she could come to publishable portraits. Although her father was the original inspiration for her style, he was only rarely its successful subject.

Distance was apparently not the solution to her troubles. Soon after she wrote "Disenchantment," Stafford began envisaging an escape from home, and eventually she managed to leave her family behind. But even safely far away, she was stymied in her efforts to portray this haunting character, who was addled by words rather than by drink: "He got up at dawn and he began before the light was full, softly orating a wild pastiche of learning and approximation with all the nouns leaping forth like pointing fingers and all the bilious adjectives insisting on their naked menace as he cherished them in a long pause." Until her last story, her explicitly autobiographical attempts went unpolished and unpublished. But the Twainian style, Stafford discovered later, offered a way to tap her roots in the "semi-fictitious town of Adams, Colorado," without facing her father directly. She ran away, and when she came back in her fiction, in her western stories and in her second novel, *The Mountain Lion,* fathers were notably absent from that childhood world, with comic and tragic results.

First, however, she had to get away, and unlike Huck she was ready to be seduced by the temptations of civilization and society and wealth: the world to the east—New England and Europe, Henry James country— beckoned. It was a seduction that John Stafford had evidently succeeded in forgetting. Certainly he had determined to repudiate it, as Stafford explained in a passage in *In the Snowfall,* describing the dilemma of her autobiographical persona, Joyce Bartholomew:

> Much of Joyce's tragedy lies in her ambivalent attitude toward [her father]; she longs deeply for all the qualities he has not got, for gentleness and a wide, inclusive love, for amiable manners, for the talent to accept the world and to be happy in it (and this says, in a sense, that she longs to reject her father unconditionally), but simultaneously, out of habitual fear and out of the residue of her childhood admiration for him, one aspect of her believes in him

implicitly: knows that the world is what he says it is, corrupt, dis-integrated, materialistic, knows that only by being alert and ascetic and unforgiving can one escape being corrupted oneself. In pitiable confusion, she hates her father for being wholly intellectual and in all other circles, she despises all those who are not intellectual. . . . She is able, that is, to recognize the worth of people who will not yield to the temptations of the easier way. . . . But she returns, as if she were in love, to the contemplation of the habits of the well-to-do and her heart, if not her mind, is in their world.

Though Stafford continued to live at home, college was the first step of her escape.

CHAPTER 2

The University

As soon as Jean Stafford began to write in earnest, her four years at the University of Colorado, 1932 to 1936, were her subject. She kept returning to them, aware that they were a decisive time in her life, certainly in her imaginative life. But almost none of what she wrote about those years was ever finished. Her manuscript from the 1940s, *In the Snowfall,* thwarted her, and she wrote several articles in which she discussed her difficulties transforming that chapter of her life into successful fiction. Corrosive memory overwhelmed creative energy every time. Though she tried to stray from the real people and experiences, she explained, she never managed to leave them far enough behind. That wasn't because her recollections were fond, but because they were frightening. It is clear that she was often appalled by her past self, by how dangerously susceptible to external influence and to self-doubt Stafford the college student had been. Yet she also suspected that the same vulnerable imagination that disoriented her in life could perhaps inspire her writing. The fragmented manuscript, though not a trustworthy memoir, is nonetheless a useful guide to Stafford's deep confusions about personal identity, which were at the heart of her preliminary explorations of a possible literary identity.

At the university Stafford faced the typical collegiate dilemma of how to fit in and stand out at the same time. Increasingly resentful of her father, dismissive of her mother, and ashamed of their circumstances, she was well practiced at being a loner. But she was also determined to discover some sense of community and of respectability. As an aspiring writer, she experimented with what it might mean to lead the "life of art" without following her father's hopeless literary path. Her own experience was far from calm. Stafford's college career closed with an act of violence—the suicide of her closest friend, Lucy McKee—that haunted her art and her life for years, perhaps until the end. It seemed, as she wrote later, to dramatize for her the fragile boundaries of the self.

When Stafford entered the University of Colorado in 1932, the beneficiary of a waiver-of-fees scholarship, she had a set of prohibitions to obey, sternly enunciated by her younger self in the guise of Vox Populi. The frivolous route of the "social-climbing sniggering hypocrites" among her classmates, who didn't deserve a university education in the first place, was forbidden: she was not to join a sorority, flunk out, or emerge a polished young American with a dilettantish collegiate air. On one level, the strictures were easy enough to satisfy, and Stafford confidently did. She was one of the "barbarians" on campus who rarely set foot in the Greek-letter mansions all over the Boulder hillside. She doubled up on courses in order to earn both a B.A. and an M.A. in four years. And she graduated a restless American, looking forward to a year in Heidelberg and a serious scholarly career in philology.

Stafford's academic career looked less smoothly purposeful from the inside. Her intellectual intensity, as she freely admitted in retrospect, was matched by real insecurity, intellectual and social. She was "restless, plunging into work, into getting honors because . . . I could not express myself in the way I really wanted to, with friends." She started out intending to study philosophy and was in devoted awe of an outspoken professor named Joseph Cohen. She was impressed less by his politics (he was a vocal Marxist, who championed, among other controversial events, a campus appearance by longshoreman leader and prominent radical Harry Bridges) than by his erudition. Cohen was the advanced intellectual on campus, the person who had always read the latest important book and who routinely intimidated the new professors. He intimidated Stafford too, but also admired her, and as philosophy often does for freshmen, his subject seemed to promise the answer to her confusions.

In one first-person draft of *In the Snowfall,* Stafford placed her autobiographical protagonist Joyce Bartholomew in a similar predicament in Dr. Rosen's class: "In my chronic inability to relate the profane to the divine, to allow the marriage of a mind which ate up Plato . . . to a body which with equal ardor ate up the sensuality of evenings in mountains, I had continued to look upon this class, philosophy, as having the atmosphere in which I was the most at ease, the happiest, the closest to fulfillment." Stafford encountered psychology in Cohen's class as well, which must have seemed to shed further light on some of the disjunctions in her life, and on the more dramatic turmoil she encountered in her college friendships. But to judge by Joyce's fictional experience, Stafford couldn't help associating Cohen with her father, even though her teacher was a far more satisfying intellectual guide than John Stafford, with his "wild pastiche of learning," could possibly be. The mental preoccupation was familiar and daunting: though "the splendor of [Dr. Rosen's] intellect did not make [Joyce] restive as her father's did," she "most secretly, despite her present situation as a candidate for an academic degree ... wondered if society would not be simpler and happier if learning were left altogether to the men." It was a thoroughly uncharacteristic hint—but only a hint—of allegiance with her mother.

Stafford was not about to act on whatever secret reservations she may have had about her scholarly aptitude, but she did ultimately turn from philosophy to study with a woman, Professor Irene P. McKeehan of the English department. In her classes Stafford seemed to find less aggressive but no less rigorous guidance. Professor McKeehan was an intimidating character of a completely different kind, a radical contrast not just to men like Cohen and her father but, perhaps even more important, a contrast to Jean's round, beleaguered mother—though her teacher was equally fastidious. In a lecture Stafford delivered at the University of Colorado in 1972, she described her starchy mentor: "Miss Irene Pettit McKeehan was the size of her middle name if her middle name had been spelled 'petite.' Her tailleurs and her hats and her shoes were accurately cut, sewn without error, and impregnable to blemish or to disarray. Her learning was so prodigious and so terrifying that during the first week of my first class with her—The Victorian Age—I could not look at her but addressed my eyes to my notebook in which I wrote down, lickety-cut, every word she said." In Stafford's third year, this Victorian guide to Victorianism led her student even further from daily confusions, introducing her to the Middle Ages and medieval languages, Anglo-Saxon and Middle English—"equipment as useless as any I can think of for our own Dark Age of the depression," Stafford commented later. She wrote her master's thesis on "Profane and Divine Love in English Literature of the Thirteenth Century" and showed that, at least within the confines of a scholarly paper, she was perfectly capable of relating "the divine to the profane." In the process she acquired a smattering of Vulgar Latin, Old French, and Gothic—and a desire, she said, to become a philologist.

But Stafford's more consuming desire, as she said later, was to "express [her]self in the way [she] really wanted to, with friends"—and in her writing—which proved to be more difficult than excelling at scholarly tasks. This self-proclaimed "democrat of the most radical species" who inveighed against "gangs" also came to college eager to discover some kind of distinctive, artistic community in which to lose or find herself— or, ideally, both. (Her literary entourage at Boulder Prep, with its Voltaire dinners and advanced reading lists, had appealed to a similar urge.) She wasn't sure just what kind of community, and her confusion was both personal and, as she emphasized in retrospect, generational.

Her maverick father was still the main source of her private confusions. His embarrassing poverty was a practical obstacle to elite fraternizing, and his inclination to asceticism was a spiritual admonishment against such a conventional, comfortable goal. At the same time, John Stafford was himself the model for her sense that there was an aristocracy of art, even if his rendition of it seemed ever less admirable. Years later, in the fragment of memoir in which she described the family's collusion in his deluded visions—"my mother spared his feelings and we believed he was an artist"—she bitterly recalled the rationale for their indulgence of him: "We understood why it was our father would not work in a mine or an office. He was sensitive and he was aristocratic." What had once been respect for her father's version of the elect life turned to resentment. His isolated intellectual and literary obsessions meant constant financial worries and a sense of social ostracism—at least they had for most of her self-conscious life with him, however idyllic the past before that might have been.

Stafford's response in college was to long for wealth, or some connection with wealth, which she associated with a refined conception of culture at odds with her father's increasingly crabbed complaints about the profligate world. In a passage of *In the Snowfall* she described her protagonist Joyce's vision of elegant civilization: " 'Culture' was a word that inhabited her like a truth or a taste; it was the agent she believed . . . could quarantine such people as her parents (her father was crazy, her mother was silly). . . . It would permit upon the premises of its marble-halled and rose-decked estates no untoward noises, no ugly appointments, no barbaric speech, no rough manners." At the same time, she evoked Joyce's ambivalence about the allure of money:

She is persuaded that only with wealth can there be peace of mind
and that it is only amongst the poor that are to be found quarreling,
hatred, misanthropy and violence, and yet she believes—because
her father taught her this in her bassinet—that only this very tur-
bulence and misery can produce things of value, that the intellectual can thrive only in want. . . . [T]o her, who cannot understand
him and cannot repudiate him and cannot love him, he is—and he
really is, more than he represents—the capricious principle of life,
and no matter how valiantly she tries to pursue order, the random
element disrupts her plans.

Understandably, Stafford's plans for seeking out friends when she arrived at college were far from orderly. The preoccupying question was
where she belonged, or wanted to belong. Her first impulse was to grav-
itate toward the bohemian set among the barbarians. She had a reputation, according to a fellow student and temporarily infatuated admirer,
as one of the literary libertines. She wore jeans at a time when they were
hardly the vogue. More shocking, she modeled nude for art classes at the
university. The contrast could hardly have been starker: the rumpled student was unveiled as a strikingly attractive young woman. In a studio
portrait taken during college, her neck is gracefully arched, her features
delicate; a much more amateurish nude sketch by a classmate shows an
equally well-proportioned body, slender yet nicely rounded. Stafford was
studiously nonchalant about her rather sensational employment; thanks
to her impecunious father, she had to work, and this was merely a high-
paying job.

Yet modeling also seemed to be a dramatic expression of deep uncertainty about her identity, as her subsequent fictional treatment of it in
her story "The Philosophy Lesson" suggested. There was a real gulf between the student who sat raptly in awe of her buttoned-up Victorian
professor and the avant-garde girl who posed nude for her artistically
inclined (and philistinely curious) classmates. In fact, her story, extracted
from *In the Snowfall* and published in 1968, implied even more profound
tensions than that. Teetering naked on the podium was a perfect emblem
of her efforts to find some balance between her sense of isolation and her
desire for connection with a wider world; it captured her fears that an
escape from loneliness might entail an equally alienating exhibitionism.

For her autobiographical protagonist (renamed Cora Savage in "The

Philosophy Lesson") to stand up on the platform undraped was at once a declaration and a denial of her independent existence in the world of other consciousnesses: she presented herself as an object of others' scrutiny, only to see herself disappear in their subjective renderings of her. Cora was disturbed by that invisibility: "Then she wandered about through the thicket of easels and saw the travesties of herself, grown fat, grown shriveled, grown horsefaced, turned into Clara Bow. The representations of her face were, nearly invariably, the faces of the authors of the work. Her complete anonymity to them at once enraged and fascinated her." Profoundly unsettled, Cora resorted to bleak Berkeleian meditations: "She concluded that she would be at peace forever if she could believe that she existed only for herself and possibly for a superior intelligence and that no one existed for her save when he was tangibly present."

This sterile vision of detachment was precisely what Stafford was looking to escape at college. When she put her clothes back on and joined her fellow barbarians, the dilemmas were posed in less abstract form. In pursuit of her artistic aristocracy, she tried out different versions of belonging as she mingled with the bohemian intellectual and literary set that was avidly discovering modernism, pretending that Boulder was Paris and the early 1930s were the early 1920s. It was an exhilarating introduction to the possibilities of creative art.

In her later writing about her college years, Stafford was eager to evoke the high excitement of the intellectual scene. She conjured up memories of her bohemian circle at some length in a lecture she delivered at the 1952 Writers' Conference in the Rocky Mountains, held at her alma mater:

In my last year at the university, I was a member of a small group who wrote and hoped eventually *really* to write and who, making no bones about it, called ourselves "the intelligentsia." We had no sponsorship and no organization and our meetings were sporadic. But once every week or so we gathered on the mezzanine of a melancholy sandwich and beer establishment on 13th Street ... where, for the Mermaid Tavern's hock or sack, we substituted attenuated and legal three point two. Occasionally we read aloud from our own work, but for the most part we read from the writers we had just discovered: Joyce, Proust, Pound, Eliot, Lawrence, Gide, Hemingway, Faulkner. Our prejudices were vitriolic and our admirations were rhapsodic; we were possessive, denying to anyone outside our circle the right to enjoy or understand *The Waste Land* or *Swann's Way* or *Portrait of the Artist as a Young Man*. We were clumsy and arrogant and imitative, relentlessly snobbish and hopelessly undiscriminating. We did not know where we were at but wherever it was we heard the thunderous music of the spheres. It made no difference at all that we were for the most part tone-deaf. Perhaps I do my friends an injustice and they were less befuddled than I, so I shall speak only for myself when I say that I was so moonstruck by the world of modern writing that had opened up before me that I saw no difference at all in the intentions of Thomas Wolfe and Marcel Proust or those of James Joyce and Thomas Mann: all of them were godly and inviolable. . . . [T]he ivory tower (a phrase that did not seem tarnished to us) that we occupied was being ceaselessly assailed by the Zeitgeist (another term we found fresh and apt). In spite of our airs and posturings and greed, we were serious and knew that ours was no golden, carefree age: we had been reared in the Depression. . . .

But hope and energy and political illiteracy safeguarded us against any real emotional involvement with these issues and while we heard the Zeitgeist wail and rattle our windowpanes, we stayed snug a while in that mild, crepuscular saloon and quoted *Sweeney Among the Nightingales*.

Two friends from the circle remembered her role as more peripheral than she suggested in her lecture, and Stafford's own portrait of the intelligentsia's gatherings in *In the Snowfall* placed Joyce Bartholomew insecurely on the outskirts. "She did not really listen to these poor, proud, scholarly boys and girls when they talked of lofty matters or read aloud . . . from T. S. Eliot or from their own works-in-progress . . . novels that sounded like Proust, poems that sounded like Pound, but she was happier with them than she was at home with her father." John Stafford apparently hovered not far in the background for Stafford even as she abandoned him for fervent conversations over beer with her new friends. In fact, the values and stance of the intelligentsia, a gathering of the poor social outsiders on campus, were in a broad way not so different from his. (In a revised version of that passage about "poor, proud, scholarly" students, featuring Cora Savage and her father, Dan, Stafford wrote: "All of [the intelligentsia] were writers, and they read aloud from . . . novels that sounded, usually, like Wolfe, poems that sounded, usually, like T. S. Eliot with undertones of Donne, and political tracts that sounded, to Cora, like Dan.") She had found an escape from her father that wasn't entirely a repudiation of him.

With greater surreptitiousness, Stafford was also exploring a more dramatic, dissolute escape. In her junior year she became a close friend of Lucy McKee, who was one of the few women studying law and a very visible presence on the campus. Nicknamed "the red-haired queen" by one of Stafford's friends, Lucy was rich and talented and presided over a distinctly different scene of daring experimentation. She was elected judge of the student disciplinary court in 1935, but it was her unofficial role as arbiter of a glamorously decadent code of behavior that apparently fascinated Stafford. Lucy's circle carried to much more sophisticated extremes the punishing libertinism that prevailed among the barbarians, whose habits Stafford described this way in *In the Snowfall:* "It was the fashion amongst [the barbarians] to scorn athletics and all other forms of physical experience since, except for sex . . . they had no uses for the flesh. . . . [B]y the time they had got their degrees . . . their stomachs were ready for ulcers and their hearts were cynical." Later in life, Stafford was usually more oblique about this darker side of her bohemian life. In fact, in her 1952 talk she explicitly denied any but the most innocent of literary intentions: "We would have been shocked and disbelieving if anyone had even jokingly suggested that we were disinterring and exposing derangements and unwholesome desires."

The truth was that at some point during her junior year, Jean joined Lucy and what Stafford later called her "limp, disreputable entourage" in exploring just such derangements and unwholesome desires in a "terrifying modus vivendi." It was evidently Stafford's literary talent that attracted Lucy, who also had aspirations to write, but their companionship was rarely quiet or creative. Stafford was soon a regular guest at the wild parties held at the house where Lucy lived with her husband and fellow law student, Andrew Cooke—whom she had married in 1933, reputedly after a friend took out a marriage license for them as a joke. Certainly marital vows weren't taken very seriously among the circle: Lucy presided over and participated in a kind of frantic dissolution, sexual and alcoholic. (She had come to the University of Colorado after

being expelled from Northwestern University, where she had been notoriously promiscuous and had contracted a venereal disease.)

Stafford was mesmerized by Lucy and the antibourgeois style of the
household, which grew more extreme during the two years of the friendship. Before long she was a favored initiate. Stafford moved in with the
Cookes, leaving the local boardinghouse where she had been living (her
parents had evidently given up trying to keep her at home). Her enthrallment entailed plenty of self-abasement. As Andrew Cooke remembered
it, Stafford and another friend who lived in the house often played the
roles of maid and butler—and the joke was telling. For all her elect
status as Lucy's close friend, she was rarely allowed to forget her lowly
origins with this high-living pair. Her central place in some of the party
"games" (which included wine enemas for the guests) was often quite
literally painful. She was Lucy's most accommodating subject in the hyp-
nosis sessions that she liked to stage; Stafford's role was to remain impas-
sive as her friend skewered her hand with a needle to prove the depth of
her trance.

Lucy was a mentor in dissipation for everyone in her entourage, but
she took a special interest in corrupting Stafford. Jean drank a great deal
and, according to another friend, tried ether. At the urging of her hosts,
she occasionally slept with the fourth occupant of the house, a friend of
Cooke's, and she became ever more dizzyingly entangled with Lucy, who
knew she had an impressionable recruit. Just how entangled was the
subject of various rumors, which implied that she was sexually involved
with either or both of the Cookes. Stafford herself, in the draft of her
novel, set a scene of deep sexual confusion and unhappiness. She portrayed Joyce as ready to agree to a joint suicide pact with the husband of
Maisie Perrine (the Jamesian name she gave to her Lucy character), and
described Maisie, desperate to escape that husband, as ready to announce
a sudden voyage with Joyce as her lesbian lover.

The truth seems to have been that there were no shocking sexual liai-
sons among the three of them. In fact, Stafford took up with Lawrence
Fairchild, a premed student who was worlds away from their circle, in
the summer of 1935. Still, her relations with the Cookes apparently acquired an imaginative vividness for her that transcended physical fact.
For Stafford, life with them was a frightening yet intoxicating experience, as her identity—none too firmly defined to start with—was threatened even more radically. If she retained her sexual independence, she

nonetheless felt herself succumb to Lucy's manipulation and glimpsed the potential for thorough disorientation. Self-destructive hedonism was the theme of Lucy's household, and it entailed perpetual disequilibrium. Just how self-destructive became clear on November 9, 1935, when Lucy, who had been increasingly unwell (she had recently had surgery for ovarian cysts), shot herself in the head with a revolver in the kitchen of her house. Andrew was in the bathroom. Jean, worried about what her friend might do, had gone to the phone to call a doctor.

THIS TRAUMA gave Stafford a tenacious fictional subject. At the same time, the experience left her without the detachment and style to execute it successfully. In her discussion of the unfinished *In the Snowfall* in "Truth and the Novelist," an article she wrote for *Harper's Bazaar* in 1951, Stafford indicated that she had hoped to elevate her story from the personal to the generational: it was to be an "explanation of myself as a specimen of my generation in the formative years." What is striking is how much that impulse to generalize seemed to be inspired by the writers of the preceding decade, the Lost Generation, and how much her portrait of the thirties in her novel overlapped with theirs of the twenties. As she had envisaged the novel while she worked on it in the late 1940s, it was to be her definitive work—much as, she said, *The Sun Also Rises* (1926) was probably Ernest Hemingway's and *The Great Gatsby* (1925) F. Scott Fitzgerald's.

The comparisons were not pulled out of a hat. Those were disillusioned novels by the younger postwar writers of the 1920s, who didn't share the political hopes or the Victorian burdens of the older, engaged writers of the decade—Sinclair Lewis, Theodore Dreiser, Eugene O'Neill. The younger writers' comparative political apathy and wild dedication to the life of art earned them some condescension from their elders, who were skeptical of the idea of the uncommitted artist. In his famous Nobel Prize speech of 1930, Sinclair Lewis (the first American winner) voiced some doubt about the art-for-art's-sake zeal of the postwar literary generation, even as he pronounced the end of American literary gentility and provincialism. "Most of them," he observed of those writers, "were a little insane in the tradition of James Joyce."

But it was just that insanity—increasingly febrile and dissolute for both Fitzgerald and Hemingway —that seemed relevant to literary college students like Stafford, for whom politics was at most a peripheral hum, and it was the younger writers of the 1920s who seemed most accessible. Hemingway had quickly become a spokesman for the war generation among those who had missed the war. Fitzgerald, though less popular in the 1930s, was the chronicler of the Jazz Age. They were both emblems, not just individual writers, and the Lost Generation they belonged to was a mythic creative community. Its influence was enormous, not least over young aesthetes at college during the 1930s, who were coming of literary age as the first portraits of that previous generation were beginning to appear. (Malcolm Cowley's *Exile's Return,* a memoir of the expatriate literary scene in Paris during the 1920s, came out in 1934.) Stafford's era of literary students felt they lacked the sense of solidarity that had inspired and united their predecessors. Among their responses was to replay the artistic ferment of the previous decade. "The aroma of Bohemianism" was thick during the 1930s, as one of Delmore Schwartz's classmates recalled of that time on another college campus, the University of Wisconsin. "Except for the gray mass of average students, 1931 was a year of vast experimentation, in which the experiences of the hip-flask decade were condensed into nine months."

Stafford intermittently invoked the larger generational context as she struggled with her traumatic material in the various drafts of *In the Snowfall.* It was an effort to tame, to distance the story of Joyce Bartholomew and her seduction into the depraved world of Maisie Perrine. Joyce entered the gates of the university in search of a life that fulfilled an inchoate desire for artistic distinction: "Maisie herself was a symbol, but rather an atavistic one as if she had been held over from the jazz age. She and her household were composed in the earlier decade by Fitzgerald, Huxley, and Coward. And Joyce, feeling herself to be identified with no time, wanted to examine these figures of history at first hand." But entering the precincts of the household, where "Bohemianism . . . must dictate every event, even the most commonplace," was not so easy for penurious, studious Joyce. "From the beginning she was called scholarly, and it amused Maisie to point out what a rare combination she was of the bluestocking and the Bohemian." The true incongruity was internal. Joyce guiltily betrayed her father and her intelligentsia friends, who were "consumed with indignation at the unfair order of things," by being herself consumed with envy of the rich and desiring "nothing so much as to imitate their ways."

But Stafford quickly abandoned any serious effort at generational portraiture in the ill-disguised fictional drama of her own ordeals. She couldn't sustain the social focus on an experience that had shaken her so personally, thoroughly undermining her sense of integrity and independence in the world. The various drafts of *In the Snowfall* are remarkable not for their social sweep or emblematic action, but for the vivid immediacy with which they reflect Stafford's imaginative enthrallment to Lucy, as if that trauma had only recently happened. Despite the intervening years, Stafford still wrote with the adolescent passion and lack of balance that belonged to her younger self. While she worked on the manuscript, which reads like a disjointed, self-dramatizing journal, she graphically relived the memory of Lucy's perverse power and of her own degrading submission to it.

It is no coincidence that Joyce's great and fatal temptation was essentially the same one that doomed her author's efforts to shape her novel successfully: unguarded confession. It was the price of admission to Maisie's society—as well as the temptation that Stafford herself in retrospect couldn't resist and that she found sabotaged her imagination. The danger of self-exposure was a theme she returned to again and again in her life and in her writing, as she careened between the urge to exhibitionism and the desire for isolation. Joyce's ethic at the outset was studiously circumspect: "My own morality was eccentric and purblind. My only code was practical, and I believed that integrity was the result of reticence, that silence was insulation and that calamity followed when protection was stripped off; secrecy was the flesh that sheathed the nerves." But in Maisie's circle, the nerves were not to be sheathed, either from experience or from the recounting of it, and Joyce was wooed by the wild words: "Maisie's history, told to Joyce, is of affairs, gonorrhea etc. Joyce is innocent, understands no society but her own family ... believes Maisie's to have been the complete life, and her own to have been insipid and unrealistic."

Under the supervision of Maisie, Joyce spiced up her pallid experience, and she renounced her reticence. "Joyce had learned that night to drink. . . . [And] quite forgetting her lifelong habits decided she had been foolish to be a listener and not a talker, for the talkers seemed to have much the better time of it. . . . [T]he former clean stinginess of her life was gone now that she had broken her pledge of self-concealment." Alcohol offered a rescue from marginality, but it also meant vulnerability. Finally Joyce's tenuous sense of integrity was utterly lost: "She did not want to know Maisie but wanted to be her; it was a suicidal thought and she shuddered. If only she could exist as vividly in the minds of those people as they existed in hers!" It was also a murderous thought, which appallingly found fulfillment in Maisie's suicide.

Stafford's fictional portrait of Lucy's circle was something of an exaggeration of the facts (of the sexual adventures, almost certainly; of her own drinking, perhaps less so). But it was not, it seems, an exaggeration of the couple's impact on her as she was drawn into a self-punishing vortex and watched Lucy drown in it. Her relationship with Lucy was a terrifying experience of the power of the imagination to shape life in destructive ways, which was to be a recurrent theme of both her difficult life and her art. She had been lured to Lucy's entourage by a vision of a decadent aristocracy of art, only to be confused about whether the derangement she discovered was the sign of a gift or a disease. Her fascination with Lucy's antibourgeois daring, with her courting of chaos, was accompanied by fear. It was a confusion that Stafford, in precarious psychological and physical health for much of her life, took to her doctors and came back to again and again in disguised form in her fiction: Does the imagination that creates art also destroy life? Does it liberate or merely isolate the self?

STAFFORD TURNED to the first of a career's worth of indirect treatments of the subject barely six months after Lucy's death. The only public literary accomplishment of her college years was a play entitled *Tomorrow in Vienna,* centered on Beethoven's death, which won first prize in the university's Original One-Act Play Contest in 1936 and was performed on campus that April. In it Stafford revisited the suicide in altered form and dramatized her ambivalence about the relation between art and a "badly lived life." Her highly declamatory scene was staged at a safe distance, in another country and another century. The spokesman of philistine, bourgeois common sense was Beethoven's doctor: "Artists are great fools. They starve their bodies to nurture their minds and what do they have ... bad liver, murmuring heart, crotchety disposition." His hierarchy of value was clear: "Health is the most precious thing you have."

In her play Beethoven's sensitive nephew Carl rejected any application of this reductive view to the great composer, but Stafford made him wonder about the justification for his own degenerate symptoms: Carl had just tried and failed to commit suicide, and his uncle had caught a fatal cold coming out in the rain to help him. "Too bad I failed, isn't it?" Carl moaned. "If I had killed myself I wouldn't have killed him. My life isn't worth a farthing and now it's going to take the place of his, the greatest life in the world." The greatest life was necessarily a desperately unhappy, lonely one, according to Carl, who castigated the doctor for his fixation on health and celebrated Beethoven's arduous dedication to fulfilling his genius: "You search the four corners of the earth for love and warmth, and your soul yells out in anguish. But the world is hostile eternally, even to those who make the most beautiful things.... Come death, come death, for the lonely man."

The implications of the rather stilted play were bleak: either your life is too sordidly insignificant to be salvaged from mundane unhappiness, or it is too great to escape spiritual torment. As the winter of her senior year arrived Stafford had guilty reason to fear the former and no reason to believe the latter: What beautiful thing had she made? In Joyce, Stafford summed up her essentially adolescent dilemma: "She believed herself to be uniquely diseased in spirit and if the fact occasionally made her proud, most of the time it made her miserable."

Stafford sought solace in religion, though years later she reported that her efforts were in vain. "I think you had left Boulder before I began instructions with Father Agatho," she wrote almost a decade later to Edward J. Chay, perhaps her best friend among the intelligentsia. "They did not, I'm afraid to say, have the result they should have, not through any fault of Father Agatho's but through my own indolence ..." (It was not the first time, apparently, that she had turned to the Church in her unhappiness. She claimed that during high school she had visited a local priest in secret.)

Then, in the last semester of her senior year, Stafford unexpectedly stumbled, quite literally, first into a more mundane source of daily comfort and then into a chance to pursue her higher literary ideals. One morning in February 1936 she fainted while she was modeling. Worried that her "undisciplined eating arrangements" were the cause of her wooziness, Paul and Dorothy Thompson, a graduate student couple whom Stafford had met through the English department, invited her to have breakfast regularly with them. Their house was a convenient stopping place on Stafford's route to the campus from her rooming house, where she lived again after Lucy's death. On Sundays, her breakfast visits would last through dinner, and the Thompsons didn't begrudge her the time and company. "We both like her," Paul Thompson jotted in the diary he assiduously kept. "She is terribly lonely, and no one much regrets the loss of study her being here involves."

The Thompsons could hardly have been less like the Cookes, and their acerbically witty but far from wild household became a refuge for Stafford. The entertainment was Monopoly, anagrams, and clever, amusing literary games—not exactly the artistic life on the edge. Apparently Stafford didn't talk much about her creative aspirations, for although the Thompsons admired Jean's play that spring, they didn't think of her as a writer—wouldn't have said she thought of herself as a writer. Her bohemian life beyond their house was something of a blur, though friends would come by for her and she would reappear later looking bedraggled and feeling sick. The Thompsons helped tend to her fragile health, which they ascribed at least in part to her unstructured habits—perhaps some dissipation, they suspected. Stafford's lifelong proclivity to disease had begun, and, it seems clear, her tendency to drink too much. She was notably frail that spring, as Paul Thompson's diary recorded: a tonsillectomy in March, an attack of appendicitis at the beginning of May and another at the end of the month, and then another in June, shortly before the Thompsons departed to spend the summer in London.

Thanks to a second piece of luck that spring, Stafford herself had plans to go to Europe in the fall. Not long after she had collapsed in art class, she had seen a notice on a bulletin board that the University of Heidelberg was awarding fellowships to American students. It looked like a practical answer to the unrealistic schemes of the intelligentsia, who longed for their turn to be a lost generation. As Stafford recalled many years later, "Landlocked, penniless, ragtag and bobtail, we planned splendid odysseys. Europe was to us the land of opportunity, and more than that, it was the world, not this halfway house in which we dawdled, where the only glory and the only grandeur were what we read about." She and Lucy had also talked of a trip abroad, and after their daughter's death, Lucy's parents evidently agreed to lend Stafford money to see that plan through.

The Heidelberg fellowship was sponsored by the German government, which was eager to refute American denunciations of the nazification of German education, but Stafford was paying no attention to the ominous political signs. It was wider culture she sought. She had had a firsthand taste of it in her own country during the previous summer, in

1935, assisting at the well-regarded summer Writers' Conference annually held on the Boulder campus under the direction of a resident poet and English teacher named Edward Davison, who had taken a personal and professional interest in her. At his urging, Stafford had mingled with the famous guests (though she missed Thomas Wolfe's vivid keynote speech, detailing his literary travails). She helped out again in the summer of 1936 after she graduated, mingled with yet more writers, and this time began work on a novel of her own. Now she was ready to go abroad. Her public and rather pedantic claim was that she was lured by the chance to study *Beowolf* under the great Anglo-Saxon scholar Professor Johannes Hoops. But the real attraction was not so esoteric as that: Heidelberg was the requisite *Studentjahr* in her literary development, the romantic break with philistine America—and with her benighted family—to absorb the beautiful things of the Old World.

Stafford had company in spinning out her fantasies for her foreign year. She had found a soul mate in James Robert Hightower, a fellow undergraduate and ex-roommate of Lawrence Fairchild, the premed student whom she had begun seeing as a junior and whom, she once announced to the surprised Thompsons, she planned to marry. In fact, Hightower and Fairchild had both met Stafford at the same party in the summer of 1935, had both been attracted to her, and then Fairchild, in the domineering way he had, promptly had usurped the field. (The roommates had never gotten along.) Just what Stafford saw in Fairchild, apparently a less than sensitive and none too literary young man, was far from clear, and she herself was mystified only a year later. Perhaps he represented a reassuringly ordinary contrast to Lucy's crowd, perhaps also a rebuff of sorts to her father, who hated doctors. Maybe, as she later said disparagingly, it was merely "physical."

The affinity between Stafford and Hightower was not hard to explain at all. He was as nonconformist as she was. A soft-spoken, attractively studious-looking man, Hightower pretended that he lived in a fraternity to keep his father happy but in fact disdained the conventional Greek-letter types. He had abandoned his own premed plans for a literary path, which he pursued with some flair—and he had noticed Stafford in literary circles and been intrigued by her. His competitive spirit was roused: here was a rare woman who posed a challenge to his literary sophistication (and who had made the mistake of taking up with his philistine roommate). But they had lost touch, Stafford swept up not only by Fairchild but also by Lucy McKee. Their only subsequent encounter had been an eerie, totally unexpected one: Hightower happened to be on hand right after Lucy's suicide when Fairchild was summoned to drive Stafford to see her parents (who had temporarily moved to Denver), and Hightower ended up taking the trip with them.

There was plenty to foster the platonic friendship that arose between Stafford and Hightower in the spring of 1936. They saw each other constantly and talked endlessly over big cheap bottles of wine, discussing their grand literary hopes, their ambitious intellectual plans, and the prerequisite to both: escape from their stultifying surroundings. Hightower, who had been studying Chinese, aspired to flee Western culture altogether, but he was more than ready to go partway. Envious of the plan of his other good friend, Robert Berueffy, to spend the following year in Paris and inspired by the ease with which Stafford had secured her scholarship (she claimed she had been granted it by return mail), he sent off an application himself. Heidelberg was happy to have him too. As the prospective expatriates saw it, life and art could now truly begin.

PART II

The Innocents Abroad
1936–1938

CHAPTER 3

Mentors

S TAFFORD'S SENSE of her personal identity had been shaken at college as she made her way among the bohemians. Her literary identity had barely begun to take shape: for all her experiments in living, she had not yet done much writing. Her literary apprenticeship started in earnest when she left Colorado for Germany in 1936, and it reached a new stage two years later when she surfaced in Boston. It was a far more tumultuous beginning than she later liked to suggest. She arrived in Heidelberg an aspiring student of philology, determined to master the science of language under the tutelage of the renowned scholar Johannes Hoops. By 1938 she was an aspiring student of fiction, struggling for a hold on the art of language and contending with the contradictory lessons of teachers ranging from Thomas Wolfe to John Crowe Ransom.

In the lecture she delivered at her alma mater in 1972, Stafford's reminiscences about Germany centered on anxiety about her grasp of language:

> In Heidelberg, tongue-tied, amazed, dumbfounded to be attending a university that had been established a century before the discovery of America, innocently drinking beer with young Brownshirts who soon would constitute the Enemy, totally at sea, I clung stubbornly to my imagined career [of philology] amid the nut-brown groves of the Indo-Germanic languages; I heard myself lecturing on Verner's Law and the High German Consonant Shift and, for the edification of awed classrooms, tracing the word "rope" back to the Sanskrit.

(At the same time, she was fumbling with German, which she found eluded her as soon as she arrived in the country.) This tension between the chaos of experience and the control of language was a central, troublesome one for her.

In retrospect, Stafford the meticulous stylist suggested that she had stood back from the flux of life early on, diligently striving for mastery of form instead. Her self-portrait in her 1972 lecture was of a rather pedantic, not passionate, young apprentice. She maintained that she started out a committed philology student who, after a year at the University of Heidelberg, wrote to Professor McKeehan to request a recommendation to "Radcliffe or Bryn Mawr or some other college for brainy women." Told by her teacher that she did not have "the makings of a scholar" and should perhaps try writing instead, Stafford claimed that she had reacted with skepticism. She was worried about earning a living, so she came home to America to look for a teaching job in 1937, and it was a year later, she said, that her literary career truly and laboriously began in Boston. "I worked and was patient with myself and by and by I got a little better and started being published"—thanks to "Miss Mc-Keehan's blunt demolition of an impossibly silly daydream." Presenting fiction as the sober alternative to frivolous philology, Stafford made it sound like a dour discipline indeed.

In fact, Stafford's literary apprenticeship was considerably more impetuous. Between the fall of 1936 when she sailed to Germany and the fall of 1938 when she arrived in Boston, the struggle between unruly experience and the rules of language consumed her. The obedient student first of philology and then of writing whom she described in 1972 is at best a partial portrait, distorted by time. Just how skewed is suggested by her friend Hightower's alternative account of her fateful conversion from philology to fiction. According to his version of events, Stafford did indeed start out as an eager young academic, but in no time she had plunged into an unfocused creative career.

Initially a favorite of Professor Hoops at Heidelberg, Stafford received encouragement to publish her M.A. thesis and evidently plenty of his attention in class. Early in the term Hoops gave a party for his students and gallantly postponed opening the wine when his acolyte failed to show up on time. (Stafford was the rare woman in the program: she later said she thought she had gotten the fellowship because the Germans mistook "Jean" for a man's name.) She never arrived. As Hightower remembered it, she decided she simply didn't feel like going. When Stafford next appeared in class, she might as well not have existed as far as her once-attentive professor was concerned. Exiled from Professor Hoops's graces, she stopped going to his classes in early November—

barely a month after she had arrived. Instead, in a skylighted room at the top of the Hotel Haarlass, where she and Hightower had found rooms, the two friends dedicated their days to writing and to reading aloud what they had written—copious journal entries, excerpts from Stafford's novel in progress, snatches of Hightower's poetry.

No longer clinging to her "imagined career" of philology, Stafford was indeed "totally at sea" as she scribbled away in Heidelberg. She evoked her sense of fundamental disorientation in an article she wrote in 1952 about the experience of being abroad, which was also indirectly a description of the immature creative imagination she first began seriously to explore and express in Germany:

> In a foreign country I know no leisure, for I am one of those visitors driven by a ravening and unselective greed for detail; at the mercy of my peeled eye and my cocked ear and my surprised palate, I do not know what to elide, I haven't time to contemplate but only to record. Everything in my prodigal picture is in the foreground, immediate, surcharged, larger than life size; the woods can't be seen for the trees. In my preoccupation with the flotsam on its surface, I am oblivious to the meanders and the depths of the river. And confronted at every turn by strangeness, I become a stranger to myself; my identity is suspended, and phrenetic as I am in my ceaseless harvest, I do not, nevertheless, participate and rapidly as I devour, I am, nevertheless, undernourished. It is not until I am at home again and have calmed down and know where I am at that I can reflect and winnow, reduce, deduce, arrange. I don't know where I've been until I have come back and the edge is taken from my astonishment.

An unexpectedly complete account of Stafford's frenetic apprenticeship has survived, largely because Hightower saved it—memories and letters, hers and his. The preservation was a labor of love and also a record of resentment: during those two years, Hightower's hopes that he and Stafford would become more than literary soul mates were repeatedly raised and disappointed. Deeply fond of him and intermittently flirtatious, she nonetheless kept rebuffing his advances when he worked up his nerve to make them. Their correspondence from the spring of 1937, when Stafford returned to America while Hightower stayed on in Paris, through her arrival in Boston, where he was by then a graduate student at Harvard, sheds rare light on her character and fiction, and on the literary culture in which both were taking shape. It catches her before she had donned what she later described as "the helmets and the masks, the arms and the armor that we take on ... [to] protect and socialize us ..." and before her writing had begun to acquire the careful style and form that later distinguished it. Open in a way that she would perhaps never be again, Stafford was strikingly impressionable and yet also aloof, isolated. As a young woman, she was both an alluring friend and a frigid mystery, to Hightower's deep frustration. As a fledgling writer, she was a responsive student as well as an impulsive rebel.

IN GERMANY, as her description of expatriate disorientation suggested, Stafford felt simultaneously immersed and suspended. She arrived in Hamburg in mid-September, expecting to be met by Hightower, who had sailed earlier in the summer. She was flustered when he wasn't there, but he left her detailed instructions for making her way to Heidelberg. She managed, and almost immediately they ran into each other on the street. After taking cold rooms in the house of an elderly German woman, Stafford stumbled onto much more comfortable but still afford-able lodgings in the Hotel Haarlass on the banks of the Neckar River. This sense of daunting foreignness and a trust in happy accidents seemed to characterize their months abroad.

The political atmosphere in Germany encouraged a kind of detached dizziness. "The great engines of war are ready, are on the rails, are being constantly enlarged and magnified," Thomas Wolfe reported on his visit in 1936, and he described "an ever-present fear ... a kind of creeping paralysis which twisted and blighted all human relations." Stafford took a curious foreigner's interest, certainly at the outset, reading German newspapers and marveling over native attitudes as Hitler ominously con-solidated his power within Germany and prepared to wield it abroad as well. She had arrived at an especially unnerving moment: the outbreak of the Spanish Civil War in the summer and the pact with Mussolini in the fall unmistakably marked the rise of fascist aggression.

In her letters to the Thompsons and to Andrew Cooke, Stafford was acute, and darkly comic, about the disturbing behavior of "a nation of madmen in the third stage of paranoia, believing sincerely that they are the New Messiah. Indeed, you cannot help admiring Hitler for com-manding the unwavering adoration of almost every man, woman, and child in the country." But if she was ironic about the extent of Hitler's sway in October when she wrote that letter, she later had firsthand reason to fear the fascination he exerted. She went to a rally in Nuremberg, and though her subsequent description of the experience—in a draft of a lecture she gave at Barnard in 1971—was again slightly flippant, it was clear she had been shaken:

> It was a grand, operatic, declamatory display. There were the army goosestepping better than the Rockettes, the masses of Storm Troopers in brown, the elite guard in black. There were thousands upon thousands of devout Germans singing "Deutschland, Deutschland Über Alles" and the Horst Wessel song. I was swept along on the tidal wave of this well-organized collective conniption fit; my cortex ceased to be in charge and the optic thalamus took over. If a recruiter had come by and asked me to pledge myself for the rest of my life to the NSDAP, in all likelihood I would have done so. And then I would have had a messy time extricating myself. My friends were equally bowled over. Once the circus was over and we were in ... the night train in the third class carriage back to Heidelberg we came to our senses and were shocked by our primitive behavior.

Most of Stafford's time and attention, however, were devoted to her labors high in the Hotel Haarlass. She was slightly dizzy and yet detached about that undertaking as well, which proved more fruitful for her than for Hightower, who worked indefatigably along with her. In fact, her high-powered purposefulness cast something of a shadow over his efforts. Not a domineering man by nature, he was nonetheless discouraged to feel daunted by her in ways that he hadn't anticipated. She made it clear, insisting on separate rooms at the Hotel Haarlass, that she didn't want their literary relationship complicated by sex. And her writing, which she read aloud to him daily, began to suggest to him that perhaps he wasn't a writer, as she obviously was.

For Stafford, the prose poured forth almost uncontrollably, and she had a goal in view. By November she had completed the novel she had begun during her second stint at the Writers' Conference in Boulder during the summer of 1936. As soon as her manuscript was done, she mailed it off to Martha Foley, an editor at *Story* magazine who had been at the conference and had taken an interest in her work. Stafford then followed up in early 1937 with a couple of telegrams. Foley's response came late in January and is the only clue that remains to the nature of the book at that point. That it was weak on winnowing, reducing, deducing, and arranging is hardly a surprise from a young writer. "It is with reluctance that we do let it go back to you but it is a little inchoate in places," Foley kindly put it and then went on to offer encouragement: "Whit [Burnett, Foley's fellow editor] and I feel that it would be better for you to put this aside and go on with other books. We feel too that parts of it parallel a little too closely Joyce and Boyle but that there is enough of your own splendid writing in it to show that you will be doing very important work."

Stafford's reply, evidently like the manuscript itself, reflected both the eager protégé and the independent spirit. "This was the first time I had ever submitted anything to an editor, and the results have been gratifying," she declared, and went on to elevate Foley to the role of mentor: "If it had not been for the Writers' Conference I should probably never have typed out the manuscript—I certainly should never have written anything again except possibly a dissertation for a doctorate. However, it's really the idea of out of the frying pan, into the fire, because writing is about five hundred times harder work than studying what's already been written."

As she confessed, the real difficulty for her was finding the right balance between reading what others already had written and speaking in her own voice, between exercising her imitative skills and resisting them—a familiar enough problem for a beginning writer, for any writer. Stafford professed to feel dangerously susceptible to influence and acknowledged that Joyce was her current tyrant. "I'm at work on a new novel," she informed Foley. "I'm trying to purge my writing as much as possible of Joyce. Strangely enough, I have never read Kay Boyle, but I'm going to try to get something at once to see what the similarity is. For the time being I'm not reading anything but Shakespeare, the newspapers, and the dictionary. It's not safe—I'm too much a chameleon."

IN APRIL 1937 Stafford sailed for home (at the urging of Lucy's parents, who were apparently impatient for Stafford to start repaying the loan they had made for her European adventure). Her eight months abroad had not simply been the studious interlude her letters to Foley suggested. Though she had kept to herself and done a good deal of writing, she had also gone traveling in search of impressions. She had taken side trips from Heidelberg, and then after a difficult December when she was repeatedly sick (stomach troubles, evidently, and fevers), she gathered her strength for a solo trip to Italy at some point during the early spring. By then Hightower had left Heidelberg, frustrated by Stafford's continued rejection of his advances and eager to join his friend Robert Berueffy in Paris. Stafford met up with them in April for a short, very happy reunion on her way home to America. She described it as the perfect expatriate sojourn, an ideal mixture of independent creativity and communal inspiration: "When I think of Paris I go soft in my stomach and want to cry. . . . We aren't geniuses, we used to say. But for a while for a few days in Paris we were happy. Oh, very happy in Paris and full of fine dreams, great ones for the three of us, very full of literature and music, and sometimes laughing hard, getting very drunk and reeling in the rain at midnight."

Back in America, Stafford indulged in nostalgia for literary companionship but also aimed to find her own way. She courted the danger of influence assiduously during the next year—and yet simultaneously, on some level, she resisted it. The internal course of a creative apprenticeship is next to impossible to chart, but in Stafford's case, the external cultural contours of this stage of her studenthood are surprisingly stark and revealing. In July 1937, two months after she had sailed to New York from Europe, Stafford went home to Boulder to attend another Writers' Conference, where the chameleon was exposed to a significant spectrum of literary life. Aside from two familiar faces (Edward Davison, who invited her to come as secretary and participant, and Whit Burnett), Stafford found teachers, John Crowe Ransom most important among them, who were a living link to the modernist masters—Eliot, Pound, Joyce— whom she had been worshiping from afar. Yet the summer after that, 1938, the writer she extolled as her model was Thomas Wolfe, the idiosyncratic American writer for whom the modernist tradition seemed largely irrelevant. She read his *Story of a Novel* (ironically, a version of the lecture she had missed at the Writers' Conference in 1935), which was in essence a declaration of his isolation in the literary landscape, and she announced that she identified completely with his ordeals. Stafford's year back home was a far from settled one: she was still traveling, no longer the literary innocent she had been when she started out.

Before going west for the conference, Stafford languished in a hospital in Brooklyn during the late spring of 1937, mysteriously ill. "It's *female trouble* which heretofore has always been good for a laugh," she wrote to Hightower at the time. "My uterus is turned over, pressing against the intestine. I have an intestinal infection. I have ovarian cysts. It will be months before I have recovered and until then I've got to be a bloody invalid of the E. B. Browning variety." Several years later, however, she told Hightower it had been gonorrhea, contracted in Heidelberg, a dramatic claim made even more dramatic in David Roberts's biography of Stafford, where he argued that in fact it was likely syphilis. The evidence for any diagnosis is thin at best, given that no medical records survive other than Stafford's letters from that spring detailing her symptoms.

As usual with Stafford, sorting out fact and fiction is far from simple: throughout her life her illnesses often seemed to inspire imaginative elaboration and collaboration. It is possible to question the truth of her subsequent confession to Hightower, the sole grounds for a specific diagnosis; she was rebuffing an advance from him, and invoking the disease served as a justification for aloofness that salved his ego. Moreover, even as she was confessing, she told him two different versions of how she got gonorrhea—first she claimed that the culprit was an Italian she had met on her trip to Italy, then that he was an American baseball player she had slept with once in Heidelberg. In general, her love life during her year abroad was a mystery she enjoyed embroidering on; she later told a friend of Robert Lowell's that she had had an affair with a German aviator, almost certainly a lie, according to Hightower.

Still, Hightower did believe her when she announced that she had had gonorrhea, and it is worth remembering that he of all people knew to be wary of her revelations (as he has been of Roberts's subsequent, much more speculative diagnosis of syphilis). Whatever the medical facts, Stafford undeniably had dark associations with her ordeal long before her retrospective claim. Being sick stirred up memories of Lucy, herself renowned for a history of sexual diseases and plagued by "female trouble" before her suicide. In physical pain and imaginatively haunted, Stafford was inclined to read her illness symbolically: she was a decadent sufferer stranded among innocent Americans.

But rather than succumb to self-pity, she portrayed herself as an ambitiously creative soul. In her letters to Hightower, who had remained in Paris with Berueffy, she was full of plans for her literary life. She enjoyed cultivating the image of the alienated American artist; at the same time, she yearned for the disciplining company of fellow creative spirits in a civilized setting—that is, in Europe. "It's hideous and I am the unhappiest mortal alive," she informed Hightower and Berueffy during the spring in the ironically histrionic style that characterized their correspondence. "I can't stay in America next year unless I completely repudiate the whole past and live in some foreign quarter. . . . I am going to try to get a job here & if I can't I'll go west & finish the novel at [her sister Mary Lee's] ranch. If I sell it I will come to Europe at once. . . . I'm miserable at the thought of never being around you guys again & being stuck in this wretched filthy Babbitt-ridden country." And she was miserable at being stuck in her "revolting body which is an old wadded up bunch of rubbish and musk and bilgewater." This romantic agony gave rise to classical inclinations, Stafford claimed: "Having had to be conscious of my body for so long, during the rare intervals that I don't hurt, I have become savagely spiritual and I swear, having realized that the only time your brain can work is when it is not bothered with a malfunctioning body, that I am going to get healthy and I want to get on the earth somewhere with some books, paper, piano, 2 typewriters and you boys"—her fellow artists, as she conceived their creative trio.

As Hightower could sense from her letters, Stafford's sights were soon trained at least as intently on more established artists as they were on her two neophyte literary friends in France. During a brief recuperating visit with her sister Mary Lee, she toyed with the idea of retreating there to write, but the isolation inspired anxiety: "I am afraid of following in my pa's footsteps," she wrote to Hightower. When she went on from the Hayden ranch to the Writers' Conference in July, she found much more promising models, worlds away from her father's anachronistic obscurity. In Boulder this time she discovered and was discovered by teachers who had come of age in the 1920s as the American literary landscape was being transformed by the revelations of modernism. In fact, the parade of authorities extended even further back, to the world of letters out of which modernism had sprung, in the person of Ford Madox Ford, the guest lecturer for the conference. "When I knew Ford in America," Robert Lowell later reminisced of his meeting with him then, "he was out of cash, out of fashion. . . . He seemed to travel with the leisure and full dress of the last hectic Edwardian giants—Hudson, James, and Hardy. . . ."

Ford had been staying at Benfolly, Allen Tate and Caroline Gordon's house in Tennessee, which had become a gathering place for the Agrarians, an ideal setting for that southern group's prescribed regimen of intense literary work amid a rural landscape. Although Tate didn't come to Boulder, the conference boasted his fellow poet and erstwhile teacher John Crowe Ransom. They had become close friends during the 1920s when both were Fugitives, members of the close-knit Vanderbilt University circle whose journal, *The Fugitive,* was devoted to publishing modernist poetry. By 1930 a larger cause inspired them—revitalizing southern literature and traditional southern ways—and they had produced a manifesto, *I'll Take My Stand.* John Peale Bishop, another friend and champion of a vital literary South who also knew the European modernist scene firsthand, was in Boulder too. So was a then-obscure face from the North: bringing up the rear of the southern entourage was a new young follower and aspiring poet, twenty-year-old Robert Lowell, who had been camping on the Tates' lawn since his migration south that spring, a detour between Harvard and Kenyon College, where he was to take up studies with Ransom. There were also a few who fell outside that fraternity: at opposite poles, Howard Mumford Jones, the old-style academic critic, and Evelyn Scott, a writer of the lush Mabel Dodge Luhan school of "carnal mysticism," whose novel *The Wave* had been a bestseller in 1929. (Sherwood Anderson also attended, but Stafford ended up having little to do with him.)

To judge by her reports to Hightower, Stafford was a model of poised confidence and ingratiating charm as she eagerly took advice and cultivated connections. She arrived with plenty of manuscripts to show around: a short story, eight poems, two hundred pages of excerpts from the journal she had kept in Germany, and one hundred and five pages of the novel she had mentioned to Martha Foley, evidently about Lucy and Andrew. She promptly, and for the most part approvingly, sized up the faculty:

This John Crowe Ransom (poet) is swell. Goes in for metaphysical poetry chiefly and is batty on subj. of Donne. John Peale Bishop is nuts on the subj. of Joyce. I shd. fare pretty well with him. I haven't seen Sherwood Anderson nor Ford Madox Ford yet. Evelyn Scott is in the background and I hope to have no traffic with her. She writes the most ponderous stuff I have ever read. The only thing I read was *The Wave* about three years ago and I don't remember one single thing from it. Bishop said today that the only important things in modern English were *Ulysses,* Hemingway and Proust. That is a joy after Davison's usual henchmen who canonize Priestley and Maugham . . .

(Revealingly, she closed with a vote for a master closer to home: "I read *Huckleberry Finn* again when I was at the ranch. It is the best book that ever came out of America.")

The faculty in turn apparently thought very highly of her and of her novel, which despite her promises to Foley six months earlier evidently remained very Joycean indeed—an intertwining of three streams of consciousness. Stafford was giddily self-aggrandizing in her letters to her friends, who were getting ready to return to America. Bishop, she immodestly (and perhaps inaccurately) reported to Hightower, "said I had an eminent nerve writing s. of c. [stream of consciousness] and thereby putting myself up to compete with the biggest boys meaning Joyce. Said I cd. however make the grade." She considered Scott's flattery worth quoting too: "Said if I can get away from the academic will become great writer."

Moreover, it looked as though the talk might be followed by action. Burnett was considering running the story and some of her poetry. Jones left with some journal excerpts to show to the *Atlantic Monthly*. Scott, whom Stafford did not in fact snub as she had planned, "says she'll browbeat Scribner's into printing my book. Whit Burnett, however, wants it himself. It's wonderful having Harper's and Scribner's fighting over me with the Atlantic in the background." Stafford indulged in a final spin, which her correspondents may well have found a little much: "Have not embellished. Am not embarrassed. Know now for sure I'm good—like hell. Will doubtless spend my life writing novels."

Not far beneath Stafford's flip confidence lurked insecurity about her literary career. Certainly her new teachers, whatever specific praise they meted out to her, preached a generally intimidating, elite view of the literary vocation. Stafford was presumably one of the few who sat through Ford's lecture, "The Literary Life," an occasion that Cal Lowell at least saw as a dramatic confirmation of the old man's main theme— the sacred nature of the literary calling and the total dedication that it demands. "I watched an audience of hundreds walk out on him," Lowell wrote years later, "as he exquisitely, ludicrously, and inaudibly imitated the elaborate periphrastic style of Henry James. They could neither hear nor sympathize." Lowell, the teachers' young attendant and acolyte, with whom Stafford struck up an acquaintanceship, doubtless also preached intense creative commitment. In his intense way, this New Englander had quickly become an ardent disciple of the Southerners, and proselytizing came naturally to him.

Lowell was probably Stafford's guide to the American mandarins (though she evidently impressed him that summer with her cosmopolitanism, somewhat misleadingly parading her mastery of German: "*Towmahss Mahnn:* that's how you said it . . . / 'That's how Mann must say it,' I thought," he wrote in a poem decades later). During his stay with the Tates he had been eagerly absorbing his hosts' and Ford's stringent teaching that the literary life was no "butterfly existence," that art "had nothing to do with exalted feelings or being moved by the spirit. It was simply a piece of craftsmanship"—arduously undertaken, producing "something warped, fissured, strained and terrific." Some years later in his essay "Techniques of Fiction" (1944), Tate wrote down what he evidently told young Lowell, and it is easy to imagine the wisdom being passed on to Stafford that summer:

> The only man I have known in some twenty years of literary experience who was at once a great novelist and a great teacher . . . was the late Ford Madox Ford. His influence was immense, even upon writers who did not know him, even upon other writers, today, who have not read him. For it was through him more than any other man writing in English in our time that the great tradition of the novel came down to us.

Firsthand exposure was an opportunity to be taken seriously, for as Tate continued: "There is an almost masonic tradition in the rise of any major art. . . . The secrets of this aptitude . . . survive in the works themselves, and in the living confraternity of men of letters, who pass on by personal instruction to their successors the 'tricks of the trade.' " The "tricks of the trade" were the opposite of facile; the craft, according to Tate and Ransom, was the arduous essence of art.

Eighteen days among the confraternity—the duration of the conference—hardly counted as a full exposure to the tradition that was so essential to the formation of the individual talent. For Lowell, the intensive initiation continued, first a stint as secretary to Ford ("As he is a very great master of English prose," Lowell announced, "the training is very valuable and I would not want to miss the opportunity"), then three years as Ransom's student at Kenyon, in Ohio. For Stafford, who reluctantly set off to teach freshman English at what she called a "charm school," Stephens College in Columbia, Missouri, the ties were considerably more tenuous, as they had been from the start. Still, she had made inspiring contact with new teachers, and she had discovered a forceful young man whose ambitions and confidence easily kept pace with her own.

Maintaining those ties was very important to her in her new uncongenial setting: teaching was merely the means to her real end, writing—and Stephens, the only place she had been offered a job, was especially mortifying. Whatever anxiety she felt about her teaching skills paled beside her disgust with the ludicrous curriculum she was required to teach: "Freshman English was known as 'Communication.' Two days a week the students were taught composition, and on the third they were taught conversation, the recommended textbook for which was the Reader's Digest." And she was scathing about the frivolous students, who brought their knitting to class and wrote themes entitled "A Short History of Fingernail Polish." Stafford wasn't making it up, and she did her best during the year to cultivate detachment from the idiocy surrounding her. She made only one real friend among the faculty, a fellow English teacher named William Mock, who knew Paul and Dorothy Thompson, Stafford's Boulder friends. Mock was equally disenchanted with the surroundings, and the two of them spent a lot of time escaping the school in Mock's car, but it was soon clear that their feelings for each other did not quite measure up. Happily wined and dined by her plump, affluent colleague, Stafford did not fall in love and envisage marriage, as Mock did. She was busily confiding in Hightower, who was now back and studying Chinese at Harvard, and apparently Lowell kept in at least intermittent touch as well.

Stafford certainly hadn't forgotten her serious teachers, and throughout the fall she kept up her connections and pursued their modernist curriculum. In December she went to the Modern Language Association (MLA) meeting in Chicago, where Ransom aired the possibility of a job at the University of North Carolina in Greensboro, where Allen Tate was teaching. ("I don't know how much you know about Tate," Stafford eagerly wrote to Hightower after the meeting, "but what I know is that he knows everybody, especially Pound and Ford Madox Ford.") Stafford only slightly exaggerated Ransom's enthusiasm, to judge by his prompt letter to Tate. "The sanest and most charming and at the same time most promising girl at the Boulder Writers' Conference last summer was Jean Stafford," Ransom wrote to his friend on January 1, 1938:

> Her best work is fiction; she has a novel pretty far along. She has had a year of graduate study of some kind in Germany (last year) and is a BA, perhaps an MA, of Colorado. She's teaching unfortunately, at Stevens [sic] College in Missouri. . . . Naturally she wants to get away next year. She would give up her salary as an instructor and take an English assistantship or fellowship at the right place. She is a fine person and a competent scholar and teacher so that no risk is involved in dealing with her. She may have a considerable creative talent, I have not seen enough to tell.

(In the same letter, Ransom relayed an even more glowing assessment of Lowell: he "is a fine boy, very definitely with great literary possibilities. I don't know whether he's better as a critic or a poet, but he's making fast progress in both lines.")

In turn, Stafford took care—and a little license with the truth—to declare her allegiance to the canon and the confraternity. She sketched a colloquial map of the terrain for Hightower: "Ford is a big man. He was chummy with Conrad and Hardy and the rest of them. He loves Ezra Pound deeply. He was the first to recognize the great value of Ulysses. He is interested only in the revolutionists. He loves Hemingway. All these boys were together in Paris. They had a magazine. Ford is pa to them all." To Ford, whom she wrote in February asking for a recommendation for a Houghton Mifflin fellowship, she sent a self-portrait as the ideal modernist disciple. Wittily disparaging about Stephens, she lamented the uselessness of the "voluminous notes" she claimed she had studiously assembled in Heidelberg for "courses I would have in James Joyce, and seminars I would have in the poetry of Ezra Pound." Stafford may not have made an altogether plausible explicator of the masters, but she was thoroughly convincing as an avid student of the Paris scene:

> Not long ago I read your preface to *A Farewell to Arms.* I was sorrier then that I had left Paris than ever before. What I wanted most at the moment was to find someone to talk to about the preface. . . . Well, I should have known better than to read anything more, but I began *It was the Nightingale* and now I am done for. When I read

I take myself very seriously, and my empathic responses are such that I not only write in the same manner as my author, but I feel that I am my author, and I am impatient to finish the book so that I can begin writing again. I am not humbled. I am just impatient.

STAFFORD HAD BEEN writing impatiently ever since she had arrived at Stephens and was evidently—and not surprisingly—finding that it was harder to write like a good student than to sound like one. She was working on the book that she had shown at the conference, the Joycean novel about Lucy and Andrew. It was entitled *Which No Vicissitude*, she told Ford—"something from a poem by Wordsworth that I've almost forgotten—'the tomb / Which no vicissitude can find.' " Amateur stream of consciousness was not exactly the most likely avenue to disciplined craftsmanship. Imitation of other approved models helped, but her instincts led to a florid manner and to autobiography, not to the taut, impersonal style and carefully hewn structure that her teachers favored for poetry. "I have done some good writing in my novel but i am sure i stole it all. there are several things I can trace directly to Eliot," she wrote to Hightower in the fall. The book, she knew, was in desperate need of pruning: "The novel is still too lush and I'm trying furiously to cut out about half of the tapestry." To demonstrate a new stylistic austerity, she sent on some fragments from a story about a cat run over by a car: "Well, I don't know if you can get any idea about what it's about, but that's the style I'm using which in comparison to the rest of my stuff is as pristine as Hemingway."

In fact, Stafford had learned a trick of the trade from Ford that might have helped her, but she was unable to put it into practice yet. It wasn't until years later that she even revealed his tip, in her 1951 essay "Truth and the Novelist," in which she acknowledged that she had made the mistake of ignoring the advice more than once. Ford's counsel was to avoid direct autobiography in fiction:

With the generosity that made him beloved of his pupils, [Ford] read and commented on my aimless and plotless short stories and on inchoate chapters of novels that were destined to die unborn. One time, in appraising a character he found disproportionately unsympathetic, he asked me how closely I had drawn the portrait from life, and when I replied that I had been as sedulous as I knew how, he said, "That's impolite and it's not fiction." He went on to observe then that the better one knows one's characters in life, the harder it is to limn them in fiction because one has too much material, there are too many facets to tell the truth about, there are whole worlds of inconsistencies and variants, and objectivity will fade when one's personal attitude is permitted excessive prominence.

Which No Vicissitude was likely the manuscript in which Ford had found that unsympathetic, barely fictional character. For all the Eliotic passages she added and the Hemingway-inspired trimming she did, it seems that Stafford's novel owed more than a little to a literary model—Thomas Wolfe—who was not exactly congenial to her modernist mentors. The only remnants of the manuscript itself are a one-page prologue, a two and a half–page epilogue, and an excerpt from one of the three streams of consciousness, all of which she sent on to Hightower in December of 1937, shortly before mailing her manuscript to Whit Burnett. "When I wrote them I thought they were literature," she told Hightower, "but now they seem almost on the pulp side." Clearly she wanted to be reassured that she was wrong. In a quaint footnote to her prologue, she voiced some anxiety about the transparency of the inspiration behind the closing lines of that section, which were indeed lush:

> Which of the three of us has died? What is the color of the hair that grows corruptly in the tomb? What is the shape of the face, what are the planes of the hands? Silence, and immaculate as dawn, the earth lies over one. A handful of flowers, a spider's life, a pulse of blood. Two mourners looked into their hands. Whose hands are these? they cried.
> Fire from the sun fills the air. Rivers and oceans run over the earth. But the quintessence dwells in the spheres beyond the moon.[1]

1. Thomas Wolfe, *Look Homeward Angel,* well i couldn't help it do you think it isn't cricket it's just that flower, spider, pulse that is so very reminiscent, isn't it?

Hightower praised the prose but also confirmed her fears about flagrant influence, telling her that Wolfe had done it all first. Not that Stafford was surprised or even genuinely disappointed; the affinity could serve as a source of legitimacy: "I read Wolfe's new book *The Story of a Novel*," she wrote back to Hightower, "and as usual he stole the whole damn thing from me. I am going to write and say will you please stop writing books you bastard."

Stafford wittily put her finger on the appeal of Wolfe as a literary model: far from being part of any exclusive confraternity, he presented himself as an amateur artlessly addressing amateurs. To imitate him was not an act of submission and appropriation but of self-expression. In place of the guilty sense of stealing from him, Wolfe generously granted a young writer the pleasure of being a fellow unbridled original. He was the influence that countenanced a kind of self-centered imperviousness to influence; he was a spokesman for the primacy of feeling over form. As Sinclair Lewis had described him in his Nobel Prize speech in 1930, Wolfe was "a Gargantuan creature with great gusto of life," at once an anomaly and an exemplar of raw American creative energy. It's easy to see how *The Story of a Novel* spoke directly to Stafford's temperament in a way that Ford and Ransom did not, for all of her declarations of discipleship.

Not surprisingly, the mixture of Wolfe's romanticism and her teachers' modernist classicism was an uneasy one. In *The Story of a Novel,* Wolfe tried to define his place in a literary world that seemed essentially alien, and the convictions he lyrically announced were distinctly at odds with the aesthetic principles espoused by Eliot and his followers—the "Wastelanders," as Wolfe called them. Even Joyce, the rare influence he acknowledged, was only a faint echo compared with the clamor of his own inner voices: "The book that I was writing," he said of *Look Homeward, Angel,* "was much influenced, I believe, by his own book [*Ulysses*], and yet the powerful energy and fire of my own youth played over and, I think, possessed it all. Like Mr. Joyce, I wrote about things that I had known, the immediate life and experience that had been familiar to me in my childhood. Unlike Mr. Joyce, I had no literary experience."

Mastery of formal technique, disciplined apprenticeship to "the tradition," did not rank high for Wolfe. "Whoever is impressed with the 'classicism' of T. S. Eliot," he mocked, "should buy immediately a copy of that other fine modern expression of the classical spirit, The Thundering Herd, by Zane Grey." As far as Wolfe was concerned, the man who suffers was the key, and the artist who creates would catch up somehow. He described a great chasm between the "whirling vortex and ... creative chaos," from which the substance of his fiction was born, and "the articulation of an ordered and formal structure"—a chasm Stafford knew all too well. Some fusion of the fire and the form might lie ahead, Wolfe said his editor told him, but the fire must come first: "I was not, he said, a Flaubert kind of writer. I was not a perfectionist. I had twenty, thirty, almost any number of books in me, and the important thing was to get them produced and not to spend the rest of my life in perfecting one book."

It is hard to imagine artistic directives less in sympathy with the teachings Tate passed on about tradition, craftsmanship, and the ideal of perfectionism—the importance of believing "each poem he finished would be his last." By the mid-1930s the Agrarian literary circle, which had initially made friendly overtures to Wolfe as a fellow Southerner, was predictably critical of him. Tate was directly hostile, saying that Wolfe "did harm to the art of the novel" and "moral damage to his readers," and Caroline Gordon denounced Wolfe's "lack of artistic intelligence." In an essay published after Wolfe's death, John Peale Bishop wrote what amounted to a critical obituary. It appeared in the winter of 1939, in the first issue of the *Kenyon Review,* edited by Ransom, and in it Bishop summed up and expanded the formalist objections his colleagues Robert Penn Warren, R. P. Blackmur, and others had already aired. "The force of Wolfe's talents is indubitable," Bishop wrote, "yet he did not find for that novel [*Of Time and the River*], nor do I believe he could ever have found, a structure of form which would have been capable of giving shape and meaning to his emotional experience." The paradoxical result was that this writer so ravenous for representative experience was reduced to solipsistic impressionism. "Incarcerated in his own sensibility," Wolfe didn't see that "at the present time so extreme a manifestation of individualism could not but be morbid."

The criticisms were close to home for Stafford. Although Bishop may have praised her for competing with "the biggest boys meaning Joyce," as she claimed, the obvious intermediary influence of that other big boy, Wolfe, apparently prompted Bishop to give her some advice about shape. He offered rather fundamental structural criticism, counseling her to tighten up her three streams of consciousness. Stafford didn't follow the suggestion, citing Ford's view that "the characterizations were pretty clearly distinct"; she also had Evelyn Scott's support for sticking to her impressionistic technique. But she was obviously apprehensive about the reception her Wolfian rhetoric might meet among her more meticulous mentors. She carefully hedged her bets as she sent off the manuscript of *Which No Vicissitude* to Whit Burnett in January of 1938: "Parts of it I am satisfied with. The prologue and the epilogue I was very fond of at the time, but since I have been working so steadily I can't get excited about any of it now, a natural disgust I think."

She was right to feel trepidation. Burnett's criticisms were blunt, accusing Stafford of producing a mere formless flow of sensibility—and a none too interesting or elevating sensibility at that:

> I do not think this book will do you much good as a writer if it is published. I imagine this reaction on my part will come to you as somewhat of a shock, but I become more and more convinced as time goes on that this whole stream of consciousness thing is a blind alley out of which a writer has got to pull himself before he becomes a writer at all. I really hope that your next book will not be done in this interior monologue framework at all.
>
> The best things about this book are the occasional objective descriptions and those for any reasonable reader are essentially the only readable parts in it. It seems a shame that the kind of writing that goes into those parts is so relatively small in proportion to the great bulk of meandering around in the inside of these people's minds. Their insides become extremely boring. And so far as the sexual elements are concerned, I do not think most of the sexual parts are at all convincing. They strike me as intended more for shock than for character delineation. The Lesbian and homosexual parts seem to me overdone. . . .
>
> All the foregoing words seem to me to be pretty brutal but I think this whole book is a miasma that should have been gotten out of your system and now that it is out of your system I say, the hell with it. You are too good a writer to stay in that pocket of exhibitionistic self-abuse.

Stafford's reaction was strikingly mature; if the twenty-two-year-old felt devastated, she was not about to betray any emotionalism. In her reply to Burnett, she sounded like a diligent craftsman who had merely been trying out some tools of the trade, not expressing her deepest passions. She showed herself capable of viewing her work with a coldly surgical eye:

> Yes, I know what's the matter with it. I agree, too, that stream-of-consciousness is dying a probably justifiable death. For four years I have been writing that stuff and for four years I have been saying to myself "Thank God, eventually I will get through with this." And I am through. I have begun my new novel and there are only a few traces of the "mutation style" left. Those I will clear out on revision. But I can't condemn myself entirely, as I imagine you had no intention that I should. I still feel that there is a certain validity in this manner of writing. An *outmoded* validity to be sure (that is, I recognize, a paradox), and I am not sorry I experimented in it. If I had not read Joyce I would never have written. If I had not written this book, I wouldn't have known anything about words. Perhaps I don't yet, I don't know.

As Stafford assured Burnett, the new book she was now embarked on was definitely not another personal miasma. It was a satire of Stephens College, she announced, and she emphasized that it had the imprimatur of approval from her stricter teachers, his friend Ransom as well as Howard Mumford Jones, whom she had seen at the MLA conference in Chicago in December:

> He, as well as most of the people there who do not, as an organization, subscribe to the modern method of Progressive education, was delightedly horrified by my tales of Stephens and said to me, the only thing to do is to keep careful notes and write a novel about the place; that I had intended, but I believe now that I have been assured that it's a good idea . . . I'll begin it sooner than I had planned.

But Stafford was not quite the undaunted protégé that she claimed to be. As the rejections flowed in during the spring of 1938—she didn't get a Houghton Mifflin fellowship, her Germany journal was turned down by Holt, by Farrar, and by Vanguard—she foundered. And then Stephens had its revenge on the teacher who so roundly ridiculed the institution. According to Stafford's somewhat oblique accounts in letters, the head of her department informed her that she wouldn't be invited back, citing complaints about her attitude from faculty and students. What was more peculiar was his insistence that she go to a doctor for a test, the implication being that she had venereal disease; the suspicion was apparently based on gossip about the various ailments (colds, headaches, intestinal flu, a face rash) that had indeed continued to trouble her through the year. Stafford lashed back with a vehement denial, and apparently no medical proof was offered then (or has been offered since). After first backing down and offering to rehire her, the college in the end simply declined to renew her contract.

In her isolation, Stafford turned for sympathy not to the confraternity but to Evelyn Scott, a far less forbidding influence. Scott was full of encouragement (and solidarity: she wrote an outraged letter to the Stephens administration). She was also ready with disparagement of the "Tate-Ransom crowd." Twenty-two years older than Stafford and an early and fervent feminist active in the women's suffrage party in Louisiana, Scott had begun her literary career in Greenwich Village in 1920 with the publication of *Escapade,* a self-dramatizing account of her six-year sojourn in Brazil with a married man twice her age. Although Scott's declamatory literary style, her romantic personal style, and her combative unconventionality made Stafford somewhat uneasy, they also answered a need. Scott spoke up for artistic instinct and impulse and criticized the intellectual and critical cabals from the outside. "Davidson's [*sic*] certainly right about Ransome's [*sic*] book—'solemnly silly' it is," she wrote to Stafford, evidently referring to *The World's Body,* a collection of essays that Ransom published in 1938. "All that Tate-Ransom crowd has set out to revive 'the mysteries' in their worst meaning, in order that same Tate-Ransoms may be sure of dictatorial officiation at the altar. And yet they have genuinely at least minor talent." She laid the ultimate blame for the claustrophobic enterprise on Pound, about whom she was scathing. "Pound has written some lovely lines that are his own," she granted,

> but to me he is the high-priest of parlor esotericism—not an artist, but a would-be Brahmin. . . . Pound grudges life—any life—which he cannot make pay toll to himself. He has a mean little ego that has been sustained by its semi-devouring of other talents—a devouring camouflaged as selfless dedication to perfectionism. I know half a dozen he has flattered into bondage for years; first learn the mumbo-jumbo of Poundism and he will support you thereafter as a worthy, but necessarily inferior, Pound. Evidently, to judge by Ransom's book, this is what has happened there in some degree.

Scott's letters at once presumed and urged a distancing from that select male circle; she addressed Stafford as a fellow outsider, and she argued that such ostracism was crucial to real creativity. At the same time, Scott presented herself as an earthy counterweight to the high priests. Her role, as she saw it, was to be an uncoercive source of encouragement, to urge artists like Stafford "to cultivate their own real distinctions independently." That did not seem to mean offering practical advice—in fact, Scott conveyed an air of ineffectualness as the spirited artist and outsider—but it certainly did mean extending extravagant praise: "Your depth of insight convinced me not only of the talents I had already recognized but of vision for their application which must surely, at last, give America one grown-up artist—one, at last, capable of more than an inchoate pioneer's challenge to Europe," Scott wrote to Stafford, and summarily dismissed the competition. "So far, the men at their best are poetic babies, the women usually temperamental schoolmarms. . . . There is a tremendous rightness about you—responding with your whole being, as the artist should, you leap ahead of the piecemeal education of years."

CHAPTER 4

Men

THE CONFLICTING LESSONS Stafford learned from her teachers involved more than artistic technique. Scott's grand endorsement
clearly implied a vision of artistic inspiration, not just of execution, of
life, not just of craft. And it was not a vision that fit very comfortably
with the outlook of Stafford's other, less impetuous mentors. Stafford
wasn't sure she could, should, or wanted to respond with her "whole
being," whatever that might be construed to mean. Scott and Wolfe subscribed to the notion that the artist's extraordinary "being" was the essence of his art, that his distinctive personal emotions made him
remarkable, that a life of suffering was in some sense a sign of creative
election. "The crucifix of the artist," Scott wrote Stafford after one of her
many spring disappointments, her bad news about the Houghton Mifflin
fellowship, "is in a measure due to the fact that his very impressionable-
ness, which heightens his sense of life generally, also heightens his susceptibility to false or dampening atmosphere."

The dictum of Eliot's that loomed behind the views of the "Tate-
Ransom crowd" sounded almost diametrically opposed: "The more perfect the artist, the more completely separate in him will be the man who
suffers and the mind which creates; the more perfectly will the mind
digest and transmute the passions which are its material." But the notion
wasn't exactly straightforward. Ostensibly erecting a barrier between art
and life, Eliot's pronouncement actually acknowledged that the artist's
personal passions were indeed the motivating material, however separate
they were from the aesthetic effect of his creation. Eliot's prescription of
impersonality rested on an intimate, if negative, relation between life and
art: "Poetry is not a turning loose of emotion, but an escape from emotion; it is not the expression of personality, but an escape from personal-

ity. But, of course, only those who have personality and emotions know what it means to want to escape from these things."

Tate's teaching was a similarly confusing guide to the relations between art and life; its contradictoriness forcibly struck Lowell when he first arrived in Tennessee. On the one hand, Tate declared that art had nothing to do with feeling but only with craft; on the other hand, his belief that "each poem he finished would be his last" implied unqualified, total commitment. "We claimed," Lowell recalled much later in life, "the whole man would be represented in the poem." For all the anti-romanticism of the formalists, they too inescapably implied that suffering was ultimately a requirement of the true artist who aimed at producing "significant" aesthetic effect, even if the connection between the "personal emotion" and the "art emotion" was impossible to trace in any useful way.

Stafford later called the summer of 1938 "the worst summer of my life." Her personal life and artistic career were in disarray, and she seemed continually, sometimes desperately, off balance. She had been rebuffed by Stephens and rejected by editors, but two men were clearly very interested in her. She and Hightower had a long-awaited reunion that summer, and their correspondence increasingly turned to questions of their future, apart or together. Meanwhile, Lowell was evidently pressing his case. Stafford struggled on paper with her experience, not sure whether her aim was to escape it or to express it. She was distracted by the dilemma she had confronted as a student, which was now posed with a new seriousness: What kind of constructive relation could she hope to establish between her susceptibility to a disorderly life and her aspirations for art? Stafford's response was, characteristically, a mixture of extremes: a desire for ascetic detachment—an escape from her personality and emotions—and an instinct for romantic self-dramatization.

Without a job and without a publisher in the summer of 1938, Stafford headed home, which now was Oswego, Oregon, where her parents had moved roughly two years earlier, following Dick, who had left Colorado for the Northwest. Stafford's destination inspired anxiety, and her trip out West was far from emotionally calm. She met Hightower in Albany, and they boarded a train to Michigan, where he was to pick up a car for his father, which he would then drive home to Salida, Colorado. On the way, he declared his love, and in Geneseo, Illinois, he booked one room in a motel for the two of them. But Stafford balked at going to bed with him. Frustrated and furious, he was tempted to put her on a bus, but he weakened the next morning: her company was too good to part with, so they carried on. In Salida, Stafford suddenly decided she was in love, and though they didn't sleep together, she and Hightower enjoyed several infatuated days. "I started loving you just after we got on the wrong road or thought we got on the wrong road up to Salida and it was a nice night," Stafford wrote shortly after her visit. "One of the things was the way your right wrist looks when it's driving a car. Another was that I began thinking and realizing that you are the only person who *always* laughs at the right things."

The cheerful mood of infatuation was fleeting. During a stopover in Boulder, her erstwhile mentor Edward Davison was less than encouraging, observing that her career wasn't going anywhere and counseling marriage as the alternative, and the Thompsons remarked that she seemed completely at loose ends. Then, after an uncomfortable train ride, Stafford arrived in Oswego, to confront again the marriage and the career that most depressed her. Her father, who worked as a carpenter in the Portland shipyards, seemed to her more eccentric than ever, and her mother more infuriatingly conventional, urged on in her banal domesticity by her sister Ella, who had come to live with them. Stafford's spirits were low as she awaited replies to the job applications she had sent out, but she did her best to rally by turning to her writing. In despair she checked the empty mailbox every morning, and with discipline she sat down at her desk each day to work, mostly on her Stephens novel. She emphasized the strictness of her literary regimen to Hightower: "I have a desk here and privacy. My books are available. The light is good. The desk is a large, rectangular table.... I cannot work when I feel I am living in a week-end; I am not a success when I am writing on the arm of a chair or on a front porch. I have to be *inside* at a stationary desk."

She also stressed her efforts to impose structure on the novel about Stephens, lamenting the laxness that came too naturally. "I am doing in it exactly what I did in *Which No Vicissitude* and it's no good," she wrote to Hightower at one point. "I realize that what Whit Burnett says is true—words, merely, unsupported by thought or action are utterly dull." She was making a concerted effort to establish a sense of distance from and control over her material: "It is funny and insofar as possible I am going to keep it on the comic side as I feel that is healthier and probably a more effective vehicle for satire," she informed Hightower, and then described her specific strategy, which was to steer clear of an autobiographical perspective. "The desperate, soulful elements will be introduced through a student. I just got that idea and think it is a good one. My protagonist is not an artist."

From the chapters of the manuscript that remain, it's clear that Stafford had real trouble sustaining her satiric distance in her portrait of Stephens. She began with well-etched comic scenes of elegantly robed teachers and scantily clad girls lining up for the opening-day procession at Neville, as she called the school. But Stafford's caricature of commercialized education was cut short, for she succumbed to the temptation to plumb the disoriented soul of Gretchen Marburg, her autobiographical protagonist, an unhappy teacher at the school. Abruptly her language loosened, the momentum slowed, and the comic edge was dulled as alienated, persecuted Gretchen took over the narrative. Perhaps sensing the problem, Stafford tried another tack on the subject, a nonfictional treatment, which would presumably enforce greater objectivity. A visit from her brother, now a forest ranger, may have helped inspire it. "A rather nice gent," as she wrote to Hightower, Dick Stafford breezed in as a model of contented anti-academicism; "the original critic of colleges," he did not "believe in working except with his hands." During the summer, alongside the novel, she wrote an article entitled "A Manicure with Your Diploma," which she sent off to the *Atlantic Monthly*—only to receive one more rejection, on the grounds that the magazine had already printed its quota of acid commentary about education.

Stafford's subject and her self-consciously disciplined literary approach to it were in stark contrast to her own predicament. She was hard at work lambasting an educational system that coddled young women who upon graduation would be supported by their fathers until they lured husbands with their cosmetic and homemaking skills. Meanwhile, she—with her advanced degree—was without a job and flailing, and her father was certainly not a protector. John Stafford was unable to support himself and his wife, much less Jean, but the trouble went further than that. He loomed as an image of the hapless, hopeless life dedicated to words. As for marriage, Stafford had begun to think about that prospect but was confronted with too many suitors to pick from. Again, though, the difficulty was more profound. Balancing art and love, she discovered, did not come easily or naturally to her.

In the one piece of published writing that emerged from that visit home—a thinly fictionalized portrait of those slow summer months in 1938 when she was in Oregon with her parents and Aunt Ella—Stafford addressed the ever-troubling subject of her father and her family. "And Lots of Solid Color," which appeared in *American Prefaces* more than a year later, in November 1939, was her fictional debut. The story shows her struggling for perspective on the subject that deprived her of any distance and inspired romantic despair. In fact, a recurring theme of Stafford's letters to Hightower toward the start of the summer was the impossibility, or inadvisability, of writing anything down about her father and his life among his womenfolk. Yet she was preoccupied with him and with the way his fate seemed bound up with hers. Her repeated resolutions to stay silent were admissions of her need to find words for her struggle with her family.

Sometimes she simply went ahead and wrote, reporting to Hightower that she was starting work on her autobiography (Evelyn Scott's *Escapade,* published when she was twenty-seven, helped inspire the precocious undertaking). Stafford was also busy jotting down notes for a novel about her "poor benighted father," a long-term project "that can wait, I think, because I can never forget the details of his misery and I can write them down bit by bit for a long time. The McKillop girls are in league against him." She was appalled by his predicament: "He sits in a corner of the couch with his legs drawn up and looks like a dwarf. He is a combination of the oldest man in the world and the youngest child. I am sick to death to look at him and to know what hell he has lived with this dreadful woman. . . . My only hope is that he will die pretty soon." More often she endeavored to banish the obsession—only to be caught in the trap of writing about precisely what she vowed to avoid. "I wish to keep to my resolve that I may have already mentioned that henceforth I am not going to write about the trivia that vex me," she wrote to Hightower in August in a particularly anguished letter about her parents, which then went on in a tumultuous stream of consciousness:

Oh God I pray that when I am away I will forget some of it I hope that I will not remember how it is how ugly it is how tragic how heartbreaking. She is not a bad woman I am so fond of her for her foolishness and I wish he would not be so cruel and I wish she would not be so cruel and I wish they would die in peace because they have never had anything but savage hostility oh it is a stone wall and my head is aching from beating myself against it and I hate unhappiness for other people I can stand my own because it proceeds from things that sometimes I can rectify. . . . I am unkind and they neither reproach nor criticize me and I understand them and they do not understand each other, oh, Robert, I want to cry forever. I said I would not write these things if I continue to put them down how will I ever forget them.

Implicitly Stafford acknowledged that she could not help putting them down, and her letters were full of ambivalent outbursts. Sometimes she was bitter about her "psychopathic" father and his delusions about his writing and pitied her mother for having to tolerate his brutally condescending treatment of her even as she worked to support his preposterous existence. Sometimes she defended him, praising his prose (which she sent to Hightower for a look) and lamenting his predicament, suffocated by his wife and sister-in-law; Stafford herself could be cruelly condescending toward them (she was recording her mother's and aunt's clichés for a projected anthology of banality). And sometimes she was resigned, even tenuously fond. She was trying out alternate tones and styles, looking for some perspective that could mediate between detachment and identification.

In another letter, written in a much more composed frame of mind, Stafford confronted with ruthless lucidity the bind she was in with her father. "I don't laugh any more. Not at all. Not about Dad I don't laugh," she wrote to Hightower:

Look, what consoles me is this: I am unpublished, and I hope to Christ that when I am published, he will be dead. What else consoles me (and this does still make me laugh) is that the same thing that has happened to him will happen to me. Will you be the watcher?

. . . I cannot explain the relationship. It is not that he is my father, my kin, but it is almost as if he were symbolic, as if he were the essence of despair and loneliness. In writing the words down I am afraid I make it worse. It is as if his presence, that pervades the whole house, were aware of what I was writing.

Yet the "consolation" of being unpublished was also a tribulation and a challenge. For Stafford to publish words would be to best—and to shame—her father, which she claimed she was loath to do. At the same time, it could be a kind of vindication of the life he had led badly, an answer to what she perceived as the philistine McKillop disdain for a literary vocation: "Today Mother said she did not understand how I could write, having witnessed Dad's thirty-year miscarriage." And of course it would be a vindication of herself.

As the story Stafford wrote that summer suggests, the resolution of her bind was far from simple. She took as the situation of "And Lots of Solid Color" the most immediate, sensitive stage of her life: she juxtaposed her own insecurity about her literary future with her family's perpetual insecurity, thanks to her father's literary past and present. That summer, on the brink of leaving home for good, Stafford was preoccupied with the question of reconciling domestic, practical values and intellectual, artistic aspirations. Her Stephens novel and article expressed one clear vision of their incompatibility: those frivolous girls would tend a house but nothing higher than that. "And Lots of Solid Color" conveyed another daunting prospect, that the price of pursuing the life of the mind was the loss of a home.

That was the theme of the simple plot, which was transparently autobiographical as few of Stafford's subsequent stories are. (Many of her observations of and indirect quotations from her family were lifted nearly verbatim from letters to Hightower during those months.) What saved it from being a self-dramatizing diary, "words, merely" atop a surge of agonized sensibility, was the prose, which was unexpectedly simple. Her protagonist, Marie Charles, awaited the arrival of the mail on a Saturday and then a Monday late in August, desperate for a letter offering her a teaching job for the fall, dreaming of the adobe house in New Mexico she would buy, with "bright solid color bathtowels ... orange teacups in blue saucers and red candlewick spreads for the beds." The other members of the family—father, mother, and aunt—hovered obtrusively in the background, each of them presenting an implicit, or explicit, commentary on Marie's predicament.

Both of her parents kindly but pathetically played along with her delusions. Her emaciated father wished Marie's predicament away: "Well, we'll be riding in a Packard pretty soon if I sell this article. I'll buy a farm and then we won't have to worry about teaching jobs. You can just read and write all the time." Her "fat, rosy" mother listened to her pipe dreams with friendly, foolish optimism. It was only Aunt Eva who spitefully punctured Marie's fantasies, sure she wouldn't be invited to live in the house should it miraculously appear—which of course it didn't. The old woman's disenchantment was doubly intolerable to Marie because it was a wizened version of the hopelessness and selfishness she herself harbored as she waited in vain for an offer. "Nothing for a college graduate," Marie lamented bitterly as she scanned the want ads and mail, "no food for them, hell, no, they could eat their educations, live on words as her father had done all his life."

TWENTY-THREE THAT SUMMER, Stafford worried about finding a fruitful balance between her personal and artistic desires not simply as a daughter but also as a potential wife. The story she wrote confirmed the fatalistic thrust of her letters—that she, the prodigal daughter, finally wouldn't be able to vindicate her prodigal father, let alone herself. Instead, she was tempted to take revenge, out of guilt and resentment, on the whole family. Such a possibility lurked beneath the surface of the story: that Marie, if she had her adobe house, would fill it with her "beautiful friends, happy and rich, not worried," rather than with her poor, unhappy relatives. She would selfishly retreat.

Stafford had an even greater fear as a lover: that she was a frigid woman doomed to love from a distance and to betray. That same summer, outside of her family, Stafford was navigating another confusing course between the competing claims of love and art, one that she didn't try turning into fiction. Not that love won out over art. The contest was far from clear. The drama was played out in letters, in which she abruptly vacillated between emotional commitment and artistic detachment. Responding with her "whole being" seemed to be impossible.

Job offers were scarce during the summer, but suitors weren't. Stafford had three. William Mock, her colleague from Stephens, was eager to marry her, but friendly though they had been that year and fond though their subsequent correspondence was, she didn't take the courtship very seriously. Robert Lowell had written to her that summer and during the rest of 1938 "wooed her something fierce," according to a friend, although none of the correspondence remains. (One possible oblique comment on the courtship, in a letter from Lowell to his friend Frank Parker that year, suggested that Lowell had decided that his work took precedence over love. "Whenever you uncover the growing flowers [of art]," he instructed his friend, "you must chew and suck them, rembering [sic] that *they* are your staple. Women until you surpass puberty are sweets, not to be ignored, not to be lived on.") The most serious, long-standing suitor was Robert Hightower, and the frequent letters between him and Stafford are a revealing record of her confusion about her identity as a woman and as a writer.

They are also a disconcerting record, for Stafford expressed her ambivalence as a violent swerving between extremes. Those fluctuations could be bewilderingly abrupt, as she suddenly switched from aloof writer defending her solitude to romantic lover pleading for emotional and physical intimacy. In part, her unsettling inconsistency toward Hightower can presumably be ascribed to deceit: she was concealing something from him—her interest in Lowell. But it also seemed to be the honest expression of a woman who truly didn't know her mind, heart, or body—whose ambivalence was so deep that the surface signs were radically unsteady. Clinging to a precarious sense of herself as a writer, Stafford was confused about the implications of aspiring to "womanliness," as she intermittently—and a little too vehemently—declared she did. Was fulfillment as a woman (whatever that might mean) a necessity or an impossibility, a prerequisite to writing or an alternative to it? Or to put the question differently, as Stafford's evident anxiety about her femininity suggested might be appropriate, was writing perhaps an alternative to committing herself to full engagement as a woman, a justification of aloofness?

To Hightower's disappointment, Stafford had started out the summer, during their trip out West, insisting on distance. Her rebuff in Geneseo was not personal but profound, she took pains to convince Hightower somewhat later, sending him a spring entry from her journal, in which she had agonized over her sense of alienation. Tacitly acknowledging his confusion, and suspicion, about her fickleness, she obviously meant the soul-baring as special proof of her openness and sincerity. In it she both condemned and excused herself in self-dramatizing style:

Always I will be thinking what shall I do, where shall I go to get away from the uneasiness, what, where, uneasy, oh, and sick inside, queer, afraid, unrelated. I won't ever marry anyone now and my desire to love someone is desperately futile because I have destroyed everything in my soul. I will not because of Ruprecht [a nickname

for Hightower, after the founder of the University of Heidelberg]
and I cannot marry him because he would be unhappier with me
than he is without me.

In the course of July, as she settled into her writing regimen and
struggled for tolerance toward her family ("Really, I don't mind it. I feel
sort of good about being kind and unprofane. I feel sort of clean")—and
perhaps received yet more letters from Lowell—her resistance to Hightower became more self-assured. He was eager to arrange a meeting in
the course of the summer and to plan the future after that; the life of a
scholar of Chinese was not the creative adventure he had had in mind,
and he was ready to abandon Harvard and set out with Stafford. Her
explanations and justifications for holding back suddenly were not those
of a wistfully doomed woman who had "destroyed everything in [her]
soul," but of a purposeful writer. "It is not that I do not love you," she
wrote to him in early July. "It is that I love both you and my novel and
for the time being any marriage of the two is out of the q[uestion]." She
rather coldly cited the unfavorable working conditions in Salida as her
main reason for postponing a visit.

In a letter two days later she lectured Hightower about the longer-
term difficulties of the marriage of the two—of him and her novel—in
unexpected and convoluted terms. Domineering demands that she re-
nounce her writing and make Hightower a home were certainly not
what stood in the way of a union: there were no such demands. On the
contrary, it was precisely his willingness to sacrifice his scholarly career
and make her a home, without seriously weighing the implications for
his own possible artistic career, that seemed threatening. Rather than a
declaration of her independence, her letter was designed to goad him
into asserting his own ambitions. Above all, she didn't want a house and
marriage on the compromised terms that had trapped her parents into
unions that she and Hightower agreed were stifling. "I will put it coldly
like this," she summed up:

> If you didn't go on to Harvard, if I continued to write while you
> were working at something you hated and suddenly I arrived, got
> published, got recognition, it would be intolerable hell for you. Or
> say I got a job teaching school (which is really more logical) and
> while I was teaching English composition to the gurls, you were

writing, and suddenly you arrived, got published, got recognition.
I couldn't stand it because I am thoroughly selfish.

I want recognition for both of us.

Stafford's thoughts on the question of competitive ambition must have
been prompted in part by her correspondence with Lowell. Unlike
Hightower, he certainly wasn't lacking in zealous dedication to his calling and was doubtless wooing her in fiercely literary terms—as fierce as
her own. That must have been a challenge, but it may well also have been
a relief to meet her match, an admirer who was equally divided about
the allure of art and of love. For there was a selfish safety in mutual
artistic determination, as Stafford clearly understood. There was also real
danger if that determination wasn't equal, warned Evelyn Scott, whom
Stafford evidently wrote for advice on her dilemma:

> And the comparative ambition—isn't that the most dangerous? If
> two artists marry they avoid the risks of such a combination only if
> each has the urge with an equal fanaticism. Otherwise, surely, the
> superior talent is half wasted by the need to pour into the possessor
> of inferior talents the conviction that comes with nature's gifts.
> Even that might be done and some happiness result if it *could* be
> done; but it seems to me inferiorities cannot be mended by any-
> body's conscious effort—the flatteries they demand as cure only ag-
> gravate the disease.

It was a less than romantic way to conceive of marriage—a calculated
alliance of artistic talent. Stafford made very little effort to couch her
attitude in emotional form, to smooth over the abrupt rebuffs. In fact,
she sometimes seemed to go out of her way to be blunt and cold to Hightower, as if her unsentimental style were a sign of her literary seriousness
and thus a justification of it. It is difficult to tell how much true confidence lay behind her surface displays of certainty in her talent, or how
much her assertive coolness toward Hightower was bolstered by a dalli-
ance with Lowell.

The likelihood is that Stafford's stern pose as ascetic writer was none
too firm, especially given how quickly it crumbled in September. Suddenly she had occasion to question her attractiveness and her talent, and
her attitude was radically transformed. First Hightower told her that in
the course of their summer frustrations he had fallen in love with a music

teacher in Salida. He delivered the news in person at her sister Mary Lee's ranch in Hayden, where he and Jean finally met at the end of August after months of aborted plans for a visit. Stafford was devastated, even though she herself had already announced that they shouldn't pretend any longer that they were in love. Soon after their visit, she left to enroll at the University of Iowa, where she had belatedly been offered a fellowship—the one good piece of official mail she had received all summer. Although it promised to be the perfect solution to her problems ("That's the place where you substitute a novel for a dissertation, so most of the year I could be writing," she happily told Hightower), she was depressed almost as soon as she arrived. "I hate all this," she wrote to him at the end of September. "I hate it like hell and I shan't like it any better as time goes on. I am not smart enough for this place. My colleagues are all intense, erudite young men with PhD's who make jokes about Gothic jan stem verbs at which I cannot very well laugh." In her misery she was up to her typical wit, but the rest of the letter suggested the extent of her desperation.

That letter was the first in a month-long succession of cries for help that could hardly have sounded less like the summer's declarations of self-reliance. To be sure, she was practiced at expressing histrionic rage at her plight, and Hightower was used to hearing it—and even to venting it on occasion, though he generally saw and put things, not least himself, in a distinctively steady, unillusioned perspective. But what was utterly unfamiliar about Stafford's stream of letters was the rhetoric of romantic love with which she responded to a crisis that clearly dwarfed her Stephens agonies or her summer troubles. "Darling (oh, hell, I can't help it. I cannot be a Modern Woman. I want you with every muscle in my body and every dream in my soul) what are we waiting for?" Framed in altogether uncharacteristic, clichéd language, her declarations of love sound unsettlingly inauthentic. It wasn't that they were purposefully deceitful claims about emotions that didn't exist. Rather, they sound like desperate efforts to conjure up feelings that didn't come naturally, if they came at all. Her dilemma was a variation on the problem of "words, merely, unsupported by thought or action" that she encountered in her fiction. In her love letters that fall she seized on the most well-worn words, counting on them, issued in overwrought abundance, to summon forth in her the sentiments conventionally attached to them. Suddenly the possibility of romantic, imaginative engagement with another person seemed to offer the only escape from the suffocation of her own sensibility, "the sickness of my soul," as she put it.

It implied a subordination of the artistic imperatives that only a month before had been paramount. Then Stafford had firmly denounced domestic yearnings on the grounds that they threatened to undermine more elevated literary aspirations; now she emphatically endorsed them. All calculated planning about which circumstances would be most conducive to creativity seemed to have become irrelevant. Stafford's proposal was that she come immediately to Cambridge to join Hightower, who was understandably disoriented by this sudden about-face. The single-minded writer had been replaced by an equally single-minded woman. "I want to be a woman," she proclaimed to Hightower in that same first letter, "and I want to be your woman." Susceptible to her avowals, he was also wary (and weary), unable to tell "if you have told the truth this time" and unprepared to endure yet another disappointment.

Her response a few days later was a revealing rhetorical performance, a four-page handwritten letter with barely a blot. It began with a calm reinterpretation of their past, in essence explaining her succession of rebuffs as a gradual progression toward intimacy, and it culminated with a lyrical declaration of her mature passion, her arrival at womanhood. It is a strange document, detached despite Stafford's efforts to convey real immediacy of feeling, studied even though she clearly aspired to spontaneous sincerity. Every love letter is a delicate balance between saying what one feels and what one thinks will sway the beloved; ideally, the two are so interdependent that the distance between them effectively disappears. The poignancy of Stafford's letter is that it was so transparently manipulative—and that the audience she aimed to seduce was not simply, or even primarily, Hightower but herself. She all but acknowledged her own need, explaining her previous outpouring and prefacing this one by telling him that she was "sick . . . of *not* being sentimental, not romantic, not womanly." An extended passage showed Stafford's anxious efforts to convey, and to feel, a sense of connection to a consciousness and a body beyond her own. But even as she reached for physical confirmation of her abstract declarations, she seemed to shy off into sentimental fantasy:

> I have been afraid to tell you before but I will tell you now: thinking of myself as your wife, my daydreams have been those of a woman

who had sloughed off all but the essence of womanliness. I have
wanted domesticity. I have wanted to be your wife and not much
more. I have wanted to bear a child for you. I have wanted you to
be sick so that I could nurse you, could rub your legs and back with
alcohol, could delicately kiss your forehead and your hands. I have
wanted to be consumed in your body. I have wanted to bend over
your desk with my clean hair brushing your back. I have wanted
you to look at the line my hips make on the counterpane. I *have
wanted* is wrong. It is I want now as I write this and shall always
want. I know I am a woman. Never so much before have I been
one. I look at myself, undressed, in the mirror and I desire your
eyes to be upon me. . . . One thing I can promise you is this: I am a
woman, Robert, a woman romantically in love with you, vibrant at
the memory of touching you, aching to know the touch again, to
know at last (so many years of love and hate! So many wasted years!
I deserve none of it!) the full articulation of passionate love. On this
paper I can only half express the need, the pain, the savage conviction that this can't end, not now, not when I have discovered such a
rapture, such a hot wish, such love for him whom I have thought of
as my friend and as my son and as my husband.

Hightower was thoroughly bewildered by Stafford's soliloquy. By now
he had reason to suspect a disproportion between what she expressed on
paper and in person, but it wasn't, as she said, that paper cramped her
style. On the contrary, distance and the mediation of written words
seemed to act as a stimulant for her—not simply to uncover buried feelings but often to invent desires and imperatives out of needs and doubts.
Hightower was hesitant to succumb to the prose, sensing how uncertain
the underlying passions were, yet the temptation was there. "I have not
read your letter again; I am afraid to," he told her in tribute to her powers of persuasion, but he also chided her for exploitation. "I hope you
realize that it was unfair. You ought not take advantage of your art in
[this] situation."

Whether or not Stafford realized it was unfair, she was frantic, and
for the rest of October they exchanged letters, hers protesting love and
impatience for their reunion, his more hesitant and practical—he had
no money, he would have to find a new place to live—though increasingly ardent. Her letters, as his reaction attested, had worked their in-

tended effect. "My love for you is as [last summer] a complex of many kinds of love, but it is as a woman that I most want you," Hightower wrote in early October. "For it is only with your last letters that I have realized you are a woman, and a woman that I am passionately in love with." By the end of the month he had found rooms and urged Stafford onward—only to receive a stunning response from her. With the same suddenness as it had begun, the romantic rhetoric ceased and the remote writer reappeared. She couldn't come, she stated flatly: "I want to be impetuous, but I know that we would be probably regretful. I hope you will receive this with a combination of relief and disappointment."

Her reasons were partly the practical considerations she had previously ignored—no money—but above all they were literary. Stafford explained that she had started writing again and touted a day-old project with the greatest confidence: "This book, I think, may sell." She eagerly outlined her theme to Hightower, perhaps realizing that it was an indirect way of acknowledging and half-explaining her schizophrenic behavior. Her subject, she explained, was the dilemma of the woman writer in search of some integration of her literary and emotional identities:

> Yesterday I began my novel over again with an idea that has been working in my mind for a long time: the question: why is it that a woman cannot write a book like A Portrait of the Artist. I mean, why it is that her experiences cannot be like those of a man. The main character, Gretchen Marburg will make an attempt to live such a life, that is with a male mind in which there is such and such a compartment for literature and such a one for love, but in the end she will be faced with the realization that a woman's mind can never be neatly ordered and every experience is tinged by every other one. It sounds a little vague, to be sure. . . . Yesterday I wrote 2000 words, the first I have done since I have been here. I shall work consistently now.

What is most striking is not the vagueness of Stafford's plan, but the certainty with which she outlined an experience of integration that so clearly eluded her. In the very same letter in which she declared to Hightower the need to establish separate compartments for literature and love, she announced as her fictional theme the fundamental unnaturalness of such a distinction. In fact, she herself directly confronted that contradiction in closing. "I know this sounds frightfully matter-of-fact," Stafford wrote in her last paragraph, acknowledging the great transformation of the romantic soliloquist of a few days before. "It is something I do not understand. Sometimes I feel that I really *do* have a masculine mind. I cannot otherwise explain how it is that loving you as I do I can separate myself from you for the sake of my book."

Or could it have been in part for the sake of Cal Lowell? Stafford was obviously very confused, and the clarity of that letter was a deceptive, and probably self-deceiving, illusion. Only a few days after declaring her intention to stay at Iowa, Stafford fled in the middle of the night, telling Hightower she was on her way. Once again, she was ready to be romantically impetuous, but it wasn't exactly pure love for Hightower that spurred her on. On her way to Boston, she met Lowell in Cleveland. She gave a rather flippant account of their meeting in a letter to her third admirer, Bill Mock: "I wrote him [Lowell] and said meet me [in Cleveland] and he did and we drank a good deal of beer and he said he was in love with me and wd. I marry him and to avoid argument I said sure, honey, drink your beer and get me another one." From there she went to New York, where she spent what she later described as "some rather scary days" alone in Manhattan (Lowell had gone back to Kenyon), not eating and staying in run-down hotels. Finally, several days late, she went on to Boston. The lure apparently was not simply Hightower waiting with an apartment, but a message from A. G. (Archie) Ogden, an editor in the Atlantic Monthly Press book division to whom she had written about her Neville novel. He had invited her to lunch with the editors.

Just what kind of a mind did she have? Stafford was clearly asking herself that question when she arrived in Cambridge, her disequilibrium no longer merely a matter of words but of actions. Once again Evelyn Scott sent on reassurances that her romantic impulsiveness was proof of her artistic spirit—proof not so different from the evidence Scott herself had provided some twenty years earlier in disappearing to Brazil. "There is nothing 'pathological' (heaven forbid such nonsense) in your having done this, though of course it is all 'unrealistic'—I mean disappearing is almost impossible as the world shrinks," she wrote Stafford on November 12:

> Your lack of realism is to me just the volume of the reaction of a person who emotionalizes in heroic terms and is confronted in youth with the inexorable meanness of general living. It is a hurt

religions at their best have existed to cure. Those who don't feel as you do neither see what is nor feel anything in full measure. The rest—the compromise involved in accommodation to the existent—is a matter of age and temperament.

That was a hopeful construction of Stafford's predicament, about which she herself was evidently feeling considerably more pessimistic.

PART III

The Bostonians and Other Manifestations of the American Scene
1938–1946

CHAPTER 5

Boston

LOOKING BACK over his own literary apprenticeship, Robert Lowell dated a turning point from the day in the spring of 1937 when he drove into the "frail agrarian mailbox post" of Allen Tate and Caroline Gordon's house in Tennessee. "I had crashed the civilization of the South," was the droll, supercilious way he put it two decades later. He got out of his car to disguise the damage to the rickety post and was promptly welcomed by the southern literary elite as a valuable rebel from New England: a renegade from the Lowell clan was a real coup for the Fugitives. The mythic status they conferred upon him—"I too was part of a legend. I was Northern, disembodied, a Platonist, a Puritan, an abolitionist"—gave him one of the literary themes that dominated his early writing and underlay all his work.

Jean Stafford's own story of arrival was a nightmarishly distorted echo. A year and a half later, home from Kenyon on Christmas vacation in 1938, Lowell smashed his parents' car, with Stafford in the passenger seat, into a wall in a dead-end Cambridge street. She was rushed to the hospital with "massive head injuries," as a friend described it, "everything fractured, skull, nose, jaw, everything." The damage would never be entirely disguised, and Stafford was soon made to feel she had "crashed" the civilization of Boston—rudely, not heroically. Lowell's parents adopted an attitude of chilling detachment from the unpedigreed interloper. Yet for Stafford the collision took on symbolic dimensions that helped give her the themes around which her emerging style matured. Inspiration did not come immediately; her head needed mending, and the symbols required time to take shape. In fact, Stafford had another unsuccessful novel to go before she found the frame and images, and the distance, to sustain a narrative.

The disastrous car ride with Lowell, a notoriously bad driver who had

probably been drinking that evening, was the climax of the high drama
that had begun two months earlier when Stafford escaped from Iowa in
the middle of the night. Soon after she finally surfaced in Cambridge
in November, she had confessed to Hightower the cause of her delay in
arriving—the rendevous with Lowell in Cleveland. Having rearranged
his life and rented more spacious rooms to welcome Stafford, Hightower understandably felt betrayed. But he trusted her claim that she
was afraid of Cal, and made clear that he was still ready to try living
with her.

Lowell certainly was far from the low-key suitor she was used to from
her years with Hightower. Cal's romantic history before Stafford had
consisted of a swift, fierce, finally aborted campaign two years earlier to
marry a twenty-four-year-old Boston debutante, Anne Dick, an unlikely
match opposed by his parents—which had only spurred Lowell on. His
father had been the victim of his violent zeal on that occasion: protesting
his parents' meddling disapproval, Cal appeared on their doorstep and
knocked his father down in the front hallway while his mother watched.

Stafford had a taste of Lowell's wild determination during a visit from
him in Cambridge over Thanksgiving when, she wrote to her friend
Mock, "he got savage and I got scared." The issue was marriage, she said,
which he insisted on and she resisted. "A friend of his, a young man from
Harvard College," she went on, "told me in a private interview that Mr.
L. wanted me more than anything else in his life and that I wd. never be
free of him, that he will continue to track me down as long as I live, a
very pleasant thought. It makes me perfectly sick because he is an un-
couth, neurotic, psychopathic murderer-poet."

How much of the account reflected her typical dramatizing is hard to
say, but she was evidently unnerved. Hightower's apartment was not a
workable haven, and she soon told him that she had better move out to
Concord to be safe. Stafford clearly wanted distance from Hightower
too, or at least couldn't manage in the flesh the intimacy she had described in her letters from Iowa. "The full articulation of passionate love"
didn't happen with the fevered eagerness she had conjured in words;
living together faltered from the start, when Stafford told Hightower she
was frigid. Whatever she meant by it, and whether or not it was true, he
understood the message. It was one more stunning reversal, but the
friendship didn't collapse.

They continued to see each other after she moved to Concord, and

Hightower planned a modest Christmas celebration. But on December 21 he received an urgent message to call Mount Auburn Hospital. He found Stafford swaddled in bandages and, learning of the accident, discovered that she hadn't kept Lowell at a safe distance after all. A loyal bedside visitor for several weeks, Hightower finally sent a letter announcing the end of their relationship, to which Stafford replied with an atypically unadorned indictment of herself: "I will say nothing, only this: I love you, but my selfishness is so all consuming that I can't help hurting you." Two weeks later, she adorned it somewhat: "I want children, I want a house. I want to be a faithful woman. I want those things more than I want my present life of a writer, but I shall have none because my fear will make me unfaithful and desire cannot now be hoped for, it is too late and I have been too much revolted." It was an echo of her declarations of frigidity and of the journal entry about her profound loneliness that she had sent him over the summer: here too she viewed herself tragically, as both victim and victimizer, maintaining that her "life of a writer" was no compensation for the emotional commitment and sexual fulfillment that eluded her.

Once Hightower had retreated, Stafford had few other places to turn during a very painful convalescence. Neither Lowell nor the Atlantic Monthly Press—the other Boston attractions that had drawn her— proved a source of much support. Lowell was not even at hand. He returned to Kenyon for the spring term of his junior year, leaving Blair Clark, a friend from his prep school days at St. Mark's, to help Stafford deal with the lawsuit it had been agreed she would file against Lowell to pay for her hospitalization. Clark was also supposed to protect her from Lowell's parents, which was a full-time job, if the rumors that reached Cal in Ohio about the Lowells' bullying conduct toward her were to be believed. "About Boston," Lowell chided his parents in the summer, "I gather many people think you have behaved shabbily about Jean's accident. Such opinion is not my concern yet I cannot feel the action of my family has in all cases been ethicilly [*sic*] ideal."

Stafford hadn't managed to establish a literary life in Boston that offered much relief or gratification either, though she had been busy making herself known at the Atlantic Monthly Press from the moment she arrived. Her Neville manuscript, based on her Stephens experience, earned her praise from the editors there, whose report judged that "she can handle the English language as a skilled carpenter handles a chisel—

with ease, deftness, accuracy, and rhythm," but they indicated that she would have to rework it completely before they would consider a contract. In fact, Edward Weeks, the editor in chief, went so far as to suggest a rough outline for a fundamental overhaul of her "ironic, heartless story of a small college community" in a memo to another editor:

> It seems to me that if the girl can link together the three points of interest now visible in her work (1) Gretchen's affection for her German professor father and her revolt from the ranch (2) college life with its stimulus and dissatisfaction (3) and her experiences in Germany where presumably she finds that there are worse things than the life she has run away from in the United States, she would have a good book. I should presume that if parts 2 and 3 were bound together with a love story, the book would have a rising interest which it at present seems to lack.

Stafford was prepared to be a docile, and speedy, student. Eight days later, on December 9, Archie Ogden sent her a check for two hundred and fifty dollars as an option on the book and said they looked forward to a "sizable portion" of the manuscript six months later, on June 1, 1939.

The guidance Stafford received didn't sound very promising. What Weeks had extracted from Stafford's ungainly Neville undertaking—a jumbled gallery of satiric portraits hung on a plot line too arbitrary and ludicrous to be compelling—was a broad (and banal) outline of her autobiography. That was exactly what she had been trying to bury beneath the more objective enterprise of a larger social satire, at the advice of the readers of her first solipsistic venture, *Which No Vicissitude*. Not that Weeks had any reason to know the creative history of this fledgling writer, but even by his own standards, which were apparently mainly commercial, his advice was dubious. After all, he and his staff had just told her that the college theme was rather narrow and overdone, and a year earlier she had sent sections of her Germany diary to the *Atlantic Monthly* at the suggestion of Howard Mumford Jones, only to meet the objection that "there is too much about Germany on the market at present."

The prospects for the book looked even less promising two weeks later, when Stafford found herself in the hospital, with a crushed nose, a broken cheekbone, and a skull fractured in several places. Ogden urged her to give "no further thought to that novel of yours until relaxation has taken every last kink out of your cranium," but relaxation didn't seem to be what Stafford wanted—and it certainly wasn't what she got. After spending roughly a month in the hospital, she had to return twice in the spring for harrowing surgery on her nose. Her convalesence was extremely uncomfortable (along with nose troubles and difficulty breathing, she was plagued by headaches). And it was lonely, though she didn't go straight back to her Concord room. She was welcomed first by the Ogdens, with whom she had become friendly; then an acquaintance put her in touch with a wealthy Milton, Massachusetts, family, who took her in. Still, she felt bereft of close companions and was apparently finding solace in solitary drinking. By the summer, she admitted, however jokingly, to some concern: "I have taken the veil and at the moment do not think I will become alchoholic [*sic*]," she wrote to Hightower.

Meanwhile, the negotiations with Lowell, not to speak of those with his parents, were far from smooth. Once again, Stafford's relationship with a man was radically unstable. His pursuit apparently continued to be unnervingly intense; he tracked her down at a friend's apartment near dawn during a visit she made to New York that spring. She in turn continued to be thoroughly unpredictable, now eager to see him, now ready to denounce him. After welcoming Lowell's company in New York, she anticipated his return to Boston for Easter vacation with trepidation. It seems that another trip to New York, during which she had seen Ford Madox Ford and his wife, had revived her fears. In a note to the Ogdens, she reported only half facetiously that the Fords, "convinced that Cal Lowell is really pathological and capable of murder, told me such horrible things about him that I am thinking of pressing Stitch [Evarts, her lawyer] into service to get out an injunction against him. He is due to arrive next week. I may have to find a hiding place." But she didn't, and when he arrived Lowell seemed "completely metamorphosed," she said later. They enjoyed a genteel time visiting his elegant relatives, and by the time Lowell returned to Kenyon to finish the spring term, they were engaged, though Stafford kept the betrothal a secret.

It was only a couple of months later, in the early summer, that they had another dramatic falling out. Under the influence of Frederick Santee, his eccentric classics professor at Kenyon who knew doctors at Johns Hopkins Hospital, Lowell abruptly ordered Stafford from Boston to Baltimore for yet another operation on her nose: Lowell was peremptory even, or perhaps especially, when he was acting out of guilt. Having arrived in Baltimore, Stafford panicked at the prospect of further surgery—to be undertaken without consulting her Boston doctors. With Blair Clark's help, she escaped on the train after a scene with Lowell on the station platform. Incensed by her and Clark's medical apostasy, Lowell leapt to the conclusion that the two of them had betrayed him romantically as well. He was quickly talked out of his delusion, and he and Stafford were reconciled. During the summer, after Lowell returned from Kenyon, they visited often, their meetings apparently made more pleasurable by being forbidden according to the terms of their lawsuit, due to come to trial in November.

In short, it was hardly the convalescence the doctor would have ordered, or the circumstances most conducive to producing a novel. Yet despite abundant medical excuses for postponing and interrupting work, Stafford was understatedly stoic—a contrast to her style in later life, when her health problems consumed her. In a note to Ogden at the beginning of May, she apologized for her slowness and treated her troubles as a passing irritation only superficially related to her work: "Part II is going at a snail's pace at the moment but I think when the effects of Dr. Butler's insufficient anaesthetic wear off, I will be able to work with vigor having no further hospitalization to look forward to." Lowell, however, seized the chance to develop a deeper connection between Stafford's external ordeals and her imaginative undertaking. An early, unpublished draft of a sonnet entitled "On a Young Lady Convalescing from a Brain-Injury but Unable to write a novel in Concord, Mass." (parts of which were subsequently reworked into "Salem" and "Concord" in his first book, *Land of Unlikeness*) is not a polished literary effort (or, obviously, a reliable factual source). But it is a suggestive projection into that mysterious realm where experience is transmuted into symbols. Lowell didn't pretend to be an omniscient mind reader. In fact, his theme was the confusion in the young lady's brain and the effort to find a form for the destructive disorder within:

> Jollying the sight, the snowdrift skips and drifts;
> Wagon-ruts show glassy in the stuttering pains;
> Screwloose, each mouselike heartbeat thumbs at rifts

Snowing deluge, monstrosity in [of] her brain's
Shutter-splintering, nerve-hallucinating drafts!
Sprung from her skull a surf of billowing heads
Oppressed by [in] their surroundings—fountainheads—
Are grounding here like the matchwood of rafts.

Concord enframes these ruptured floes of lot
In a cracked setting—Concord where Thoreau
and Emerson were preachers—named for peace
And famed for its embattled farmers' shot—
Confusion—Characters storm in her brow
For the scrawled characters of her release!

After the fierce octave based on dynamic nature analogies, Lowell's cadence suddenly slowed in the sestet, and he suggested a more static, historical set of symbols to give shape to the chaos: the New England images that eventually dominated the final poems inspired by this draft. But here the image of Concord was only introduced, its ironic implications—named for tranquillity, it was famous for rebellion—merely suggested before violent confusion returned.

Certainly Stafford hadn't yet worked out her symbolic geography, in which cold New England (a setting of both tranquillity and rebellion for her, too) would occupy such a prominent place, when she began to write again in the turmoil of early 1939. She was nonetheless able to write—in fact to prove herself a "fast worker," as Ogden had described her to the Atlantic Monthly Press's business office. But Lowell's poem emphasized what Stafford herself didn't tell her editors: the writing was far from painless. The bland landscape that Weeks had sketched in his outline didn't offer the creative release she needed, to judge by the manuscript that was emerging; the characters were indeed storming in her brow, but scrawling them out on paper was no liberation. The section she delivered to Ogden in April bore little resemblance to the upbeat bildungsroman the Atlantic Monthly Press staff had suggested. Confiding to Stafford (even though it was against the rules) that the initial editorial report was less than favorable, Ogden tried to suggest the problem, which was one she had been told about before: the story, he said, was heartless. Whit Burnett had bluntly made the same criticism more than a year earlier about *Which No Vicissitude:* "Verbally I think you are one of the most brilliant persons I have ever read, but I think all of these people are not merely lost, they are damned and I must say pretty repulsively damned at that."

Ogden put it somewhat more gently. The reader, he said,

> is impressed with the cleverness of the writing and the technique of the story, the gradual development of the pattern, but his emotions are not involved nor his sympathies engaged by any one character in the book. Artistically this is perhaps not a fault, but from a sales point of view it most certainly is. There must be one character with whom the reader can laugh and cry, rejoice and regret. It all sounds sticky and sentimental, but I trust you understand what I mean and I do not doubt that you will have such a character in the book by the time you have done your final revision.

Rather than the conventionally encouraging story of revolt and reconciliation that Weeks had outlined, *Autumn Festival,* as the novel was titled, was the record of a tortured consciousness. And the revised manuscript that she submitted in September, after which she left for two months at Mary Lee's ranch in Colorado, was not much different. It was more of the "exhibitionistic self-abuse" she had vowed to avoid after *Which No Vicissitude,* and yet it was also a kind of perverse precursor to *Boston Adventure,* the novel she ended up publishing five years later. There, playing off an almost mythic image of Boston, she found a successful way to tell her unconventional story of social ostracism and then infiltration, which eluded her so long as she struggled with a German setting.

In *Autumn Festival,* a draft of which survives, Stafford took Weeks's outline and gave a morbid twist to each of its proposed optimistic episodes to produce a portrait of radical alienation. Her protagonist, Gretchen Marburg, endured an unhappy childhood in America, full of ambivalence about her German father, Hermann Marburg. Mocked as a "Hun," she felt excluded and marked forever: "There was never a time she did not know that she was largely German. . . . Next to Bolshevik, that had been the worst thing in the world to be." Her adolescence was similarly loveless and insecure. Her brother's friends laughed at her, and her one frail effort at romance turned to hate when she was rejected.

The focus of the story was Gretchen's year at the University of Heidelberg, her father's alma mater, where she went after college in 1936, at the age of twenty-one, with her brother, Karl. She wasn't appalled by far worse things than she ran away from at home, as Weeks had prescribed. On the contrary, she discovered a strange salve for her self-loathing loneliness in Nazism, to which she subscribed with desperate fervor. "In America, Gretchen had been kithless; in the country of her own blood, she felt assimilated with a nation." As for the love affair the Atlantic Monthly Press proposed for "rising interest," Gretchen's attachment to the young Nazi aviator Rheinhard Rössler was a chilling union, contrived mainly to ensure her acceptance as a loyal Nazi. For this was a young woman in search of a violent, punishing embrace: "There might be, as the aviator said, here something to take in your two hands; maybe you could wrench a tree by the roots. You could believe in something hard and brutal like the Hebrew God that could scare the daylights out of a sinner and scorch the sinews of an idolator."

But Gretchen also aspired to revenge against the world, convinced in her loneliness that she was sinned against as well as sinning. She found a pretext for it in her frantic determination to prove her faithfulness to the Nazi cause. "Like the Catholic in whom the ritual grows and grows until it becomes all, so she rejected nothing of National Socialism." In fact, she went so far as to inform on her own brother, an anti-Nazi, as well as on several of his friends and an old humanist at the university, Professor von Reisenhoff, her father's mentor during his student days. While Rössler was being killed in Spain, soldiers were pillaging on the home front as well: they stormed Professor von Reisenhoff's apartment, thanks to Gretchen's tip. Appalled by what she had done, in self-defense she murdered a drunken Nazi in the mêlée that ensued. But the writing leaves it far from clear that her eyes were opened in the process. After a brief and fearful refuge in drunken oblivion herself—the novel is full of "drinking and howling and flirting with strangers" as an escape from self-hatred—Gretchen was rescued by the chance to leave Germany, arranged by one of Rössler's friends.

The novel was an exercise in venting self-disgust and revulsion with the world. It was an outpouring that Stafford seemed to be powerless to redirect in more positive directions, even though that was her own creative aim, not just the commercial desire of her editors. During the previous summer she had exhorted herself, in correspondence with Hightower, to purge her writing of its defeatist strain. That she found it very hard to avoid was suggested by the insistence of her rhetoric: "I will not write any more books that are discouraging; I will not be a writer of defeat.... I will not teach anyone a doctrine of futility, and I will not delight anyone with violent burlesque.... It is wrong to put futility and disease down on paper." The remedy she had usefully identified was comic irony, which she tried with very uneven success in her Neville novel. The trouble with *Autumn Festival* was that she doomed any effort at tragic ironic tension by rendering her protagonist in such profoundly unsympathetic terms. For a brief moment, during the fall of 1938 when she had written to Hightower about embarking on her portrait of the artist (which she apparently quickly abandoned), Stafford had managed to feel fondness for a heroine with the same name—and had remarked upon it: "I like Gretchen Marburg now as I did not before." But sympathy eluded her when she set to work on *Autumn Festival* in 1939. Instead of the protagonist pulled between love and literature whom she had described to Hightower, what emerged was a character incapable of love who in her guilty, agonized isolation concluded that "You could anaesthetize yourself in one of the two German ways: the Reich way or the way of books"—and chose the Reich way.

Stafford may have assumed that making Gretchen a Nazi automatically ensured a certain ironic distance, much as Gretchen seemed to feel that becoming a Nazi could rescue her from the burden of being herself. But it is precisely that parallel that undermines any consistent possibility of irony: Stafford's merciless narration, like Gretchen's merciless indoctrination, reads like an act of self-punishing will rather than an act of self-transcending imagination. Instead of irony, there is an air of futility, as one of the Atlantic Monthly Press readers vividly complained, remarking that Gretchen

> is so completely negative that I can't feel very much interest in what happens to her. The whole business seems futile, morbid, and slightly unpleasant. There is hardly a page without a bad smell of some kind on it, and the result is so unsavory that it obscures the genuine merits of the piece.
>
> I don't know what the remedy for all of this may be, but I suspect that one cause for it is that Miss Stafford has been reading too much Joyce.

She had been reading Joyce almost obsessively, and this influence lay behind some of the "genuine merits" of the manuscript as well as its excesses. Stafford was still readily carried away by abstract "words, merely," seduced by their sound as much as by their meaning, but she was also striving for greater concreteness and often attaining it. Working her way out of the old loose introspection, she displayed a new, if sometimes less-than-nuanced, concern for form. She had taken pains to impose structure on her enterprise.

In fact, the central theme of her novel was the necessity of form, however brutalizing, to give meaning to otherwise undirected experience. Like Stephen Dedalus, who was "proud and sensitive and suspicious, battling against the squalor of his life and the riot of his mind," Gretchen turned on the world and herself in rage and guilt. But instead of the portrait of the artist that Stafford had in mind when she wrote to Hightower, she turned Weeks's instructions into a pretext for writing what amounted to an anti-*Kunstlerroman.* Where Stephen's battle had a triumphant artistic outcome in *Portrait of the Artist as a Young Man,* Stafford denied Gretchen such release. Stephen turned his back on the Catholic priesthood after suffering turmoils of the flesh and spirit, to become instead in his own mind "a priest of eternal imagination, transmuting the daily bread of experience into the radiant body of everliving life." Gretchen discovered no transcendence but remained trapped in an unwieldy body and a mind racked by guilt. She occasionally considered the possibility of elevation through art but was inhibited by what felt like an incompatibility between the roles of writer and woman: "It was the same old horse and cow debate, which was better, a creative woman or a homebody." She couldn't reconcile the creative woman with a body: "She thought of the ink stains on the sleeves of her blouse . . . of her room which had no gender and belonged, as did the ink stains, to a desiccated Marburg, and she wondered if she looked like a woman . . . if she was as unsexed as her mother, who was as uninteresting as a plain white linen pincushion."

Instead, the only vocation Gretchen could claim was not a creative analogy to the Church, but a destructive parody of it. Throughout the novel, Stafford adumbrated a parallel between the zealous Catholic and the fanatic Nazi. At the close, the religious framework became explicit in the symbolic superimposition of Golgotha on Heidelberg and the arrival of Lent: "The great grave of Golgotha, the ostentatious mausoleum and the carnage primly covered and marked with a Christian cross to which four extra arms had been affixed, was a charming town cut by a beautifully twisting river." Here, as throughout, Stafford's irony is almost impossible to gauge, but this awkward image effectively undercut any suggestion of imminent redemption for Germany or for Gretchen. This Lent wasn't likely to end in any resurrection into "everliving life."

As it turned out, Stafford herself was denied any reward after writing two drafts of the novel, a labor that must have been a masochistic ordeal. It is not hard to read into the manuscript Stafford's own anxieties about ostracism and her ambivalence about literature as a salvation from corrosive self-doubt and hatred, magnified to nightmarish proportions. Despite Ogden's championing of what he admitted was a "curiously tortured story," the Atlantic Monthly Press rejected *Autumn Festival* in December 1939. In a sense it was a fitting fate for an anti-*Kunstlerroman*, just as the publication of a portrait of the artist can be its own self-fulfilling conclusion. It was also a familiar fate for Stafford; she had been turned down before. Once again, she reacted with impressive resilience. Earlier she had shown herself eager to be taken in hand, even harshly, and now, though she had made obvious strides since *Which No Vicissitude,* she seemed to know she needed to be goaded to avoid that "doctrine of futility," as she described her tendency to Hightower.

Years later, in 1952, Stafford offered this rather strange retrospective assessment: "The war came along and [the novel's] slant wasn't topical enough. Thank Heaven, oh, thank Heaven, its author apostrophizes. It was not, in retrospect, a book she would like to have written." Her declaration is striking not only for its subtle distortion of the circumstances of rejection—actually, the book was all too topical, though its slant would definitely have been unpopular—but also for her emphatic relief that the book was buried. *Autumn Festival* evidently was a disturbing skeleton in her literary closet, which she only later found ways to flesh out more successfully and acceptably.

At the time, the impact of rejection may have been softened by a development in another quarter: she made public her engagement to Lowell when he returned from Kenyon for Christmas vacation and they saw each other in Cambridge, where she was now sharing an apartment with two Vassar graduates. It is even possible that Stafford's publishing setback played some part in encouraging her to solidify their plans. In December of 1939, the same month that her manuscript was turned down by the Atlantic Monthly Press, she wrote to Hightower to announce, "I am engaged to marry Cal Lowell," a prospect that she described in chilling terms: "You said it would happen . . . and I did not believe it. Then I hated him but he does what I have always needed to have done to me and that is that he dominates me."

It is possible to wonder whether Lowell the college senior would have been able to dominate—and whether Stafford would have been so sure she needed it—had he confronted an author who had just sold her novel. For it seems clear that creative aspirations and anxieties played an important part in their relations, which from the start had obviously thrived on great strain. To say this is not to minimize the psychological interplay that Stafford herself saw at work: her masochistic inclinations and his aggressive impulses fueling each other. Perhaps the best clue to the interwoven artistic and emotional tensions of their far from tender courtship lies in a story called "1939," written many years later by Peter Taylor, Lowell's Kenyon roommate and the closest mutual friend of Stafford and Lowell throughout their lives. It seems to have been inspired by Lowell's Thanksgiving visit of the year before, but the story suggests the peculiar embattled intensity that continued to mark their relations.

Peter Taylor's story is a fondly comic drama that is more about literary competition between its protagonists than about romantic incompatibility, though the two are not easily separated. Above all, it is about immaturity. The story is not true in any strict sense; when it came out in 1955 in *The New Yorker,* Taylor wrote to Stafford, "It is full of lies about us all, with just the modicum of truth necessary to make the lies worth telling." The key to its main characters is clear enough: the first-person narrator is Taylor, his Kenyon roommate Jim Prewitt is Lowell, and Prewitt's girlfriend, Carol Crawford, is Stafford. The action roughly follows fact as the two restless Kenyon boys set off on the long drive from Gambier, Ohio, to New York to join their girlfriends.

There are, however, salient alterations of fact that make the story even more revealing about reality: when the boys arrive in the big city, Carol has just had a novel accepted, two parts of which are about to appear in *Partisan Review,* and when they leave she has jilted Jim. In fact, the Atlantic Monthly Press jilted Stafford—the success Taylor described didn't come until five years later, with the appearance of *Boston Adventure*— and she accepted Lowell's proposal. But Taylor's distortions are in the service of that "modicum of truth," for they help convey the mixture of ambition about literature and ambivalence about love that characterized that part of their lives. The story offers the male perspective on the awkward stage, but essential to "1939" is the prevailing irony about the in-adequacy of "the boys'" view. Taylor gleefully noted the conflicting reactions to the story. "Those two nice boys, and those *awful* girls," some said, but there is another possible response: those poor girls, those lucky boys.

For Taylor's story is double-edged. On the one hand, it is about two bookish college boys who are endearingly eager to display their indepen-dence and acquire the "mature and adult experience" essential to their literary vocation. They are rudely disenchanted when the girlfriends they admire for their "'critical' and 'objective'" view of life condescend-ingly dump them in favor of finer attractions—in Carol Crawford's case, the blandishments of the bohemian literary set open to her once she has sold her novel. (Nancy Gibault, the narrator's girlfriend, decides she isn't an artist and suddenly sees the appeal of an older, richer hometown boy.) On the other hand, Taylor is tough on the self-pitying boys and subtly sympathetic to the girls. The "independents" (as the boys think of them-selves), foiled in their quest for the mature experience that would mix love and literature, don't have much cause to complain about the New York fiasco. In fact, they can be somewhat relieved: they have the com-fortable haven of their college house (modeled on Douglass House, the literary enclave at Kenyon where Lowell, Taylor, and Randall Jarrell, among others, lived) to return to. There they have the camaraderie they profess to hate as well as a respite before they have to be anything more than aspiring writers—and not least, they have an escape from those unconventional, potentially competitive, creative girls they claim to ad-mire. There is an air of slightly pampered gentility about these rebels, with their rumpled respectable clothes and horn-rimmed glasses.

The girls, as Taylor describes them, can't afford such luxurious im-maturity. They are confronted with a profoundly significant choice, which the boys completely fail to comprehend. Nancy announces her realization that she isn't an artist, which the narrator fliply and cruelly endorses: "When we were at lunch yesterday, you know, with Jim and his girl," he tells her, "it came over me suddenly that you weren't an artist. Just by looking at you I could tell." Carol has come to the opposite real-ization, that she is an artist, and Taylor digresses to offer the mature, retrospective portrait of her even more difficult predicament—an under-standing that eluded him as a youth:

Poor Carol Crawford! How unfair it is to describe her as she was that Thanksgiving weekend in 1939. Ever since she was a little girl on a dairy farm in Wisconsin she had dreamed of becoming a writer and going to live in New York City. She had not merely dreamed of it. She had worked toward it every waking hour of her life, taking jobs after school in the wintertime, and full-time jobs in the summer, always saving the money to put herself through the state university. She had made herself the best student—the prize pupil—in every grade of grammar school and high school. At the university she had managed to win every scholarship in sight. Through all those years she had had but one ambition, and yet I could not have met her at a worse moment of her life. Poor girl, she had just learned that she *was* a writer.

Taylor's version of Stafford's youthful single-mindedness is purposely exaggerated to call attention to the truly independent, hardheaded effort she had expended. In oblique contrast, the cosseted boys are both expecting checks in the mail from home when the story opens. And Carol's arrival at her goal entails yet more hard work of a different kind, as the story shows: now the self-made girl has to be one of the boys among the bohemian set. The task is strenuously to cultivate connections and camaraderie with more established writers. In the succession of Greenwich Village apartments to which Carol drags Jim, the ambience is male and the tone intimidatingly, judgmentally intellectual. The style is calculated knowingness; everyone goes by surname only and is adept with the sophisticated put-down ("*so* naive, *so* undergraduate") as well as with the ingratiating bow to those better ensconced. Carol is thoroughly caught up in the scene. Suddenly the outsider has had a taste of the inside, and Taylor suggests how much more important that loomed for the girl from the provinces than for the boys from the genteel families and the Kenyon circle, who already knew the pleasures and perquisites of belonging.

In fiction, Taylor simplified the asymmetry and sent the boys and girls on their separate ways after that fateful weekend, Crawford forging ahead to the greatest fame of them all. In fact, at the end of 1939 Stafford's literary career was uncertain, and far from spurning Lowell, she had declared that she needed his dominating influence. In a sense she was straddling the choices that Taylor had divided between Carol and

Nancy, which turned out to be perhaps the most difficult course of all. Stafford had discovered that she was a writer—had been told by editors and teachers that she was a writer—but she hadn't yet proved that identity with literary accomplishment. As important, she wasn't altogether sure just what price she was willing, or dared, to pay for that proof. Her letters to Hightower testified to the tension she felt between the poles she labeled love and literature. On the one hand, she energetically pursued her writing career and literary connections; on the other, she proclaimed her need to be a dominated woman. In Lowell there was a possible resolution. She could have her assertive hometown boy—from the home she wanted to claim as her own, literary Boston, not Colorado—and be a writer, too. With the independent but pedigreed Lowell, she could be a rebellious author but also an established wife, an insider.

In a letter to Merrill Moore, a peripheral member of the Fugitives and a friend of Lowell's parents (they had appointed him Cal's guardian that summer while they went to Europe to escape the scandal of the car accident and the lawsuit), Lowell outlined his intentions in terms that suggest the ambition and sense of embattlement that played an important part in his match with Stafford. "I am confident that given anything like an even break, I shall in the future achieve things of considerable value," Lowell announced to Moore, and went on to describe his new, mature strategy, which sounds as though it might well have been conceived in the course of his forbidden summer meetings with Stafford:

> By an even break I mean chiefly to be able to act without the autocratic guidance of friends and parents.
>
> My carreer [*sic*], I hope, will be exceptional rather than queer. That is I have become more and more aware of the need for an at least surface conformity, dressing inconspicuously and neatly, living by a stable economy, flaunting [*sic*] convention by penetration rather than by eccentricity.

By an entirely different route, Stafford had arrived at a comparable aspiration. For Lowell, the subversive challenge was to stake a claim to originality without overtly abandoning tradition, which was for him incarnate in his family; he aimed to play unruly genius off against gentility. Stafford's urgent need, as the ordeals of her autobiographical character Gretchen suggested, was to lose her sense of queerness in submission to some form of convention, preferably a stern and alien one. (It is not hard to see a disturbing parallel between Gretchen's infatuation with the domineering Nazis and Stafford's desire to cast Lowell in the role of dominating lover.) Aristocratic Boston would make a fine proving ground for Stafford the "hick," as the Lowells had made clear they considered her. Not that she aimed to submit docilely by any means; motivated by an uneasy mixture of self-hatred and self-interest, Stafford was evidently attracted by the idea of belonging, but not of simply obeying.

The match answered the upstart inclinations of both of them, and Lowell also had guilt about the accident to contend with. Yet mutual fascination probably shouldn't be underestimated as the motive that clouded all others. In retrospect Stafford claimed that they had had a "glorious affair" before they were married, a curious characterization, given the peripatetic year between the accident and their wedding, but one that suggests perhaps the dizzying intensity of that time together. "Glorious" certainly hadn't meant serene. On the contrary, struggle seemed to increase their interest in each other, and once marriage plans were announced, opposition served to bolster their resolve—opposition from the right, benighted places. Boston was aghast, Lowell's parents informed the couple, and they did their best to rouse condemnation elsewhere as well, insinuating none too subtly that their son had been trapped by the injured Stafford. Their displeasure was made known at Kenyon, and though Ransom obliged by making it clear that Stafford would not be welcome on campus for Lowell's last semester, he didn't disapprove. In fact, he promptly started pulling strings to help set up the couple after Kenyon. "Lowell is more than a student, he's more like a son to me," read the recommendation Ransom wrote for his protégé. Allen Tate, Lowell's other surrogate father, thoroughly flouted parental wishes by giving Stafford away on April 2, 1940, at St. Mark's Episcopal Church in the Bowery, where the small wedding took place. There was no immediate family present.

It was not a marriage launched in happy peace. At least that was how Stafford portrayed it to Hightower, who lived around the corner from her in Cambridge and who had been restored to the position of confidant. The version of events she presented to her rejected suitor is obviously not the most reliable record. Still, several letters convey a sense of confused dread about the course that she was embarking on and about the self-doubt that was driving her. The first, written on March 31, 1940, from the Hotel Albert in New York, where the couple was staying two days before the wedding, was the most explicit, though not altogether articulate, expression of anxiety: Stafford was drunk when she wrote it. It had been an awful day, and she was sitting with a solacing bottle of rum, she explained. "[Cal] should not have left me tonight and yet at this moment we are so irritated we hate each other," she scrawled in far looser script than usual (on hotel stationery adorned with the motto "Where Courtesy Dwells"). A sense of duplicity and insecurity evidently overwhelmed her, prompted by a relatively minor confession: she had admitted to Lowell that she didn't really know German well at all. Unnerved, she proceeded to a desperate and somewhat cryptic postscript:

> Say a novena for me—you've got to. Our lies—yours and mine—have to remain forever and our truths must always be implicit in a casual affection and implicit only to us—and I shall never know, I suppose, how vain I am. I am a great fool and incidentally Cal knows it. . . . I told him about the German and he was absolutely stopped in his tracks & revolted. What wd he do if he knew me? P.S. He just came in and said you've got to stop drinking and I mean even 1 drink and I was panic-stricken for fear he wd take my rum away. It was very definite, very true and yet I shall perhaps not marry him & if I do not I shall be invisible for the rest of my natural days.

Stafford was much calmer when she wrote again, two days after the wedding. She and Lowell had parted in Cleveland, where they had gone by train after the wedding—he heading for Kenyon (where she wasn't welcome), she for her sister's ranch. "I am beginning to see what comfort there is in being married. He will, I think, make an honest woman of me," she wrote from Chicago, a lyrical fondness leavening her foreboding. But she was quick to undercut any suggestion of simple domestic harmony; comfort would not come easily to this less-than-malleable wife. Stafford might fear invisibility, but she had no illusions that she was helplessly vulnerable. Once again, she acknowledged her own skills as victimizer, of herself as well as of others: "How typical that I should have had a honeymoon on a train and in Cleveland. And while I may lay it all to external circumstances in my soul I know it is only my peculiar genius for the uncomfortable. Poor Cal! What a life he will have with me."

In a third letter Stafford displayed yet another perspective, suddenly neither desperate nor wistfully fond. Instead, she declared herself coldly resigned to her fate. She now viewed her admission of her inadequacies in German to have been a moment of sincere self-exposure that she regretted: "It was an absolutely needless confession." Similarly, she revised the warm tone of her Chicago reflections, reporting on the "utter dreariness of our leavetaking in Cleveland, he on a bus to Gambier and I on a train to Chicago thinking in our numb way that now we were married and the worst was over." Her mood was bleak: "I have no very terrible fears. I have had only one letter from him, and that chilled me to the bone." Meanwhile, she heard plenty from the other Lowells, firsthand and secondhand: "Gossip that is said about me in the Chilton Club and so forth, initiated by Mrs. Lowell and turned into neat phrases by Merrill Moore before she publishes them in the club as well as in letters. The Tates stand by us but they are our only support.... I have been stirred up continually by the evil predictions for Cal's destruction through me...."

Yet for all the apprehension that Stafford obviously felt—and that, for obvious reasons, she emphasized to Hightower—she also had fulfilled an ambition. The first letter Lowell wrote as husband to his wife had perhaps "chilled" her, but to judge by one he sent to his parents at roughly the same time, he was taking the occasion of his new married maturity to display exactly the peremptory determination that had attracted her. There was to be no veering off into invisibility for him, that was clear. "You may enjoy talking about my sacrificed fellowship [to Harvard] and forced marriage," Lowell wrote to his mother:

> The first is uncertain and the second untrue. Naturally I find such gossip very undignified and annoying....
>
> I am not flattered by the remark that you do not know where I am heading or that my ways are not your ways. I am heading exactly where I have been heading for six years. One can hardly be ostracized for taking the intellect and aristocracy and family tradition seriously.

That was precisely what Stafford yearned to take seriously and found mortifyingly skewed in her own obscure heritage. Not that Lowell was uncritical of his elevated background, or that Stafford was either. Taking the tradition seriously entailed applying a critical perspective—as Lowell made clear in his valedictory address at his Kenyon graduation: "Customs are not a culture, Boston is no longer Athens. I am emphasizing a

glaring problem, our aristocracy . . . has special advantages but no superior way of life." In the Agrarian vision of the ideal hierarchical literary
order, Lowell had found rigorous prescriptions for the true cultural, critical elite that society required. Strenuous discipline not decadence, energy not enervation, were required for the artistic labor of transforming
recalcitrant experience into aesthetic form. In fact, arduous struggle was
perhaps the most important sign, and justification, of exclusivity; "dualism, division, tension, and conflict, the clash of desires, evil and pain," as
two New Critical theorists, W. K. Wimsatt and Cleanth Brooks later put
it in *Literary Criticism: A Short History (1957)*, were the key to the mature
literature and criticism required for a sound society.

Stafford's accounts to Hightower made clear just how central struggle
was to her relationship with Lowell, and she emphasized that she was in
a sense well equipped for it, with her "peculiar genius for the uncomfortable." But she was also conscious of that "genius" as an ambiguous
attribute. It was "peculiar" because, as the rest of that passage suggests, it
removed her from the role of accommodating woman and wife, or of
facile woman writer. She certainly was not one of the "Cambridge ladies
who live in furnished souls," women who are "unbeautiful and have
comfortable minds," as E. E. Cummings caricatured the staid, sentimental scribblers whom the modernists scorned.

But her readiness for rigor didn't mean that her course was clear, that
admission to the exclusive circle of Lowell's teachers and friends was
straightforward, especially for someone as defensively sensitive about belonging as Stafford. Once again she turned for counsel, and encouragement, to the only woman among the literary guides she had cultivated,
to the writer who was well aware of the antifeminist inclinations of the
"Tate-Ransom crowd." In a letter to Evelyn Scott not long after the wedding, Stafford must have expressed her disappointment about her rejected novel and her confusion about what lay ahead, confessing
insecurity about having crashed not just Boston, but the southern literary
elite as well. On April 30, 1940, Scott sent her a letter with reassurances
and advice:

> The tale is dismal and I am so sorry. Dismal, that is, in the literary
> sense. I don't think the marriage sounds dismal; and my observa-
> tion bears out the frequent lasting success of alliances originating in
> an atmosphere of scraps and calamities. I think nature rather likes

these. The ego seems to gratify some double craving, when, out of external and emotional turmoil, arises the edifice of a new, unanticipated relationship. . . . [T]ry out Mr. Ransom's suggestion [that she work at the *Kenyon Review* and Lowell teach a course in English and one in Latin]. He has a real interest in your husband and is willing, I gather, to make paternal efforts for his talents; and you may persuade him (Ransom) that "feminine" art is not, after all, any more femine [*sic*] in his meaning than "masculine" art is masculine in the same sense—in short that not all women writing exploit their sex in ways external to art (as he has suggested of Edna Millay).

Scott was charging Stafford with a rather intimidating mission, which revealed the awkwardness of her predicament now that, through Lowell, she had entered the inner orbit of the southern writers, whose campaign to spread their formalist literary views was shifting into high gear. In essence, Scott suggested that Stafford make the most of her connection to their star protégé to persuade Ransom that women writers don't exploit their sex. Her ego, capable of forging an alliance out of turmoil and strain, Scott implied, would be part of her proof that women do not simply "[live] for love," as Ransom had written in his essay on Millay, "The Poet as Woman," in *The World's Body*. On the contrary, she could show that they can claim some of the calculating discipline he assigned to man, whom he defined as "an intellectualized woman."

Just how uncomfortable a predicament she had gotten herself into, Stafford seemed to realize with sudden and devastating force when Hightower wrote to tell her he was marrying Bunny Cole, one of her former roommates in Cambridge. In a succession of bitter letters to him, Stafford condemned Cole for her frivolous female qualities—she was a mere "ornament," a "cottonhead," stupid and "untaught." Stafford claimed to be insulted—at least she had had the decency to betray Hightower for someone who prompted "respect . . . awe of a superior mind and a shining talent"—but the truth was more complicated. In a moment of merciless self-revelation, Stafford confessed to Hightower her sense of exile from the softer qualities, from love:

I'm a bitch, yes, and I've hurt you and brutality is my way because tenderness frightens me and I'm no hand at accepting what does not benefit me. I'll always be brutal to you and humorous, except when under the influence, and, under the influence, my maudlin incoherence will be the exhibit of a fool but in reality the release of my heart-broken, inconsummate love, which, being inconsummate must be friendship but it preserves the jealous tenderness of romantic love. If I am ungenerous, it is because I am passionate. If I am unforgiving, it is because I can only hate what comes between us. . . .

In myself, I am not a bad woman, but my appearance in people's lives is usually a disastrous accident.

Her appearance in Lowell's life literally had been marked by an almost fatal accident. But as she indirectly acknowledged, the fact that she hadn't disappeared from his life was the result of dogged will, hers and his. And as Scott suggested, their future together was likely to entail more tenacity than tenderness. "Thank God we are both writers and have as a model the superb marriage of the Tates," Stafford wrote to Hightower as she looked ahead. That model did not augur peace, but it turned out to be, certainly for Stafford, a remarkable prescription for productivity.

CHAPTER 6

Catholicism

LOWELL'S SURROGATE FATHERS saw to it that he and his new wife had somewhere to go after graduation. Hoping to keep them close to home, Ransom tried to arrange a teaching stint at Kenyon for Lowell and a job for Stafford on the *Kenyon Review*, the literary quarterly he had launched two years after coming to the college in 1937. The prospect was not quite as perfect as it looked. Though the magazine was already well known as a home for serious poetry and for the New Critical approach to literature, dedicated to close textual readings, Stafford's role was to be lowly: a typist. And Lowell, though championed by Ransom, was finally rejected as too immature by Kenyon's president. An alternative plan was promptly devised, and the couple ended up safely ensconced with another branch of the literary family. In the summer of 1940 Stafford was offered a secretarial job in Baton Rouge at the *Southern Review*, the Agrarian quarterly where the New Criticism was also in the ascendancy, and Lowell began taking classes at Louisiana State University on a junior fellowship. As Ransom wrote to the Tates (who had suggested the fallback plan of setting up house in Tory Valley, in Dutchess County, New York, where, Caroline Gordon remembered, "we spent our first year of wedded life. It was tough but healthy"), the arrangement was the next best thing: "I told [the president of LSU] I would have only envy of him if he got that team (Cal and Jean) as it was precisely the team we'd wanted here."

Instead of remaining with Ransom, the senior guide of the southern literary circle who was known for his courtly kindness, Stafford and Lowell found themselves among his followers, who tended to be fiercer. The physical climate in Baton Rouge inspired sluggishness—Stafford liked to exclaim over the preposterous heat, and everybody liked to drink a lot—but the intellectual climate was invigorating. The two years they spent in the South were a formative time for Stafford. She was fascinated and appalled by the landscape. "Louisiana, on the whole, is lovely, but it is lethal, teeming with serpents, disease, spiders, tainted meat. I've never seen anything so lush, and I've never been anywhere that I was so little tempted to go barefoot." She was equally divided about her other discoveries that year. She was learning the full extent of her husband's intensity, as Lowell turned from zealous literary criticism to zealous Catholicism. And while she coped with her secretarial chores, she was finding out how disciplined a student, of belief and of fiction, she could be. The Lowells' start together was tough, as Gordon characterized her own first year of marriage, but not healthy. Stafford was sick—with fevers, a bad cough, flu, and kidney infections—a good deal of the time.

The main draw in Baton Rouge was Robert Penn Warren, one of Ransom's former students, as well as a great friend and protégé of Allen Tate and one of the contributors to the Agrarian manifesto, *I'll Take My Stand,* in 1930. With Cleanth Brooks, Warren was co-editing the *Southern Review* in the proselytizing spirit Tate had endorsed when the quarterly was founded in 1935. The editor, Tate instructed in "The Function of the Critical Quarterly" (1936), "owes his first duty to his critical principles, his sense of the moral and intellectual order upon which society ought to rest." Meanwhile in the classroom, Warren and Brooks were unsettling the LSU English department with their heretical interpretive techniques, which had been codified two years earlier in their influential textbook *Understanding Poetry* (1938).

The Lowells had arrived during an important transition for the erstwhile Fugitives: they were consolidating in a new cause, one that consumed them through the 1940s. Their Agrarian goal of restoring the traditional hierarchical society they revered in the Old South had been derided in both the North and the South; the urban, industrial economy showed no signs of giving way before the imprecations, however eloquent, of "Twelve Southerners" in *I'll Take My Stand.* So they increasingly devoted their attention to a more manageable crusade. Their aim was to reform the teaching of English in American colleges and universities, where literature, they argued, was buried under the weight of erroneous readings. Historical scholarship had to give way to a new focus on textual criticism, on the intrinsic elements of a literary work rather than on extrinsic influences and sources. Above all, the southern explicators emphasized the linguistic and structural tensions within the literary work, issuing in irony, ambiguity, and paradox. And, following Eliot, they championed a new perspective on English poetry that elevated the metaphysical poets as models of the "unification of sensibility" essential to poetry—intellect and emotion maturely joined and rendered effectively indistinguishable. In 1940 the New Critics were still on the outskirts of the academy, rebels scattered through English departments in the South, but they were determined to make inroads.

Stafford and Lowell were perhaps not quite the wholehearted recruits Ransom judged them to be. During the spring, in the turmoil following their marriage, they had talked dramatically of escape from the opprobrium of Boston, from the philistinism of America, and not least from the claustrophobia of the academy. As Hightower and his new wife prepared to leave for China, Stafford sometimes dreamily, sometimes desperately, spun out fantasies of joining them. It was an old rebellious plan dating from her days in Boulder with Hightower; they had made it as far as Heidelberg, but they had told each other the real goal was to flee the West. Now Hightower was making good on the adolescent scheme as he entered adulthood. Stafford was envious, and Lowell, she told Hightower, was as ready to take a momentous step as she was.

In fact, it was really she who was frantic to flee during the low weeks after their wedding, and she was briefly convinced that above all she needed to escape from Lowell. As she prepared to go to Kenyon for his graduation in June 1940, she wrote to Hightower, pleading with him to come see her on his way out West en route to China. They ended up meeting in Omaha in the middle of the night at the end of May. Stafford's cry for help was reminiscent of the agonized letters she had sent him in the past: she didn't love Lowell, couldn't live with him, and had discovered, she claimed, that her earlier avowals of frigidity were in fact true (she admitted that she had been lying, or thought she had been lying, before). She wanted only Hightower, and she proposed that they both abandon their spouses and disappear. Hightower wasn't interested, and Stafford wasn't really surprised. Fatalism quickly set in: "I feel exiled and it breaks my heart to think I am extraneous to your life," she wrote to him as she proceeded along the path that had been laid out for the wife who was now part of Lowell's life.

She and he moved South flattered by the solicitude of Lowell's mentors yet somewhat disappointed that their situation was so academic. And Stafford couldn't even look forward to teaching or taking classes:

she was not enthusiastic about the secretarial duties that awaited her. Newly arrived in Baton Rouge in June, she wrote to Hightower and tried to conjure up the atmosphere for him. "This place, Robert, is a university and it is like every other university I have seen," she began in a world-weary tone, but as the rest of her description revealed, the place was in fact more caught up in its own divisive affairs than most campuses. The debate over the teaching of English was in full swing:

> Talk in academic gatherings is of . . . (1) language requirements for the degree PhD (2) the deficiencies of the Freshman English curriculum and (3) the necessity of subordinating historical scholarship to criticism or vice versa. And Cal says, I wish we had gone to China. Sat. night we ate at the Brooks's . . . and had food on our laps in a brightly lighted and much too small room and we were there for six hours hearing those three things. . . . Now mind, they were all delightful, charming, amusing people *but* it is a university. It is academic. It is that and nothing more.

The spirit in the *Southern Review* offices was similarly combative. "The place is revealing," she wrote to Hightower the same month. "Letters from contributors are rec'd with shrieks of laughter, mss are sneered at, rejection slips go out furiously. The Atlantic Monthly looks like a bunch of kind old ladies." The quarterly was gearing up for a major offensive in the New Critics' campaign to convert the academic world, or at least to establish a respectable place for their kind of criticism in it. During Stafford's year at the *Southern Review,* its issues were crowded with articles making the case against historical scholarship and in favor of close commentary and the modernist approach to literature. The culmination of the campaign came in a symposium entitled "Literature and the Professors," conducted jointly with the *Kenyon Review* in the autumn 1940 issues of the two magazines.

At LSU, Lowell experienced the pedagogical and critical ferment firsthand. His initial response, like Stafford's, was a degree of detachment from all the academic earnestness. "I am not looking for a vocation or marking time," he wrote to his grandmother, sounding nonchalant. "If war comes and they want me, I'll gladly go; if not, I'll continue in this peaceful and sedentary occupation of university work. I suppose writing is something of a career, something that steadily grows more secure and substantial." In a letter to Robie Macauley, one of his Kenyon housemates, he began in a similarly aloof manner: "About L.S.U. I have taken as my motto, 'In Rome consort with the Romans and never do as they do.' Here reign the critical approach, 'the aesthetic approach,' 'metaphysical poetry,' 'drama in the lyric' etc. The students are weak and worthy." But then his letter took an unexpected, elliptical turn:

> Brooks and Warren / Brooksandwarren are excellent. Especially Warren; result: I am reading English theology.
>
> This, as perhaps Randall Jarrell would say, is not as crazy as it sounds, but it's pretty crazy and must not be amplified. My poetic terminology using: heresy, diabolic, frivolous gnosticism etc, should worry the solemn and liberal English majors.

The letter was an oblique augury of what was to come: chafing in the role of student, Lowell was inclining toward discipleship, a discipleship that went beyond the expectations even of his English teachers—and beyond his own. Contrary to what he had claimed to his grandmother, he was looking for a vocation; evidently it was not so easy to wait patiently while his writing efforts grew steadily (or unsteadily) "more secure and substantial." He needed a calling, not "something of a career."

At first Lowell found a satisfactory mission in distinguishing himself from the "weak and worthy" students. He quickly earned the respect of Warren and, especially, of Brooks. He was not one of the dilettantish college boys but a colleague engaged in the project of establishing criticism as a profession, for that was essentially the New Critics' intent: to stake the claim for the study of poetry that was implied in Eliot's claims for the writing of it—that it was not a personal, impressionistic, belletristic endeavor, but an occupation anchored in tradition and guided by exacting, prescriptive principles and techniques. It was a discipline that demanded total dedication and required a pure, formalistic approach that historicist and other critics failed to appreciate. "The opposite of the professional, the enemy, is the man of mixed motives, . . ." Eliot wrote. "Surely professionalism in art is hard work on style with singleness of purpose." That was the kind of uncompromising prescription that Lowell thrived on.

Stafford's predicament was rather different, and so was her perspective. Rather than musing about her writing career, much less about a literary vocation, she was starting a job, which right away meant hard work on shorthand. Her assessment of her situation was a wry echo of

Lowell's report to his grandmother. "My life seems annually more fogged and my retrogression is steady—now I'm a secretary," she wrote to Hightower in June. "And will the next be a telephone operator or will I be the receptionist in a city laundry? This is not gloom, merely curiosity." Wryness continued to dilute resentment. She was quite amusing, and cutting, about her labors and her colleagues. She followed the critical controversies from her clerical perch, then wrote letters that mixed skepticism with obvious excitement at being in the midst of the ferment.

She readily assumed the role of housekeeper as well as breadwinner. Though she enjoyed complaining about unpacking in the heat, fixing up their apartment was a preoccupation that gave her pleasure. As the wife of a promising young poet in 1940, Stafford fully expected that domestic distractions would hem in her own writing life. She was prepared to be the comparative amateur, to dilute artistic motives with practical ones. But her role was not simply socially ordained. Stafford found domestic details and duties very seductive—she was, as she acknowledged, her mother's daughter in her willing absorption in the homely sphere of orderliness. She sometimes suspected that her nesting zeal was a reaction to the sense of uprootedness she had felt as a child, thanks to her father's fantasies. Her domesticity was doubtless also encouraged by Lowell's utter abstraction from such concrete concerns, his penchant for high, austere discipline. Not least important, there were models for their respective roles: cerebral Allen Tate and capable Caroline Gordon, who was renowned for running crowded households with one hand and writing crowded novels with the other.

Renowned but not, for the most part, doubly respected. The writer wife had to be intense about her literary work (or she would never get any done), and yet according to a critic whom Stafford herself admired, the competing pressures of home and writing meant that she was unlikely to be intellectual enough about her art. "To be intellectual," Ransom wrote in "The Poet as Woman," "is to be disciplined in technique and stocked with learning, a very great advantage for every purpose, and even for fertilizing the pleasures of imagination." It was, he continued, an advantage largely denied women "because they are not strict enough and expert enough to manage forms,—in their default of the disciplines under which men are trained." Granted, there was a certain compensating literary gift that accrued to women as the keepers of the house, as Ransom acknowledged in his essay "Sentimental Exercise":

It will probably be agreed that women have much more aptitude for cultivation of sentiments than men do.... A good housewife ... makes a point ... not to have merely useful or abstract relations with the things and persons of her ménage, but to seek in addition a delicious knowledge of them as individual objects.

But it was a gift that women writers, lacking discipline, were in danger of indulging to excess, he suggested. At least at the outset, Stafford threw herself into the management of her ménage, which in true Tate fashion quickly became crowded and complicated. There were problems with the woman whom they hired to clean. There was lots of socializing, not just with the Warrens and Brookses, but with numerous friends and literary figures passing through—among them the Jarrells and, awaited with some trepidation, the British critic I. A. Richards and his wife.

And there were two boarders—"a great gauche lummox of a girl from Memphis who is my assistant," Stafford wrote to Hightower, and Peter Taylor, who was by comparison "considerably more attractive but wants a brain." In fact, that fall Stafford and Taylor became the close friends they turned out to be for life. Though they and Lowell proved to be a sturdy trio, relations were not without strain, especially at the start. There was an obvious and immediate affinity between Stafford and Taylor that, as Robie Macauley observed, left Lowell feeling slightly excluded. The two of them were great talkers, their style witty where Lowell tended to tongue-tied ponderousness. In the prevailing literary hierarchy, their interest—prose—was less elevated, and they could both joke about their want of brains as no poet, or certainly not Lowell, would.

The emotional ease and directness between them doubtless stood out as Lowell grew ever more intellectually preoccupied—but not too preoccupied to notice and finally to intervene. Stafford's description of the scene, in a letter to Hightower in October, was flippant but revealing: "Peter & I got incredibly drunk and exchanged words over the extent of Peter's love for me & the peril of it so that Cal, who spent the evening talking with Mr. Brooks about belief, did not speak to Peter for 1 week thereafter." Lowell was the stern pedant in the household—though he also had a comical streak, too often overlooked. In Baton Rouge he introduced Stafford to one of his favorite games, featuring a humorous cast of animal characters called "berts," pronounced "bear" in French fashion.

He was Big Bert, she was Bigless Bert, alter egos through whom they could be wittily expressive with each other—and droll with the friends whom they initiated into the game.

But as the fall progressed, Lowell's preoccupation with belief intensified as he read theology, plowing through Étienne Gilson's *The Spirit of Medieval Philosophical Experience* and his *Philosophy of Thomas Aquinas,* then turning to E. I. Watkin, John Henry Newman, Jacques Maritain, Blaise Pascal, Gerard Manley Hopkins. He began to take instruction with Father Shexnayder at LSU. The leap from reforming the English curriculum to reforming the soul was not as large as it looked. Implicit in the formalist literary mission, as Eliot's own conversion had already suggested and Tate's would later, was a religious conception of the word as the way to truth. Though the critics didn't play up the religious dimension of their views as they vied for influence in English departments, it was perhaps no surprise that Lowell readily fastened on to it. "The religious mind would seem, in the end," the critic W. K. Wimsatt wrote much later, "to be more hospitable to the tensional and metaphysical view of poetry than the naturalistic mind is able to be." Elsewhere he and Cleanth Brooks summed up the perspective lurking behind their literary position as "the vision of suffering, the optimism, the mystery which are embraced in the religious dogma of the Incarnation." And as Lowell's teacher at St. Mark's, Richard Eberhart, had remarked years before, his protégé's early efforts at poetry showed that "his mind was heavy and that it was essentially religious."

Lowell was increasingly adamant about the new order and direction in his life and insistent that his devotional regimen embrace the whole household. That meant two rosaries a day, Mass in the morning, benediction in the evening, only suitably serious books, fish on Fridays. A pious attitude was required, and impious habits (smoking and drinking) were fiercely discouraged. Stafford, not surprisingly, was deeply ambivalent. She too had recognized religious inclinations in herself and had acted on them. But her sessions with Father Agatho during college (a failure, thanks to her "indolence") had led her to suspect her mind wasn't naturally "heavy" and disposed to rigorous discipline (as her English teacher Miss McKeehan had also gently suggested in another context). In the last story published in her lifetime, "An Influx of Poets" (1978), the most directly autobiographical she ever wrote, Stafford put more emphasis on the desperation of her youthful search for faith, but still there was an air of futility about it:

> My mission had not been accomplished, despite my fervor and my need. Later on, from time to time, I tried again in different churches of different towns at different seasons of the year and different hours of day and night. But I was God-forsaken; the shepherd could not hear my bleating, for I was miles astray in the cold and the dark and the desert. And at last I vanished without a trace; with a faint shiver and a faint sigh, I gave up the Ghost.

In Baton Rouge, a deep passivity seemed to come over her in the face of Lowell's fervent mission. This time, instead of straying from the path, she was pulled along by Lowell. "An Influx of Poets" dramatized her unconsciously acquiescent detachment as her husband, whom she called Theron in her story, swept her up in his all-consuming new cause:

> Like Father Strittmater [Father Agatho], Theron's instructor was Pennsylvania Dutch—a coincidence that only mildly interested me but one by which my husband set great store: Our Lord (he adopted the address with ease) had planned likenesses in our experience.

Stafford's protagonist was both observant and distracted, accurately sizing up Theron's teacher but then stunned to discover her own situation: the priest's "austerity was right up Theron's alley, and before I knew what had happened to me, I had been dragged into that alley which was blind."

What Stafford left out of the story was her own alternative mission, writing. She was groping there, too, but it was clear that she felt her efforts at literary discipline, at greater control of her craft, offered a more congenial route to order and meaning than the religious observances that Lowell urged ever more forcefully. She was also skeptical of the emphasis on criticism. She worried that Lowell was neglecting his poetry: "Cal is to make a new edition of Herbert which will be published by LSU Press. He is immensely respected here, particularly by Cleanth Brooks who asks his advice on all literary questions," she wrote to Hightower proudly, but she went on to express apprehensions. "Cal has not written any poetry for five months and I would rather have him a poet first and by his merit establish his invulnerability." She knew how difficult it was to claim writing as her priority amid her many mundane preoccupations, and yet it was an important source of stability and self-definition for her; she was afraid of the effect of divine preoccupations on Lowell—and on herself. Through the winter and spring, while her daily life with Lowell became more difficult and the devotional routine more demanding, Stafford was at last experiencing a literary breakthrough of sorts. Her faith was frail, and a source of conflict with Lowell, but her religious struggles proved to be important inspiration for her writing.

EARLY IN THE FALL, Stafford evidently tried to explain to Evelyn Scott something of her newly structured approach to writing. To judge by Scott's alarmed reply, Stafford emphasized impersonality—not what her former teacher wanted to hear. Apparently she didn't, however, mention the growing role of Catholicism in her life with Lowell. Her quest for some external discipline and vision to guide her writing seems to have been cast in more general terms. As she had at the Writers' Conference, Scott urged rebellious independence and vigorous self-expression:

> I can't bear hearing you say it [Stafford's fiction] sounds "heavy." I'm getting horribly fed up with the way people with gifts are being shaken everywhere in their determination to be expressive in terms of the experienced and not in dictated terms of some externally compelled pattern invented by others. If you don't stay soundly adamant on this core, I will build a wailing wall, and weep for the whole generation—generations!—born after 1905.

But Stafford was clearly in a humble, methodical frame of mind about her writing. She was prepared to be a ruthless judge of the inchoate outpourings that had so far proved unpublishable. She was determined to address a creative dilemma: she needed a larger framework of meaning and symbolism for her writing, yet also a closer focus on concrete detail. In the same letter to Hightower in which she had worried over Lowell's neglect of his writing, she calmly assessed her own literary situation. She was heartened by progress on a story that drew on a daydream of a peaceful room that she had obviously discussed with Hightower before:

> As for myself, I am writing at a tortured snail's pace.... I worked 7 months on the suicide story and it, I was very proud of, but al-

though the style was sustained and the rhythm carried, it lacked, still, much precision and all imagery. But the present one—you remember my queer room daydream—is almost successful, though it is awkward. It is obscure, allegorical, and the prose is loaded. I am a great fool to write you this way, but this way is habitual and I, under no illusions about myself any longer except that I have a gift, want you most particularly to know that at this stage of my life, the note is steadily sanguine.

She was right that the "present" story was a turning point. Based on her experience in the hospital after the accident with Lowell two years earlier, the twenty-seven-page manuscript (never published) was in a sense her answer to Lowell's poem "On a Young Lady Convalescing from a Brain-Injury but Unable to write a novel in Concord, Mass." It was a story about that convalescence, in which she discovered a key scene for her first novel, *Boston Adventure,* and sketched a draft of what was to become perhaps her best-known story, "The Interior Castle" (1946). She had, in fact, found the deep symbolic landscape that informed her fiction for many years.

St. Teresa of Avila was her inspiration. Stafford's account in "An Influx of Poets" of her discovery of the saint is revealing. "Theron once told me that I was going through the dark night of the spirit and I should meditate and read John of the Cross. I did, with a certain kind of recognition, read St. John's friend Teresa's 'Interior Castle.' . . ." The emphasis was on a disobedient independence of mind: told to read St. John, she read St. Teresa instead. Her need was less for abstract meditation than for some sense of empathy, and she gravitated to the more accessible Spanish saint, and a woman, to find it. It could hardly have been more symmetrically scripted. While Lowell set about mastering the intellectual intricacies of Catholic doctrine, Stafford made her way to a mystic—and not to the Thomistic St. John recommended by her husband but to untutored, colloquial Teresa.

St. Teresa was a very suitable teacher, well known for her merciful concern about recalcitrant creatures. In particular the saint sympathized with certain weaknesses of the soul that Stafford felt she knew well. St. Teresa didn't assume a focused, contemplative intellect, and she was notably lenient about two other handicaps, a wayward will and a vivid imagination. In fact, she took pains to explain that she was not writing for those with methodical minds and good concentration. "It would be a mistake if you pay attention to what I say about prayer," she told the clearheaded, recommending instead the standard texts about discursive meditation as useful instruction for them. Her audience, she emphasized, consisted of those with "souls and minds so scattered that they are like wild horses no one can stop." And she understood that discipline, though essential, was best applied less stringently to these at once fierce and fragile wills.

St. Teresa's tolerant, practical attitude as a teacher was mirrored by her tone as a writer, which made her a particularly good guide for Stafford. Teresa's style was marked by its wit and colloquial intimacy. She was not an intimidating adept delivering gnomic insights, but a woman struggling to give some expression to the ineffable, some structure to amorphous mysteries. Sympathetic to the weaknesses of her students, she acknowledged versions of them in herself—or at any rate set out to accommodate them in her own methods. Thus she made no pretense to rigorous intellectual presentation. Instead, she emphasized her humble role as amateur thinker, putting pen to paper only because she had been instructed to do so, and even then being constantly distracted from her task by all sorts of other business. Throughout her most famous work, *The Interior Castle,* she lamented how often she had been interrupted and she apologized for losing her place, for repeating herself, for failing to be clear.

But the greatest distinction of St. Teresa's style was its metaphoric profligacy. Though all mystical writings necessarily work through concrete symbols and analogies, Teresa was renowned for her extravagant recourse to elaborate imagery—certainly compared with her follower John, whose poetry employed spare, archetypal symbols and whose prose tended to more abstract terminology. ("To judge by his language alone," the editor of his complete works commented, "one might suppose at times that he is speaking of mathematical, rather than of spiritual operations.") Where John devoted himself, in a large proportion of his classic, *The Ascent of Mount Carmel,* to urging a vigilant mistrust of the imagination and its visions as impediments to true communion with God, St. Teresa based her classic, *The Interior Castle,* on a trust in vision. She urged her readers to imagine "our soul to be like a castle made entirely out of a diamond or very clear crystal, in which there are many rooms, just as in heaven there are many dwelling places." And she proceeded to describe the edifice, its dangers and its potential delights, in vivid detail.

St. Teresa's colloquial welcome to the wayward spirit and her invitation to the imagination clearly spoke to Stafford as little else on Lowell's Catholic reading list did. She was looking for some form in which to conjure with the pain of consciousness, the sense of estrangement that was the emerging subject of her fiction—and the persisting fact of her life. In *The Interior Castle* she found a powerful set of images to help her translate the kind of psychological agonies she had visited upon her character Gretchen into the terms of a spiritual ordeal. Teresa's supremely tantalizing and inaccessible castle—a series of glimmering, receding chambers, beset by wicked serpents at its walls—provided Stafford with a central symbol: the bounded circle of the self, in thrall to darkness without and in search of illumination within. Teresa taught the way from the outer, cloudy chambers where the senses were besieged to the inner, irradiated room where the soul met God. For the devoted and blessed among her students, the prison house became a transcendent palace.

The castle was an encompassing mystical metaphor for Stafford to work into her own, more mundane writing. As she acknowledged to Hightower, her first efforts were "obscure, allegorical." But she was striving for greater concreteness, and it seems clear that William James in *The Varieties of Religious Experience* (a title she later considered borrowing for a novel she never finished) helped her make the crucial bridge between the empirical and the spiritual. It is no surprise that she would have turned to him in her religious travails, for she, like so many others in the 1940s, was avidly reading his brother; it was the peak of the Henry James revival in America. William James's acute description of the physical, psychological, and epistemological qualities of religious consciousness offered a perspective that might well have spoken to Stafford as she tried to adjust to life with Lowell the convert. In particular, James's chapter on mysticism seems to have provided one footnote that was evidently just what she needed.

The chapter turned to St. Teresa, whom James cited as "the expert of experts" on the ultimate mystical state, but first he paused to probe a more accessible stage of mystical experience. "I refer to the consciousness produced by intoxicants and anaesthetics, especially by alcohol," he explained, and elaborated: "Sobriety diminishes, discriminates, and says no; drunkenness expands, unites, and says yes.... It brings its votary from the chill periphery of things to the radiant core." Stafford certainly would have recognized this route to illumination, or at least warmth, through alcohol. She had been drinking far more than casually ever since college. But it was James's reflections on more presentable, medical anesthetics that seem to have pointed her toward a profane, literary approach to divine Teresa. In a lengthy footnote James quoted the firsthand account of "a gifted woman [who] was taking ether for a surgical operation"—a woman, clearly, with whom Stafford had something in common. "I wondered if I was in a prison being tortured, and why I remembered having heard it said that people 'learn through suffering,'" the woman began, "and in view of what I was seeing, the inadequacy of this saying struck me so much that I said aloud, 'to suffer *is* to learn.'" She then proceeded to describe what she saw, which "was most vivid and real to me, though it may not be clear in words." Her experience was of merciless torture suddenly issuing in enlightenment:

> A great Being or Power was traveling through the sky, his foot was on a kind of lightning as a wheel is on a rail, it was his pathway. . . . I seemed to be directly under the foot of God, and I thought he was grinding his own life up out of my pain. . . . He bended me, turning his corner by means of my hurt, hurting me more than I had ever been hurt in my life, and at the acutest point of this, as he passed, I *saw*. I understood for a moment things that I have now forgotten, things that no one could remember while retaining sanity.

Stafford too was a gifted woman who had become well versed in the varieties of anesthetic experience, and of pain, thanks to operations on her head after the accident. While her skull was aching as she worked on *Autumn Festival,* she explored the path from physical suffering to some kind of metamorphosis of the spirit, however fleeting. There was a curious trial run of the notion of anesthesia as revelation in the manuscript of that novel. The passage stood out, an incongruous digression in her narrative. Stafford didn't try to integrate it, but was intrigued by its possibilities:

> Time was passing slowly. It was like ether coming down, coming spicy blue in a downward surge, and the anaesthetists saying, don't struggle, don't struggle, don't trouble yourself and the roaring

drunken sleepiness. Or it was like half awake dreaming when the conscious mind almost meets the unconscious on its threshold, that sort of sixth sense that can discover the essence of things. The awake mind can name the mystery of the naked thing only in terms of what its five senses behold: darker than darkness, lighter than light. But the other mind sees, understands, knows what is inside. Now some people describe this mystery by such terms as no-thing, Nirvana. Heaven is the Christian word.

Almost two years after the accident, in the fall of 1940, Stafford's memory of the pain, and doubtless also of anesthetic release, was refreshed. On a trip to New Orleans with Lowell's school friends Blair Clark and Frank Parker, who were down in Louisiana for a visit, Lowell hit her, breaking her nose again. A surreal, horrible night, it seems to have stunned them all, including Stafford, into an oddly understated appraisal of the event: arguing with his wife about something (no one remembered what), excitable Cal had simply forgotten his own strength. In the rush to get Stafford to a hospital—Clark, as usual, came to the rescue—none of them paused to consider at all seriously what it might suggest about Lowell and about their marriage. If worries surfaced afterward, they were kept quiet. Stafford made no mention of the incident, or of the ordeal of further surgery on her face, in her letters to Hightower. But it seems she was working on her experience of suffering, recently renewed, turning it in an unexpected direction. Her story about her "queer room daydream," which built on the accident, was a story about a votary, not a victim. Putting St. Teresa's metaphor to use, Stafford found metaphysical meaning for her travails. She charted the soul's path from bodily woe to a moment of spiritual release.

The story was divided into two parts, two stages in the lessons of suffering. The progression loosely followed Teresa's *Interior Castle* and is worth tracing in some detail, for the story's structure, themes, and style laid the groundwork for much of Stafford's fiction to come. In the first section, the nameless patient lay silently in her hospital bed, cultivating aloofness from the outside world and alertness to the motions of her mind. It was an all-consuming occupation, which required a willed self-absorption but promised some ultimate repose. "She fancied the consummation would resemble her present obliviousness to all but the abstract exercises of her mind, but that the external world would be altered; it would no longer be necessary to discipline her privacy, for the trespassers would be exterminated. But she forever pondered what the steps to this treacherous Nirvana would be." Memory, as Teresa instructed, played a crucial role in the progress of the soul away from the distractions of the world. It summoned up reminders of the contingency of material things, strengthening the soul in its determination to turn away from them. In the opening half of Stafford's story, her patient dipped down into ether dream states where she drifted among memories, some recognizable, others mysterious. One image in particular stood out, and here St. Teresa's metaphor of chambers entered explicitly. In her mental meandering, the patient stumbled upon a room, soothingly shabby and bathed in a restful autumnal light—a vision of material decay that seemed to offer sanctuary:

> The room was a refuge like a church which she had impetuously deserted only to find better comfort nowhere else. . . . The inspiration was without passion but it nonetheless partook of the atmosphere of religion in its calmer weathers. However, though the temptation to construe the room's meaning as religious was strong and, at times, even irresistable [sic], she withstood it, feeling that the process of arriving at this explanation, had been too simple, at least too slovenly.

For Stafford's patient, this reddish room, though alluring, remained somewhat elusive: permitted no further than the threshold, she continued to inspect the apparition like a psychologist, resisting any religious interpretation. The process turned up a disturbing memory that was perhaps its source—of a real room in New York where a moment of "tranquil mortal melancholy" was suddenly transformed into an experience of loneliness, of cosmic homelessness. Though all the furnishings seemed to connote death and decay, and an eerie isolation, the patient was calmed by the chamber:

> This she knew: if it were anything more than a phenomenon which could be clinically dismissed, it was a sanctuary whose auspices were merciful. Having rejected a supernatural agency in those auspices, she came to look upon them as belonging to herself: that for her instincts she had made a tamed-down sitting room, that as an architect and decorator aware of the needs of his tenants, she had been scrupulously somber in her choice of appointments.

But like St. Teresa's pilgrims in the preliminary stages, Stafford's protagonist was in a precarious position, her progress away from the world still only tentative. She had managed to will her detachment only because the external world—a quiet hospital room, with a chilly landscape beyond its windows—"made on her so few demands, distracting her so little from herself." Similarly, she had found that her will could take her only so far in her journey toward the interior world: "Though the room was ready and was appropriate, as far as she could judge, in every respect, she could not gain entrance to it again. Her dilemma was exasperating: she could not destroy the room and neither could she evoke it."

In the transition to the second section of Stafford's story, the will's true trials began, as St. Teresa instructed they must on the route to salvation: "Doing our own will is usually what harms us." The will was chastened by greater physical suffering: an assault from without enabled the necessary surrender within. For the path to God, the mystics taught, was passivity. The soul did not *gain* entrance to God; it was admitted if he so willed. For Stafford's patient, the liberating ordeal came at the hands of her nose doctor, who barged in one morning, disturbing her meditations, and announced that it was time to operate. Forced to endure anesthetic cocaine packs stuffed into her injured nostrils—a procedure that Stafford described in excruciating detail—the patient lost all capacity to concentrate on her beloved room. Her crisis began to convert her from a psychological to a spiritual perspective on her plight:

> Because her nose was palpable and her room was hallucinatory (or would be called so by this nose-bigot and his sedulous acolytes) the removal of cartilage was to take precedence over her salvation. Now when there was no hope of recovering the room so long as she was in the possession of pain imposed upon her from the outside . . . the need to enter it, to do more than observe it from the threshold, became as acute and raw as the pain itself.

The second section of the story was a meticulous description of the surgery on her skull and a metaphorical evocation of the seizure of her soul. As the doctor cut close to her brain, piercing tissue unprotected by the anesthetic, the patient in her agony was suddenly delivered into her room. Stafford's effort to put that moment, that decisive turn, into words recalls William James's "gifted woman" who strained to find adequate expression for her experience. Like her, Stafford groped after geometrical imagery: "Her solitude was pyramidal: its peak was the snarl of un-sheathed nerves. It was a naked pain, a clean and vivid pain, causing her to be reduced to a focal point. She had no existence beyond it." And then she tried again: "Her solitude was a sustained shriek, an infinite line, a light of incommensurate intensity. It was a minute sharp edge, a metallic malice, a flame from the hottest fuel."

In the room itself, the calm seemed almost anticlimactic: "She was so loving she felt she could not ever leave." Stafford's vision of faded gran-deur was quite different from Teresa's brilliantly sparkling inner cham-ber, but she closed her story with the image of a jewel familiar from the saint. In her commentary on imaginative visions, Teresa likened the cul-minating revelation to sudden admission to a secret reliquary that housed a precious stone. Stafford's patient came into possession of a pearl: "Now she lay upon her gentle bed with her aches stroked out and her fever cooled by the pacific maturity of her room. Her bleeding brain was sealed and rounded, was like a loaded, seamless ball, the agony's wonderfully perfect pearl."

Stafford's story was the map of her formative efforts to find some ac-commodation between writing and religion—an accommodation im-plied but not spelled out by the New Critical teachers with whom she was now so closely associated. Lowell had already blurred the line when he began not only sprinkling his poetic terminology with words like "heresy" and "Gnosticism" but exploring some connection with the Church. He had barely begun to prove that he could be Eliot's "classicist in literature" when he turned to the other element of Eliot's equation, becoming "Anglo-Catholic in religion"—and not just in theory but in single-minded practice. For Lowell in 1940 the terms of the accommo-dation were temporarily clear: he wasn't writing poetry at all. His reli-gious convictions explicitly took precedence over his literary craft and would dictate its direction when (and if) he resumed. His piety was a matter of fierce will, and so would his poetry be, its formal structure and its metaphors the occasion for yoking together the abstract and the con-crete, the spiritual and the material.

For Stafford the terms were not so straightforward. Faith eluded her, and her will tended to be fickle. She explored her predicament, stylisti-cally as well as thematically, in her story. She introduced the central sub-ject of her fiction: the isolation of the self. Her outwardly passive patient was in a sense the extreme archetype of many of her future protagonists, under assault from without yet also secretly plotting an escape within. And Stafford focused on the double-edged faculty that dominated her characters: the imagination. In a world of opaque selves, it was the only power that permitted any semblance of interpenetration, any possibility of transparency. Thus it could claim near omnipotence. And yet, inescapably subjective, the imagination wasn't simply to be trusted. Following St. Teresa, Stafford suggested deep ambivalence about its status. The most seductive of faculties, the imagination granted vision, but it also increased vulnerability. To see into the alien world was not necessarily to master it; to be at its mercy was perhaps more likely. The imagination threatened entrapment at the same time that it promised transcendence.

The other faculty that complicated matters was the will, if anything even more unsteady than the imagination. On the one hand, it helped define the rootless self, establishing its identity in embattled relation to the rest of the world. Stafford's patient, all alone in the hospital, deliberately ostracized herself from her surroundings and consciously worked at cultivating a private, self-protective realm. On the other hand, the chief allure of that realm seemed to be that it offered a respite for the will—a place of repose. Moreover, ultimate access to that realm required a surrender of the will. In her story, Stafford introduced the uncanny dynamic at work in so many of her characters. They start out on the arduous route to self-creation, which turns out to be the path of passive self-abnegation.

In the curious play of will and imagination that Stafford set up in her characters, escape could seem a kind of imprisonment and imprisonment a kind of escape. For her patient, the red-tinted room was not a simple refuge, and the return to the real world was a very ambivalent resolution. Playing the therapeutic and theological perspectives off against each other, Stafford discovered a rich source of irony and tension, qualities that she counted on in her writing—which were also the key literary ingredients in the New Critical recipe. The double identity of the victim/votary provided her with a suggestive set of oppositions—body versus mind, outer versus inner, active versus passive. The most important opposition of all for Stafford was innocence versus experience, as her patient yearned for enchantment and faced disenchantment. It so happened, though doubtless not by explicit design, that the contrasts answered to the prescriptions Brooks and Warren were shortly to announce in *Understanding Fiction* (1943), the companion to their influential volume on poetry. The oppositions were encompassing and morally ambiguous, and thus productive of the complex conflict that was an "essential aspect of fiction." They were central to all-important irony, which "in its most sophisticated form," Brooks and Warren explained, "concerns the alignments of judgments and sympathies on the part of the author—the problem of his own self-division."

That division was reflected in Stafford's style as well as her themes. In the course of the story, her prose underwent a striking transformation. She opened in an abstract, discursive, rather mandarin style, but by the second section, she had shifted to concrete, imagistic language and was inclining toward a colloquial tone. It was an evolution entailed by the shifting focus of her subject matter. The first section, as the patient lay undisturbed in her bed, was introspective and meditative. The second, when she was ambushed by the doctor and his knives, was interactive and dramatic. But the shift was itself also part of the subject matter, for in probing the place of the self in the world, the story also probed the role of language in linking the mind to physical and metaphysical reality.

The Latinate discursiveness of the first half conveyed a mistrust of metaphor, an insecurity about how to relate the subjective and the objective, the abstract and the concrete. The ungainly grasping after, yet holding back from, analogy or allegory often resulted in heavy obscurity—the "words, merely" problem that was all too familiar to Stafford: "The steadfast plant was like an allegory of her body in which comfort followed pain in progression syncopated with retrogression. The sameness of her occupation was, indeed, as unrelieved as the winter sky; yet she was not so mournful as the scene, nor was the protracted interruption of her activity suitable to arbitrary categorizing." Stafford's discovery in the second half of the story was an increasing confidence in concrete detail as a vehicle for metaphysical meaning. She had set herself perhaps the most difficult challenge of all in the use of metaphor: to give expression to pain—that is, to find for the most subjective of experiences some objective form. It meant venturing out onto the poetic verges of metaphor, as she did in her geometric allusions. As important, it meant creating a more solid, prosaic context to set off those poetic excursions. Stafford was inspired to a mixture of the mandarin and the mundane, of elevated and lowly diction and imagery, which came to be a staple of her style:

As the unworldly creature lay strapped to the table and in her mind divorced from all accoutrements and all the claptrap of the surgeon and his entourage, a murmur, anguine and slowly perceived, reached her, and after the words had been spoken, she recalled them as though they were echoed: "Careful, careful, I'm near her brain." Instantly she became an animal and though her attempt to escape was abortive, she jerked her head, and as she did so felt the pain flare.

"Relax!" cried the surgeon angrily.

Now she heard the busy scissors clipping the cartilage like tough old toenails. That place where her thoughts originated was buried shallowly and the points crept around the bones, through the tunnels to her brain.

As Stafford wrote to Hightower in the fall of 1940, she felt she had made a breakthrough, but also knew it was only a beginning. She got just the right kind of reading from Evelyn Scott, who proved for once that she could offer more than extravagant tributes to a potential talent. She stepped back to sum up what she took to be Stafford's intentions, rather than simply focusing on the technique, the execution—though she was also ready with specific suggestions:

The surgical second section, the pain-delivery episode ... is *great* writing. And I *mean* great. It is as harrowingly real as the best Dostoievski. ... It is physical & emotional agony translated into immortal terms. ...

The story begins with a rather wordy effect. ... Your "room" is exquisitely purveyed. But its symbolic importance seems dependent on its character as "room" in a perfect category, and that is why the episodic references to the flat in New York ... struck me as wrong. ... [T]he minute you begin tying the room down to a specific instance of a room in which action takes place—specified— the eternal moment feeling the reader has threatens to be shattered. ...

The defect [some] call "lack of focus," I would call maladjustment in tempo. The infinite deliberation of first [*sic*] section refuses to relate itself *inevitably,* as it should, to the dramatic timing of section II. ... You get the net impression of two distinct *blocks* of feeling—two sorts of densities—adjusted in mosaic pattern, but not *fused.*

Scott suggested shortening the first half and making it "a precipitate of section two."

IT WAS GOOD ADVICE, which Stafford eventually—six years later—took in rewriting the story. But as 1941 opened, "lack of focus" and "maladjustment in tempo" proved to be problems that went beyond her story. Like the patient in that story, Stafford was distracted in her efforts at disciplined meditation. Her writing was not the refuge she had hoped from religious confusions and pressures—or from social domestic demands. Soon illness (a persistent fever and a cough) got in the way, too. "My life has become subordinate to all other lives to which I am related," she had written to Hightower late in the fall of 1940; it "has become a monstrous pattern of struggle against rules and frustration so that my desire for anarchy has never been so passionate and the possibility of it has never been so remote." In February she followed up her dramatic declarations, with which Hightower was by now familiar, with a more concrete account of her sense of claustrophobia and its cause: it was the first she had told him of Lowell's conversion. Sitting alone in her *Southern Review* office one morning, manning the telephone, she summed up her situation in her deadpan style of desperation:

> Cal is becoming a Catholic. He is being baptized in a couple of months. A real one with all the trimmings, all the fish on Friday and the observances of faith and confessions and grace before meals and prayers before bed, and while I can stand off and even admire what he is doing, I want to have none of it for myself. It sickens me down to my soul to hear him talking piously and to see in him none of the common Christian virtues [such] as pity and kindness but only the fire-breathing righteousness that belongs, not to an unbaptized lay brother, but to a priest. I am so tired of moods and disapproval and complaints that if I were any less tired I'd not put up with them. I'm boxed up and I'm hopeless and there is no one to talk to. "It is not important to me to be a writer," he says. "If I cannot write devotional poetry, then I will not write poetry." And it's becoming not important to me to be a writer because it is absurd

to think of it, having no time to do it. Someday I'll send you the stories, but God knows when. There's no time for anything.

Yearning for anarchic release, Stafford instead succumbed to sickness. She herself noted the correlation between external pressures and internal problems: when literary guests and demands descended on her, her insecurities and her fever rose. And she appreciated the perverse resourcefulness of her imagination and will in cultivating this uncomfortable yet somehow alluring limbo. "My particular brand of hypochondria is highly impractical," she observed to Hightower in March after she had been on her back with a mysterious fever for three weeks. "Well, I imagine all kinds of diseases, sick, I refuse to pamper myself. I have been in bed only because Cal saw the doctor himself and enforced the order." But in bed and feeling overburdened—too much mindless work, too many visitors, too much Catholicism—Stafford, like her patient, was about to turn a corner. Her formative story still unfinished, she found a focus and a tempo that inspired more writing. In a sense, she now did the opposite of what Scott had advised, saving her old teacher's counsel for a later effort. Instead of shortening the first, introspective section of her story, Stafford set to work on a novel that relied on precisely such probing: she embarked on the chronicle of a curiously aloof yet alert consciousness.

Though Stafford later said that she began *Boston Adventure* when she first arrived in Baton Rouge, it seems clear that work began in earnest during the spring of 1941. Being ill seemed to bring Stafford a sense of liberation, or at least of detachment. Sickness apparently served as her response to and also her release from external pressures, for in bed she felt paradoxically less "boxed up." Not that the devotional regimen relaxed. That April, Lowell was baptized and they were remarried in the Church. Routine observances remained a time-consuming affair. As for her writing, she found "great compensations," both concrete and abstract, in the course of being sick and convalescent on and off throughout the rest of their year in Baton Rouge. (With customary hyperbole, she claimed she had a fever for seven months straight and regularly referred to her disease as tuberculosis, as indeed it had been diagnosed by one doctor, though it turned out to be pneumonia.) She had time to write and read, since the *Southern Review* editors let her go home (grudgingly, she thought) and Cal commanded rest. Then in the spring her illness served as a reason to escape the South and to spend a couple of weeks in the salutary air of Colorado at her sister's ranch. In retreat, she seems to have been able to reflect on the spiritual claims of Catholicism rather than simply react to its daily demands.

The balance between reflection and rebellion, between passive and productive resistance, was precarious, as she conveyed in her correspondence with Hightower. By March the frustrations of February had modulated, and the tone was calmer: "I have some new opinions of life," she wrote,

> the pattern, however, remains the same. I know the solution, but I cannot bring myself to affiliated [*sic*] myself with the agent. That is, order obviously cannot be set up in an individual life without some higher authority. I know that Cal is doing the sound thing by going into the Church and going the whole way, but it is the perverseness of my nature to fight against any therapy advocated for me without my first having discovered it. I may come around in time. Certainly I see no other institution as rewarding. Your anarchy, orderly as it is, is finally as worthless as my chaotic variety.

In April she sent two letters, the first proclaiming that "turnabout as this may sound I believe Cal's Catholicism has been the best thing that has happened. . . . I still object to some of it naturally, but have come to realize that anarchy, even our ordered anarchy, is no good. Also, even though my view of it is still far from objective, I am apprised of sin and no longer believe my history of it is too old for reparation. Don't misinterpret me— I have not become pious and I deny having such notions every day of my life." The second was written a week later. Stafford was drunk, and it was a frantic cry for escape: "State some plan. You and me, I mean. No ties. . . . Get rid of your encumbrance, because oh dear God I cannot live this way without your help."

Then in early May of 1941 she retracted her unhappiness almost cavalierly: "I never, of course, meant any of it. I'm actually very happy." But she followed up with a serious and sincere meditation on her shifting perspective:

> I think I can still scoff at aspects of the Church, but I have come to believe in the Passion. And this, I hope, will not sound like pious cant. . . . Sin (and by sin I mean the behavior we have so often deplored in ourselves) is inescapable without dignity. I believe that you

have attained dignity; I imagine you to be much altered and I wish we had not, in foolish years, scorned the word "respectable" for its meaning is only fully clear to me now.... Speaking, you understand, of conduct. I am neither dignified nor respectable. I am formless. What else *but* orthodoxy? My life terrifies me. I am saturated with meaningless experience. I hope to have faith eventually.

Her last letter to Hightower from Baton Rouge—a very long one, in August, obviously written in several sittings—ranged over almost the whole spectrum of attitudes. Stafford acknowledged at the outset the inconsistency of any attempt at summary: "Oh, Lord ... I cannot give you an intelligible account of this period of my life at all." Initially, her tone recalled the old fierce frustration, as she tried to convey the extent of Lowell's zeal and of her own sense of precarious balance. She was full of dread at what lay ahead—moving to New York, where a job with the Catholic publishers Sheed and Ward awaited Cal. That represented "the first stage of our entrenchment, which I regret to say looks as though it will be permanent and deep," a daunting sequel to their already intense introduction to the Church. "I couldn't begin to tell you, convincingly, the extent to which [Cal] will go for a conviction. I have been *absolutely* without choice and I have whitewashed the thing to you because I must take all possible precautions against cracking up completely, which I have done several times anyway with nearly disastrous results." She itemized the strictures of their lives, which she felt she had no alternative but to obey—aside from all the prescribed observances, "choice of movies according to the Censor, choice of books in the same way, and talk of *nothing* but the existence of God." Once again she confided the urge to escape, to "do an Iowa City disappearing act" once they got to New York.

Yet by the end of the letter she was defending the virtues of discipline and devotion against Hightower's skepticism, reiterating her own need for a source of order, her desire for submission rather than rebellion:

Nevertheless, when I cry out against all this, I am convinced ... that there is at least the possibility of a heavenly book of records where my misdeameanours will be added up, in the end, to my ruin and damnation. Ideally, I suppose the religious attitude is composed of terror and love, humility and adoration and when, after my confession, saying in the Act of Contrition, "I detest all my sins because I dread the loss of Heaven and the pains of Hell, but most

of all because I have offended Thee, my God" I do not then more
than any other time believe but I see and am appalled at the *possibility. . . .* When I am alone at Mass or more particularly when I am
doing penance after confession and no one else is in the church, I
approach something. The obtrusion of opinion, argument, ramifi-
cations distresses me.

She could abstractly admire the large, austere structure of the thought,
but she was put off by the "provincial, pious, *embarrassing*" style of the
practice. "While I may agree with Eliot's prescription—a Christian society—and may admire the intellectualism of the Thomists, I no better
than the thousands of other liberals like me can speak of Christ as 'Our
Lord.'" She could not "swallow the vernacular of Sunday sermons," she
said, preferring a notion of the Church as "a composite of ritual and
philosophy in which God, the saints and the angels remain timeless, absolutely timeless." Yet, as she said, her mixture of philosophy and ritual
was far from standard or steady. Stafford perhaps captured her perspective most accurately in an allusion to Keats's "Ode to a Nightingale": "I
think I will always be in alien corn," she told Hightower. She was sum-
ming up her relation to Catholicism, but her declaration of estrangement
not only expressed her distance from religion but also suggested what
drew her to it. She was a straying creature, in search of some sense of
home.

While looking vainly for refuge in belief that spring, she found it
instead in fiction. "You would not recognize me," she wrote to Hightower in March. "This present book is first person and is the first un-
autobiographical piece I have done." A month later she reported that she
had finished a 175-page outline of the novel "which is religious." Though
St. Teresa was an abiding presence, two other, secular influences seized
her imagination: Henry James and Marcel Proust. Along with Dostoy-
evsky and Tolstoy, they were among the select authors who made it onto
Lowell's short list of acceptably serious literature. Stafford certainly took
them seriously. Reading them, as she described it, was not exactly a restful convalescent occupation.

"Proust outstrips everyone," she announced, and he was demanding:
"He wears me out physically. His intensity demands complementary energy which in me is limited, but I know of no intellectual exercise so
rewarding as reading him carefully." She quickly amended that claim:

"That is, no exercise performed with another novelist unless it is James who in a way is better." Then in rounding off her assessment, she called a halt to the competition between the two masters: "But the methods, inductive and deductive, are diametrically opposed and a comparison between them is precarious." She had identified the contrasting approaches that she had begun to explore in her surgery story and that she was about to pursue in her novel. The loose, subjective Proustian progress from specific experience to generalizations lurked behind the opening section of her story, in which she strived to extract some kind of transcendent significance from sensual ordeals. But she was also attracted by James's pursuit of appropriate particulars to illuminate his implicit theme, of drama to display the presiding intelligence in his stories. Her second section was a kind of exercise of that more directed and disciplined method.

By August, it was clear that Proust had gotten the upper hand, though Stafford's impatience with James seemed to be a symptom of more general restiveness. Apprehensive about the consuming Catholic regimen that lay ahead for her and Lowell in New York, she was not looking for more constraining structure in fiction. In fact, she was in the mood to denounce it quite categorically. It was luxurious texture that held great allure: "Having been reading them simultaneously [I am] finding Proust lengths ahead on every score. James is never a pleasure to me and P. always is. There is a peerless luxury about him and a flavor that produces absolute satisfaction. James's protagonists usually irritate me and he often seems 'fixed up' and improbable beyond the limits of his careful prose." But finally, she wasn't ready to write James off so summarily, concluding rather lamely: "I nevertheless much admire him."

Just what the shape and structure of their lives in New York would be was far from clear, but Stafford at least had the prospect of potentially more time to herself to write. The Lowells were no longer student and secretary. She and Cal were setting forth on newly independent footing, and this time he was the one heading for the daily job. Stafford had been turned down once more for a Houghton Mifflin fellowship, but with her outline in hand and Proust foremost in mind, she was poised to plunge into her novel. Her illness had provided her with the preliminary momentum. She knew it would be a struggle to sustain it, given the bustling life in their household, which she acknowledged she hadn't managed gracefully: "It has been a dreadful arrangement here and I have not been

good about it. It enraged me during the winter to come home at noon &
find both [Cal] and Peter Taylor still in their pajamas, having spent the
morning reading or writing while I had been cutting stencil and wrestling with 'Accounts Receivable.'" Now she and Lowell could wrestle
with new balances and imbalances.

BEFORE THEY HAD SETTLED on New York, the Lowells had been
thinking of returning to Cambridge—but not, Lowell was emphatic, to
the familiar fold. "We must avoid, [Cal] says, social Harvard and literary
people and must be surrounded by Catholics," Stafford wrote to the
Thompsons, her Boulder friends, in the summer of 1941. It was a droll
scenario but also an intimidating one. The incongruity of a popish enclave in Puritan New England, presided over by a Lowell, clearly appealed to Stafford's comic sense; but the intensity of belief and
rebelliousness she could predict from Lowell, especially at such proximity to his family, didn't.

By comparison, New York was a relief. Not that life was relaxed and
tolerant, but the Lowells succeeded in mixing religion and literature.
They were surrounded by critics as well as Catholics, and the critics were
not just the familiar southern faces. In the city, Stafford and Lowell associated with the literary circle around the *Partisan Review,* very different
from the Fugitive set and worlds away from the Brahmin, Harvard ambience. Yet despite the surface opposition between the urban Jewish intellectuals and the southern Agrarian critics, there was, as Irving Howe
observed in his memoir *A Margin of Hope,* an underlying affinity—the
critical energy of the marginal. "I came to feel that," Howe wrote,

> clashes of opinion aside, there was something symmetrical in the
> situations of the writers from Nashville and the writers from New
> York—both groups semioutsiders starting to break into the central
> spaces of American culture, yet unwilling to succumb to its slack-
> ness, its small optimisms. There was enough disagreement between
> the two groups to create tension, enough respect to begin friend-
> ships.

Tension and friendship certainly were staples of the Lowells' New York
sojourn from the fall of 1941 to the summer of 1942.

Stafford was still sick when they arrived in New York (where a doctor
finally diagnosed pneumonia), but she did her best to get herself and

Lowell settled. She found an apartment at 63 West Eleventh Street, and Lowell was especially pleased because the landlords were Catholic. The two of them began working at Sheed and Ward, Jean part-time. "We are both excited at the moment about proper editing," she announced.

More exciting, though, was the literary company they quickly came to know. Right away they had invitations from the Tates to visit them at Princeton, where Allen had been hired on a grant from the Carnegie Foundation for an experimental program to teach the creative arts. Through them they met Richard Blackmur, who had taught with Tate in 1939, Tate's first year at Princeton (and whom Tate later accused of having a hand in his firing in 1942). The Tates were also their entrée into the *Partisan Review* crowd. The older couple introduced them to Philip Rahv, the co-editor (with William Phillips) of the magazine, and his wife, Natalie, "both of whom are very nice," Stafford judged—not quite the adjective most of Philip Rahv's colleagues, least of all Tate, would have used. As Howe observed, Tate and Rahv made perfect opponents, both zealous for battle, which didn't stop them from also being close— but far from calm—friends; "nothing but ideas stood between them." Randall Jarrell was in and out of New York that fall, staying with the Lowells between trips to lecture at Princeton and to see Edmund Wilson on the Cape. Delmore Schwartz was teaching at Harvard, but they in-evitably heard plenty about him. He had been the talk of the *PR* circle, and the Southerners, ever since he had published *In Dreams Begin Re-sponsibilities* in 1938. "Your poetic style is beyond any doubt the first real innovation that we've had since Eliot and Pound," Tate had written to Schwartz. Not least important, the Lowells also met Robert Giroux, a young editor at Harcourt, Brace, shortly after they arrived.

This fluid circle of semioutsiders welcomed the young protégés of the Nashville writers. As she had back at the Writers' Conference in Boul-der, Stafford made a good impression—on the Catholics as well as the critics. Frank Sheed, the founding editor of the Catholic publishing house, was always ambivalent about Lowell and his messianic manner, but he doted on Stafford. The Rahvs seem to have assumed something of the same parental role that the Tates did toward the Lowells. Stafford gossiped and mingled with agility, distinctly more polished than Lowell.

But she also stood apart, the outsider among the semioutsiders. At the same time that Stafford successfully aimed to be socially captivating, she instinctively resisted being brought entirely into the circle herself—

lonely though the Colorado girl often felt "in alien corn." Her distance was evidently a source of insecurity, but it also gave her a vantage point from which to play the ironic, incisive observer of the literary alliances, more and less precarious, around her. Her continuing struggle with Catholicism, which threatened to be all-consuming, was also grist for satiric storytelling. In a letter to Peter Taylor in October, she reported on Catholic developments and delivered one of the deadpan anecdotes that were her specialty; the more uncomfortable the circumstances, the more comic her rendition of them was. Her role in the stories was well turned. She was the docile victim, but also the understated commentator:

> I should tell you about the Catholic Worker. . . . Cal insisted that I do Catholic work so finally I went down to the offices of the newspaper which is run, as I suppose you know (or ought to) by a woman who used to be a communist and has written her autobiography which is called "From Union Square to Rome." The first time I went down, I was terrified just by the approach to the place. It is a block from Pell St. and two from the Bowery, just off Canal. I had to walk seven blocks through the kind of slums you do not believe exist when you see them in the movies, in an atmosphere that was nearly asphyxiating. The Worker office was full of the kind of camaraderie which frightens me to death and I was immediately put at a long table between a Negro and a Chinese to fold papers, a tiring and filthy job. The second time, it was about the same except that Mott St. seemed even more depressing and that time I typed. After I had described the place to Cal, he immediately wanted to go down and live there. I vainly argued against it. Finally a priest whom he admires told him his work should be intellectual. And now we are quite happy here in a respectable neighborhood and henceforth I do not have to go to the Worker but instead I have to go to work in a friendship house in Harlem under a Baroness de something.

Cal's fanaticism, as Stafford wittily told it, was an offense against taste, and she cast herself in the role of fastidious (even racist) snob. And then she concluded with an all-lived-happily-ever-after cadence. But the truth was, despite the note of self-mockery about her aesthetic delicacy, she was viscerally repelled by the clamor on the streets, as a later journal entry suggested: "We went to look for an apartment on Mott Street. The pressure of people was almost entirely physical and the noises nearly drove me mad."

Nor did devotion to the intellectual dimension of Catholic endeavors suit her much better. In a diary entry that apparently dates from several years later, Stafford recalled her work with Sheed with a different kind of shudder:

> I remember the translation of [the Confessions], 12 hour days, from dark and wintry seven until seven in the small, English-cool bare and cluttered office in that old house with its broad, commanding marble stairway, our smudged windows overlooking 5th Ave. as it peters out below 14th St. The tea, as dark as broth, in pasteboard containers and the yeast buns came from the luncheonette, handy on the corner. My typewriter was tall and stiff and Sheed, forever in overshoes and sometimes in a dinner jacket in which he had slept in the back office, translated indefatigably and excellently and with so little evident delight that everything about him—including his faith—came to me to seem learned rather than experienced.

Where Lowell seized on to Catholicism as, among other things, a bridge—however fragile at times—between learning and experience, between spirit and fact, Stafford often found herself looking into the chasm between them. Her religious travails seemed to call attention to her discomfort both with faith and with the vulgarity of the physical world.

Literary mingling, however intense, could offer a kind of refuge from zealous Catholicism. It was company in which the goal was more congenial—some harmony between life and art. Though Stafford sometimes found the bookish camaraderie quite frightening in its own way, she didn't complain to Taylor about the impinging crowds of writers (as she had the year before to Hightower). After she recovered from her pneumonia, there was no word of fevers in the autumn. She felt equal, it seems, to the literary scene. Jarrell was "a rather exhausting joy to see," she reported jauntily. She urged Taylor to try to make it to a cocktail party being held by the Rahvs for Robert Penn Warren, "because it ought to be kind of fun." She eagerly kept her eyes and ears open on their trips out to Princeton and summed up her impressions with typical, far-from-intimidated tartness: "We met Blackmur later in the evening. He talked to no one even when he was speaking, not even to Tate. The most interesting thing he said was that you could get all of James unbound for about 7 dollars."

But for all of the literary socializing, Stafford was also obviously pleased to be able to report that when Robert Giroux came to dinner for the first time in October, he "said that it came as a complete surprise to him that I was at the Southern Review, that I knew Mr. Ransom . . . in fact, that I was anything but a quiet talented mole working year after year on a novel down on 11th St." She liked the idea of having connections, of being a protégé with access, but she liked perhaps even more the chance to claim all that and yet remain a solitary, independent outsider pursuing her own course.

That fall she was steadily at work on *The Outskirts,* the working title for the novel that eventually became *Boston Adventure.* The semioutsiders didn't distract her, and Lowell's continuing pursuit of piety rather than poetry didn't deter her from the project she had under way: an anatomy of the real insiders—the Bostonians who were safely two hundred and fifty miles north. "It's a conscious imitation of Proust, or as Cal says, of Moncrieff's Proust," she wrote to Hightower in September. "He is an exacting master, but Ransom (I don't put much stake in this since he doesn't like and doesn't read novels) wrote that I had sold him on Proust. Actually, there may be an uncomplimentary ambiguity in his remark." She cheerfully admitted to imitation, and then jokingly to bad imitation, out of an evident confidence that she was embarked on a literary endeavor that at last suited her.

Stafford was obviously working hard and productively. By early 1942 she already had a manuscript in shape to submit to Harcourt, Brace. As Giroux recalled it, Frank V. Morley, the editor in chief, passed him Stafford's manuscript one Friday with a note attached: "It is well written in a way that creeps on relentlessly, giving the interior life of the heroine, Sonie. I found that it kept hold of me; but will it keep hold of a public? Other opinions on this—RG, please?" When Giroux boarded the train that day for a weekend in Connecticut, he settled in with the manuscript—and was so absorbed that he missed his station. Shortly after that he persuaded Morley to take on the book and was assigned to be Stafford's editor (as he remained until mid-year, when he left to become an officer in the navy). In April at the Tates' house in Princeton, where Stafford and Lowell had come with Giroux to hear Jarrell lecture, Caroline Gordon seized the chance to make the signing of the Harcourt,

Brace contract a witnessed event. She set out candles on her desk, and Stafford closed the deal in flickering light among friends. With that secular ritual, her literary vocation had acquired an external sanction. From secretary, she had not progressed to receptionist in the city laundry, the path she had predicted to Hightower in Baton Rouge. It was a real contract, she wrote to the Thompsons, "not the twaddle I had with the Atlantic Monthly"—two hundred and fifty dollars on signing, two hundred and fifty dollars on delivery.

CHAPTER 7

The Tates

ARMED WITH HER manuscript and contract, Stafford and Lowell left New York in July of 1942 to set up house with the Tates, who were leaving Princeton for Monteagle, Tennessee. Tate had not been rehired, and he and Gordon loved the small village and quaint summer resort where they had spent a productive stretch several years earlier. "We always start working like hell as soon as we get here," Gordon said, and both Tates were wound up to write. Allen wanted to start a sequel to his novel *The Fathers,* which had appeared in 1938, and Caroline was at work on *The Women on the Porch.* It was the right recommendation of the place for Stafford, who was poised to proceed with her novel, and apparently Lowell too was suddenly ready to write again. Sheed and Ward was cutting back on staff, and Lowell planned to undertake a biography of Jonathan Edwards. "We will just hole up in a cottage on the mountain until we have finished our respective books," Gordon wrote to Malcolm Cowley.

It was obviously not so simple as that, but it was a strikingly productive year, from July of 1942 to the next July—"the winter of four books," was the way Lowell remembered it. Tate and Lowell, in fact, barely got started on the books they had intended. Stymied with their projects, together they began editing an anthology of sixteenth- and seventeenth-century poetry. Then, inspired by the "formal, difficult poems," they turned to writing poetry again themselves. Lowell later looked back on that year, during which he wrote all of the poems in *Land of Unlikeness,* as a profoundly formative one, just as his first southern summer, in 1937, with the Tates at Benfolly had been. "In the beginning," he later told one of his biographers, Steven Gould Axelrod, Tate "was not only an influence but often *the* (my) style of writing." And the young poet's comprehensive debt to the Tates transcended style; they also inspired him with a theme, and, as Axelrod put it, with "something greater than either of these—a vision of a life totally committed to art, and an assurance that he too could achieve such a life."

For Stafford as well, the year—the middle year of the roughly three she spent hard at work on *Boston Adventure*—was crucial. But her view of the experience was less glowing, more in line with Ford Madox Ford's reaction to the Benfolly summer: "Consorting with the Tates," he said, "is like living with intellectual desperadoes in the Sargoza [*sic*] sea." Work and play were fierce. For the Lowells, the industrious days began, at Cal's behest, with attendance at Mass. Then it was time to retreat to their typewriters, though it wasn't all quiet creativity among the foursome. There was plenty of noisy criticism as well, of which Stafford took the brunt: Gordon later recalled "how often we all took a whack" at Stafford's novel. Their evenings were filled with gossip, mostly literary and very mean—and, of course, with drink. Too much drink, Stafford acknowledged at one point: she had broken a vow to cut back, she told Taylor, and had seen "for the millionth time what a prize jackass I am when I drink."

By the spring Stafford had collapsed, sick once more, but what is most striking is how creatively resilient she seemed to be, despite the hard-driving company. She had arrived in Monteagle in the summer of 1942 with a draft of her novel already in hand, which gave her a clear sense of direction as well as important momentum, and she managed to leave in the summer of 1943 with seven hundred pages. Stafford's themes, style, and vision of the creative life, like her husband's, owed plenty to the Tates. But as *Boston Adventure* showed, she was a protégé who wandered from the paths of her patrons.

THOUGH STAFFORD doubtless refined her themes as she pounded away at her typewriter on the third floor of the big house, they had been worked out long before she arrived in Monteagle. "Cal was very right when he exclaimed one night in Louisiana, 'I've just discovered Jean is writing a Catholic novel,'" Peter Taylor wrote to Stafford in the summer of 1944 after he had read her finished manuscript. He went on to characterize the religious perspective that Lowell had seen at the outset and that he saw at its completion: "I had not realized (this will sound stuffy) that you have honestly integrated your Catholicism and your natural aestheticism by which I mean—however poor a choice of terms—your natural revulsion to the coarseness of most human beings and the grossness of their lives." *Boston Adventure,* as its original title, *The Outskirts,* suggests, was a story of exile—of social, but also of spiritual, exile. It was a version of the story that Stafford had tried to tell in *Autumn Festival,* and her protagonist this time, named Sonie Marburg, was a relative of Gretchen, like her an outcast from her family, searching for salvation in an alien society.

But in Sonie, Gretchen's temperament was tamed by a more mature imagination—her own and her creator's. Where Stafford's earlier heroine had been consumed by adolescent self-loathing and disgust with the world around her, Sonie was more patient and ironic in her explorations of her alienation; if Gretchen was a damned soul, Sonie was a spirit in purgatory. It marked the kind of tempering of sensibility that, interestingly, was not much in evidence in Lowell's *Land of Unlikeness,* which consisted largely of poems that emerged under the Tates' roof at the same time that *Boston Adventure* was taking revised shape. As R. P. Blackmur wrote of Lowell's poems, "There is not a loving metre in the book," echoing the Atlantic Monthly Press's reactions to Stafford's earlier novel. "What is thought of as Boston in him fights with what is thought of as Catholic; and the fight produces not a tension but a gritting. It is not the violence, the rage, the denial of this world that grits, but the failure of these to find *in verse* the tension of necessity; necessity has, when recognised, the quality of conflict accepted, not hated." Stafford had discovered the tension of necessity in Sonie's narrative. In mesmerizing prose, she created a character who confronted the divisions in herself with an eerily calm, fatalistic curiosity.

Stafford's novel was not religious in the same sense that Lowell's contemporaneous poems were. She was not working with explicitly Christian symbolism, aiming to articulate an apocalyptic religious myth, as he was. (He said later that he had been "much more interested in being a Catholic than in being a writer.") But her basic inclination, like that of her teachers Tate and Ransom (and, behind them, T. S. Eliot), was to see, as Taylor observed in his letter, mankind as fallen and art as a kind of redemptive witness to that plight. And like Lowell, Stafford was fascinated by the opposition between Catholicism and Boston. Dividing her novel into two parts, she juxtaposed an Old World vision of spiritual damnation with a New World vision of social salvation. Sonie hoped to escape her lowly, blighted past and redeem herself amid high Boston society. But Stafford didn't grant her such a simple pilgrimage. Boston was hardly the salvation Sonie expected, and Stafford offered another alternative, the life of art—only to deny her that as well. Stafford was not proposing Sonie's tale as a portrait of the artist as a young woman. The only prospect of transcendence she held out for Sonie was a contemplative, not a creative, retreat from the corrupt world—a retreat that threatened to mean losing her mind rather than finding her soul.

Sonie's spiritual and social journey began in Chichester, a little village across the bay from Boston where she lived in near destitution with her tormented German father, Hermann, a lapsed Catholic, and her histrionic Russian mother, Shura, immigrants with nothing to cling to in the New World. Her odyssey took an unlikely turn when her childhood fantasy was fulfilled. She was invited to live in the well-appointed Pinckney Street house of Miss Pride, the embodiment of Boston propriety (and, it turned out, of petrifaction) who regularly vacationed at the Hotel Barstow in Chichester and had become Sonie's idol. For years the child had been consumed with admiration of the impeccably bred visitor, and with envy of Miss Pride's niece, Hopestill Mather, Sonie's age and a lucky inhabitant of Pinckney Street. The image of the spinster's old house—hallowed in Sonie's mind by tradition, by association with some vague ideal of civilization—emerged as the presiding symbol of the book. In her daydreams Sonie adorned those solid, orderly rooms with concrete details, drawing on her knowledge of Miss Pride's immaculate Hotel Barstow room, which the child cleaned when her mother, the chambermaid, wasn't feeling well. But the cruel recognition crowning Sonie's quest was that darkness and isolation existed in the aristocratic order of the Boston elite too. Her life with Miss Pride proved to be anything but a liberation. Garbed in civility and enlightenment, the solitude there was even more chilling.

For the Southerners, the North, especially New England, played a crucial role in the drama of deracination, and both Stafford and Lowell were fascinated by the myth of the "abstract-minded, sharp-witted trading society" of New England versus the "simple . . . personal and dramatic . . . sensuous" southern mind, as Tate put the contrast in his essay in *I'll Take My Stand*. But their allegiances were, understandably, not so clearcut. Though Stafford, the Westerner (and now a New Englander by marriage), was acutely aware of the formative power of place, she could also become exasperated with the dogmatic views of her hosts. She had listened to countless conversations about the importance of regionalism, a favorite topic among the Tates and the assorted company that gathered at Monteagle. The chauvinism was sometimes expressed in an appealingly humble style. "Thank God for being a Southern writer," Caroline Gordon exclaimed to a friend in 1937, citing the Civil War as a rich source of inspiration. "I do feel at times that in comparison with the rest of you we are sitting in at a game where the cards are already stacked. . . . Our stuff due to the upheaval of '64 is lying around loose for any fool who has a big tow sack to pick it up. . . . If you are from other parts of the country it seems these days that you have to use much more skill to strike a vein of the real stuff and get it out." But sometimes the smugness roused Stafford to indignation. "We had this statement 'I cannot feel that anything out of the south is of any consequence,'" she reported in a letter to Taylor:

> What appalls me is not the statement but the fact that it was said in dead earnestness, not under the influence either of alcohol or chauvinism. It was declared that nowhere but in the south are people conscious of the land and when we objected, we let loose a storm against New England. All of this reads like a book to me and not such a damned good book.

Like Lowell, whose ambivalence about New England emerged in the poems he was writing at the time, Stafford was evidently inspired in part by the southern prejudice about the North to write about the place herself—make a better book of it. Unlike her husband, however, she wasn't writing from the inside. In Baton Rouge, Stafford had written to Hightower announcing that her new novel was her "first un-autobiographical" effort, which was in an obvious sense true. It was not as though she could portray New England from intimate knowledge: she had lived in Cambridge and skirmished with the Lowells only briefly, and her reaction had been confused. She had been at once enthralled and repelled by the clannish elite that had given her such a cold shoulder. But if Sonie's lurid Chichester childhood and her frigid Boston coming-of-age bore little resemblance to Stafford's actual life, the progress of Sonie's mind reflected the growth of Stafford's own. *Boston Adventure* was the portrait of an adventurous yet vulnerable imagination struggling to make sense of the world. It was steeped more in literature than in life—especially in Proust and James, an intimidating tradition but one that Stafford wasn't afraid to turn to her own uses.

In an important essay on James published in *Partisan Review* during Stafford's Monteagle spring, "The Heiress of All the Ages," Philip Rahv focused on the development of James's principal heroine, his daring young American woman. She was the star of his international drama, which turned on issues of central interest to the southern critics, who were among the first advocates of the James revival. James offered not merely a model of formalism but a version of the conflict of values they identified in their own national drama. His juxtaposition of innocent, idealistic Americans with sensuous, experienced Europeans was not so different from the Agrarians' opposition between Northerners and Southerners, for as both Tate and Ransom made clear in their contributions to the Agrarian manifesto, *I'll Take My Stand,* the South was America's Europe, the repository of tradition, of landed attachments, in an otherwise shallow-rooted country. James's contrast was evidently helpful to Stafford as she worked to complicate the conflicts in Sonie's Boston adventure.

Not that she simply followed his lead. Instead of a Jamesian heiress, a "passionate pilgrim" sent forth from innocent New England to encounter in Europe the "social successful worldly world," as Rahv called it, Sonie Marburg was a pauper on what looked like the reverse journey. She started out across the water from Boston with her European parents. Physically she was not far away: "On a clear morning, looking across the green, excited water, littered with dories and lobster-pots and buoys, I could see Boston and its State House dome, gleaming like a golden blister," Sonie began. But spiritually she was miles away, her life in Chichester a socially unsuccessful impoverished world. Sonie ended up in the heart of New England, but it was far from innocent.

If James was one lurking literary model whose international theme Stafford in a sense transposed, Proust was the presiding influence. Here too Stafford inventively adapted. "With its first page, tuned to the glazed and dying night-music of Proust's Overture," Alfred Kazin wrote in his review, "'Boston Adventure' brings us into the mind of a young girl so high in her style and so low in society that one's first impression is that Gorky's tramp characters have stolen into the cork-lined room." The strange tension at the center of Stafford's novel was the disjunction between Sonie's sensibility and her circumstances. She sounded, as Stafford herself said early on, like C. K. Scott Moncrieff's translation of Proust—elevated and archaic—yet her origins and her destiny were a world away from Marcel's. Although *Boston Adventure,* narrated in the first person, was proof of Sonie's prodigious imagination, Stafford emphatically denied her character the fruitful circuit that Proust granted Marcel. Sonie was Miss Pride's disillusioned secretary—an amanuensis charged with a hopeless project, the old lady's memoirs—not a real writer. She never enjoyed Marcel's miraculous triumph of simultaneously renouncing the corrupt world and possessing it in the creation of a work of art.

That is what made Sonie such a peculiar, and powerful, heroine. Stafford's Proustian and Jamesian ingredients resulted in an idiosyncratic mix. Sonie was neither an artist nor really an heiress. What stood in the way of art was that she aspired to be an heiress—that she wanted to be, and then was, adopted by Miss Pride—more than she wanted to pursue a literary life. What undermined her role as heiress was that she had the ironic spirit of an artist, the imagination to see the distance between pretension, aspiration, and reality. She made not only the opposite of James's journey, but also the opposite of Proust's journey—that is, she chose society over art, even though society was an imprisonment. Yet Stafford shared with both writers a focus on disillusionment, on spiritual alienation and social subjugation. In fact, her vision was completely dark. She allowed no bridging of American and European values, no synthesis of art and life.

Neither heiress nor artist, Sonie was an odd combination of dreamer and critic. She was a rather mystifying narrative presence, as Lambert Davis, Giroux's successor as Stafford's editor at Harcourt, Brace, pointed out to her that spring in Monteagle. He sent Stafford a preliminary editorial report, which was full of praise but also posed questions about her elusive heroine. How does Sonie, he asked,

> become the master of a polished and intricate prose style and a cool ironic insight into character? ... Sonie as she appears in this book is a curiously passive creature.... One asks to know why she is telling this story: what springs of pride or frustration or anger or ambition or love lie at the source of this outpouring, what violent inwardness is under the cool surface of the style?

These were not questions that would have been asked of Stafford's earlier, heated style. That Davis asked them now was a sign of how far Stafford had moved from the subjective agonies of her first efforts and from more conventional psychological portraiture in general. Her answers did not make for a standard saga of developing identity. Instead, Stafford unfolded a sort of mythic progress of the soul, or rather of the imagination.

IN BOOK ONE, "Hotel Barstow," Stafford set in motion Sonie's liberation from Chichester and traced her problematic imaginative heritage. She lived surrounded by—suffocated by—disappointed hopes. Her mother, brought up in horrifying misery in Russia, berated her father for sabotaging her dreams of a lavish life in America. Her father, once a proud craftsman and now a poor shoe repairman, was tortured by self-hatred and shame at his fall, not only from his vocation but from Catholicism. As Edmund Wilson wrote of Proust's Combray residents, "all are sick with some form of the ideal." As a child, Sonie knew all too well the symptoms of this sickness. Violence and hatred rocked the Marburgs' dilapidated cottage, especially at night, when from her pallet on the floor she heard her parents rail at each other in bed. As the narrator, she understood the different sources of the common affliction: "My mother believed herself persecuted by everyone she had ever known. . . . But [my father] knew, and was powerless to rectify the fault, that all his torture came from his own flabby will which swung him like a pendulum between apathy and fretful indecision."

The odds were heavily weighted against this half-Russian, half-German child, whose lineage was even more outlandish than Gretchen Marburg's had been. To be half Hun was "infamous beyond pardon," but to be part Russian was "utterly improbable." Sonie was in unwilling thrall to her big-eyed histrionic mother, whose story of betrayal was "so fantastic that not even I, a little girl, could believe it." Stafford's great accomplishment was to convey Sonie's enraptured resistance to Shura's lunacy. The two inseparable figures, mother and madwoman, loomed over Sonie, unbelievable yet unquestionable.

Shura Marburg grew more and more fantastically disoriented as the novel progressed, Dickensian in its exaggeration. Impregnated and abandoned by Hermann, she gave birth to a son, Ivan, whom she detested and destroyed, while Sonie struggled in vain to protect the epileptic child, a little monster grown hateful from hate. The scenes—Shura shivering with cold in front of a blazing fire, embroidering birds without tails on every cloth surface she could find, painstakingly picking lint from wicker chairs at the hotel with a hairpin, staring at her son until his eyes rolled back and he succumbed to a foaming fit—made no pretense at realism, but were compelling in their symbolic intensity:

> I looked upon my mother with sheer fright. It was as if I looked upon naked evil in the person of that woman whose beauty so far surpassed any other I had ever seen that it was almost divine, as if she had come directly from the hand of God, but had, immediately afterwards, been inhabited by a ravenous and indefatigable fiend. Or perhaps she was not alive with wickedness but was dead with it: an empty vessel, or an excellent hull holding a withered fruit. I wondered how deep she was and if my own depths ... were the same.

Where her mother was an incarnation of the dark urges and fears that Sonie was strong enough to restrain, Hermann Marburg embodied the ambivalent desires and needs that threatened to undermine Sonie's determination, as they did his own. "My father was not a man whose misery could be mitigated by a change of environment or an increase of worldly goods or an establishment in a society," Sonie judged, and ascribed his suffering to his sensibility, "refined by what influences I could only conjecture. And this sensibility had led him away from the traditions of his religion and his work and neither the one nor the other could stand alone." The artisan was tormented by what Stafford suggested was a deep, and hopeless, desire for transcendence. His scenes, too, turned into tableaux of high drama, which Stafford often deftly undercut. This damned man spoke a variety of tongues, but only one tone—a desperate rhetoric that left his daughter reeling, sometimes from physical blows that accompanied his verbal violence:

> Then he put his head down until his forehead was in his greasy plate and shouted, "*Confiteor Deo omnipotenti, Beatae Mariae, semper Virgini ...* " but he could not go on. He rolled over until his face was pointed upward to the ceiling and he wailed, "*Gott! Gott, warum hast Du mich verlassen!*"
>
> "Papa, do you want some cheese?"

"Cheese? Yes, that's the remedy! Give your father a spoonful of cheese and that will get him out of hell!" He took me by both arms and shook me until my dizzied eyes began to hurt. "We're fit for nothing!" His eyes, afire and yet still as cold as ice, looked upon me with such hatred and so terrible a threat that I commenced to cry.

He fantasized that the American frontier was his escape from hell. His favorite book was Zane Grey's *Riders of the Purple Sage,* which he loved to read to Sonie (if he wasn't urging Latin on her). When, sixty pages into *Boston Adventure,* he fled his wife and family, he was presumably headed out West.

Thus Stafford gave plenty of evidence of the "violent inwardness" that lurked under Sonie's cool style, though it didn't come packaged in familiar psychological form. This was not subtle introspection at work, but a kind of poetic projection, a drama that called attention to its mythic, religious dimensions. Her parents were not simply the source of certain symptoms in her, but symbols that dramatized her divided nature. In casting Sonie's predicament this way, Stafford couldn't avoid a static, almost surreal quality in the first section of her novel.

What suspense there was in the plot lay in the question: Was Sonie, unlike her father, someone whose misery could be mitigated by "a change of environment or an increase of worldly goods or an establishment in a society"? That was certainly her dream as a child, as she announced on the first page of the novel. Huddled in the same room with her haranguing parents, her secret wish, cultivated in great detail in her head, was "that I might have a room of my own, and the one I imagined was Miss Pride's at the Hotel Barstow." With the echo of Virginia Woolf, Stafford was playing off the expectation that Sonie's transcendence might lie in literature, and she continued to point tantalizingly to that path for Sonie.

But as the soulless nature of Miss Pride's room suggests, Sonie's primary aspirations were, in fact, the opposite of aesthetically liberating. Her fantasies were of a potentially suffocating order. The Boston grande dame displaced Shura in Sonie's dreams, an antimother if there ever was one. Miss Pride was repression incarnate, which the child interpreted as desirable aristocratic rigidity. Surrounded by violent passions, Sonie yearned for a kind of serene passivity that seemed ominous. "It was not until then, in the summer of my 10th year, that I learned, in what terms of childhood I cannot remember, that peace was to be desired above all things," she announced, and showed herself eager to submit to Miss Pride's tyranny.

Against Miss Pride, the heroine of Sonie's childhood, however, Stafford juxtaposed another force, or direction, in Sonie's adolescence: her Jewish neighbor in Chichester, Nathan Kadish. He represented the path of rebellious creativity, which had almost as much allure for Sonie as the route to social success, so commandingly staked out by the well-connected Bostonian. Precocious Nathan's combative dedication to learning, which was his way of high-mindedly rejecting Chichester, thrilled Sonie. He dogmatically lectured her about his life's course, much of which he cribbed from George Moore's *Confessions of a Young Man,* which he pressed on Sonie, too. She was captivated but confused: How could this iconoclastic vision of culture and self-definition fit with her ambitions toward Pinckney Street?

I had not read much of [*Confessions of a Young Man*] yet, but its effect on me was already marked, and I was anxious for the next week-end to come so that I might tell Nathan that I understood why it was he wanted to go to Paris. Shivering in the icy room, I thought of the book and wished that I were a young man, queer enough to keep a tame python, clever enough to educate myself at the Nouvelle Athènes where the painters and poets gathered nightly as a learned and bibulous academy. I thought how simple my actions would be if I were a great, confident pagan egoist like George Moore. Would I not, if I were a young man, leave Chichester and my foolish mother? But I was not fitted for such a life, not only because I was a girl, but because I was an ignoramus. I nearly cried aloud thinking of the sloth of all these past years that had prevented me from reading less than a tenth of what Nathan had read. Here, only two years older than I, he was a store-house full of books. Even at my own game, he surpassed me, for he spoke and read German with twice my facility. To be educated was the privilege of our class, he had told me. That was the weapon whereby we could conquer the bourgeoisie. I did not know precisely what he meant. Whenever I dwelt upon his words, I could only imagine myself dazzling Miss Pride with my culture; I had no desire to overthrow her, only to make her welcome me.

It was a tension that Stafford knew firsthand in life and that she came back to often in her fiction—fascination with wealth and status in conflict with dedication to independence of mind. Sonie understood that she was pulled between two contrasting poles: "Between these two astronomies, the young man's whose earth was plural, and Miss Pride's whose solitary world was Boston, round which the trifling planets revolved at a respectful distance, I could not choose, for both were true." Here Stafford drew more directly from her own life, as she introduced another character to serve as a possible bridge between the two: Dr. Philip McAllister, a young Bostonian who mixed Miss Pride's breeding with Nathan's rebelliousness. He seemed the fulfillment of Sonie's ideal, the independent insider who aimed to disconcert but not to destroy the smug establishment, and who thus could offer a potential solution to her dilemma— much as Lowell did for Stafford. In one of Sonie's Boston reveries, Stafford conjured up this ideal young man in terms quite clearly reminiscent of Lowell. Sonie's dream man was a literary radical—a reader of Donne, a writer of unconventional poetry—who posed an overt challenge to the old lady with her impossibly provincial views.

But Stafford finally didn't allow a constructive synthesis, though at first it seemed she might. A man with a taste for transcendence, Philip McAllister enabled Sonie's liberation from Chichester by helping her to commit her mother to a mental hospital. In Boston, however, he failed her. There he was too late in warning her against Miss Pride's tyranny, distracted from Sonie's troubles by his fascination with, and then marriage to, Hopestill Mather.

True to the injunction that art ought to be impersonal, Stafford had cast Sonie's predicament in ambitiously encompassing terms in Book One. Though the facts of her own life were discernible, she was notably successful this time in transforming them into inevitable forces in her characters' lives. The parents represented the most extreme metamorphosis. Sonie's crazed mother was a kind of demonic inversion of Stafford's own long-suffering, matter-of-fact mother. The father figure, violently embittered in his disappointment, had to disappear early in the novel: he was so daunting, Stafford recognized later, that she couldn't confront him straight on in her fiction. The domineering, aristocratic woman was the mother Stafford didn't have but acquired through marriage, and to whom she then felt masochistically susceptible: Mrs. Lowell lurked not very far behind Miss Pride, an emblem of social power and ruthlessness and an enemy of creative energy. (Miss Pride's aesthetic views seemed to echo letters from Mrs. Lowell, who considered serious writing a thoroughly unsuitable pursuit for a well-bred Bostonian. "I think he writes doggerel," was Miss Pride's assessment of Eliot. "I have never quite got his connections clear. All I know of him is that he was born in Saint Louis, even though he really was an Eliot.") The younger men, too, could be assigned their counterparts: McAllister as Lowell, Nathan as Hightower. Moreover, the deeply ambivalent view of Boston reflected not simply Stafford's personal dilemma but a preoccupation of her husband's as well. At any rate, that was how Lowell sometimes told it, as he worked alongside Stafford on poems in which he couldn't quite decide whether the Puritans were forces of enlightened rebellion or of benighted authoritarianism and inhumanity.

I N B O O K T W O, "Pinckney Street," Stafford shifted the scene from Chichester to Boston and settled the question. This was her Proustian anatomy of corruption, though as Dr. McAllister explained to Sonie, the drama of decadence among the Bostonians was wan: "Boston was something in the days when hell was immediate, altruism was ruthless, and justice was Mosaic. Now, cured of its chills and fevers, its blood watered down, it was no longer exciting. Still puritanical, it tried to imitate Sodoms and Gomorrahs in their decenter fashions, but the result was only dowdiness." The inward, subjective perspective gave way to a more objective approach as her heroine matured. Delivered to the Boston of her dreams, Sonie now had to face the disintegration of her ideal. She had escaped the wild frustration of the powerless, her parents, only to discover the more decorous desperation of the powerful.

On one level, "Pinckney Street" was the more manageable part of Stafford's enterprise. It was scathing social portraiture in a well-established tradition, a novel of manners about an often-caricatured corner of America. And though Stafford hadn't penetrated Boston society very deeply, she had been formatively exposed to it, directly and indirectly. In short, it was less a challenge to her mythic imagination—as "Hotel Barstow" had been—and more a task for her analytic, satiric powers. And certainly she had those in abundance. Stafford's principle was once again juxtaposition, this time between crowded social scenes, in which Sonie was more observer than participant, and intimate encounters, in which Sonie watched—and was in turn watched by—Miss

Pride, Philip, and, most important of all, the renegade Hopestill Mather (a name as unsubtle as Miss Pride's). Miss Pride's niece and ward, Hope was the offstage object of Sonie's envy throughout Book One. In Book Two she became her dark alter ego.

Precisely because she was so naturally gifted at lampooning the "pilgrims' heirs" in Boston, Stafford had more trouble managing the tension for Sonie between creativity and gentility in Boston than she did in Chichester. As a child, both Sonie's outlandish imagination and her yearning for aristocratic rigidity cohabited uneasily but credibly. It wasn't hard to see how this imaginative girl's vision of escape featured the repressive Miss Pride, whom she saw as admirably rigid. But in Boston, it was more difficult to balance Sonie the social aspirant and Sonie the detached outsider. Perceptive satire came so readily to her (as Hope acknowledged, "It takes an outlander to trap us alive") that her continuing myopic adulation of Miss Pride strained credulity.

Stafford did her best to deal with this problem by developing in Book Two the tension that she had introduced in "Hotel Barstow" between Sonie's social and artistic aspirations. Although Nathan had drifted out of the foreground temporarily, George Moore was still at her bedside, unsettling her Boston reveries. "I read him constantly . . . out of the desire to prove to myself that the 'best' Nathan had wanted for himself and for me was in reality only second best." Sonie was clearly struggling. Her yearning for propriety and order had to do battle with a zeal for vital experience that she found hard to suppress:

> My talents were not artistic, not creative. I felt that they were assimilative and analytical, that what I saw in Boston, what I had seen in Chichester I understood, but that I could not reassemble my impressions into something artful. I could not ennoble fact. It was experience of the most complex order that I desired, and while there were times when . . . I wished my knowledge to include the cafes and *ateliers* and quays of George Moore's Paris, the wish was diluted as I turned home and thought of my room, of Miss Pride, and of our conversation over the sherry glasses. She, I thought, was worth all the freedom and all the abandon, worth, indeed, all the triumphs.

It was in the intimate scenes, which directly or indirectly centered on Hope, that Stafford tried to fine-tune Sonie's perspective on Pinckney

Street and her own fate. By setting up a doppelgänger relation between Sonie and Hope—two black sheep, one the insider, one the outsider—she found a way to have both drama and detachment in her story's plot and in her protagonist's psyche. It was a structural and thematic strategy she used again in her fiction after *Boston Adventure*. Through Hope's melodramatic relations with Miss Pride and Philip, Stafford gave Sonie vicarious exposure to the real, brutal Boston, while still sustaining Sonie's own eerily distanced and submissive presence amid the clan.

Hope was not a realistic character any more than Sonie's parents were. She was an emblematic figure, the product of psychological and spiritual pressures that arose from a larger social situation. Hope was the culmination of bad blood and rebellion in the Brahmin enclave—the daughter of a philandering, drunken brute who died when thrown from his horse. But as with the Marburgs, Stafford spared no effort on the vivid particulars; for all the caricature, she was also drawing on a reality even stranger than eccentric stereotype. (She included an outlandish detail from the Lowell family history that surfaced in a poem of Lowell's a decade later: to spare the ears of her husband, Hope's poor mother was forced to play on a dummy piano, a punishment actually visited upon Lowell's Great-Aunt Sarah, as he wrote in "My Last Afternoon with Uncle Devereux Winslow" in *Life Studies*.)

Hope's story was a familiar one of self-destructive revolt. To the horror of her family, she disappeared to New York, where she spent time with psychoanalysts and fast-living bohemians who were more dedicated to drink and general decadence than to art. Her fate among them was the predictable one. She got pregnant by a cad beneath her station, a Machiavellian social climber with plenty of money but no class and no conscience. She returned to Boston and successfully plotted a solution to her dilemma. She maneuvered her way into marriage to Philip, ousting Sonie from her position as the doctor's confidante and companion (and, though Sonie hardly dared admit it to herself, aspiring lover). And then Hope's rapid decline began, as Philip, his love transformed to hate, exacted his revenge with the Puritan rigor that had lurked in his idealistic character from the start. In the end Hope, a passionate horsewoman, committed suicide in the Mather tradition. She goaded her horse to throw her late in her pregnancy.

As Elizabeth Hardwick observed in "Poor Little Rich Girls," a piece she wrote for *Partisan Review* after the novel came out, Hopestill Mather was a "literary convention [out of] the novels of the twenties": she was the "romantically wayward" and theatrically jaded flapper. Hardwick assumed that the convention was being unselfconsciously employed. By Sonie, it was, at least up until the end of the novel. She saw Hope, the aristocratic rebel, in her most symbolic dimensions, because that was how her untutored, ambitious imagination worked on the facts of Boston. But Stafford's own perspective is less easily pinned down, a problem posed by many of her exaggerated portraits: Just where does the irony begin? In part, she seemed to share Sonie's rapt immersion in Hope's lurid life, and her fascination is not hard to account for. As she herself wrote to an old college friend much later, "Hopestill in my book is Lucy. Miss Pride (and I did not connect these things until the other day) is named Lucy." Behind the Bostonian decadence, and Hope's suicide, was the frightening memory of Lucy McKee and Stafford's own loss of distance and control in that relationship. No wonder irony sometimes eluded her.

Yet Stafford was also very much in control of her characters and of the relations among them. If Hope on occasion escaped her grasp, for the most part Stafford successfully, and consciously, exploited her as a literary convention. The stereotypical quality of Hope's character highlighted the contrast between her and Sonie, whose reverse aspirations—to join precisely the Bostonian gentry that Hope revolted against—were played out so unconventionally. If Sonie had been the typical arriviste, she would probably have shared some of Hope's salient qualities: feverish energy, manipulative skill, and a calculating understanding of power, along with some vision (however delusory) of autonomy. There is a natural kinship between those literary favorites, the highborn rebel and the lowborn arriviste. But Stafford's purpose was to subvert the conventions in Sonie's case. She was not simply the provincial who triumphed in the city either by mastering its manners or by seeing through them. She did both, and yet she remained convinced that she was the one who had been mastered and seen through. Disillusioned, she was still in thrall. Peace and powerlessness exerted a seductive appeal for this heroine.

Where Hope was finally driven to death as the escape from the merciless sway of Boston—the conventional, dramatic response—Sonie's reaction to Boston was highly unconventional and hardly dramatic in the standard sense of the term. Miss Pride's ruthless pursuit of power was belatedly revealed to Sonie (our class, Hope helpfully whispered, lives for power). Betrayed by her ward, Lucy Pride had hired her secretary not really to write her memoirs, but to tend her through the terrors of a lonely old age. Sonie was indentured unto the death of the indomitable lady, the same fate she had faced in Chichester with her own, real mother—and then faced again when she learned from the doctors in the asylum that Shura was improving and might be released. All at once, the world closed in on Sonie, as two crabbed women claimed her freedom, and her only choice, as she saw it, was between enslavements.

Until, that is, she stumbled upon a strange escape in reverie. Late in Book Two, Stafford turned to the "red room" of the surgical story she had written in Baton Rouge, inserting whole sections of the meditative vision she had developed there. This time the suffering that impelled retreat to the inner sanctuary was not physical (surgery on her flesh) but mental. Sonie was not a patient in need of release from vivid pain, but a nurse in need of respite from less tangible oppression. The setting for Sonie's first visionary experience, however, was similar. She was in the cool, white asylum visiting her mother—the undistracting surroundings that permitted that first step on St. Teresa's path, the willful cultivation of memories. Instead of the surgeon's knives, it was Miss Pride's eyes that propelled Sonie into the more terrifying culminating instant when the will retreated and the corner was turned. That moment arrived in the midst of one of Hope and Philip's cruel cocktail parties, at which the hosts quietly tortured each other and the guests feigned oblivious- ness. Sonie slipped into her sanctuary, only to discover that she was trapped by her mistress's gaze:

> The eyes, like a surgeon's knives, were urged into my brain. The edges of the knives screamed like sirens; their sound curled in thin circles round my hot, pink brains. I crouched in a corner of the room, down behind the bookcases, safe, I thought. But I was plucked up by the burning yellow flares that went in a direct path like a sure blade. Miss Pride blinked her eyes. The room vanished. I had not moved but I felt an overwhelming tranquillity as if my brain were healed again, was sealed and rounded and impervious, was like a loaded, seamless ball, my hidden and wonderfully per- fect pearl.

Once again, there was an ambivalence at the heart of the escape, for it was a kind of imprisonment of its own. In liberating herself from exter-

nal experience by retreating to her internal chamber, Sonie acknowledged that she was not just cutting herself loose but cutting herself off:

> I cannot say how long the "vision" of this red room lasted, but while
> it did, I experienced a happiness, a removal from the world which
> was not an escape so much as it was a practiced unworldliness. And
> it was a removal which was also a return. The happiness was not
> unmixed: as I gazed at the red evening sunlight winnowed through
> the brick chimneys of the court, I was filled with a tranquil, mortal
> melancholy as if I were out of touch with the sources of experience
> so that I could receive but could not participate.

Sonie's subsequent portrait of her room, a variation on a similar passage
in Stafford's original story, was, if anything, more chilling. "It was a sanctuary and its tenant was my spirit, changing my hot blood to cool ichor
and my pain to ease. Under my own merciful auspices, I had made for
myself a tamed-down sitting-room in a dead, a voiceless, city where no
one could trespass, for I was the founder, the governor, the only citizen."
Where Stafford had previously left it at the cozy enough "tamed-down
sitting-room," she now ominously amplified the room of her own to suggest a postholocaust city. There was a high price to pay for escape.

   In her novel, unlike in her story, Stafford treated the room as a prelude
not to spiritual readjustment—whether fulfilling or disillusioning—but
to insanity. Sonie dreaded succumbing to her mother's fate. The drama
here was not simply one of mind over matter, of a patient coming to new
terms with the material world through the experience of physical pain;
it was one of mind versus mind. For the problem was that Sonie's brain
was not healed, "sealed and rounded and impervious." Her imagination
was all too permeable, confused between facts and fantasies. She knew
all too well "the fear of my own mind which had conceived so awful a
possibility." More frightening than the confusion between subjective and
objective worlds was the confusion between subjective worlds. By virtue
of its penetrating power, the imagination itself was rendered vulnerable.
It could see into other minds, and thus it had to assume that other minds
could see into it. For someone as hypersensitive as Sonie, there was nowhere to hide from the tyrannical eyes. Sonie the child had watched the
deadly gaze that locked her mother's and her brother's wild eyes. Sonie
the young woman closed with this ominous, understated image of mind-
forged manacles: Miss Pride "looked again as she had done when I was

five years old in Chichester; her flat, omniscient eyes seized mine, grappled with my brain, extracted what was there, and her meager lips said, 'Sonie, my dear, come out of the cold. You'll never get to be an old lady if you don't take care of yourself.'"

TAKING CARE OF HERSELF was not Stafford's priority that year in Monteagle. Taking care of her novel was, and that was taxing work. Stafford's thematic ambitions, which had taken at least rough shape in the manuscript that had convinced Harcourt, Brace to offer her a contract, were demanding. By the time she joined the Tates, her labors were evidently devoted above all to problems of style and structure: there was more than a year of arduous revising ahead of her. The first stretch, spent at Monteagle, was the formative stretch of rewriting, and if the Tates didn't direct her style in quite the domineering way they did Lowell's, they were nonetheless a presiding influence. Stafford worked zealously, apparently spurred on by the productive household and in turn intimidating them with her intensity. Writing to Katherine Anne Porter, Caroline Gordon described the exhausting scene: "Four of us here on this mountain top, leading what would be an idyllic existence if it weren't for the news from the outside world and for the surges of creative energy which shake the house. I guess I'm identifying Jean's typewriter with her Muse. Sometimes it sounds like the sea breaking on rocks or a small explosion."

Stafford was nobody's docile student, but it seems fair to say that along with her muse, her mentors and their literary views helped to guide her energetic typing and retyping. Certainly the reigning ethos of laborious craftsmanship left its mark. The New Critics wholeheartedly subscribed to Eliot's view that "the larger part of the labour of an author in composing his work is critical labour," as he wrote in "The Function of Criticism" (1923); "the labour of sifting, combining, constructing, expunging, correcting, testing: this frightful toil is as much critical as creative." Lowell recalled years later that he had kindled to Tate's insistence that "poetry . . . must be tinkered with and recast until one's eyes pop out of one's head."

Critical prescriptions for tinkering with fiction were less dogmatically formulated. In fact, Tate sounded downright lax about the techniques of fiction in an essay by that title published in 1944 (the writing of which probably dates roughly from the Monteagle year):

There must be many techniques of fiction, but how many? I suppose a great many more than there are techniques of poetry. . . . The
novel has at no time enjoyed anything like the number and the
intensity of objective conventions which the drama, even in its comparatively formless periods, has offered to the critic. The number of
techniques possible in the novel are probably as many as its conventions are few.

Such a refreshingly informal perspective was surprising from a man better known for his insistence on high discipline and strain. But in practice,
the openness seems to have left plenty of room for meddling in Monteagle, and not only by Tate. As Caroline Gordon acknowledged in retrospect, Stafford had by no means been left alone. When Gordon set
about revising her own novel during the summer of 1943, not long after
the foursome had disbanded, she wrote to Stafford, cringing at the memory of the younger woman's revision ordeal and offering a glimpse of the
ruthless critical method in the Tate household. Apparently Tate was the
reigning arbiter, despite Gordon's more extensive experience with fiction.
"I am so sorry about your fever coming back," she wrote to Stafford, who
was by then having a difficult time at Yaddo, the writers' colony in Sara-
toga Springs, New York:

The hell of it is that you had hardly got on your feet. I am in a
position now to sympathize with you even more deeply than I did
when we were all taking whacks at your novel there on the mountain. Allen has finally finished reading mine and I have started the
revision. But there are two chapters that he thinks are perfectly
foul. I don't like them either and had already rewritten them several times. The other day I hauled off, took a fresh start and wrote
a substitute chapter, which, according to Allen, had exactly the
same faults as the original. God knows how many times I'll have to
repeat this performance. I don't mind the suffering so much, or
rather I can stand it, but what worries me is that whenever I get
stuck on a place like this it shows.

The Monteagle treatment of Stafford evidently had been memorably
rough, for Gordon came back to the subject again in the fall: "I have
decided that your mysterious fever came not from sinus or anything else
but from having your novel torn to pieces by fiends in the guise of
friends," she wrote apologetically.

If the flexibility of the New Critical approach to fiction meant that Stafford was inundated with advice, the absence of a prescribed, intensive method was perhaps what saved her. Certainly she prospered creatively with all the help, even though she felt beleaguered and got quite sick. (And she was bitter, years later, at Lowell's imputation of excessive dependence on her mentors. "I have not ever forgiven him and I do not know if I ever shall for saying . . . 'Just remember that Boston Adventure would have been *much* poorer than it was if it hadn't been for the Tates,'" she wrote to Peter Taylor after she and Lowell had separated.)

More than a decade later Philip Rahv saw occasion to take issue with the New Critics' aggressive inroads into the criticism of fiction. In "Fiction and the Criticism of Fiction" (1956) he maintained that the "effort to deduce a prosaics from a poetics is *au fond* doomed to fail, for it is simply not the case that what goes for a microscopic unit such as the lyric poem goes equally well for the macroscopic compositions of the writer of narrative prose." Though Rahv may have been right that by then the New Critics' method had hardened into an excessive emphasis on style, his article also serves as a reminder of the underlying interest that had animated them at the outset, that inspired Rahv himself as well, and that was crucial to Stafford's revisions. Rahv denounced the New Critical preoccupation with style in the name of a novelistic virtue that Ransom himself had heartily endorsed in his essay "The Understanding of Fiction" (1950): concreteness. At the heart of that most empirical of genres, Rahv believed, there should be "solidity of specification." Ransom put it only somewhat differently. He suggested that the novel's power was to express and appeal to the affections over the intellect by transforming the "world of utility" and abstraction into "the world of objects built up in the fulness of their actual being."

As for the New Critics' obsession with symbols and mythic patterns, which Rahv also felt was misplaced in treating fiction, Tate at least had expressed a distinctly moderate view in comments about his own novel, *The Fathers*. His main aim, he said, was to accommodate both symbolism and concreteness, stressing that realistic texture took primary place: "I wished . . . to make the whole structure symbolic in terms of realistic detail, so that you could subtract the symbolism, or remain unaware of it, without losing the literal level of meaning . . . but if you subtract the literal or realistic detail, the symbolic structure disappears." Although it's arguable that his symbolic touch was not as light as he hoped in his own novel, he seems to have offered useful advice to Stafford. In a couple of letters to her during the spring of 1943, Lambert Davis emphasized how helpful it must be to have Tate's suggestions and mentioned that he had talked with Tate about one particular problem of symbolism—the choice of book (in the end *Riders of the Purple Sage*) to represent Sonie's father.

The successful balance in *Boston Adventure* between carefully structured patterns of symbolic imagery and density of specific detail was doubtless the product of Stafford's endless revisions, begun under the auspices of the Tates. In a crucial step beyond her old "words, merely" problem, she had found not only themes but a newly concrete style that suited her natural inclination to captivate through carefully wrought language rather than through the representation of raw experience and action. The central symbolic pattern of the novel, which must have required plenty of tinkering to get right, sheds light on the organic relation of Stafford's stylistic method and her themes. Sonie's vision of Miss Pride's Hotel Barstow room and her actual experience of it, then her vision of Miss Pride's Pinckney Street room and her experience of it, and finally her vision and experience of her own "red room," give the novel its underlying structural unity. The imagery links Books One and Two, establishing ironic cross-references between them, and it helps set up the key counterpoint of the novel: the play between internal and external worlds. Sonie's fascination with these evocative chambers, which seem to speak to her of some peaceful tradition that she has been born without, has a metaphysical as well as a social resonance. Stafford had found a place for her meditation on St. Teresa's castle of receding rooms.

The room that began its existence in Sonie's mind (Miss Pride's room) became in the end an image of that mind (the "red room"). As Stafford developed the symbol, it acquired a new dimension: house evoked head, the outer room became an inner chamber, windows were linked to eyes. For Sonie the Chichester dreamer, Miss Pride's room offered an escape from subjective hell into objective calm. Yet for Sonie the Bostonian, it became an objective hell from which she tried to retreat to subjective calm—only to discover that there was no real escape. Miss Pride could peer in through the windows. Just as no room in the world was the salvation she dreamed of, so the mind was not the asylum she hoped. In fact, it might be precisely the asylum she had feared all of her life: Miss Pride's small, piercing eyes evoked Shura's huge, terrifying eyes. Thus

Stafford implicitly returned at the close to the little cottage, barely bigger than a room, rocked by raging passions, where the stove blazed in the middle of summer. With this tour de force, Stafford proved herself an exemplary student of symbolism who was faithful at the same time to the world of objects.

As it was for Lowell, the year with the Tates was for Stafford not only an education in technique. It was also a lesson in life. The Monteagle household was her first extensive and intensive exposure to the life devoted to art. For all of her desire to consort with sensitive artists, Stafford was less at ease amid the creative, often claustrophobic, tumult than she perhaps expected. At Yaddo, where Stafford spent the summer months of 1943 after leaving Monteagle, she collapsed. It was the culmination of anxieties that had evidently been building. Stafford had been especially shaken by a bad quarrel she had had with Gordon in the spring (about what it's not clear): "I guess it wasn't as serious as I make out," she wrote to Taylor, but she evidently felt that she had completely lost control: "it gave me a violent attack of vertigo and completely bewildered me because it's the first time I've burst out like that at anyone but Cal or my family." The fight, as Stafford herself suggested, was the eruption of her ambivalence about her Monteagle "home": she fought because it felt like family and then found herself the stunned, stranded outsider again.

The life of art exemplified by the Tates was a taxing one. To judge by their relationship, the dynamic between married writers was not simple or smooth. And the Tates were a particularly pertinent model for the young Lowells. From early on in their marriage, Cal especially had looked to the older writers as guides on the literary path they hoped to follow. Some of the parallels were obvious. Gordon wrote prose, Tate poetry and criticism. Both were strong willed, combative, and addicted to gossip, especially literary gossip. Tate, like Lowell, tended to be abstract and impractical, while Gordon and Stafford prided themselves on their mastery of the mundane details of household management, and of career advancement. Gordon, with years of practice at feeding, housing, and organizing crowds of literary company on meager budgets, set dauntingly high standards for Stafford. Caroline was an autocratic organizer, who doubtless didn't make it easy for Jean to find her useful niche during the Monteagle year (just as Stafford later complained about the intrusive wives in her kitchen when she had her turn at playing hostess of an equally rustic salon).

But there was a subtler, internal parallel as well. For ten years, Gordon had worried about Tate's comparatively dry stretch, when he was writing next to no poetry. She felt "a little guilty," she had written to Katherine Anne Porter at one point, "the supposition being that he might be writing if he were married to someone else." She had also felt creatively somewhat cut off from him: "He really has no interest whatever in the modern novel," she had written to Josephine Herbst a decade earlier; "I never even think of showing him anything I write unless he hounds me into it." Tate's friend (and one of Stafford's teachers at the Writers' Conference in 1937) John Peale Bishop had once probed the lurking competitiveness that Gordon alluded to: "I wonder if Caroline's success hasn't had something to do with your silence," he wrote to Tate. "I don't mean that you begrudge it to her, nor that she doesn't richly deserve it, and more. But the relation between a man and a woman is very complicated." On the surface the relation seemed to be simplified that year in Monteagle, when Tate was suddenly engaged again, both in his own poetry and in her prose—and Gordon was eager to defer to his judgment. A withering critic in her own right, as her students and letters attest, she was notably self-effacing and willing to labor long and hard when it came to her husband's criticisms. But as subsequent years were to show, friction between them was far from resolved.

A similar assessment might have been made of the younger couple, and Stafford, it seems, tried to take her cue from Gordon in coping with the tensions. The mixture of household dominance and literary deference came quite naturally to her, and she too was relieved at Lowell's return to writing—though she expressed some skepticism at the outset. "He has commenced to write poems again," she wrote to Taylor in the fall. "But I have long since ceased to be hopeful about these fits and starts." Yet when he continued, she was not just hopeful but energetically helpful, typing poems to be sent out for submission, charting acceptances (three taken by *Partisan Review* by early 1943: "We are hoping that this will make that party in Gambier Ohio [Ransom at the *Kenyon Review*] stir his stumps"), assisting as Cal worked on assembling a manuscript to send off to Eliot. "I have intended all week to write you," Stafford wrote to Taylor in the spring, "but between cleaning up after the kittens and typing poems for Cal I have had very little time. We got the manuscript of his book off to Eliot yesterday—Allen thinks he may be able to get it published by Faber and Faber."

While Stafford presided over the daily, practical order, Lowell imposed the higher vocational discipline. During the Monteagle year, as Taylor remembered it, the couple's productivity—for the first time since their marriage, both of them were enjoying a fertile writing stretch at the same time—did not mean peace or easy companionship between them. It was a perpetually combative union. Lowell was stern, not least because Stafford was drinking a good deal (he had stopped). Back from a bibulous visit with Taylor, who was stationed at Fort Oglethorpe, Georgia, Stafford wrote Peter a chagrined letter, which revealed more about the strains between her and Lowell than she perhaps suspected:

> When [Cal] asked me had I been drinking I automatically said no (or rather humph-uh) which falsehood I will be glad to have perpetuated by you, although I cannot tell you the shame I feel in making such a request. The fact is that he has forbidden me 1) to drink ever again 2) to read the newspapers 3) to read any novels save those by Dostoievsky, Proust, James and Tolstoy 4) to get a paying job when he goes into the army. In making these prohibitions he is quite justified if tyrannical and I am not complaining. . . . The point of all this is that I have no fear of his indignation or scolding, but rather that I don't want him to worry about me when he goes into the army.

Imperious about the regimen of life, Lowell presumably joined in the criticism of Stafford's art as well. He certainly was not a shy critic of his teachers. Tate credited him with, among other things, "constant criticism" of his translation of the "Pervigilium Veneris." Gordon, too, was apparently attentive to the suggestions of a young man who impressed her more and more. As for Stafford's fast-growing manuscript, Gordon had emphasized that there had been *three* whackers at work on it.

Sick on and off at Monteagle (as was Gordon), Stafford was suddenly laid low again by her mysterious fever during the summer at Yaddo. But the suffering, she acknowledged in a letter to the newly married Taylors, was more than physical. (During the spring at Monteagle, Taylor had wooed Eleanor Ross, a poet and former student of Gordon's who had come to visit the Tates.) In July, not long after she had arrived at the writers' colony, Stafford wrote in distress, her jauntiness forced: "Imagine the Bean Bert [a nickname from Baton Rouge days] having a nervous breakdown. It is too grotesque and I am real cross at myself. My humor has departed. Everything seems bitterly grave. This is caused by Yaddo." In August she elaborated on her symptoms—continuing fever, continuing loss of weight—the diagnosis of which was still unclear: "Either a tubercular or a streptococcic infection of the kidneys," a doctor had evidently told her. On top of that, she was worn down by "nervous exhaustion." She offered some concrete reasons that she found the literary surroundings uncongenial, however luxurious the setting (which she relished describing). She took an immediate, perhaps slightly competitive, dislike to Carson McCullers, with whom she shared a bathroom, and she was clearly not in sympathy with the prevailing politics of the assembled company: McCullers "is by no means the consumptive dipsomaniac I'd heard she was, but she is strange. . . . They are all left. Perhaps the most irritating of all is Mrs. McCullers who, although she is a southernor [sic], passionately hates the south. . . . [Another] loathes Allen's criticism and thinks Ransom is impossible, . . . regards Blackmur as a person of no significance whatever."

But these complaints don't adequately account for Stafford's extreme unhappiness and her profound sense of dislocation—a real crisis. Some of the vaguer phrases in her letters to the Taylors over the summer seem to come closer to capturing her unease. The trouble wasn't really politics or a particular personality. Stafford recoiled from a deeper sense of alienation from the literary company, who struck her as abject souls. "Mrs. Ames," she wrote, referring to the kindly proprietress of Yaddo, "will, I am certain, protect me from these lost and desolated people." In the same vein, she wrote a month later: "I could stay here—Mrs. Ames is very good to me—and lie abed all day and perhaps come down for dinner in the evening. But in this rarefied atmosphere with the vibrations of these tragic lives I simply cannot. I suppose I am on the verge of some sort of nervous crackup which the fever is not helping any."

Just how disturbing she found this "desolated" company is suggested by a diary entry written years later, on December 27, 1949, the day after she had arrived for a second, shorter stay at Yaddo: "As the taxi brought me up the long road yesterday, winding between the lakes through the lines of trees joined to one another by dense fog, I felt the spooks of this place as I had done when I arrived for the first time, seven years before.

The company is difficult and strange. . . . Poor, unsuccessful, lonely, they embarrass me." Stafford's response both times recalls Sonie's ambivalence, entranced by Nathan's visions of the artistic life yet also daunted by its uncomfortable loneliness.

Not that Stafford was under any illusion that she could avoid loneliness. She recognized that her own sense of exile was at once a source of inspiration and of terror. In cringing at her literary colleagues, she was cringing at herself—and at what was ahead. For Stafford, only twenty-eight, the life of art had already been tumultuous, and here at Yaddo in the throes of still further revisions of her seven-hundred-page manuscript, she looked around her and was apprehensive about what lay in store. Perhaps added to the lost souls unnerving Stafford was the least successful, most lonely and desolate writer of them all, her father, whom she was letting down once again. He had sent her money to come visit him in Oregon that summer, she wrote to the Thompsons, but instead she had gone to Yaddo. It was a double betrayal: ignoring his plea for companionship and pursuing the fate that had so frustrated him.

As if she sensed Stafford's fear of contagious desolation, Caroline Gordon kept in touch throughout the summer, playing the role of mother, not critic—though she took care to bolster Jean's literary confidence. (Oddly, Stafford didn't mention Lowell, who had gone to New York to look for a job, in any of her letters.) Mrs. Ames, Gordon wrote, "is doing something for art when she stands by you," and she chimed in with a condescending dismissal of McCullers: "her trouble is not with technique but lies too deep for words." But mostly she conveyed her maternal concern; she had sent Stafford off in ill health, and look what had happened. Gordon freely admitted, in fact emphasized, her intrusiveness, as if she wanted to make sure Stafford took note of her unusual efforts— hoping to reassure Jean that she hadn't been abandoned. "I wrote [Mrs. Ames] a note this morning, telling her how grateful Allen and I were to her for making you so welcome. A bit meddlesome of me, perhaps." But the real target of Gordon's efforts was Stafford's mother-in-law. "I wrote Mrs. Lowell in desperation the other day, what I tried to make a very tactful note," she reported to Stafford:

> I deplored the fact that the children (I spoke of you and Cal as if you were babes whom I had had under my care all winter) . . . had

had such heavy doctor's bills. I myself was not very good at managing my own affairs so hesitated to give advice but it had occurred to me that it would be better to have a doctor's bill to end doctor's bills. . . . Allen pondered the letter and said he thought it was tactful, but of course he's not much of a judge. If she doesn't offer to pay the bill after the letter, she's a—rock-ribbed New Englander. I hope I haven't done wrong to horn in but I have been so worried and felt that something ought to be done.

Gordon was doing her best to make up for the rather different kind of meddlesomeness and lack of tact that had characterized their year together.

FOR THE LOWELLS, the life of art took a dramatic political, public turn in the fall of 1943. Cal had tried to enlist in the army throughout 1942, and in the spring of 1943 he had filled out an army employment questionnaire. (His answers were riddled with bizarre errors—he claimed, for example, that he had a dependent—which Stafford duly corrected before mailing off the form.) But suddenly he decided he wouldn't serve. The day before he was due to be inducted, September 8, 1943, he wrote a letter to President Roosevelt, with a "declaration of personal responsibility" attached. His case was in essence the conservative, anti-Communist one: the United States, bent on destroying Germany and Japan, would leave Europe and China "to the mercy of the USSR, a totalitarian tyranny committed to world revolution and total global domination through propaganda and violence."

It is impossible to know how this stand had matured in Lowell's mind, much less what Stafford thought of it. Tate, who had expressed reservations about the destruction of European civilization, was high among those blamed by Lowell's mother. It's true that a strange letter from Lowell to his grandmother suggests that Agrarian notions figured somehow in his decision: "You know more about American history than I do and can certainly judge whether our recent actions in this war are justifiable," he wrote to his grandmother. "I think only a Southerner can realize the horrors of a merciless conquest." (In his declaration he cited the Civil War as a warning about the perils of a war "carried through to unconditional surrender.") But a letter from Tate to Stafford in November made clear that he was as taken aback as everyone else. In fact, he took the occasion to give a short lecture about Lowell's evasion of responsibility, the implicit message being that the creative life is no excuse:

> You know, Jean, that I am greatly distressed that I cannot feel as much sympathy for Cal in his plight as I might have felt a year ago. I have already told you about this, and I need say but little more. Early in the summer he was casting about for an escape from his social responsibilities, and I am sure that he would have gone ahead then had he not met the rude interference of Caroline and me. Then, later—after he had been in New York for a month—he told Caroline that *she* was to blame for your illness, that her cruelty to you at Monteagle had brought on your breakdown. He had no connection to it apparently—as indeed possibly he did not; yet I cannot conceive that Caroline did either. Then his resistance to the draft completed the pattern in my mind, a development towards complete escape from his obligations. Try as I will I cannot see it in any other way. . . .
>
> You are involved in an enormously complicated situation, and all our sympathy is with you whether you want it that way or not. Cal will never really suffer—unless, of course, he gets into his mother's clutches again.

Lowell didn't see it that way at all. He evidently thought of his stand not as an evasion but as a shouldering of responsibility, which he was eager to broadcast. He and Stafford made numerous copies of his statement and distributed them widely. And he later said that it was "the most decisive thing I ever did, just as a writer," though he emphasized that at the time "it was not intended to have anything to do with that." Yet in some sense, it clearly did, as his mother realized, blaming it on his "poetic temperament." He conceived of it as part of his revolt against moribund Lowellian, establishment traditions in the name of higher, creative principles. It was as though he and Stafford that summer each suddenly had a very different intimation of what lay ahead—uncannily prophetic ones in retrospect. While Stafford was panicked by the lonely, marginal life dedicated to art as she looked around her and thought of her father, Lowell was inspired by the opposite perspective. Though he had been reared on a notion of poetry that was explicitly not politically engaged, he had been taught that art took the "whole man." It was an "aggressive stance," and after fighting on paper with words, he had seized a chance to fight his parents and other people with words and deeds.

Sentenced to a year and one day for draft evasion in October 1943 and transported to prison in Danbury, Connecticut, Lowell left Stafford to wage both battles. She had more revisions to do on *Boston Adventure,* after a break from the manuscript due to illness and the "declaration" drama. She was daunted by the prospect, she wrote to the Taylors in October:

> I have not started any writing yet at all. Yesterday Lambert Davis talked to me on the phone and said ominously that they would probably want some more work on the novel. It made me thoroughly sick at heart but I gathered, at least, that the manuscript is definitely accepted and after this vacation from it I suppose I'll be able to go back to it, heavy-hearted though I will be. They are anxious for Allen to read it but since I have only one copy, they don't dare let it out of the office. . . . Allen was terribly sweet and we were again completely devoted to him and to the whole household.

She had funny stories about some of her further revision travails. She had visited Bellevue Hospital to find out about paupers' burials (Harcourt, Brace complained that Ivan's burial was too implausible) and had been given a comical runaround. She had to cut, and diminish the melodrama of Hopestill's ending, and she worked hard. To the Thompsons, she later painted a bleak picture: "It was a rather bad winter for brooding—there is probably nothing more desolate than living in a New York apartment alone. . . . I spent the better part of six months huddled in front of the fireplace working on revisions of the book and almost never leaving the house."

In fact, she did leave the house (she had rented an apartment on Stuyvesant Square) and had a break from her brooding. Two of her closest friends that fall and winter were Gertrude Buckman, who had separated from Delmore Schwartz earlier that year, and especially Cecile Starr. In getting to know Starr, who hailed from a cultivated Nashville family, Stafford took evident pleasure in renewing her southern connections. Starr's uncles, Milton and Alfred, had been members of the Fugitives, and her close friend Patrick Quinn had been a friend of the Lowells at LSU. At the same time, it was a relief to her that Cecile Starr was not part of the New York literary scene. Their relationship was uncluttered, as few of Stafford's were, a respite from the competitive cultural scene. She had a kind and solid friend in Starr, and counted on her for support, psychological and practical.

For being back in the New York literary whirl was not the exhilarating experience it had been the first time around, in 1941–42, during the Lowells' Sheed and Ward year. This time Stafford ventured out alone, without Cal, to face the intimidating *Partisan Review* crowd—and then found she had to defend him in absentia. It was the kind of fight she felt completely inadequate to wage. In a long letter to the Taylors in November, she graphically dramatized her predicament. She had just been to Danbury to visit Lowell and waxed uncharacteristically romantic: "He is the most attractive and lovable man I know. . . . And I cannot tell you how glad I am that I am married to him and how sick down to my bones it makes me that he isn't in this room and won't be for ages." As in her earlier letters to Hightower, she seemed better able to love at a distance, and on paper. But the mood was quickly shattered:

> I have had *such* a revolting experience. After I got back from Danbury, I went to a cocktail party at the Rahvs. I got there very late—never should have gone, of course; I was wretched and should have gone home with my wretchedness and spent the evening looking at the snapshots of Cal—and not only was everyone quite drunk, but Philip Rahv had told everyone about me and Cal. (I should say here, by the way, that the greatest snobs in the world are bright New York literary Jews and the name Lowell works like love-philtre.) So that total strangers came up and asked me how Cal was. A certain Mr. Sidney Hook said to me, "Your husband is a heretic. He cannot be a conscientious objector and a Catholic for he is going against the dictates of the Pope." This happens to be untrue and it is an un-nice thing to be told by a logical positivist that your husband is a heretic. We had a little set-to over Saint Augustine (I was on steady enough ground here because I have recently been reading the confessions and reading them hard.) and had a generally distressing conversation. Of course he had everything at his fingertips and I daresay he is a distinguished man—if you go in for that kind of distinction. At any rate, when the crowd thinned out, a few of us went to dinner and then to a PR editor's house to go on drinking.

Mrs. Sidney Hook ... commenced to bait me and when I said "I can't discuss the Spanish war with you because I don't know enough about it. I know only the Encyclicals. But I am very sure there is something to be said for Franco," she screamed across the room, "Sidney, there is no point in talking to this girl. She thinks there is something to be said for Franco." And suddenly, as if there were large onions before my face, tears began to stream down my cheeks. They were automatic tears and very large ones and I couldn't stop them. Finally the woman gave me her handkerchief and presently they left.

In the middle of the distressing scene—a snapshot of the legendary, unending *PR*-style party—Stafford was still able to watch it and then recreate it, deftly inserting irony alongside the agony. Her comment about Franco seems to have emerged unbidden; she was perhaps parroting a throwaway line of Lowell's. Once again the literary world had undone her, but this time she saw more clearly than she had at Yaddo the degree of her ambivalence. She went on to give the Taylors her postmortem of the event, sizing up her situation with acuity:

> This morning when I woke up I felt like something out of its shell. *Crying* in front of people! And I analyzed it out and realized that what had happened was that I was lonely and isolated and that there had never been such a stupid move on my part as to go amongst such cruel people immediately after seeing Cal. For I had been told by ¾ of the men there that Cal was a fool or was hysterical, etc. etc. And suddenly everything broke like a glass and there I was, in tears. . . . I wish I could talk to you long and completely about literary people in New York. They are such cut-throats, such ambitious and bourgeois frights and yet I, in my stupid lack of integrity, continue to see them.

And it wasn't just *Partisan Review* people whom Stafford had to battle on Lowell's behalf. Perhaps even worse, she had to face her mother-in-law. In a couple of remarkable letters, Charlotte Lowell—"Charlotte Hideous" to Stafford—coldly lectured her daughter-in-law about the inadvisability of drawing on Lowell's trust fund while he was in prison (as Cal had wanted) and insinuating none too subtly that Stafford was to blame for letting "Bobby" get into this fix. "He will be completely penniless when he is released if you care to impose upon his generosity," she warned. "I hope, Jean, for your own sake as well as for Bobby's, that you will see in the present situation an opportunity for courage, selfdevelopment, and integrity of purpose."

In finishing *Boston Adventure,* which she was on her way to doing by the turn of the year, Stafford had shown all three—though Mrs. Lowell would hardly have seen it that way, not least because the product of Stafford's perseverance was a spirited satire of Mrs. Lowell's own precincts. But in February of 1944 as Lowell's sentence neared its end (he was granted parole in March), Stafford's courage faltered and her sense of Lowell's own self-development and integrity was shaken. According to a retrospective account of the year, she had "great trouble with the church . . . could not believe and suffered great tortures." Whatever new wave of doubts she may have had, they were augmented by the increasing religious zeal Lowell displayed in prison. She talked with a priest in New York who also knew Lowell, who confirmed her impression that Cal had become "more Catholic than the church," but as she confided to Peter Taylor, that was small comfort. Ahead of her loomed life with a man whose fervor dwarfed even his previous religious dedication. Her letter to Taylor spelled out the specifics, and it tends to confirm her later declaration that the term in jail was not so hard for Cal, for he was "crazy" (she was not being merely figurative). Certainly his plans were outlandish:

> It is not right for me to burden you with this just before you go overseas, but you are probably Cal's closest friend. I see I've given you no facts. Roughly this is it: after the war, what Cal wants to do (he cries, "This is to be my life and I will not be hindered.") is to be a sort of soap-box preacher with an organization called the Catholic Evidence Guilds which operate in city parks, etc, preach and answer the posers of hecklers. I cannot write this down without seeing you smile. . . . And when I inquire of him how we will live, he points to the Gospels and says that we must not worry about that, that God will take care of us, that one cannot be a wage-slave but must have leisure in which to serve the church. . . .
>
> I am frightened, feel that it will be three years before Cal has recovered from the pleasurable monasticism of the penitentiary.

Once again, it was an eerily prophetic pronouncement. Not that Lowell took to the soapbox, trusting to God's support. On the contrary, Lowell and Stafford turned again to writing, and Stafford spent a great deal of time and energy worrying about how and where they would live. But it was less than three years before it was clear that neither of them could recover from the unhappy monasticism of their marriage. If one can credit unprovable claims and rumors, the sexual side of their relationship had long since deteriorated (the Tates gossiped about it at Monteagle, and Stafford herself later declared that sexual relations between them had ended when Cal became a Catholic). They had cultivated their separate retreats, which also served as punishments, of themselves and of each other. Lowell had not only the "monasticism of the penitentiary" but his Catholic observances; Stafford her retreat at Yaddo, her domestic preoccupations, and her drinking. Yet over the next three years, despite distractions and unhappiness, they also adhered to their other devotion, writing, and they produced work that arguably ranked among the most important of their careers. Being cloistered together was far from simply destructive.

CHAPTER 8

Connecticut

W HEN LOWELL was released from prison in March of 1944, Stafford undertook what was to become an increasingly preoccupying project over the next couple of years: house hunting. She searched Connecticut for a place to rent, well aware that she and Lowell were about to settle in greater solitude than they had yet known in their married life. This time there were no patrons, either critical or Catholic. They would be living by themselves, and they would be a train ride away from the literary bustle of New York. She found a house with a picturesque address—Harbor View, Ocean Avenue, Black Rock—and the right pedigree. It was owned by a Roman Catholic priest. The reality, however, was far from bucolic. Relishing the unsavory details, Stafford sketched a comic portrait for Cecile Starr:

> I myself have nothing to report although I could on request write volumes on the odor of low tide in this unpleasant fen known grandiosely as a "harbor." At present the tide goes out some time after midnight and when the process is complete, our rooms are instantaneously invaded by a stench that wakens us like gunshot. It lingers in our hair and clothing and coats the caramels and gets into the apples. It does not more closely resemble a stockyard than a small boy who traps skunks, nor is it more like a condemned privy than an ice-chest in need of attention. It is an essentially *organic* odor, and probably the most powerful I have ever experienced.

What she really longed for was a beautiful house to buy, and her daydreams were fed by Harcourt, Brace's efforts on behalf of her book. Her publishers had decided to promote *Boston Adventure* vigorously, evidently gauging that it had a potentially wide readership. Stafford had every reason to think that she might actually make some money on her first novel. It was not a prospect familiar to her circle of poets and critics (or, for that matter, novelists: neither of the Tates had earned much from their fictional labors). Stafford was more than a little distracted by high hopes during the spring and summer, and somewhat sheepish about her fantasies. Certainly her optimism and domesticity were out of tune with the times, as a visit from her brother, who was about to be shipped off to France to serve in the airborne field artillery, must have reminded her. But rather than dwell on worries about his future, she marveled above all at the ease and pleasure of their time together after such a long separation: they hadn't been in touch since their short reunion in Oregon six years earlier, after her return from Europe. She was aware of the fragility of her contented visions, but couldn't banish them: "Our dreams are probably the most dangerous and very likely will all collapse, for we have based them on my book," she wrote to Eleanor Taylor in June, describing the advance publicity and the Hollywood interest that *Boston Adventure* was attracting. "You will understand the violent spasm this has flung us into. We so passionately want a house that we have become very unattractively materialistic."

The "we" seems not to have been Stafford's imperial projection of her own desires onto Lowell. Her worst fears about his unworldly aspirations, which she had confessed in her letter to Peter Taylor in February, had not been fulfilled. Despite his prison rhetoric, Lowell gave little indication of yearning for the soapbox and the ascetic religious life (though both he and Stafford went on a satisfyingly rugged Trappist retreat in June). On the contrary, once he had completed his parole stint cleaning the nurses' quarters of St. Vincent's Hospital in Bridgeport, Connecticut, he turned to poetry with zeal after months of not writing. And, completely contrary to Stafford's expectations, he seemed ready for a stretch of pleasurable domesticity. He too was eager to dream of countrified comfort—and was greatly disappointed when he saw the view that went with the scenic Black Rock address. He had looked forward to a wide vista of ocean.

But Lowell's house reveries took second place to his writing. Stafford, by contrast, admitted that her work was completely derailed. It was a well-earned lapse in concentration. She had a winter of intensive revision to recover from and laurels to rest on: in addition to her forthcoming novel, two stories had been published by the spring ("The Darkening Moon" and "The Lippia Lawn") and another was scheduled to appear in the fall ("A Reunion"). Still, the fallow stretch was hard. "Cal . . . is working with the same intensity that he did in that great period of fertility in Monteagle," Stafford proudly announced to Peter Taylor in July. To Eleanor Taylor, she went on to confess that his productivity had its corrosive effect on her: "Cal has started writing poetry again and his intensity and industry make me feel completely worthless. I have done nothing at all this summer. However, I rarely do work in the summer but that's no excuse." Her imagination, she emphasized again, was devoted to house fantasies so vivid that she couldn't resist describing her dream to Eleanor: "I imagine it as being on one of the tongues of land that project into Long Island Sound and fancy a lawn going directly down to the water. I wish it would be a hundred years old with its original floors and many fireplaces and with the tallest possible trees. This is the shocking way I spend my time!"

The domestic vision generally seemed to take the Tates as a model. That is, Stafford had in mind artistic fraternizing within her dream house, though for the time being she and Lowell were enjoying the experience of married life, just the two of them, far more than she could have anticipated: "Despite the ugliness and the heat we continue to enjoy this solitude. It may be a sign of age in us but whatever it is I'm glad we have become so happily independent. And now, after this summer of finding so much pleasure in one another's society, New York is unthinkable. A house is mandatory." But she didn't intend the house to be a haven of solitude. A letter to Eleanor Taylor sheds some light on a deep-seated paradox in Stafford's sense of her relation to a larger literary world. Surrounded by writers, she felt her fever rise, but without them she felt abandoned, uncreative. "Actually I think few things are more stifling to creative energy than loneliness," she wrote to Taylor. "I wish we were established somewhere in a roomy house and you could come live with us and do nothing but write." The sense of isolation that was a main wellspring of her imagination was at the same time, she knew, a source of paralysis. A house of her own seemed to beckon as one place where the tension might be eased—somewhere she could retreat and yet also feel rooted, enjoy both independence and camaraderie; somewhere she could perhaps find fulfillment as both a writer and a woman.

THE THREE STORIES that Stafford published that year—"The Darkening Moon" in January in *Harper's Bazaar,* "The Lippia Lawn" in the spring issue of the *Kenyon Review,* and "A Reunion" in *Partisan Review* in the fall—all treated the central theme of exile. In fact, the image that lurked behind all of them was banishment from the garden, a religiously evocative drama that Stafford gave three very different secular treatments. Although the stories were doubtless all begun before *Boston Adventure* was finished (it is hard to fix just when and in what order they were written), none gave any sign that Stafford had that ambitious novel in her. Each tends to rely on rather heavy-handed manipulation of symbolism, but together they offer an overview of this stage of Stafford's stylistic development and an introduction to the origins of the preoccupying theme of homelessness.

It is striking that all three stories focused, directly or indirectly, on the figure of the father, who was virtually to disappear from Stafford's fiction after Hermann Marburg's comparatively brief appearance in *Boston Adventure.* "A Reunion," though published last, was the least mature of the stories, harking back to her early static, histrionic efforts; it was a kind of companion to "And Lots of Solid Color." This time it was the father figure whom Stafford exposed in his heartless myopia. The plot was not taken from life, though the portrait of the protagonist's self-pitying father in part was. The first-person narrator of this story, whose mother had died at her birth, returned to visit her father after a seven-year absence, wondering if their lifelong estrangement would have altered at all. But in his eyes, and in her own, she remained the guilty daughter, an unwitting murderer. Though he welcomed her into his garden, it was a shrine to the dead mother, and she was an intruder—likened, in a less-than-subtle closing image, to a beetle her father injured and then left to die.

The lush garden of "A Reunion" recalled the Covina, California, paradise, which was explicitly invoked in "The Lippia Lawn" (included, as was "The Darkening Moon," in Stafford's *Collected Stories*). In the 1970s, in a brief sketch of her California origins, Stafford claimed that she had only recently come upon the name for the kind of lawn that had surrounded her Covina house, though she had spent years perusing horticulture books. As she must have known, her own fiction gave the lie to that claim. "The Lippia Lawn" took as its starting point and symbol the search for—and discovery of—the elusive name of the plant, lippia, of her childhood. In fact, Stafford's subsequent claim of forgetfulness is an illustration of the theme of the story: nostalgia for a purportedly Edenic past is dangerous. It is better not to remember the lost paradise.

In place of the overwrought meditation of "A Reunion," Stafford was now in control of the intricate yet concrete introspective style she elaborated in *Boston Adventure*. The first-person narrator of "The Lippia Lawn" summoned up memories of her past, jogged into the rumination by an arbutus plant she came upon during a walk with an old man on the Cumberland Plateau (a setting inspired by Stafford's Monteagle stay). She realized that the trailing arbutus reminded her of the lippia lawn of her youth, a past that she had evidently done her best to bury. In a scene that suddenly acquired symbolic intensity, she found herself wrestling with the tenacious plant, aiming to retrieve a cutting for the old man (another unsympathetic father figure, as the story proceeded to reveal). "It was as though the root was instinct with will. There was something so monstrous in its determination to remain where it grew that sweat, not from exertion but from alarm, streamed from my face.... Something prevented me from cutting it, ... a sort of inexplicable revulsion at the thought that the knife might not cleave through." The plant had become a sinister symbol of a past that couldn't be domesticated. While her companion ranted nostalgically about the once lush landscape—"It's a crime, I tell you! When I was a boy this place was Eden!"—she was thoroughly unsettled by memories of the past. His constant refrain of rootedness was like "a phrase of music once admired and now detested." To recall her own Eden vividly would be to confront her exile; her fall from innocence was best left unexamined.

In "The Darkening Moon," Stafford turned to a dramatically different terrain and style, harbingers of the texture of *The Mountain Lion* and of Stafford's subsequent Colorado stories. This was the first of her western stories, featuring a twelve-year-old character named Ella and told by an omniscient narrator who favored exact, objective description over subjective meditation, a colloquial over a refined manner. The story was about the dawning of a divided consciousness, the moment of maturity when Ella suddenly recognized the end of an unreflective unity between herself and the external world, her mind and her body. Nature abruptly turned ominous and unwelcoming: she was cast out.

This time the garden was not a tended enclave but the looming, rugged country of Colorado. Ella began the story courageous and comfortable in that world, thanks to her deceased father's lesson years before on a night fishing trip, when he left her alone by the riverbank with these reassuring words: "There ain't nothing to harm you, sister. The animals is all there is and they won't be looking you up." But this night, babysitting for a neighbor, Ella let her imagination take over from her senses, and she was profoundly disoriented. Unnerved by the mystifying eclipse of the moon, Ella was revisited by a darker version of her childhood fishing trip. She had fallen into the river up to her waist, and the fish had "swarmed slimily" all over her. At her father's instruction, she had picked up the "fat slithering blobs in her bare hands," and to her terror, the fish blood had been smeared on her. "The horror of the reptilian odor" came back to her now, and Ella cried out for her father, but there was no comfort. The imagery of the story was unmistakably sexual: Ella's own body was about to become unfamiliar; the moon's rhythms and new fears and desires were about to hold sway. The old Edenic confidence had become part of the irretrievable past.

Despite the common theme, the stories were strikingly different in formal execution. It was as though Stafford had decided to practice a variety of techniques and tones as she continued to revise *Boston Adventure,* where her very different task was to unify the parts of that ambitious whole. And she was sampling different literary outlets. She had been welcomed in the quarterlies of both the New Critical and the New York camps, and somewhat to her chagrin, she wrote Hightower, she had dipped down to *Harper's Bazaar,* which clearly didn't rate with her literary circle (though it paid well). She was drawing on material from the relatively distant past—her family, not her current life. It was only when her novel was finally in her editors' hands that she turned to the present, or near present, for inspiration for the rest of the short fiction she wrote during their year and a half in Connecticut. But before she was ready to turn to those quite different stories, she faced a tumultuous autumn, beginning with the appearance of *Boston Adventure* in September of 1944.

"A REUNION" appeared in the same fall 1944 issue of *Partisan Review* as a review of *Boston Adventure* by Andrews Wanning, dramatizing the distance Stafford had come: the author of comparatively slight exercises in sensibility had produced a Proustian epic. Most of the reviewers, like Wanning, had high praise for the unconventional ambition of the novel, though several confessed to being mystified by the peculiarly passive heroine. Just what Sonie's fate might be, once she had dreamed her way out of her un-Edenic childhood to the pinnacle of New England civilization, only to be drastically disenchanted, was far from clear.

Stafford's own fate looked very promising, though she was genuinely modest about her artistic accomplishment. Her novel did very well very quickly: forty thousand copies were sold within a few months of publication, and as a Book League selection, *Boston Adventure* went on to sell almost two hundred thousand more copies. A condensed armed services edition of more than 125,000 also appeared. But Stafford played down the success. As she—like her mentors and friends—hastily emphasized, commercial success was hardly a measure of merit. Stafford had evidently been worried all along that Harcourt, Brace might be taking a lowbrow approach, and had consulted Philip Rahv about the popular title her publishers had proposed. He suggested some tonier possibilities, acknowledging the delicate line she was treading: "Your book struck me as the best first novel by an American writer that I have read in quite a few years. I am sure it will be a great success. Congratulations!" he wrote to her, endorsing bestsellerdom. But he also advised a more refined presentation: "I've thought about that title rather intensively, and all I can manage are the following: 1) A Boston Venture (takes the sting out of "adventure," I mean the sting of romantic and popular appeal). 2) The Siege of Boston 3) Late Pilgrimage—or Belated Pilgrimage. I like the first title best."

Stafford was also eager to subordinate her noisy debut to Lowell's virtually simultaneous, more elite publication with the Cummington Press. "Cal's book [*Land of Unlikeness*] . . . came out just three days before mine and I cannot tell you how relieved I was to have him beat me into print. His is a 'fine' edition, very beautiful and so expensive that he's sure no one will ever buy it," she wrote to the Thompsons. There were clearly some competitive tensions as their two careers were launched, but Stafford seemed more than happy to defuse them with modesty. To Hightower, she was excited but self-effacing: "The success of this book is both ludicrous and disgusting. It would never, never have happened at any other time in the history of publishing, but books, all books, are selling like mad." (Perhaps a little envious, Caroline Gordon somewhat tactlessly emphasized the hype involved: "It looks as if it would certainly sell. I believe they are spending enough money on it to make it sell," she wrote in the early fall.)

Just in case anyone thought she might be corrupted by popular success, Stafford outlined her plans for a highbrow sequel. As she described it to Hightower, it was going to be a literary leap beyond *Boston Adventure,* and the subject was not exactly best-seller material:

> I hope it's going to be worlds better. It will, if I can do it right, be at any rate a good deal more profound.... I want you not to jump to conclusions when I tell you the scene is laid in Heidelberg. It is not that foul old thing I did for Archie Ogden. It is Heidelberg physically. And that's about as far as it goes. It is to be another satire, this time on expatriate Americans. But the body of it is to be a religious conversion and my principal character is a Benedictine monk named Dom Paternus.

Sonie's fate wasn't going to have the sting of popular or romantic appeal. Her future was apparently to be a religious one; Stafford planned for her to discover the spiritual significance of her "red room."

If commercial success was somewhat suspect among their circle (Lowell hastened to write Tate that "we are neither respectable nor rich"), it was an even more delicate issue for Stafford among her family, in particular her father. She might have been able to skirt the subject; she had put many miles between herself and him, and seen to it that they were not in close touch. But that fall there was a family crisis. In early October, as she was in the midst of organizing yet another move (to Westport, to another rented house, which they called The Barn—this one closer to her dreams), Stafford received the stunning news that her brother, Dick, had been killed in France in an ambulance accident. Though she and Dick had not been close for years, their two brief and happy reunions, one so recent, had obviously stirred up the past. For her it was a relationship dominated by imaginative nostalgia—he was the idol and elusive ally of her youth—which perhaps helps explain the momentous blow his death was for her: dead, he became an immutable, even more imposing presence.

Stafford promptly made plans to go out to Oregon to be with her parents and sisters. "I am so glad, in this terrible thing, to be a Catholic," she wrote to Mary Lee. "And you must believe, as we all have got to

believe, that he is just somewhere else. . . . I long to be with you. Cal is
wonderful, but he didn't know Dick." On her return to Connecticut in
mid-November, she wrote a mournful letter to Peter Taylor, obviously
struck by how little she herself knew Dick, or her parents, and yet how
bereft she felt:

> The shock was the greatest I have ever known. I did not feel the
> grief that I would have felt if I had heard of such misfortune for
> you, because I did not know my brother so well. Even so, it went
> deep. . . . I went west. . . . The trip was hard and long and the visit
> was sad: one does, as I think you've remarked, value one's parents
> more as one grows older. And it is so bad of us not to know them
> well until the last years of their lives!

The "image of a modest schoolteacher" while she was in Oregon, according to her sister Marjorie, Stafford certainly did not play the role of
triumphant novelist on her trip home.

But there was one person who paid special attention to Stafford's commercial success, and that was Mrs. Lowell, who couldn't avoid at least a
grudging acknowledgment of her daughter-in-law's worldly accomplishment. The reception of Stafford's novel in Boston was a very mixed
one, not surprisingly, but the clan had to take note. Stafford could no
longer simply be the wife beneath notice. In a letter to Cecile Starr, Stafford caustically reported the reactions they had encountered during a
visit to Marlborough Street:

> It was not a very good trip; we always expect things to be different
> and they never are. There are the same lectures and moral general-
> ization and refusals to countenance the way we live and the dredg-
> ing up of all the mistakes of the past. I am more thoroughly, more
> icily, more deeply disliked than ever on account of my book, even
> though it is generally admitted that it's a damned good thing Bobby
> married someone who makes money writing. This is the only way,
> you see, writing can be justified. And my inimitable mother-in-law
> who, as always, would stop a clock, said to Cal that his poetry was
> nice but valuless [*sic*] since "one must please the many, not the few."

BACK FROM OREGON, Stafford settled into a comparatively uneventful
winter and spring in Westport with Lowell in the spacious house they
had moved to after Black Rock. Once again, they were not alone, perhaps

a sign that they were ready for some distraction from each other. Not that the guests were easy to manage: Albert Erskine (who had been business manager of the *Southern Review* when Stafford worked there and was now an editor at Reynal & Hitchcock) and his wife moved in with them, and there was a steady stream of visitors. Stafford admitted that the company was often a trial: "I have bad nerves and entertaining large numbers of people does me in," she wrote an old friend. "Inevitably I drink too much." In the spring Stafford took a job teaching creative writing at Queens College, another academic stint that proved to be a big mistake. She was no more comfortable in front of a class than she had ever been, and the commute between Westport and Flushing, which must have taken at least two hours, was a nightmare.

Meanwhile, Lowell's creative stretch continued, and his next book, *Lord Weary's Castle,* steadily took shape as he revised old poems and wrote new ones. Stafford's writing was not proceeding so smoothly. In December 1944, she told Peter Taylor that she hoped her old energy was back; she was feeling inspired by, among other things, F. O. Matthiessen's new book *Henry James: The Major Phase.* "The book on James together with native conscience have roused me from my stupor and I am eager to get to work again. I did finish a story which was not altogether satisfactory but was something so entirely different from anything I've ever done before that I did feel a certain sense of achievement." It was not an assessment brimming with confidence, and she went on to confess a more pervasive sense of inadequacy, surprising in the wake of *Boston Adventure.* "I am still so inchoate in my perceptions, something that you, I believe, have never been," she wrote to Taylor, perhaps thinking of the endless revisions of her novel and the unfocused manuscripts before that. "I think you, like James, see your story entire in the initial symbol. I see nothing but the symbol." To Hightower in March, she also mentioned a story that was "something completely new for me" and reported that her new novel was going badly. "My new novel is progressing at a snail's pace," she wrote to another old friend, "and I'm not yet certain I want to write it at all; I'm sick of the way I write." She planned to put it aside and turn to three short stories.

Stafford's stories after she finished *Boston Adventure* were more ambitious than her earlier short fiction. She was not as barren as she feared. In the two stories that appeared in 1945, "The Home Front" in *Partisan Review* in the spring and "Between the Porch and the Altar" in *Harper's*

Bazaar in June, Stafford tackled more serious subjects: the war and religion. She was evidently pursuing themes suggested by the new, recalcitrant novel about Sonie that she had started, and she was turning away from her past to address preoccupations in her life with Lowell. In fact, the two of them seemed to be drawing on at least superficially similar sources of inspiration. In two poems Lowell was working on at roughly the same time, he chose (for one) the same setting and (for the other) the same title. His "Colloquy in Black Rock" is set, like "The Home Front," in Black Rock by the stinking harbor and similarly involves immigrant Hungarian Catholics who work in the local defense plant during the war. And Lowell's dramatic monologue, "Between the Porch and the Altar," takes its title, as Stafford's story does, from a phrase in the Book of Joel, the Ash Wednesday chapter.

Without suggesting anything like an intimate parallel, it's possible to point to general links between Stafford's story of a young girl on her way to the first Ash Wednesday Mass at five o'clock on a cold February morning in New York and Lowell's four-part poem that dwells on mother domination and adultery. Both convey the confessions and confusions of youthful believers, struggling to reconcile the flesh and the spirit, the disorder of life and the order of religion. Stafford had shown Tate a draft of the story in the summer of 1944. It wasn't a formal submission to the *Sewanee Review*, where he was then editor, but perhaps she hoped that he would accept it. If so, she was disappointed. Tate's response was typically to the point; "BETWEEN THE PORCH AND THE ALTAR is beautifully written, but I don't think it is successful." His complaint was that it was too elliptical, that the reader never learned enough about the girl to "place" the sudden conversion of feeling she experienced at the end. Her abrupt clarity of soul might work in a lyric poem, he told Stafford, but not in a story. "I wish you would write a full-length story and let me have it," he wrote somewhat impatiently. "I am determined to publish you only at your best." Stafford evidently worked further on the story; at least she smoothed the transition to the concluding revelation.

The story was strikingly well written, a happy balance of exact description of the external world and an unexpectedly concrete evocation of her protagonist's thoughts and feelings. Throughout the story Stafford effectively counterposed ritual and real life, both of which pulled at her protagonist, whose loneliness was made palpable. Heading for church with careful plans for distributing her alms (some for the poor box, some for candles in memory of her dead mother and two friends interned in China by the Japanese), the girl was distracted by other, grubbier demands on her money (a poor beggar, an old crone). She was disoriented: "She was not assured in her heart and she prayed with a dry compulsion." The story teetered toward skepticism, for structured piety seemed wan and irrelevant compared with clamoring life. Yet at the same time Stafford's "natural aestheticism," as Taylor had called it, prevented anything so simple as an endorsement of "the coarseness ... the grossness" of daily existence. The girl gave her dime to the crone, rather than spending it for a candle as she had planned, but she was repelled. When her trials of charity were over, she wiped away the official ashes, "leaving herself alone possessed of the knowledge of her penance"—a penance that brought ambivalence, not complacency. Catholicism was not a matter of easy motions for either Stafford or Lowell.

Patriotism was an equally fraught subject during those years. It lurked behind Lowell's "Colloquy at Black Rock" and was at the center of Stafford's "The Home Front." The surfaces could hardly have seemed less alike. Still, some underlying affinities were clear. Lowell's poem, originally titled "Pentecost," was an impassioned religious meditation on the incarnation that, as one critic observed, looked forward to apocalypse not redemption. In his version of the Pentecostal ritual of the bird falling from the church roof, Christ descended to destroy the body, not redeem it ("my heart, / The blue kingfisher dives on you in fire"). At the same time, the poem, with its evocation of the poet's great agitation as he watched the war efforts of the Hungarian immigrants ("My heart, you race and stagger.... / Till I ... / Am rattled screw and footloose"), was an anxious meditation on human guilt and destruction and on martyrs; there was perhaps a trace of Lowell's uneasy reflections on his decision to stand by while others fought.

Stafford's "The Home Front"—the story she had described as "something completely new" for her—featured an unfamiliar protagonist: a late-middle-aged German-Jewish doctor exiled in Connecticut during the war, who Ian Hamilton, Lowell's biographer, has suggested was "quite clearly Lowell." That is too reductive an autobiographical reading, but the story's theme was close to home. "The Home Front" was about unpopular permutations of patriotism, about the unredeemable destruc-

tiveness of human nature. The whole point of the story was to complicate
"sides." The Hungarians who ran the doctor's boardinghouse were loyal
contributors to the war effort, yet they were anti-Semites. The doctor
was a Jew watching the war from the sidelines, but he was also a German
full of nostalgia for the old, civilized Germany and full of crude loathing
for the dirty Hungarians. The war between the doctor and his landlady
was played out through their pets, a cat and birds respectively, none of
whom made out well.

The story was unnerving, for it was unclear where—if anywhere—
Stafford's own loyalties lay. Though her imagination obviously kindled
to memories of Germany, the result was that cold lack of compassion in
her writing that she had worried about to Peter Taylor the year before—
and that editors had complained about long ago with *Autumn Festival*.
But *Partisan Review* was impressed by it, naming the story the "second
prize-winning novelette in the *Partisan Review*–Dial Press Contest." Randall Jarrell's reaction, in a letter in August of 1945, spoke to the sinister
ambiguity of the story. A great cat lover—and a war poet—he was immediately drawn in:

> Anything happening to one's cat is the most painful subject in the
> world, so far as I'm concerned. I liked your story in *Partisan* ex-
> tremely, Jean ... and felt indignant at their giving first prize to
> Schwartz's much inferior (but ideologically *so* much more conge-
> nial to *P.R.*) story. *But* I had the horrible feeling all through the
> story that so far as I was concerned—it was a subject nobody *should*
> write about; that's crazy, but, boy, that was the way I felt.

That same summer Allen Tate registered a characteristically uncompromising assessment, though he leavened his reaction with praise for the
other story Stafford wrote during 1945, "The Present" (which appeared
in her *Collected Stories* under the title "The Captain's Gift"). "Since I like
this story ["The Present"] so much," he wrote to her, accepting it for
publication (it didn't appear in the *Sewanee Review* until the spring of
1946), "perhaps you won't mind my saying that your story in the next to
last *Partisan* is very bad indeed, and I can't understand why either you or
Philip would want to see it in print."

"The Present" was also about the barbarity of war, but here Stafford
had mastered an extraordinarily polished irony. Recounted in the present
tense (one of only two such stories in her *Collected Stories* volume), the

story was a mixture of familiar themes presented in the compacted Jamesian style that came to characterize much of her fiction. The protagonist, Mrs. Chester Ramsey, was another in an expanding gallery of elderly characters whose salient quality was their resistance to change. Miss Pride–like, she immured herself in her brownstone in New York, unaware of the world and above all of the war: "The ivory tower in which she lives is impregnable to the ill-smelling, rude-sounding, squalid-looking world which through the years has moved in closer and closer and now surrounds her on all sides." Stafford's irony was effective because Mrs. Ramsey's delusion was not simply folly by any means. It was presented as a dignified aesthetic reaction to a sordid reality. Just as the appeal of Boston snobbery was clear in *Boston Adventure,* the allure of the widow's self-protective cocoon was obvious.

Yet its inadequacy was also obvious, and the suspense of Mrs. Ramsey's inevitable disillusionment propelled the plot. Her ultimate shock was, as Caroline Gordon judged in a letter to Stafford about the story, vivid in precisely the right way: Mrs. Ramsey's favorite grandson, a young captain off fighting in Europe who thus far had faithfully and cheerfully kept in touch with her, sparing her the facts of combat, one day sent her a fateful package. When the old woman eagerly opened it, out fell a thick, blond braid. "You have concentrated on that golden braid," Gordon commended Stafford. "It's very real and its reality invokes overtones, makes the story go on sounding in the head, conveys, I feel, all the implications you want conveyed." It was a symbol, yet it was also a particular object, "cut off cleanly at the nape of the neck," as Stafford described it. "It is the sensuous aspect of the braid that does it," Gordon told her, and went on to set that praise in the context of a more sweeping criticism:

> What I am trying to say ... is that I don't think you observe things closely enough, or perhaps it's that you don't observe them passionately enough to render them the way I like to see them rendered. ... I realize that fiction, considered from the standpoint of technique, is, after all, only the combination of long and short views. You do the long view so well. Those long sentences, with their sudden shifting of view point, their detachment from the scene, do exactly what you want them to do. It's your short views I criticize. They aren't sensuous enough. The rhetoric that you use so well in the long views often creeps in and blurs things. ... But Cal

knows all this so well and can put it to you so much better than
I can.

It was a telling criticism in general, comparable to Tate's emphatic
teaching to Lowell that poetry was *"ideas* tested by experience, by *direct
apprehension."* Lowell too was seduced by rhetoric, but at the same time
he inclined—perhaps more than his mentor—to the fiercely concrete
over the abstract. And in the poems he was working on in 1945, the
emphasis was increasingly on experience, as he winnowed out the more
intellectual poems in *Land of Unlikeness,* revised the ones that Tate had
judged "richer in immediate experience," and wrote new poetry more
firmly grounded in fact. Stafford's progress too had been steadily away
from the "words, merely" difficulty of her early unpublished efforts. In
her stories of 1944 and 1945, which introduced her major protagonists—
disoriented old women, lonely young women, sensitive but stalwart children, uneasy expatriates—she was taming some of the Proustian orna-
mentation that had cluttered parts of *Boston Adventure.* She was
perfecting her gift for the well-selected detail with symbolic resonance,
and she was working at mixing more colloquial cadences into her Jamesian style.

In the spring of 1945 she received two awards. The National Institute
of Arts and Letters gave her a one-thousand-dollar prize for *Boston Adventure,* and the Guggenheim Foundation granted her a fellowship to
write the sequel to that novel. (Lowell had wanted to apply for a Guggenheim at the same time, but the Tates had discouraged him. No couple
had ever won in the same year, and they judged Stafford the likelier
candidate.) The prize was one more recognition, from the right highbrow quarters, of her past accomplishment. Even more important, the
fellowship was an endorsement of her future efforts. In fact, nobody on
the Guggenheim committee—nobody who had read Stafford's work so
far—could have foreseen the completely different kind of novel that she
was about to start.

CHAPTER 9

Maine

IN THE SUMMER of 1945 Stafford was ready to act on her home-owner dreams, thanks to her windfall from *Boston Adventure*—roughly twenty thousand dollars by then. This was now house hunting in earnest. The Lowells' lease at The Barn was up in July, and they headed for Maine. The couple rented a cottage in Boothbay Harbor, and the search for the ideal house began. Stafford found it in Damariscotta Mills, roughly fifteen miles inland from the coast. The fantasy she had described to Eleanor Taylor a year before had all but come true. "It is about 100 years old," she wrote to Cecile Starr in late August, "has a barn attached to it which we are going to make into two vast studios, has fine old trees, a 12 mile lake in the back yard and within a stone's throw, the oldest Roman Catholic church north of southern Maryland." The white clapboard house also had the old floor and numerous fireplaces that she had prescribed.

It needed a good deal of work as well, and home improvement was a preoccupation that Stafford was eager to introduce into her life. For the next six months, she coordinated repairs and renovations, often at long distance, since it was clear that she and Lowell couldn't live there through the winter. In fact, they didn't envisage living there full-time for quite a while, as Stafford explained to the Thompsons: "I imagine it will be some years before we can live in it the year round—we can't afford to yet and we're frightened about isolation anyway." Their Connecticut year had been surprisingly calm, given their less than placid marriage, but a small village in Maine was a true rural retreat—and the nearest city, Boston, was more problematic than New York. As the home of Lowell's parents, it hardly provided a welcome relief for either Cal or Jean.

So at the same time that Stafford undertook elaborate home-improvement plans, the Lowells undertook elaborate house-sharing plans with the Tates once again. They decided they would spend the fall and winter in Sewanee, Tennessee, with the Taylors for company along with the Tates, while work was under way in Maine. "Two families living together always get in each other's hair," Gordon wrote jauntily in August, "but as far as we are concerned we would love to have you and Cal living with us again. We like living with the Lowells better than anyone else we've ever tried." "The winter of four books" was the galvanizing memory.

The Monteagle sequel never happened, though amid the disarray that ensued instead, it proved to be a winter of two books. In December of 1945 Lowell sent off the manuscript of *Lord Weary's Castle* to Philip Rahv, who forwarded it to Lambert Davis at Harcourt, Brace a few weeks later; Stafford had previously shown the poems to Giroux, who became the book's editor. Then in January of 1946 Stafford herself signed a contract with Harcourt, Brace for *The Mountain Lion*. She had shown a draft to her editors, and she finished the novel that spring.

In retrospect, the collapse of the Sewanee arrangement—in fact, the whole course of that fall and winter—looks like an augury of troubles to come for Lowell and Stafford, as the Tates showed the way toward domestic chaos. All of a sudden in September Caroline and Allen announced that they were separating, so the Tennessee plan was off. Though unexpected, the abrupt separation (soon to be just as abruptly reversed) was not a total surprise. If anyone knew the Tates' stormy marriage, it was the Lowells, and Allen's girlfriends were legendary. For the next couple of months the Lowells heard all about the marital troubles— a divorce was planned for December—in letters from both Tates as well as from endless secondhand gossip.

In November Stafford was drawn into the drama. The Lowells had invited Gordon to camp out at Damariscotta Mills while they were in New York and Boston, and Stafford joined her one late weekend around Thanksgiving while Lowell stayed on in Boston. Doubtless abetted by drink, the visit unraveled into violence in a scene that outdid the traumatic fight between them in Monteagle. Gordon quizzed Stafford about Tate's infidelities, and Stafford made the mistake of all too willingly supplying the names she knew. "Everything crashed in a most terrifying event," as Gordon began throwing and breaking things, prompting Stafford to call the police in a panic that once again seemed out of proportion. When her intimates (now Gordon, in the past Lowell) lost control or perspective, she was seized by the fear that it was she who was losing her grip. "I shouldn't tell you all of this, for it will frighten you," Stafford wrote to her sister Mary Lee in great distress, "but Cal will protect me and if I crack up, I will go to a sanitarium." Her dread that she was losing her mind seemed outlandish—a Sonie Marburg nightmare—but in retrospect it, too, looks like a warning of troubles in store.

One extended literary family had been disastrously shaken. In mid-January of 1946 the Lowells tried another arrangement while they waited for winter to subside. They joined Delmore Schwartz and his cat (he had been divorced from his wife, Gertrude Buckman, two years earlier) on Ellery Street in Cambridge. "One might think that this was not a household but a literary movement," Schwartz wrote to Helen Blackmur, exulting in the trio's productivity. In "To Delmore Schwartz" in *Life Studies* more than a decade later, Lowell was fondly, grandly nostalgic. It was a household in disarray—the poem was filled with drinking—but the poets were possessed, which was what they were convinced poets should be. The image of the mad artist prevailed in the poem, which implicitly predicted greatness and, as important, agony for its heroes. "Underseas fellows, nobly mad, / we talked away our friends," the speaker recalled. And Schwartz was given the dark variation on Wordsworth's lines: "We poets in our youth begin in sadness; / thereof in the end come despondency and madness."

Stafford the prose writer, though conspicuously absent from the poem, smoked and drank and typed along with them. And she joined in the talk, about their friends' lesser fates and their own momentous ones. As John Berryman later wrote about his own sojourn in Cambridge with Schwartz, the heady expectation of fame was never far from their thoughts. Glory was to be not simply a reward for their labors but a guide for their lives. Berryman described the intoxicating ambience in a "Dream Song" addressed to Schwartz:

> . . . You said "My head's on fire"
> meaning inspired O
>
> meeting on the walk down to Warren House
> so long ago we were almost anonymous
> waiting for fame to descend
> with a scarlet mantle & tell us who we were. . . .

They fed each other's ambitions, anticipating a public dimension for their private lives. Schwartz, who had already known success, relished the role of the encouraging mentor (he was trying to arrange a Briggs-Copeland lectureship at Harvard for Lowell). And it is safe to say that he led the way in conceiving of his life in heroically representative terms and in suggesting by example that autobiography could be the center of art. With his long poem *Genesis* (1943), he had aspired "to 'express' the 'Spirit of America.'" His autobiographical protagonist proclaimed: "No matter where he was, what he felt, what event, he was to himself / The center of the turning world." The mythologizing was not all golden. The poets, "nobly mad," thought of themselves as in some sense in tune with the dark currents of their time, a theme Lowell later developed much more fully.

Stafford, who had tasted fame too, was caught up in the dramatic generalizing about themselves and about the zeitgeist, as she recalled five years later. Among her contributions to the discussions was her Lucy story, a "suicide that had come at the end of a spectacularly ugly life"—a dark tale that struck her and the poets as emblematic of the thirties: "The actions were motivated by the dislocations of the twenties that had still not been set right, by the depression, by the end of prohibition, by the New Deal." It was her life written large, and "my friends said I must write it down, that it was obviously my next novel and that it was, so to speak, ready made. I should write it, they said, just as I had told it to them." She couldn't start right away, since she was trying to finish *The Mountain Lion,* but she was inspired, as they were, by the prospect of tragic generational portraiture.

The manic harmony on Ellery Street lasted roughly two months. After a visit to the elder Lowells on Marlborough Street, Schwartz's lurking envy of Lowell's background turned to open resentment. The Brahmin surroundings and the implicit anti-Semitism were too much for him. The mentor became a tormentor, endlessly mocking the Lowell family. More serious, he began, according to his biographer, "circulating malicious rumors" in an effort to undermine the Lowells' marriage. (His gossip was apparently about Stafford's supposed interest in other men, among them him, which few friends credit as being serious.) To judge from a letter Stafford sent to Cecile Starr from Cambridge, this was not the first sign of tension. Dental work was keeping her in town, but Stafford had been feeling jittery in their temporary household for some time

and was ready to leave. In fact her letter, which progressed incongruously
from jauntiness to bleakness, suggested a state of real agitation:

> We shall probably go home as soon as I am through with the den-
> tist. The carpenters are through and I am perishing to see the new
> kitchen floor, to say nothing of my fabulous desk. We have had a
> really splendid time here, but I am working very badly and in a
> state of depression, I really need my house to keep me from stulti-
> fying gloom. My new book seems hideously pallid and loose-
> jointed and to escape the thought of it I have been visited lately with
> my really neurotic sleeping, hours and hours of such oblivion that I
> don't even dream. . . . I am in an untrustworthy state and if my
> depression continues, I will be fit company for no one.

It is a revealing letter, which sets up correspondences among Stafford's
house, her work, and her health that are central to an understanding not
just of this formative phase of her life with Lowell, but of the rest of her
life as well. The house seemed to be the key element, which could distract her from and yet also support her in her creative and physical ordeals. Both she and Lowell were preoccupied (in significantly different
ways) with the image of the castle at this point, a metaphor that points to
the contrasting visions that seemed to be guiding their lives and work
during this unsettled stretch. Stafford had been reading St. Teresa's *Interior Castle* again during the summer of 1945 and probably reworking her
accident story, in which she developed the analogy between chambers in
a mansion, or castle, and the head. The castle, though under assault,
offered refuge; the head, though buffeted by distractions, contained the
safe inner sanctum where the soul could experience transcendence.

Lowell's book of poems took its title, *Lord Weary's Castle,* from an old
English ballad, which he understood to tell a very different story from
St. Teresa's—the story of the apocalypse, as Steven Gould Axelrod has
explained. In the ballad Lord Weary denied payments to Lamkin, the
man who built his castle. Spurned, Lamkin came to the castle and killed
Lord Weary's family. The allegory Lowell intended, according to Berryman in his review of the volume in *Partisan Review,* was the end of days:
Lord Weary's castle was the modern world, a "house of ingratitude, failure of obligation, crime and punishment," and Lamkin was the Lord
who destroyed "the faithless house He built." On the title page of the
manuscript, Lowell wrote, "Death comes when the house is built."

The Lowells called the house at Damariscotta Mills Lord Weary's Castle, though for Stafford—at least at first, while it was being fixed with her money and her loving attention—it promised liberation. For Lowell, always more ambivalent about domesticity, it seemed to mean imprisonment. He and Stafford were increasingly tense around each other that winter, her drinking and his efforts to curb it a source of constant quarreling. Her obsession with the Maine house meant her withdrawal from him, and he found as many pretexts for escape as he could. He went on another Trappist retreat in late March, began taking long bird walks when he was at Damariscotta Mills, and went as often as possible to New York, where both Taylor and Jarrell were living. On his return from one trip to the city, he certainly didn't repay his Lamkin in gratitude. Stafford described his reaction to her improvements in a letter to Taylor: "When he came back and found the house fresh with all its wallpaper and its new paint, he exploded and said that it was cheap, that it was immoral, and that I had done the whole thing out of a sadistic desire to stifle him."

Stafford by contrast was rejuvenated. Her letters about the ordeals of life in her unfinished house were filled with exhilaration and an uncharacteristic hardiness. She flipped the metaphor around: she likened the castle to her body, rather than her body to a castle—except that where the house was touchingly infirm, its habitually sickly proprietress was suddenly flourishing: "We have had a taste of really rigorous country life: our pipes freeze and burst in the most heart-rending fashion," she wrote to Allen Tate in January when they spent some time in Maine before going to Cambridge.

> We were without water for two weeks until an ingenious plumber came and moved every vital organ in the house. It has been between 17 and 20 below several times. But I have never been in such top-notch shape in my life and do not even complain of the cold, a transformation in myself I do not altogether understand.

She used similar anthropomorphic imagery for her invalid house in most of the homesteading letters she sent her friends that winter and early spring.

And though she wrote to Cecile Starr, in terms similar to those she used for her house, that her new novel was "pallid and loose-jointed," the truth was that she was nearly finished with the most vivid and taut novel she ever wrote. Her work, like her body, seemed to be thriving while her house was convalescing. As Stafford herself later said of her first and second novels, "They were entirely different books, those two." She could hardly have strayed further from the sequel to *Boston Adventure* she had initially planned. As she explained it,

> There wasn't any basic change in me; the material was so different in each and required different treatment.... The first one is leisurely, a good deal more embroidered. It's contemplative. I think *Boston Adventure* is old-fashioned; it's filled with digressions, for example. *The Mountain Lion* is a more symbolic book. The symbols are apparent, though I didn't know what they meant at the time I wrote.

Though she emphasized the contrast, Stafford recognized that her second novel did not represent a radical transformation in her as a writer. On the contrary, she felt that the two books expressed two poles of her imagination, equally important. "What I would like eventually to do," she said, "is to fuse the two manners." From James she had traveled to Twain, an incongruous pair of models who had seen nothing in each other but in both of whom Stafford found a great deal.

The Mountain Lion was Stafford's emphatically American book. She had discovered a colloquial voice that could barely be glimpsed in the elegance of her earlier prose, and she had perfected her gift for staging small epiphanies in her choice of concrete details. In her trim new novel she let those details do their work and dispensed with the discursive integuments she had favored in *Boston Adventure*. She was "less inclined," as Lambert Davis at Harcourt, Brace praised her, "towards some of those baroque effects that we talked about in connection with the first book."

At the end of that book, she had left Sonie on the brink of maturity after what amounted to a protracted adolescence, in which Sonie watched but did not participate in a decadent drama of another woman's coming-of-age. In fact, each fateful step Hope took toward sex and marriage meant greater passivity for Sonie, who was deprived of Philip and exiled to the periphery. Hope's death left her facing adulthood, disillusioned and disoriented. Sonie's future seemed to require some form of transcendence, but Stafford left it far from clear that art was the answer. Her subsequent plans suggested that she had decided religion might hold out hope for her.

But from the start Stafford had trouble pursuing her *Boston Adventure* plot: she couldn't carry Sonie forward into the future. Instead, she ended up replaying the past, with a new set of characters, in *The Mountain Lion.* It was a novel about childhood, and about the death of childhood. In a sense, it was a radically revised version of Book One of *Boston Adventure,* with a denouement that solved the larger question: for Stafford's new heroine, there would be no maturity. The key to the revision of Sonie's childhood was Stafford's shift from a mythic rendition of the ordeals of childhood to a much more directly autobiographical treatment. Set in California and Colorado and drawing on her own family lore, the novel was nonetheless far from nakedly confessional: she did not abandon the edict of impersonality. But like Lowell, who was beginning in some of the poems of *Lord Weary's Castle* to attempt more personal themes, Stafford now seemed more prepared to consult her own experience. Still, it had to be experience at some remove, and her childhood proved to be an accessible subject. By contrast, she evidently had difficulty drawing from her more immediate, mature life of religious and marital turmoil—and of artistic success—as she contemplated her original sequel. It was a problem that had first presented itself years before in her initial unpublished efforts, *Which No Vicissitude* and *Autumn Festival.* Writing about her recent past—her college and German adventures—she had found herself struggling unsuccessfully to overcome a solipsistic self-loathing.

In *The Mountain Lion* Stafford discovered a new comic and symbolic clarity with which to tell a tragic story. The shaping vision, as she said more than once, came almost unbidden. The novel does seem to have been written more directly from the subconscious than Stafford was used to, certainly more than her first book was. Begun in the summer of 1945, it was finished roughly nine months later, in April of 1946—remarkably rapid progress, especially given the many distractions of that fall and winter. To be sure, it was not half the length of *Boston Adventure,* but it was written with a degree of polish that suggests longer labors, particularly for as dogged a reviser as Stafford. When she wrote to Cecile Starr in March about its loose jointedness, she gave no hint of arduous readjustments she had already made—and made with astonishing swiftness. Between January and April (she had one particularly productive stretch alone at Damariscotta Mills, while Lowell was off on one of his trips), she apparently reconceived the basic structure and dynamic of the novel in a radical way. This time, the transformation was definitely not to tame her story—as she had needed to do with *Boston Adventure,* correcting for its melodramatic tendencies. Instead, she reworked the novel so that it addressed even more directly a theme that had lately surfaced as an especially fraught one: her relationship with her brother, whose death had evidently roused powerful memories.

In a letter early in 1946, Robert Giroux, back from the navy and again her editor, exclaimed over Stafford's revision and offered a quick reading of the newly aligned novel. His analysis makes a good introduction to the strange and poignant love story of ten-year-old Ralph and eight-year-old Molly Fawcett, brother and sister, whose path to maturity led them away from their California home to the rigors of Colorado—where, when the story closed six years later, they were lost to each other:

> Your major change—the Ralph-Molly conflict instead of Ralph–Uncle Claude—does wonders to the book and, as I wired you, the ending comes off beautifully. I see the whole book now as Ralph's struggle—the struggle to escape from the Bonney side of the family, from his mother, from Covina—all of which he manages to do when Grandpa Kenyon dies & Uncle Claude takes him to Colorado. But of course he doesn't escape from the one thing that really troubles him & which he scarcely admits or perhaps even realizes (except subconsciously)—Molly. . . .
>
> Those weeks at Lord Weary's Castle have been really profitable, Jean.

Giroux emphasized what few readers do: that Ralph's story was really in the foreground, rather than Molly's. At least that was the way Stafford had originally structured the novel, as Giroux's letter indicated. And in fact, it was true of the finished novel as well, in which Molly's character emerged largely through Ralph's perceptions of her. Yet as Stafford revised and Molly loomed larger, it was that "creature of funny precocity and awful pathos," as the poet Robert Fitzgerald characterized Molly in a review, who gradually usurped the more memorable place in the novel. Much of her power derived, in fact, from her peripheral and passive position. And Molly's pathos was awful rather than sentimental because Stafford successfully distanced her, even as she granted her a growing role. It was a difficult feat. As Stafford revealed in a distraught letter to Lowell written a year later from the hospital, where she had gone in a state of nervous collapse, Molly was a creature far too close for comfort. In the midst of psychological turmoil, Stafford saw the book, that girl, and her own life as inextricably and tragically connected:

> Gradually I became Molly. I was so much Molly that finally I had to write her book (in which it was my brother, you will note, that destroyed me—the guilt was still operating so strongly that I left the father out. In almost all my stories the father is either dead or is cruelly driven away; only in that little story "Reunion" is there a blameworthy father and even he is exonerated by detesting his daughter because she caused her mother's death). All the self-mutilations came back; for I had mutilated myself constantly when I was a little girl in order to gain pity and love. My father was too cold and awkward to give me affection; my brother soon resented me because I tagged along everywhere; my mother was too busy; my sisters found me too young; is it any wonder that I wanted to marry Laddy [the Staffords' dog]? And on one of those last nights in Maine, you will remember that I ground out a cigarette on the back of my hand: I was then completely Molly. I had gone all the way back, I was an angry, wounded child again. . . .

Precisely that agonized identification was what Stafford avoided in the novel itself, where a kind of merciless sympathy was at work. As one critic has noted, it is a "double bildungsroman"—the intertwined stories of siblings who journey from childhood union to adolescent conflict to a final resolution, in this case tragic. For Stafford, this pairing was a variation on the device of doubling that already in her first novel had been a key to dramatizing the idiosyncratic development of her autobiographical protagonist. Both Nathan and Hope served as foils to Sonie, characters who lived out alternate fates while she watched from the sidelines, frustrated—and yet also in her peculiar, self-punishing way fulfilled—by her own marginal status. Using these second selves, Stafford had found a way to avoid the monstrous solipsism of Sonie's predecessor, Gretchen Marburg.

In *The Mountain Lion* the doubling was much more explicit. These two bespectacled misfits were equally sickly, ugly, precocious, and unconventional, and they shared pride in their pariah status, defiantly scornful of their conformist mother and two older sisters (Mr. Fawcett had died years before). But Ralph, two years older, was beginning to feel the pull of a world beyond their idyll of estrangement, whereas Molly was unable to imagine any other life. Her devoted solidarity with Ralph increasingly seemed to him an imposition rather than a gift, and he felt guilty for his apostasy:

> He looked at his weedy sister with dislike as she crouched on her heels, plucking the lilies all around her, and when she looked up at him, her large humble eyes fondling his face with lonely love, he wanted to cry out with despair because hers was really the only love he had and he found it nothing but a burden and a tribulation.

Through Ralph's ambivalent vision—he was disoriented by the distance he felt opening between him and his sister—Molly's hopeless loyalty emerged as a moving mixture of the noble and the neurotic. As the novel progressed and Molly slipped further into her own isolated world, Stafford used the peculiar pair to offer different perspectives on her alienation, the view from the outside and from the inside. Ralph, growing into a newly vigorous body and strong desires, watched his sister barricade herself within her eccentric mind, denying maturity. If Stafford had wanted to test that quality she feared she didn't have, compassion, she couldn't have set more exacting conditions for herself. She succeeded in making Molly—"this scrawny, round-shouldered tall thing, misanthropic at the age of twelve," saddled with brains and bitterness and "a savagely satiric nature"—a tragic figure. In Stafford's pages, the suffering of children could not be more serious.

Doubling was the principle of the entire, studiously symmetrical novel—which itself was a curiously inverted reflection of her first novel. As Giroux's letter indicated, the basic dichotomy of *The Mountain Lion* was between the Bonney merchants and the Kenyon men, between effete California and rugged Colorado. The division oriented the world for Ralph and Molly, who started out the novel eagerly awaiting the annual visit of their favorite relative, Grandpa Kenyon—and who were devastated when he collapsed, dead, on the front porch. The rest of the novel traced their troubled shuttling between the two poles—between their tame California home and the Colorado ranch where they began to spend summers with Grandpa Kenyon's son, Uncle Claude.

It was the redskin-paleface distinction of *Boston Adventure* viewed this time from the Twainian, rather than the Jamesian, perspective. And this time the raw frontier won out over the cultivated city. Sonie yearned for an escape to the orderly capital; Ralph and Molly dreamed of escaping from the "sissy life" presided over by their mother and sisters and their ancestors on the Bonney side of the family, about whom they had heard much moralizing lore. To them, Grandfather Bonney, their mother's father, represented all that was hypocritically genteel. Their bond with Grandpa Kenyon, their mother's stepfather (Grandfather Bonney died young, and Mrs. Bonney made an "unseemly second marriage"), was an incongruous one: two gawky, sickly children smitten with a leathery old man—a rough rancher from Colorado who was for them "half legendary," ruddy like an Indian and imposing like a "massive, slow-footed bear."

The echo of Hermann Marburg, who entranced Sonie with tall tales of the West he had never seen but yearned after, was clear. But Stafford thoroughly revised the scene of childhood. An almost too idyllic walnut farm in California supplanted the hell of Chichester. In place of Shura Marburg stood fussy Mrs. Fawcett, her clucking no comparison to her predecessor's manias. And this time the father was gone from the start. Stafford commented on the omission, but in fact *The Mountain Lion* marked a step closer to the charged subject, for Ralph and Molly were looking for a father—unlike Sonie, who found a mother substitute in Miss Pride. Once again, Stafford's Twainian style allowed her to address, however indirectly, her own search for some accommodation with her father.

Not surprisingly, there was no easy resolution to the quest, particularly for Molly. The most fundamental alteration in Stafford's revised version of childhood lay in the fates of the siblings. In *Boston Adventure* it was the brother, poor Ivan, who was sacrificed so that Sonie could go on and confront maturity. He was the victim Sonie might have been, and though she couldn't protect him (a male, he was for Shura a devil by definition), she herself could and did weather the turmoils of their childhood. In *The Mountain Lion* it was Molly who was sacrificed so that Ralph might emerge into the wider world. This time it was femaleness that was at least part of the handicap, for the world to which Ralph awakened was masculine terrain—the rugged West of ranching and hunting. It was not a place where women thrived, especially odd creatures like Molly, who became more weedlike and solitary as Ralph grew more fit and handsome. Haunted by his innocent, fiercely asexual sister,

Ralph couldn't resist trying to corrupt, and ultimately destroy, her. The end of the novel, at once contrived and compelling, had a mythic western setting: during a hunt for the golden mountain lion that had become his own and Uncle Claude's grail, Ralph accidentally shot his sister instead.

But it is a mistake to read the novel in programmatically feminist terms, as critics have been increasingly inclined to do (to Stafford's evident impatience, judging from her marginal comments on one such reading—a reconsideration of the novel in *The New Republic* in 1975). To be sure, Stafford was interested in the broader social and sexual implications of her story. The setting was carefully chosen. In developing the contrast between the rough-hewn West and the refined East (which included California on Stafford's map), Stafford was commenting on a disunity in the American identity, a conflict of social values that warps personal identity. Molly and Ralph were caught between a masculine ideal of the frontier that entailed a destructive crudity—a "virile opacity" Stafford called it at one point—and a feminine ideal of the civilized establishment that implied hypocrisy and an absence of real culture. The time, too, was subtly but constantly emphasized: this was the mid-1920s, prewar America, a country that didn't quite realize it was on the brink of maturity. Old traditions were vanishing, and there was a sense of drift. Uncle Claude's immature pastime was stalking the mountain lion, an animal then almost extinct; Mrs. Fawcett's plan for a grand tour with her eldest daughters was an effete farce. Growing up for Ralph and Molly meant a struggle to find a path amid inadequate possibilities.

On one level, their fates fit the patriarchal paradigm. Molly died in an accident that was also, as critics have pointed out, an initiation ritual for Ralph. She was a symbolic element in his life—the feminine side of his nature that he had to suppress if he was to come of age in the world, the childhood that he had to destroy in order to enter maturity. The tragic ending marked a kind of fulfillment for him, while it sealed Molly's decline. Unlike Ralph, who found consolation for his estrangement from Molly in comradeship with Claude, she had nowhere to turn after their breach. The only kinship she could feel was with Magdalene, the blasphemous old black cook at the ranch, "always smoldering with an inward rage or a vile amusement over something sexual or something unfortunate," who she decided must be her mother. Full of rage herself, Molly added name after name (including Ralph's) to her "list of unforgivable" people: "She hated them all for the same reason, but she could not decide what the reason was. You could say, Because they were all fat." Molly was determined to deny the corrupt world of the flesh.

Finally she added her own name. "She burst into tears and cried until she was hungry, and all the time she cried she watched herself in the mirror, getting uglier and uglier until she looked like an Airedale." The self-loathing that had always lurked beneath her contempt for others surfaced in a death wish, which the novel proceeded to fulfill. Molly could thus be cast as the perfect prototype of the female protagonist who was rejected by the world, and then rejected herself, "bereft in an unadulterated masculine environment and denied the guidance and example of acceptable female models," as one critic has put it.

Yet Ralph and Molly's story was more complicated. In bringing Molly toward the center of the novel, Stafford was not merely filling in the hopeless half of a double bildungsroman and clarifying a message about gender. She was trying out another portrait of the artist, a variation on Sonie's strangely frustrated career. To consider Ralph's and Molly's aspirations, as opposed to their fates, is to see the novel in a rather different light. In fact, Ralph was far from the conventional hero whose path into the active world was clearly marked out for him by society and family. He was not like George Eliot's assertive Tom Tulliver in *The Mill on the Floss,* who expected and received the entrée into the wider world that his sister, Maggie, vainly dreamed of. On the contrary, Ralph's view of himself and of his relations with Molly and with the world was notable for its unaggressive ambivalence.

Ralph's situation was, unexpectedly, closer to the predicament of an undirected female. He was acutely aware of a division within himself, a desire for independence alongside a continued yearning for a deep, dependent bond with his sister. His consciousness, the reigning one of the novel, was highly other-directed, empathetic rather than assertive: caught between his conventional family and his eccentric sister, he was painfully aware of (and confused by) their opposing perspectives. Nor could he easily accept Uncle Claude as his alternate model. The more time Ralph spent with him, the more reservations he had about the rough maleness that defined his uncle's circumscribed world: "Ralph was troubled by the loss of his desire to enter Uncle Claude's world completely." Male bonding became even less appealing when sexual maturity crept up on Ralph: "Because his own masculinity was, in its articulation, so ugly, and he could therefore take no pleasure in himself, neither could he respect it in anyone else." Ralph was oppressed by his lack of clear direction and drive, felt there was something wrong with him—not least because Molly had in abundance the ambition he lacked, when it should have been the other way around. "If he did not become Uncle Claude's partner, what would happen to him?" he wondered at one point. "He had no variety of ambitions as had Molly who, in the course of a week, would plan to be a salesman for the *Book of Knowledge,* a grocer, a government walnut inspector, a trolley conductor in Tia Juana; of course her real vocation was writing and these were to be only sidelines."

Molly was not simply a victimized female, a misfit crushed by society's narrow expectations of feminine development. This was a portrait of the artist as a young girl, whose alienation transcended the defensive aloofness of a precocious, unpopular female child. She was the inner-directed rebel who was ready to proclaim her independence with a brutal finality Ralph could rarely manage: "'My literature is more important to me than you are, Ralph Fawcett,' she said coldly and left the room, pausing in the doorway to make donkey's ears and say 'Hee haw.'" The literary vocation extracted a high price, and Stafford was inclined to emphasize the burdens of art more than of gender, though she acknowledged those too. Molly's obsession with reading and composing strange stories and odd poems (on that favorite theme of Stafford's, heads: "Gravel, gravel on the ground / Lying there so safe and sound, / Why is it you look so dead? / Is it because you have no head?") was considered inappropriate behavior for a dutiful daughter. "Everyone said she had the brains of the family, but as Mrs. Fawcett was not interested in brains, she thought this a handicap rather than otherwise and often told Molly there were other things in life besides books." But it was not clear that Ralph would have met with much more approval had he displayed a similarly idiosyncratic imagination and vocational obsession.

The artistic temperament, as Stafford told it, was necessarily in tension with conventional society. It had its source in a sense of ostracism, and as it developed, the distance only increased. If the novel had a message, it was that the cost of growing up female and artistic was far greater than the cost of being a boy ready to make his peace with a conventional future. As in *Boston Adventure,* Stafford emphasized that self-destructiveness, a readiness to forsake ordinary comforts and calm, seemed to be an inextricable part of artistic aspiration. Where Sonie admired but shrank from the disorderly bohemian life, tempted instead by Pinckney Street propriety, Molly took the high, hard road. The child's uncompromising desires—to love and be utterly loved, and to be utterly devoted to her writing—spelled lonely unhappiness. Disappointment in love fueled her literary ambition, and her literary zeal alienated her further from Ralph, from everybody.

The painful cycle seemed to be especially destructive because Molly was a girl, more dependent on love and more suspect for her unconventional ambitions. Yet Stafford gave plenty of evidence that had Ralph been the poetic one of the pair, the predicament would not necessarily have been any easier. A creative, reclusive boy on Uncle Claude's ranch would have violated expectations even more dramatically than Molly did. It would have been, if anything, less acceptable for Ralph to cling to the imaginative purity of childhood—as the artistic temperament so often dictates. Thus although Ralph succeeded in growing up and Molly was defeated, Stafford suggested an unconventional reading. Of the two children who started out in search of integrity in a hypocritical world, one, Ralph, faced a future of terrible guilt at the end and the other, Molly, had been liberated.

Liberation by death is not a triumph by worldly standards, of course. But Molly was not a worldly creature. Her vocational rigor, as Stafford emphasized in Molly's central and exceptional scene—her bathing ritual—was religious in spirit. The detachment that art required, Stafford implied here as she did with Sonie, was near not only to neurotic isolation (Ralph worried that Molly was going crazy) but also to religious retreat. Molly's bath was her refuge from the eyes of the rest of the world—she carefully pulled the shade "though there was nothing outside but night" and blocked the keyhole though no one would come peeping at the ranch—and also from her own eyes. Her regimen was straight from a medieval nunnery (though Freud clearly hovered over Molly's rites). She cloaked herself in a wrap while she undressed, then slipped on a maroon bathing suit, and when she finished bathing, "she dried herself and bound her stomach with a piece of outing flannel. She wrapped it so hard and pinned it so tight that it gave her a pain and she had to lie down on the floor to get her slippers because she could not bend over. Then she put on her long-sleeved, high-necked pajamas, and the nightcap she had made over her drenched hair. It was her desire to have tuberculosis." Molly's self-mortification could also be more public and dramatic. When Ralph punctured her dream of marrying him someday, she poured acid on her hand. "The pain was not severe; it was the knowledge that the pain was *eating* her" that revolted this child whose body was so ill at ease in the world.

Molly, repulsed by the physical world in all its corruption—its "fatness," as she named it—wanted to waste away to spirit. Stafford once again blended religious and psychological perspectives on her character's spiritual, social, and sexual alienation. Molly was the austere novitiate and the incipient anorexic, the fanatic creative soul and the confused preadolescent. Stafford's skill in this colloquial novel was to evoke Molly's metaphysical dilemma in idiosyncratic detail, to seize on the comic particulars of her tragedy: "For the most part, [Molly] was not conscious of her body (she was never conscious of it as a *body* and had never spoken this word aloud and almost died when one of her sisters would jokingly say, 'Don't touch my body'; Molly thought of herself as a long wooden box with a mind inside)."

Similarly, Molly's category of "fatness," which applied to the rest of the world—all body and no mind—was at once her own droll childish curse and a metaphor with well-established religious and psychological associations. St. Teresa's style and teachings seemed to lurk behind Stafford's portrait of asceticism. In the ongoing war between the flesh and the spirit, the world and the word, the concrete and the abstract, Stafford, like Teresa, was a committed materialist as she wielded her pen. The flesh must be acknowledged in all its grossness and weakness. Concreteness was crucial in her account, and the strength of a symbol lay in its specificity. However archetypal their journey might be, Molly and Ralph were two children whose souls and pains were imagined by someone who had never forgotten what the loss of childhood felt like.

"In some respects it is a better book than *Boston Adventure*," Philip Rahv wrote to her after he had read *The Mountain Lion,* and his praise called attention to what a model of New Critical tautness the novel was:

Though less ambitious and narrower in scope and invention, it is more unified, more complete and convincing as a work of art. What is particularly admirable is the density of detail, its rightness and completeness. The various motives of the story are articulated through the detail with great naturalness and ease; and the symbolic meanings come through the experience you describe without strain or distortion. The ending is wonderful, and not only for its dramatic power—it integrates plot and meaning in an extraordinary way. Here for once is a novel about childhood and early adolescence which goes beyond genre painting, overcoming the limitations of personal biographical experience and converting its theme to the larger and more fundamental uses of literary expression.

Stafford "had gone all the way back," but what is remarkable is the distance she maintained from the "angry, wounded child." As the first part of *Boston Adventure* had shown, childhood was a subject that liberated Stafford's great gift: irony. She told an interviewer years later that "My theory about children is my theory about writing. The most important thing in writing is irony, and we find irony most clearly in children. The very innocence of children is irony." And echoing her New Critical teachers, she added, "Irony, I feel, is a very high form of morality." In *The Mountain Lion* Stafford had mastered a wide range of irony, from the broad social satire with which she developed the Bonney/Kenyon dichotomy to the self-irony she granted Molly. As a child writer, Molly was blessed, or rather burdened, with a double dose of alienation—from the world and from herself. "I know I'm ugly. I know everybody hates me. I wish I were dead," Molly told Ralph not histrionically but "in a cold, level voice." That moment of awful self-condemning clarity culminated in the proclamation that echoed throughout Stafford's fiction: "I haven't got a home."

Stafford's return to the Covina and Colorado of her childhood was another exploration, as *Boston Adventure* and before that *Autumn Festival* had been, of her sense of homelessness—written, very quickly, in the midst of arduous homesteading. Later in life, far smaller bouts of energetic housekeeping served as lengthy distractions from her work, but the whirlwind of restructuring and redecorating at Damariscotta Mills seemed to carry over into her creative life, not to detract from it. That's not to say that the writing was easy—or, for that mater, that the renovations went smoothly. *The Mountain Lion* was the product of considerable tumult, but it seems that the exploration of her past and the construction of her present and future in Maine were linked in an important way for her.

In a letter to Lowell from the hospital a year later, the same letter in

Dick Stafford and his sister Jean riding a bicycle.
Courtesy University of Colorado, Boulder.

John Stafford.

Sketch of John Stafford, presumably a self-portrait,
on the fly-leaf of his thesaurus.

Ethel Stafford with her son, Dick, in Covina, California.
Courtesy University of Colorado, Boulder.

*Andrew Cooke and Lucy McKee
in the Colorado Rockies, 1931.*
Courtesy Andrew Cooke.

Jean Stafford at sixteen.
Courtesy Robert Giroux.

Jean Stafford at the University of Colorado.
Courtesy University of Colorado, Boulder.

Jean Stafford's first passport photograph, 1936.
Courtesy Robert Giroux.

Jean Stafford and James Robert Hightower in Europe, 1936 or 1937.
Courtesy University of Colorado, Boulder.

ABOVE:
*Robert Lowell, Jean Stafford,
and Robert Giroux in front of the
Lowell's house in Damariscotta
Mills, Maine, 1946.*
Photograph by Charles Phillips Reilly.
Courtesy Robert Giroux.

LEFT:
*Jean Stafford and Peter Taylor
in Sewanee, Tennessee, 1942.*
Courtesy University of Colorado,
Boulder.

Jean Stafford and Robert Lowell in Damariscotta Mills, Maine, 1946.
Courtesy Houghton Library, Harvard University.

Jean Stafford and her sister Mary Lee Frichtel in Westport, Connecticut, 1950.
Photograph by Oliver Jensen. Courtesy Oliver Jensen.

Jean Stafford in front of the mountain lion cage at the zoo.
Courtesy Robert Giroux.

Jean Stafford at the beach in Jamaica during her honeymoon with Oliver Jensen, 1950.
Photograph by Oliver Jensen. Courtesy Oliver Jensen.

Oliver Jensen and Jean Stafford.
Photograph by Kay Bell. Courtesy University of Colorado, Boulder.

Jean Stafford in Westport, Connecticut, early 1950s.
Photograph by Oliver Jensen. Courtesy Oliver Jensen.

ABOVE:
Jean Stafford with her cat
Elephi, early 1960s.
Photograph by Janet Malcolm.
Courtesy Janet Malcolm.

LEFT:
Jean Stafford doing
needlepoint, 1956.
Photograph by Margaret Bourke-
White. Courtesy *Life* magazine,
© Time Warner Inc.

*Jean Stafford and A. J. Liebling sitting out behind
their house in East Hampton, 1961.*
Photograph by Therese Mitchell. Courtesy Joseph Mitchell.

Jean Stafford, 1975.
Photograph by Bernard Gotfryd.
Courtesy *Newsweek* magazine.

which she poured out her feelings about Molly, Stafford ruminated far more explicitly, and darkly, on the connection between her writing and her house—and her marriage and her father:

> For ages (and indeed until now) I have not known what you meant by saying that my success was bad for me. I am not sure that you know exactly how it was, but I see it in this way: that suddenly, having got money and comfort, I remembered with all the bitterness and hatred of my childhood my early poverty which had been needless; I remembered all the humiliation, the half-hunger, the shabby, embarrassing clothes, the continual oppression, my mother's tears and my father's dreadful laugh. And when you cautioned me to be prudent in my spending, I whipped around as if you had insulted me; I thought that you were trying to deprive me of all pleasure just as my father had done when I was a child and out of defiance of my father, I spent the money wildly and I began to drink more and more, still paying *him* back.

The absent father haunted, and inspired, both her book and her house frenzy. She was writing the story of children in search of a father figure, of a force to mediate between effete Bonney values—the McKillop side of Jean's family—and harsh Kenyon standards, the Stafford side. Molly's idiosyncratic choice of a misanthropic, literary course was in fact the childish version of the course embraced by John Stafford. The role model Molly didn't have was the model that Jean herself did have, and far from clarifying her life, he profoundly confused it. Admiration for her father's uncompromising, cantankerous path continued to be mixed for Stafford with ever greater doses of bitterness, and even hatred. He had perversely chosen to abandon the responsibilities of maturity, leaving his family to suffer the consequences. Molly's fate was in a sense a comment on his failures: the young writer died on the brink of maturity, prevented from repeating them.

But Jean Stafford's own fate was quite different. She had grown up and written a best-selling book, and she found herself, as her letter to Lowell acknowledged, reacting quite differently to her father's failures. She threw herself into establishing a home, precisely what John Stafford had never been able to do once he had embarked on his writing career, consigning his family instead to a succession of boardinghouses. It was her McKillop moment, her gesture of solidarity with the feminine world of stability and domesticity. And it was her replacement of the Covina idyll that her father had squandered. Jean's utopian dreams for Damariscotta Mills echoed her father's response to his first windfall, inherited in his case rather than earned. Her drama of triumphant defiance was spurred by Lowell's ascetic reaction, which was the perfect stand-in for the paternal stringency she was rebelling against. Yet guilt undercut the triumph. Her success couldn't help being a devastating comment on her father's failure, and lurking in her utopian dreams was an urge to have it all fall apart, as it had for him—at least this was how she saw it a year later, as she wrote to the Thompsons in the spring of 1947: "I felt perpetually accused and guilt-ridden and it was partly the guilt itself that made me spend all the money and so madly, to get as quickly as possible back to the familiar state of poverty, of literally not knowing where the rent was coming from. I was accused both by Cal and by my family, particularly by my father who wrote me (and writes me now) that he was glad of my success because he himself had been such an awful failure."

STAFFORD FINISHED *The Mountain Lion* in the spring of 1946, as the house too was being completed. She wrote to the Taylors early in April, full of the familiar plans for a communal literary idyll, this time on her own territory: "Come as soon as you can and plan to live with us for at least five years," she wrote, her confidence perhaps masking a sense of desperation. She then went on to address the practical details, obviously aware of the precariousness of the proposal:

> We shall have to work out some sort of domestic arrangement, as I do not intend that Eleanor and I shall get cross with one another. . . . The house is really quite a convenient one and I think we shouldn't have the least bit of trouble. We are much too fast friends, the four of us, to run risks at all and consequently—as I know you both will agree with me because we've discussed it before—we must be frank from the start. Then it will be nothing but pure pleasure and profit.

But true to the epitaph of Lowell's draft of *Land of Unlikeness,* death did come when the house was built. The troubles began in the spring, and they culminated in "That awful summer!" That was how Stafford opened the short story, three decades later, in which she presented a version of the events that led to her collapse, and the collapse of her marriage to Lowell.

"An Influx of Poets," extracted from Stafford's last, unfinished novel, *The Parliament of Women,* and published in *The New Yorker* in November 1978, has understandably enough been mined for facts. It was clearly an autobiographical story, an appropriately stylish record of a season that in retrospect stood out as a turning point not only in Lowell's and Stafford's lives but in the collective life of a loose literary circle—the promising writers whom the newly established Lowells overeagerly invited to come visit. The Rahvs and the Blackmurs were part of the literary Maine circuit that year too, but the ferment was taking place at Damariscotta Mills. It was a summer when the younger writers were on their own turf, away from their mentors, declaring their ambitions to one another—a memorable moment of high hopes. John Berryman, one of the steady stream of visitors (which included the Taylors, Robert Giroux, Patrick Quinn, Eileen Simpson, Delmore Schwartz, Gertrude Buckman, and others) called it his "last summer of innocence." From the exhilarating heights of the crowded summer, the Lowells' subsequent fall seemed to mark the border between promise and reality: with their house in 1946 and then with their second books in 1947, they stepped into their own—and it was clear that the way was not going to be smooth. Their books were successes—Lowell's won him the Pulitzer Prize; Stafford's was well reviewed—but their lives were difficult.

Stafford's story merely alluded to the spring, which was the traumatic start of the troubles between her and Lowell. It was such a harrowing time, perhaps, that it could not be tamed into a story. "It has been the most confused and difficult spring of my life, I do believe," she wrote to Cecile Starr as it ended. "I have got so accustomed to the confusion that now, when there is quiet and little to worry about, I am still unable to be calm." Her letters gave only a general clue to her distress. For the most part, she played the role of long-suffering but resilient hostess. But shortly after she finished *The Mountain Lion,* there seems to have been a violent scene between her and Lowell, who had just returned from a Trappist retreat. She called it "the incident," as distinct from "the accident," the other memorable shake-up at the hands of her husband (the New Orleans episode, when Lowell broke her nose, never seemed to figure in her memories): she claimed that Lowell beat her up and threatened to kill her. Clearly something happened that was disturbing enough to surface later in one of her stories, "A Country Love Story," in 1950 (originally titled "When the House Is Finished, Death Comes"), and in Lowell's *The Mills of the Kavanaughs*. The scene was strikingly similar in both (though Stafford excised it from her final story): the husband, in a seizure of jealousy, tried to strangle his wife in bed. So were the details of the setting—the Damariscotta Mills house looming, as Stafford put it, "as if it were their common enemy, maliciously bent on bringing them to disaster," the snowplow clanging in the quiet night, its lights ominously blinking. And a larger theme lurked behind both of their portraits of marital crisis: the fear of mental collapse.

Whatever actually happened between Lowell and Stafford, they were profoundly estranged. The tensions of the winter had mounted to a breaking point. All the distractions they created for themselves and all the energy they devoted to their writing could not, evidently, cure or deflect their unhappiness with each other. As she wrote in the story, "it seemed to her that love, the very center of their being, was choked off, overgrown, invisible." Her novel finished, her husband aloof (and then, immediately after "the incident," his parents in Maine for a visit), Stafford lost what equilibrium she had had. During the spring she was "seized with the terror of losing my mind," as she wrote to Lowell a year later. "This is not a casual statement nor is it a common experience, and it is, of all the terrors I have had, the very worst." She was drinking a great deal (Lowell was not), tensely dependent on her trips to and from the nearest liquor store in Bath. (They had no car, but the local sheriff was her willing chauffeur.) Insomnia returned, and she was plagued by terrible headaches. At the recommendation of a doctor she was then seeing, she left to rest at a farm in Pennsylvania but quickly fled what she described as a "nest of ex-Communists." After spending a few lonely days going over the galleys of *The Mountain Lion* in a hotel across from the Algonquin in New York, she returned to Maine—and "that awful summer" began.

"An Influx of Poets" is remarkably free of bitterness. It had taken a long time—decades—for Stafford to find the right tone and perspective to write about what had happened in Maine. The immediate circumstances had been galling: her husband's flagrant flirtation with one of her erstwhile best friends, Delmore Schwartz's ex-wife, Gertrude Buckman. The repercussions had been long-lasting. Stafford's marriage to Lowell always loomed as the formative chapter of her life, its collapse as a traumatic event. It would not have been a surprise had she, with her "tongue of an adder," dedicated the story to fierce revenge. In fact, that was the hope, or at least the expectation, of many of her friends (some of them remnants of that old literary circle, others of them allies from subsequent, very different, milieus). Certainly her anecdotal tendency, with rare exceptions, was to cast Lowell as the villain, herself as the victim. But on paper, she once again discovered the detachment that so often eluded her in life—and that enabled her imagination to work, dramatizing a more complicated account.

Her inspired narrative strategy was to juxtapose her younger self (Cora Savage in the story) with an older Cora who was telling the story many years later. Both were subjected to the same satiric irony that informed the story as a whole, and the facts were altered just enough to give the two of them a philistine air to set off the poetic pretensions of the rest of the company. Thus young Cora was not a writer, though she had an ornate style. She was merely the wife of a poet, and she had bought her house with a legacy from her aunt, rather than with the proceeds from a best-selling novel. Not that authorship would have elevated her much. In a survey of the Maine literary scene, Stafford made clear that prose writers were at the bottom of the heap in any case:

> There was an influx of poets this summer in the state of Maine and ours was only one of the many houses where they clustered: farther down the coast and inland all the way to Campobello, singly, in couples, trios, tribes, they were circulating among rich patronesses in ancestral summer shacks of twenty rooms, critics on vacation from universities who roughed it with Coleman lamps and outhouses but sumptuously dined on lobster and blueberry gems, and a couple of novelists who, although they wrote like dogs (according to the poets) had made packets, which, because they were decently (and properly) humble, they were complimented to share with the rarer breed.

The young Cora, suffering from headaches and unhappiness, was distinctly on the outskirts, estranged from her poet husband, Theron Maybank, and skeptical of "Theron the poet's poet friends. He was beside me and they were in all the rooms around me and in the barn, but I was dead to their world, and they, thereby, were dead to mine." She was like a ghost hostess, actively arranging the domestic details of the influx but passively aloof from the artistic, erotic intrigue. Not that she was unaware of it. Cora saw, as through a hazy scrim (of drink, she acknowledged, and depression), all the flirting and flattering going on— especially between her husband and Minnie Rosoff, the Gertrude Buckman character whose visit was the most fateful of the entire influx. But out of a perverse instinct for escape and for self-mortification (precisely the opposite of the poets' self-preening inclinations) she could only abet the adulterous romance: "I helped in every way to make the match which was already a fait accompli and which, when I discovered that it was, was to hurtle me off the brink on which I had hovered so long into a chasm."

The older Cora was very much present, recounting and commenting on events, in an outspokenly colloquial and rather curmudgeonly style that established the distance she had traveled since that summer. Where the young Cora was blind and self-destructive, the older Cora had a therapeutic clarity. She was not venting bitterness; her tone was too entertainingly farcical for that. She was simply setting the record straight with satiric zeal. "(Mine! Remember, Cora Savage, if you forget all else, that this is *your* house)," she scolded her past self in one of the conversational parenthetical asides that litter the story. "(God almighty! Never was a man so set on knocking the stuffing out of his bride!)," she exclaimed at another point. The effect, along with her device of casting the poets (and herself) as children, was to knock all of them off their pedestals, to offer an irreverent look into the legend. The "baby bards," as she described them, were infantile in their self-absorption—but not innocent, by any means. This was the point at which their flailing ambitions were becoming more focused. "(Though they were no longer enfants terribles, the blood of despots was in their veins and they would very soon usurp their elders' thrones and their dominions)," the older Cora reported, looking back.

Young Cora was oppressed by the poets' self-importance, but docilely played her role as helpmeet, typing endless revisions of Theron's poems and listening to endless recitations of poetry. In the story the older Cora wasn't docile at all and was perfectly prepared to risk philistinism in declaring her position. "I was in this throng of litterateurs (three poets in one medium-sized room constitutes a multitude), enjoying nothing." The once-loyal typist was none too respectful: "(I admit they were brilliant poets, if you happen to be interested in that sort of thing), but if they changed an 'a' to 'the' the whole sonnet had to be typed over again. And I grant that such a change can make all the difference in the world (if, that is, you happen to be a poet or a lover of poetry), but why couldn't the alteration be made by hand?" The once-silent auditor, trapped into "listening to the poets listen to themselves and not to one another," confessed that "she took a drink as the poetry was read, but drink didn't help."

But this was not a simple feminist complaint against the elitist, overbearing bards. One could doubtless be written, as Delmore Schwartz suggested in a poem he wrote just before his marriage fell apart:

> All poets' wives have rotten lives,
> Their husbands look at them like knives . . .
> Exactitude their livelihood
> And rhyme their only gratitude,
> Knife-throwers all, in vaudeville,
> They use their wives to prove their will—

Marjorie Perloff has played out the suggestion in her essay "*Poètes Maudits* of the Genteel Tradition," in which she points out the pattern of "the prodigal poet, the unselfish and forgiving wife or mistress" that seemed to characterize the private lives of these same poets (and was then presented for public consumption in their poetry). In a sense Stafford's story could be read as the record of the emergence of that pattern: aside from the Tates' troubles and the Schwartzes' divorce, the Lowells' Maine turmoils were the first of the dramatic marital difficulties that were to become a theme of Lowell's and Berryman's lives in particular. Stafford was more than ready to point the finger at the poet-husband: she drew on Theron's outrageous behavior for much of the colorful, witty drama and repartee of her story.

But at the same time, almost as if offering her autobiographical story as a commentary on the autobiographical poetry that the poets—especially Lowell—had been writing out of their personal troubles throughout the 1960s and 1970s, Stafford undercut any effort at self-vindication or inflation of the episode. She, unlike the poets, was not about to project her private troubles as historic turmoil, or to write herself a tragically heroic role. The story was finally less about the poets' injustices to her than about her injustices to herself. There was no clear-cut victim and

victimizer. It was her own psychological distress, not the poets' pretensions, that afflicted her most: "I knew—although I did not want to
know—that I could not honestly attribute [the headaches] to too many
iambs and too many dithyrambic self-congratulations by the baby bards."
It was her own passive will at work, bidden by an inchoate desire for
escape, that undid the marriage as much as Theron's peremptory moves.
Not that Stafford substituted a kind of ennobling self-castigation for self-
justification. Her strategy was satiric deflation throughout. Her failure
to plead her case, to have a straightforward revenge, infuriated at least
one of her friends, Nancy Flagg Gibney, who felt she had missed a historic opportunity:

> But great as you are, Madam, I have for once a bone to pick. This
> story must be read as autobiography, not fiction, and I wish you had
> written it as such. Cora Savage like hell, heavenly though her name
> is. Robert Lowell is up against precisely Jean Stafford, no little hap-
> less schoolteacher in over her head, inheriting goading cash from
> antipodal aunts, but a blazing genius with better looks and taste
> and sense than he has, and the achieved success that he only longs
> for. Of course he had to beat the stuffing out of you, and of course
> he couldn't do so. Not quite. You were a woman so liberated that
> you could afford to be a slave. No matter how many fish you fried,
> how many dishes you washed, how hard you tried to expiate your
> sins of superiority, he knew it was a gag, and so did you. You say—
> "the man I wanted to flee because, in failing to commit myself en-
> tirely to him, I knew he would not commit himself to me." But
> surely you know that he was entirely committed to you, and to your
> destruction. . . . You had the war between the sexes fought out on
> the highest possible plane Miss hydrogen-bomb-bearing Savage,
> and I wish you had reported it straight.

But precisely what seems to have liberated Stafford years after the Maine
summer to rework this section of her stalled novel for publication was
the sense that she no longer needed to see it as a war. Time had allowed
a cooled perspective. She was free to let irony replace the agony of betrayal. In this case, the domestication was devastating, as she cast the
episode comically as a story about children and a bygone time, not about
important poets whose lives had acquired the status of cultural symbols.
  The truth, of course, was not so comical. And the power of "An Influx

of Poets" is that, for all its witty shapeliness, it does capture some of the shapeless confusion, the real desperation of that summer. The trouble was clear to the earliest visitors, John Berryman and his wife, Eileen Simpson, who glimpsed the marital tensions and Stafford's distress beneath the mostly convivial, intensely literary stay. Jean's "somber mood was growing more obvious every day," Simpson remembered in her portrait in *Poets in Their Youth,* which captured Stafford slipping from ordinary depression into more serious disequilibrium. Caustic as always, and a solicitous host, she was nonetheless drinking more and more and sleeping less and less. Lowell certainly seemed dead to her unhappy world, endlessly verse swapping and talking with Berryman, and Stafford became ever more distant. She drank against his wishes, from bottles hidden around the house, and she was awake at night, her insomnia a solitary vigil (though one night she told her Lucy story to a sleepless Berryman, the third poet to urge her to put it into prose). A letter in June from Stafford to her sister Mary Lee, to whom she often confided her unhappiness at this stage of her life, conveyed her mixed mood, which easily shifted to real bleakness:

> Everything is going much better in one way—so that day to day existence is easier—much worse in another; it will be harder to make the break. In my absence [in Pennsylvania and New York] Cal realized the horror of solitude. Now I do not know what to do. In some ways the problem is not terribly complex. I am suffering from years and years of accumulated fatigue not only from working too hard but from knowing too many people. Being a writer and being married to a writer is a back breaking job and my back is now broken.

Stafford cast her predicament in literary terms. The allure, and burden, of being married to a promising, difficult writer—and being one herself—had been clear to Stafford from the start. And the tension between dreaming of the communal literary life and dreading the arrival of litterateurs was a familiar one, dating back to her feverish days in Louisiana. Now the allures and dreams seemed to have faded almost completely. It was clear that Stafford was looking for a way out. She announced her verdict in a flip tone, but behind it lurked serious intentions: "I've now decided," she told Mary Lee, "that writers shouldn't be married and certainly women writers shouldn't be unless they are married to rich responsible husbands who fill their houses with servants." She sounded almost like the older, wiser Cora Savage speaking, who had put those poets behind her.

By August neither Lowell nor Stafford was sounding remotely flip, and an end was in sight. Gertrude Buckman had arrived in a plane and captivated Lowell while Stafford watched, her passivity a spur to their affair. Lowell wrote to Taylor, leaving out the specifics but emphatic about the impossibility of life with Stafford:

> I don't care for confessions, but I suppose I must tell you that everything is chaos between us. Jean is driving like a cyclone and we both have had about all we can stand and more. Right now I think I'll go to New York sometime in September. . . . Jean has a lot of plans, none of them too good, including going to Hollywood. Anyway, we have got to *leave each other alone* and the future to time.

Stafford, writing to Cecile Starr, sounded much less composed and wasn't yet ready to announce the end. In fact, she claimed she felt some calm might be at hand:

> There has been such a stream of visitors ever since Memorial Day that I was half out of my mind and so was Cal. I was half out of my mind with all sorts of anxieties and was drinking too much—as I do, you know—and had got no work done at all since April and in general I thought I was at the end of everything in my life. Now that everyone has gone and no one else is coming and the leaves are beginning to turn . . . I feel as if I were recovering from a long and feverish sickness, one that has covered a great many years, and I have some kind of hope that I will at last be able to pull myself together. . . . Our plans are as vague as they have always been.

When she wrote a little later to Peter Taylor, the hope had faded, the recovery seemed out of sight again. Stafford too was silent about specifics—there was no mention of Buckman—and, far from blaming Lowell, she shouldered responsibility for the disaster, though it was clearly more complicated than that. Neither of them stable at the best of times, both had drastically lost their balance. That Stafford still had the poise to bear the guilt for the failure was a sign of hard-won maturity, but at the same time a last act of self-punishment:

I have wanted to write to you ever since Cal told me he had written but there have been so many people here and besides I have been rather too miserable to be coherent. It is just barely possible that if I can ever pull myself together something will work out for us but I love Cal too much now to allow him any longer to be subjected to what seems to amount almost to insanity. I am very much afraid of the future, but I will pull through somehow. What I most need now is to go far away somewhere to a place where I know no one and cannot therefore be influenced by the wrong people.

I am almost altogether to blame for my life being the ruin it is.

She was right, her sickness wasn't over, and its course continued "like a cyclone," sweeping away a house and a husband. Stafford was left to rebuild a life, which inevitably was a literary life, despite her vows to avoid the creative company. But it was a strikingly different literary life, a world away from the poets and critics among whom she had come of age.

PART IV

Manhattan
and Other Islands
1946–1979

CHAPTER 10

Patterns

IN SEPTEMBER 1946, Stafford and Lowell left Maine by train, and as she told it in "An Influx of Poets," the trip from Damariscotta Mills was the culmination of their estrangement. It was a bleakly symmetrical ending to a marriage that had begun less than smoothly with a train ride: they had spent their brief honeymoon en route to Cleveland in 1940, and when they had separated in the station (Lowell on his way to Kenyon, Stafford to her sister's ranch), Stafford had been full of doubts about the vows she had just taken. Now the lonely fall of 1946 continued to echo past scenes. In New York, Stafford soon went to the New Weston Hotel, and the next several months were full of "scary days." That's what Stafford had called her nightmarish stay in New York after fleeing from Iowa in 1938; this time she was even more disoriented. Then she had been wondering when and how her literary career would begin, and she had been entangled with two men, Hightower and Lowell. Now she was wondering if that career had peaked, and she was distraught over her husband's betrayal. And this time the frightening days lasted much longer than they had eight years earlier. As she described it later, the fall in New York was an abyss of rage and humiliation, and above all of loneliness. She drank wildly—suicidally, she said in retrospect—and ate and slept very little. Finally she turned to doctors for help, recalling yet another New York scene from her past. In 1937 she had gotten off the boat from Heidelberg alone and feverish and had spent most of her time in the city as a patient in Brooklyn Hospital, writing despairing letters to Hightower. This time, in late November, in more psychological than physical trouble, she signed herself into the Payne Whitney Psychiatric Clinic at New York Hospital.

Amid what looked like a notably unsteady life, there were uncanny patterns and correspondences. In a letter to Peter Taylor the month she entered the hospital, Stafford expressed her fear of the inauspicious shapes her life seemed to take. "There was something wrong in me to marry [Cal]," she wrote, "for he was so much like my father whom first I worshipped and by whom I later felt betrayed." Recognizing this central echo in her life, she shuddered at all the other reverberations:

> This is not psychiatric cant even though the psychiatrists have told me that this is just what I did, married my father, just as the same perverseness made Cal marry his mother. . . . I disobeyed him as I disobeyed my father; he was cold as my father had always been and he was economically and domestically irresponsible as my father had always been. And he read his poems aloud to me as my father had read his stories for the pulp magazines. And his manners were courtly or they were uncouth and he was slovenly, as my father was. My father didn't have his wit nor his brilliance. They were both violent men in every way. This pattern terrifies me. All the patterns of my life terrify me and this is why, in the constant torment of my fear, I have had to seek someone who really *can* be my father and can protect me.

For the next year and more, psychiatrists were Stafford's source of support (as doctors of one sort or another were to be for the rest of her life). She was not, however, a simple and tractable patient. Her attitude toward psychiatry, as her phrase "psychiatric cant" suggested, was at base skeptical, a view she shared with many of her friends, certainly with Lowell, who at this stage was less than sympathetic, as Stafford indicated in "An Influx of Poets": "He was, despite his eccentricities and his rebellion, an intransigently conventional man," she wrote of her character Theron; "thus his diehard repudiation of psychiatry as poppycock, a Viennese chicanery devised to bilk idle women and hypochondriacal men."

It was Robert Giroux and Cecile Starr, two of Stafford's most loyal friends during the frightening autumn, who urged her to try psychotherapy, less out of faith in that course than out of desperation. Starr had welcomed Stafford to her apartment when she arrived in New York, and had tried in vain to help her stop drinking and begin sleeping again: "If it had not been for Cecile," Stafford wrote to Lowell later, "I would have killed myself." (At one point they retreated to Connecticut for some peace and distance from the hard-drinking literary crowd, whose company only added to Stafford's anxieties, Starr could see.) More drastic measures were clearly called for, and before long Stafford's unhappiness overcame her resistance. She was ready to find help wherever she could, even though enlisting doctors seemed to her an admission of defeat, as she wrote in the early fall to her sister Mary Lee. It was a letter of confession, but also of warning; she wanted no comfort or visits from close relatives:

> I have finally had to face the fact that I am very ill and I now must face a long and arduous and tormenting cure, but it is the only way out of my despair. I am full of self-hatred and disgust for I have always scorned people who could not help themselves to become adjusted, but my heart breaks for all of them now: I understand fully what "nervous breakdown" means. I do not know what will happen. . . . I shall be alone and shall be lonely, but it is all better than what might otherwise happen to me. There is now nothing that anyone can do for me but myself and an expert. . . . I cannot, in my present state, burden anyone with my half-mad society.

When Stafford came under the care of Dr. Mary Jane Sherfey, a young doctor on the staff of Payne Whitney, she felt she had found the person she needed. Stafford had already had a dizzying tour of assorted other doctors, all well known and very interested in the gifted young writer. Robert Giroux had put her in touch first with Dr. Carl Binger, whose books on psychiatry were published by Harcourt, Brace, and whose recommended treatment was more drastic than she was yet prepared to consider: no more alcohol, he insisted, and he urged a brief stay in Payne Whitney Psychiatric Hospital. Then she turned to Dr. Gregory Zilboorg, who earned her enmity by sending her in October to a Detroit sanitarium, from which she promptly fled to Denver, where she was met by Mary Lee. Proximity to her family was, as she had predicted, the worst cure. Her sister was distraught, especially about Stafford's drinking, and there were battles, as well as one unhelpful visit to the local doctor, the son of Stafford's childhood doctor. She hurried back to New York, moved into progressively cheaper hotels, and tried yet more doctors (and yet more drink: sleepless, she would close the hotel bar, then pour herself applejack in her room). Again at the suggestion of Giroux, she talked with Dr. Henry Murray of Harvard ("my marvelous man—I wish he were our father," she wrote to Mary Lee), who unfortunately had to return to Cambridge. Finally at the end of November, she was ready to admit herself to Payne Whitney (Giroux was to release her if she decided she wanted to leave), where she was initially treated by Dr. Oskar Diethelm, psychiatrist in chief, who then entrusted her to his student Dr. Sherfey.

As Stafford herself seemed to recognize, psychiatry occupied much the same place for her that Catholicism once had. In fact, while she was frantically touring doctors, she also consulted Father Dougherty, the priest whom she and Lowell had relied on in New York, and whom she had especially counted on during her lonely days while Cal was in prison. Father Dougherty urged her to try a convent in New Jersey run by German nuns, an implausible plan that the nuns vetoed before Stafford had to make the decision. She clearly needed an authoritative structure to guide her, but a more therapeutic discipline than religion could provide. Psychiatry presented a prescriptive regimen against which she could continually rebel but on which she could also rely. It offered a system of explanation, a possible way to overcome the confusion and lack of control that she knew all too well, in fact sought out. Stafford's impulsive testing of experience was an exhilarating part of the creative life, and yet it also "terrified" her, she had written to Hightower earlier: "I am saturated with meaningless experience." Her sense of a centered self was precarious, she confessed in journals and sometimes in letters, and her ever active imagination made the world around her an infinitely distracting, often threatening, place; Cecile Starr thought of her as internally combustible, because she was so susceptible to so much outside. Alcohol, as Stafford alternately admitted and denied, was an additional deadly ingredient. Drinking beckoned as an anesthetic, only to betray her; its pleasures were short-lived, and instead of dulling internal and external anxieties, it multiplied them.

Stafford knew she needed a domain of order as a refuge from disorientation. Her domesticity was one practical source of stability; her identity as a woman with a house and the responsibilities that went with that role were clear. Yet that realm, so painstakingly constructed, had quickly crumbled in the fall of 1946. Now the hospital offered a haven. The position of patient, disciplined and tended to, was a relief, and psychoanalysis held out the prospect of easing some of the burden of dizzying experience; it could point out patterns in her life, not to entrap her, but instead perhaps to liberate her.

Although liberation was the goal, Stafford also worried that freedom from her demons, if it was possible, might destroy or dilute her creative gift. As a writer she depended on hypersensitivity to her surroundings and on contact with her subconscious. Despite her need for her "red room," as she sometimes referred to her hospital retreat, she was ambivalent about admitting psychiatrists into the inner sanctum. Her doctors, most of whom had read her novels with great interest and admiration, were all too eager to parse them for symptoms. Dr. Zilboorg, Stafford reported to Lowell, had told her that "Boston Adventure was 'the product of one of the most tormented minds in a woman of my age' that he had ever seen." Stafford's initial response was icily to remind him that she was not an agonized neurotic, but a writer with particular aims. When Dr. Sherfey told her that *The Mountain Lion* was "excellent from a psychiatric point of view; so is the mother in Boston Adventure," Stafford's reaction was decidedly mixed. She had had no conscious intent to produce perfect neurotic specimens, and the diagnosis seemed to turn imaginative characterizations into mere case studies. At the same time, she had to admit that *Boston Adventure* was intimately connected to her own deep-seated preoccupations and insecurities, whether or not she had consciously seen the connections in the process of writing. And the autobiographical anxieties were closer to the surface in *The Mountain Lion,* she acknowledged; she told Dr. Diethelm that she "felt [the novel] had very much to do with my collapse. . . . I do not know why the collapse did not come last spring when I finished the book."

In an unfinished manuscript of a short fictional sketch entitled "A Personal Story," which seems to have been written sometime in the fall of 1946, perhaps after Stafford had entered Payne Whitney, she pursued the theme of patterns and proposed an unconventional relation between her writing and her life—one that sheds an unusual light on her career. A thinly fictionalized reminiscence of her and Lowell's year in Maine, the story began as a meditation on the thrall of memory. The protagonist was a traumatized, solitary woman; "almost more than anything else, it was the thought of the summer and of the house when it was 'finished' that had taken her up in a possessive embrace." Yet after a few pages of the woman's despairing nostalgia, which she admitted was not new to her life, the sketch ended with an echo of Stafford's letter to Taylor about haunting patterns, and a shift from memory to prophecy:

Still, the torment had never been so concentrated as it was now and she had come to believe that she was possessed. She was terrified by the patterns of her life and by her prophetic dreams and her prophetic insights, by the fact that she had imagined and had written much that had happened later.

Stafford reversed the usual relation between art and life. Her books, she suggested, shaped her life as much as, if not more than, her life shaped her books. It is a point too rarely acknowledged about writers' relations to their creations: plumbing a life for psychological clues to the writing that emerges from it, critics and biographers sometimes neglect to observe that a life is in turn altered by writing. That is clearest on a public level: a book that is a great success, or for that matter a marked failure, obviously looms over a writer's subsequent career. Sudden fame, as Stafford discovered with *Boston Adventure,* can inspire confidence but also insecurity. That novel behind her, she was watched as a promising young writer by a much larger circle; she now had a reputation, and a distinctive one, to live up to. Yet there is also a more private, psychological level on which writing can influence a life. It was that more mysterious intermingling that Stafford invoked in "A Personal Story." For a writer as imaginatively impressionable as Stafford was, creative fantasy, dream, and reality readily blur. The fantasizing mind can exert surprising power over, as Stafford put it, much that happens later. The confusions and fates she worked out for her characters on paper, whatever they owed to her past, also seemed to influence her future in indirect ways.

In a digression in "An Influx of Poets," Stafford called attention to the power of words to influence experience—in particular the power of lies to entail suffering: "So ignorant and sheeplike is my flesh," Cora Savage announced, "that if, at the eleventh hour, I telephone my hostess to say that I cannot come to her party because I have a headache, at the twelfth hour a fang of pain strikes deep within my skull, and by the time the party is over and the guests are at home in bed asleep, I am haggard with suffering." Stafford's susceptibility to psychosomatic illness, the most obvious instance of mind over matter for her, suggests the overweening role her imagination could play. Not unlike her little medical lies, her large-scale literary fictions seemed to her to have a kind of independent life within her life, altering as well as reflecting its course. Suffering was usually the result, which was doubtless what terrorized her.

During her year in the hospital, her two novels haunted her in different ways. In *The Mountain Lion* the familiar relation between life and art prevailed. It was a novel steeped in memory, for Stafford had drawn deeply on her childhood, but it also cast a shadow over adult life, especially over that year. She associated the ordeal of writing about Molly with her collapse in Damariscotta Mills, and the painful childhood memories were doubtless kept vivid as she probed her psyche with a succession of doctors at Payne Whitney. *Boston Adventure* was a stranger case. Unusual for a first novel, it had tenuous grounding in autobiography. It was the book that Stafford wrote before one would have expected her to be able or inclined to. After all, she had barely penetrated the Boston enclaves that she set out to dissect. It was a novel written more thoroughly out of the imagination, a book that then exerted a kind of prophetic power over Stafford's life. The sequel that the novel's ominously inconclusive ending seemed to call for—and that she kept trying over the years to write—always took on quite transparently autobiographical shape. Sonie and Philip's subsequent life, as Stafford tracked it in various abortive drafts and outlines, was essentially her life with Lowell. She couldn't make it work in fiction. The real sequel was perhaps Stafford's own life, as she lived out some of the implications of what she had written in her first novel.

Certainly during that fall in New York, when she had lost Lowell, her Philip, to another woman and when a retreat to her "red room" beckoned urgently, Stafford felt the book haunting her. "All I can feel now," she wrote to Taylor in her unhappiness, "is Pray God the day I can forget my Boston Adventure will not be long in coming." And in the course of her trip back from Denver after her stay with Mary Lee, the novel instigated a traumatic reckoning with the life she had imagined in it and had lived while writing it. Or at least that was the dramatic story she told. In the train station in Chicago on her way to New York, she wrote to Lowell, she was overwhelmed by the sense that she could

> not go any further. I must hand myself over to a policeman and tell him that I am no longer responsible, that the state must now take care of me. . . . And then I did a pitiful thing. . . . I had not been able to read anything for weeks and so, in the station, when I still had some hours to wait, I bought a dollar edition of Boston Adventure and I tried to read it. I went into the women's room and tried

to read it there and when I could not, the tears poured out and in a perfect rage I threw it in the trash container. It was, in its way, a little suicide.

Her convulsion seems almost too neatly scripted to be true. Whether she had imagined or actually lived that "little suicide," it was a scene more in keeping with Hopestill's dramatic life than with Sonie's, as Stafford's entire time in New York was. She had described Hope's disoriented, self-destructive life in the city with some wryness in the novel. In search of peace with herself, Hope had become immersed in a psychiatric milieu worlds away from her Calvinist relatives in Boston. Stafford's own life was not so different. In fact, the memory of Lucy McKee, the model for Hopestill, loomed over her during her ordeal—and so did thoughts of her father (just as Sonie's father continued to haunt her). "If only I could sleep," Stafford wrote Taylor in November, still suffering from the insomnia that had plagued her before entering the hospital. "But I shall learn [to] again," she assured him, and herself, as she summoned up optimism about her future, "just as I shall learn to eat again and to face reality on my own two feet without the crutches of alcohol and sleeping tablets because if I do not learn again, I shall destroy myself in one way or another. It will not be so hard now that my father has departed from my life and as soon as I can really lay Lucy's ghost [to rest] I will not have to flee my guilt."

But her father hadn't departed from her life, even if at moments she might feel she had successfully banished him, and Lucy's ghost was not so easily dispelled. It was Sonie's analogous predicament that gave the end of *Boston Adventure* its inconclusive feel: Hope's death had hardly liberated Sonie, and Miss Pride was clearly no father substitute. In the hospital Stafford was relieved to be in a sense suspended in time, "safe between innumerable locked doors," focusing only on establishing a mundane, healthy routine: eating well, not drinking, dressing neatly, and being amused by the ridiculous routines of "Luna Park," as she called it. But she was also probing her past, and she couldn't help wondering what the sequel to her life so far would look like. Above all, she hadn't abandoned thoughts of the writing that might lie ahead. Work on the *Boston Adventure* sequel continued to vex her, but she embarked—or at least announced that she was embarking—on a different book, which was another approach to laying the persistent ghosts to rest. It was the book that she had outlined to Lowell and Schwartz in Cambridge and then stayed up late recounting to Berryman in Maine: *In the Snowfall,* the story of Lucy's suicide, which was also the story of her own escape from her family, in particular from her father, during her college years.

It's not clear when (or whether) during her year in Payne Whitney she actually began work on it, but by the summer she was referring to a novel, one that she was having real trouble with. The trouble was familiar from her earliest fictional efforts, as she acknowledged in a journal entry: self-hating solipsism. "I think the stumbling block in both the novels I am writing—writing the one to escape the other—is my dislike of both my heroines who are, as they have always been, myself. I can only write of loneliness—when I don't I offensively attack—only of a half-mad separateness." *In the Snowfall* was a novel written about a past that cast its shadow far into the future for Stafford: Lucy and her father were, as her efforts on the novel suggest, two images of her own fate—the loveless woman and the frustrated, bitter writer. Those were the patterns that perhaps terrified her most.

The novel shaped around those images languished, but they were among the dominant themes of the torrent of letters she sent to Lowell while she was in Payne Whitney. The correspondence (none of Lowell's letters survive) proved to be Stafford's main literary work during her stay. The letters, essentially a long plea that they give their marriage another chance, were remarkable for their fluency and their fierceness. If they were the product of one draft, she was in amazing control of language in the midst of her misery. The well-crafted sentences rolled out smoothly, and there was barely a correction in letters that sometimes ran as many as nine single-spaced typed pages. Still, the correspondence was far from measured. Stafford's tone shifted radically, sometimes almost hysterically, within and between letters. Her irony for the most part had fled, and she became histrionic, as she was sometimes able to recognize.

It was in her letters to Peter Taylor—who kept in close contact with both her and Lowell throughout, devastated by their separation and even offering at one point to serve as intermediary in an effort to clarify the situation between them—that Stafford managed some distance from her distress. "I warn you that I am fanciful these days and that I am so starved for consideration which I am not getting, for affection of which I have been entirely deprived for months," she complained dramatically, but caught herself up, "that I am, in short, so beside myself that I cannot help but exaggerate." In a short note, she put it simply and poignantly: "I have had many very hideous things happen to me which I hope I can be funny about some time."

And it was Taylor who early on that fall gave Stafford advice that spoke to her fears about her identity as a writer and as a woman. He understood her ambivalence about a single-mindedly literary life and urged her to avoid the total immersion she had experienced so far. She ought, he advised,

> to get yourself a community of your own where people would care for you as a person not as a writer, to develop an interest in a career other than writing (I said that being liked because one is a good writer is the same as being liked because one has a handsome face), to begin to make a life of your own. . . . You will have to develop a sense of irony toward yourself and your life that few people would recognize as human. In the end you will be much more than you have ever before been. You'll no longer be JEAN STAFFORD or MRS. LOWELL. You'll be that girl in that picture holding the prize won in the essay contest. As I remember her eyes, they were evaluating her experience with a child's objectivity.

Taylor invoked an ancient but appropriate moment: Stafford at fifteen, when her essay "Disenchantment" had been awarded first prize in a statewide competition among high school students. That disenchantment was with her father, who had uprooted his family and consigned them to a life of boardinghouse instability. She had been able to turn a sense of loss into polished satire and had apparently taken her prize in the same spirit of calm detachment and control. What her father, the villain of the piece, might have thought of it all did not ruffle her. Neither did the fact of the prize.

It was not a poise that came so easily to her in Payne Whitney after the great disenchantment with Lowell. She had lost yet another home, which, as Stafford wrote to Taylor, was much more than a beloved house: "a symbol to me of all I ever wanted, it is the symbol of my marriage to him which I wanted, I desperately wanted to be complete." She was frantic in the face of her abandonment by Lowell, who apparently came to the hospital only rarely. Other friends did make regular visits, which she awaited eagerly, but she needed some reaction from him, some contact, to stave off thorough disorientation: "I must be believed in," she wrote to

Cal, "you must believe in my objective existence." She sent the same message to Taylor. "Once again I have been visited by the fear . . . that I have no objective existence. . . . I continue to pray . . . for the realization at last [from Cal] that I am in a *hospital,* that I am *sick,* that I am a woman, that I am a reality and not an abstraction. . . ." (She took one occasion, the publication in *The Nation* of his poem "Her Dead Brother," with its suggestion of sibling incest, as a rare communication from him—precisely the kind that proved his utter insensitivity, for she felt he had plundered and slandered her life. The poem "appearing in the Nation a week before the publication of my book with its dedication [to Lowell and her brother, Dick], with its theme of latent incest, at a time when you have left me and I am in the hospital," she raged, "seems to me an act of so deep dishonor that it passes beyond dishonor and approaches madness. And I am trembling in this presence of your hate.")

Gone was the child's self-sufficient objectivity. In the many agonized letters Stafford sent to Lowell, she constantly looked to him for an acknowledgment of her unliterary, feminine identity—an identity she felt he had always rejected. She tried again and again to explain to him the sense of extraliterary integrity that was so important to her, and her insistence suggests that it wasn't just Lowell she had to convince, but herself as well. "Cal, let me point out one thing finally," she wrote to him at one point:

> In your letter you say that you hope I will be recognized as the best novelist of my generation. I want you to know now and know completely that that would mean to me absolutely *nothing.* I respect myself as a workman and as a human being and what I have done, I have done to save myself for myself. I shall be grateful for whatever praise I get, but I shall never be so confused as to think that this is life or that, if one looks closely, it bears any resemblance to life.

Stafford was struggling to define herself on more stable and ordinary ground as the celebrated Stafford-Lowell literary and marital alliance dissolved. (Their reputation was far-flung: Cyril Connolly, surveying the American scene in 1947, reported that "last year's authors . . . are pushed aside and this year's—the novelist Jean Stafford, her poet husband Robert Lowell or the dark horse, Truman Capote—are invariably mentioned.") She was insecure about sustaining on her own the intense creative ambition that Lowell had brought to their life together. "I am only a part of Cal's very fabulous life and a time will come when I shall be glad that my role was taken away," she wrote in an elegiac vein to Cecile Starr from the hospital. But her assertion of simple humanity was far from merely defensive. She was also trying to clarify what she saw as a dangerous confusion between art and life that she identified in Lowell—and that had lurked behind some of the tensions of their marriage. "I have never, as you well enough know, regarded my writing as being as important as yours," she wrote to him. "But now, while this is still true, I regard myself as being as important as a *writer* as you. I am, I mean, as valuable a human being whose vocation happens to be writing." She was trying to assert the existence of values that arguably transcended even the most obsessive dedication to art; not all of life could be subordinated to art, made mere grist for the creative spirit. It was not the last time Lowell heard that plea from a wife.

As perhaps the most painful letter of the painful correspondence suggests, the truth was that Stafford desperately needed some confirmation that she was in fact a valuable human being. "What do I care if Randall likes my book? Or anyone? Why should it console me to be praised as a good writer?" she challenged Lowell, rejecting what must have been his offers of literary praise. Those were no substitute for love withdrawn— were in fact only reminders of what she was missing. "These stripped bones are not enough to feed a starving woman. I know this, Cal, and the knowledge eats me like an inward animal: there is no thing worse for a woman than to be deprived of her womanliness. For me, there is nothing worse than the knowledge that life holds nothing for me but being a writer." It was a version of the declarations she had made to Hightower years before in the stream of letters she had sent him from Iowa—that within her hid a needy feminine nature, waiting to blossom.

Now, as then, it was as if she hoped that by proclaiming her womanliness, her ripeness for love, she could call those qualities into being. What seemed to lurk behind her pronouncements was a fear that Lowell had put into words. He had left her, Stafford confided to Peter Taylor, saying that she was "incapable of being loved by anyone." It was a devastating verdict that summed up all of her doubts about any extraliterary life as a wife and, perhaps, mother. Citing those fears, which Taylor the faithful intermediary clearly understood, he urged Lowell to wait on a divorce: "Jean has suffered a lot in her lifetime from the feeling that she is unwanted. It is a theme she returns to in her conversation and in her writing. The effect of a divorce on her might be disastrous."

The problem, as Stafford recognized, was not one-sided or new. It was another pattern, one she knew all too well. She acknowledged just how difficult she found any real intimacy, and despite her professed interest in children, she must have sensed—as she later said—how ill suited she was for motherhood. ("I love children," she wrote toward the end of her life, "but I chose to have none because I knew I would be an abominable mother, by turns indulgent and cold.") Not long after her separation from Lowell, she confessed in her journal a sense of fraudulence in her expressions of love. "I have never been able to demonstrate love except when I have been drunk and the love I have shown then has been trumped up out of the bottle." It wasn't just drink but also, as her letters to Lowell and to Hightower revealed, emotional crises that brought out the protestations of love so extreme and elaborate that they couldn't help seeming false.

Stafford had plenty of occasion in the hospital to meditate on the sources of feeling unwanted, and she traced the sense of loveless isolation to her past. That seemed to be Stafford's dominant memory of her family life—though she was the first to admit, as she did in a letter to Mary Lou Aswell, her friend and an editor at *Harper's Bazaar,* that her memories, however intense, were not the most reliable: "Partly because I was born with a monstrous talent for exaggeration and partly because I write fiction, I am never the least bit sure whether I am telling the truth in all these explorations of the past." And she was prepared to acknowledge that rejection on her part, not just on theirs, had played a significant role in the estrangement she felt.

STAFFORD'S EXPLORATIONS of the past led her outside the walls of Payne Whitney twice in 1947. Both journeys revealed just how ensnared she still was in the unhappy patterns she had hoped to escape, and she hurried back to the protection of her doctors, overwhelmed by the need to drink. In February Stafford received the news that her mother was dying and, full of apprehensions about whether she was up to the trip, she got permission from the hospital to fly out to Oregon. By the time Stafford arrived, her mother had died of malignant melanoma, and she remained to mourn with the assembled family. It was a trauma that brought back her family past even more vividly, and Stafford's response—like her reaction to so much else during that difficult time—could hardly have been more ambivalent. She said she experienced a transcendent reconciliation with her mother, speaking of it in both mystical and psychological terms. On a page of her diary headed "My mother's death," she experimented with some lyrical imagery: "A mind, no more inseparable from its body than a pilot from his plane, sang in its bone-cell: DEUS TE AMO. Purblind it nosed like a mole through splendid mansions, hearing a chorus in ecstasy, within an inch of god." She clarified her experience in a letter to Lowell: "I received (and I do not use the word inaccurately) a kind of spiritual and consuming rapture that I had never known before in all my life; freed of guilt toward my mother, I was free to love her and to take a most wonderful joy in her peaceful death and I myself felt no fear, no hatred, nothing but this tranquil exaltation and the certain knowledge that I was prepared to die." To Taylor, she spoke in more standard therapeutic terms: "I grieve that I did not get there to efface my past unkindness, but my guilt is leaving me slowly and this time I am not hurting myself. I know this sounds unfeeling, as if I counted myself the most important person—yet, curiously, in forgiving myself at last, at last I love my mother."

Yet Stafford's claim to have been liberated from guilt about her mother had a hollow ring—further protestations of newfound intimacy grounded more in rhetoric than reality. It was clear that she also continued to feel trapped in the old, antagonistic way. A journal entry apparently written shortly after her mother's funeral, as Stafford looked forward to leaving Oregon, showed how susceptible she was to a return of the intolerance and insecurity that had made her adolescence at home such an ordeal. Despite the years she had spent far from home, her family could still promptly reduce Stafford to the resentful youngest child; the past, however completely she had aimed to put it behind her, was always there just below the surface, poised to engulf her again. She began her journal striving for mature distance—and then failed to find a merciful vantage point:

> I try to see under the bad taste to the poverty beneath and under the inhumanity to the misfortune, but it seems as willful and senseless as it ever did. My father has never been more stunningly boring. His larger-than-life-size conception of his role in Mother's illness maddens me in the terrible and familiar way and I feel a

perfect bitch because I am unable to make allowances for his grief
and loneliness. . . . In his egomaniacal hatred of doctors (and I am
shaken with fury to remember such things as the sewing machine
needle in my finger and the blister he would not believe was anything but a blister and each day he lanced it with a blunted bodkin)
he would not give her the medicines that had been ordered.

Her memory was "pitiless," she had written to Lowell, and as the rest of
the passage revealed, Stafford couldn't help reverting completely to her
childhood role:

It is assumed by my father and by Margie that I will come out here
to live. . . . Margie is such a hopeless fool. . . . She said at once that I
had got fat (at this point my father looked at me the way he has
always looked at me, as if I were a large dog or a small horse, and
observed that I had, indeed, got fat and he fancied I was almost as
tall as he. I have been four inches taller than he since I was seventeen years old) and she immediately revived the childhood jokes
about rubber underwear for me and reducing pills and phonograph
records of reducing exercises and I responded inwardly in the
childish way and wanted to pull her hair. . . . She went on from my
obesity to the fact that I was adopted and would presently be kidnapped.

It is not hard to read the journal entry for telltale references to some
of Stafford's lifelong preoccupations and problems—her dependence on
doctors, her ambivalence about food, and her search for surrogate-
daughter relationships. Her responses to the ancient feeling of being
unwanted were open, as Stafford would probably have appreciated, to
less-than-subtle analysis. ("Deep-rooted as it all is," she wrote to Taylor
of her propensity to feel rejected, "it appears to me at least to be so clear-
cut a kind of perversity, so really up the alley of psychiatry that it
shouldn't be too hard for them to help me.") Her cold father disapproved
and deprived his family of doctors; his daughter sought paternal reassur-
ance in doctors. Her sisters teased her about fatness (while her round
mother urged food on her family); she became a "problem feeder." They
suggested that she didn't belong; she set about proving that she was an
outsider.

And yet, as the next few sentences in her journal showed, this defiant
self-definition left Stafford feeling as stranded as ever: "There are no

pictures at all of me in the album," she wrote—she had evidently spent time perusing the family record—"except for one in which I am dressed in some man's clothes . . . and my father's hat and am carrying his black-thorn stick. This is my father's favorite picture in the album." The picture was the one of Stafford dressed up as a literary agent come to deliver her father to fame and fortune, a picture that he loved more and more as time passed and that Stafford liked less and less.

It was a photograph that exposed his delusions, delusions that she felt had destroyed the family's life; and it implicated her in his fantasy. Writing to Mary Lee from the hospital shortly after the Oregon visit, Stafford expressed the worst version of her fears: that, like the literary agent in the picture, she should devote her life to her now-solitary father—the nightmare she had tried to escape by leaving home as soon as she could. "I felt awful about Dad and I still do. Wrong as it is and always has been, it still isn't possible not to feel torn to pieces by the spectacle of his loneliness and I only hope, for everyone's sake, that it will not last long," she wrote, sounding more sympathetic than she had in her journal. But even if her embittered seventy-two-year-old father lingered on only a short time, she couldn't face it, a confession she relegated to a footnote, though the message was clearly more than an afterthought: "PS: I know I should go out there and keep house and I suppose that by not going I will be tormented with the guilt I *should* feel and won't as much as I would be if I went. But I know that I couldn't live with him without drinking."

The other trauma of the spring was a trip up to Damariscotta Mills to prepare to sell the house, a trip that left her, she wrote to Taylor, "mutilated with woe." She couldn't face that without drinking either, she confessed to Cecile Starr, describing her collapse: "Faced with its loveliness (I never owned anything so beautiful, nothing was ever so completely *mine* as that house and those trees and those marvelous scenes from all the windows) and with all the misery that my pitiless memory disinterred for me, I could feel myself falling headlong and helplessly. . . ." The journey wasn't made any easier by the knowledge that Lowell was celebrating great literary success with the publication of *Lord Weary's Castle* (he was awarded a Pulitzer that spring, along with a Guggenheim and an award from the National Institute of Arts and Letters) just as she was commemorating their marital failure with her trip back to the castle. "The pictures of him that one sees in all the papers are not the pictures of my husband but of someone else, a professional poet," she wrote to

Taylor, sounding slightly stunned. To Mary Lee, she allowed herself to sound more thoroughly devastated: "I went alone . . . and all the anguish of last autumn—and the whole summer and last spring—came back . . . in all the cold and desertion at the very same time that Cal was coming joyfully into all his national glory." She retreated to the hospital to mend.

And sometimes, as she wrote to Lowell, even the hospital didn't seem a remote enough sanctuary. The seductive exile she had created for Sonie in her novel was one that she herself was tempted by. Sonie's Boston adventure had driven her to seek refuge in her "red room," a prophecy of Stafford's own response. But unlike her fictional character, she struggled against succumbing to her desire for total isolation. "It would be, right now, easy for me to enter the Red Room and to shut the door tightly and forever," she wrote to Cal, knowing that he was familiar with the terrain of her spiritual landscape:

> When I told you long ago that if I had been instructed by a particular priest, I could have become a nun, I was not making a schoolgirlish and self-dramatizing statement, but the truth of it has never been more real to me than it is now. Far as I have retreated already, I wish to retreat ever farther. It is my courage which operates in spite of me that keeps me here where some business, little as it is, of the world intrudes.

THE ALLURES AND DANGERS of transcendent retreat were a theme not just of *Boston Adventure.* In *The Mountain Lion,* Stafford had created in Molly a far more unworldly ascetic than Sonie; she was a child who might have become a nun, who turned away from the corruptions of the world to the loneliness of her own mind. And the theme was at the heart of her story "The Interior Castle," which came out in *Partisan Review* in the winter of 1946, as Stafford was entering the hospital. In fact, it had been in a draft of that story, six years earlier, that she had first begun exploring concrete, literary expression for the symbolic inner chamber that became a centerpiece of her work. Another pattern asserted itself: this story inspired by Stafford's first hospital ordeal in late 1938 and 1939, after she and Lowell had run into a wall, appeared during her subsequent hospital stint, after she and Lowell had encountered a different kind of wall. It seems likely that she had been reworking the story during the year before, a time of confusion when it was becoming ever clearer that the chambers of Damariscotta Mills were unlikely to offer the refuge she had dreamed of—and when, as "An Influx of Poets" attests in retrospect and various letters suggest, the allure of retreat to the chamber of her own head was irresistible. She had resorted to an anesthetic readily available outside the hospital, alcohol. But her drinking did not, evidently, impede the revisions that produced perhaps her best short story.

In "The Interior Castle" Stafford took the advice that Evelyn Scott had offered years earlier, dispensing with much of the Latinate abstraction and refining the concrete description of the protagonist's ordeal. It was the author of *The Mountain Lion* at work, letting symbols emerge naturally from specifics, making an abstraction like pain speak through physical details; with unerring intensity, she worked metaphor and simile hard. Stafford stepped further back from her protagonist, now given the exotic name of Pansy Vanneman, and thus gained objectivity, though not at the expense of vividness: it is difficult to read Stafford's account of knives ravaging Pansy's nose and skull without cringing.

Her distance did, however, introduce a new note of skepticism into the story. There was irony in Stafford's perspective on Pansy's arrogant zeal for retreat, a suggestion that the glorious inner chamber she visualized was perhaps not the ideal escape from pain and the lesser distractions of the mundane world that Pansy assumed it would be. At the same time that Stafford lavished perfect prose on the chamber, she implied a solipsistic inadequacy in it:

> What Pansy thought of all the time was her own brain. Not only the brain as the seat of consciousness, but the physical organ itself which she envisaged, romantically, now as a jewel, now as a flower, now as a light in a glass, now as an envelope of rosy vellum containing other envelopes, one within the other, diminishing infinitely. It was always pink and always fragile, always deeply interior and invaluable. She believed that she had reached the innermost chamber of knowledge and that perhaps her knowledge was the same as the saint's achievement of pure love. It was only convention, she thought, that made one say "sacred heart" and not "sacred brain."

There was something loveless in Pansy's worship of her own head, and the conclusion of her quest took a turn rather different from Stafford's original ending. Pansy's revelation was the product of resignation, as St. Teresa instructed, but this time it was not eager acquiescence to God's will but reluctant acquiescence to the claims of the world. Pansy's glimpse of her inner treasure came only after she had bowed to the doctor's designs, recognizing that "the time would come when she could no longer live in seclusion, she must go into the world again and must be equipped to live in it; she banally acknowledged that she must be able to breathe." She had her moment of ecstatic repose, her visit to the "red room": "This time alone she saw her brain lying in a shell-pink satin case. It was a pink pearl.... It grew larger and larger until it was an enormous bubble that contained the surgeon and the whole room within its rosy luster." Unlike the story of six years before, which left the patient with her "agony's wonderfully perfect pearl," Pansy was only granted a moment to marvel that "never had the quiet been so smooth." The self-important world intruded, and in the closing sentence, Pansy was left disenchanted: "She closed her eyes, shutting herself up within her treasureless head." Transcendence or retreat could only be transitory relief, Stafford suggested with great ambivalence; the story conveyed bitter impatience with life in the trivial world, yet also doubt about life in the solitary head.

A therapeutic realism had diluted her former spiritual rigor, as Stafford acknowledged in an article that stands as a companion piece to "The Interior Castle." Aside from two other short stories ("The Hope Chest," about a crabbed old woman's loneliness, which appeared in *Harper's* in January 1947, and a story set in the West called "A Slight Maneuver," which *Mademoiselle* printed a month later, both interesting mostly as variations on themes Stafford dealt with more successfully elsewhere), the only writing of hers to appear that year was in a new vein: journalism. As she did later in life, she turned to outlets worlds away from the *Partisan Review* end of the magazine spectrum, obviously with money foremost in mind.

The piece she wrote for *Vogue,* which came out in the October 15, 1947, issue, shortly before she was released from Payne Whitney, was hardly a conventional women's magazine article. An account of her battle with insomnia, "My Sleep Grew Shy of Me" was a short tour of St. Teresa's *Interior Castle,* to which Stafford credited her cure—not exactly the sort of thing *Vogue*'s readers were used to. It was a harbinger of some of Stafford's later journalism, in which she domesticated her own ordeals, transforming personal difficulties into occasions for idiosyncratic advice columns. In this case, her mental breakdown was reduced to a sleeping problem, which certainly had been a part of her agonies, but hardly the whole.

Stafford wrote as though her troubles were long behind her. It was a confident tone adopted for her audience, and it glossed over the sense of precariousness she acknowledged to friends on leaving the hospital that fall. Her style was deliberately archaic and poetic, the appropriate accompaniment to her anachronistic cure: "And now that my insomnia has passed, I have liked to borrow [St. Teresa's] divine figure in my profane reflections and similarly to see myself moving at a snail's pace from the exterior wasteland where I kept a violent vigil to the safe place where I now sleep." Stafford traced her progression from mansion to mansion, describing the transformations in her attitude that permitted her gradual penetration to the inner sanctums.

It was as though she were laying bare the outline that guided the shaping of "The Interior Castle," doing the close reading of St. Teresa that preceded her far freer use of the saint's work in her fiction. She explicitly addressed the analogies she used to such powerful effect in the story: the relation between a literary and religious perspective on the one hand and a medical approach on the other, between illness as a figurative and as a physical state. Her article described the evolution of her views that seemed to be reflected in the second version of "The Interior Castle," a journey toward greater acceptance of a therapeutic, psychological understanding of her plight. It culminated in an embrace of the merciful science she had discovered: "I honored the good practice of psychiatry as I had heretofore only honored religion and the arts, and [began] to see that its intention is profoundly moral in the most splendid and intelligent sense because it aims to create happiness."

Its aim, she understood, was to return her to the world, which meant that she could not linger in the Fifth Mansion, of "convalescence, the charming antechamber to health." Its allures were great, and Stafford recognized her special susceptibility to them. She needed urging to relinquish its lovely oblivion: "Perhaps this is the happiest house of all to live in because there is an immediate contentment, a sort of rapturous anaesthesia." But she did move on, and her description of the final chamber avoided the ambivalence in her story. She offered the upbeat resolution suitable for *Vogue*. The chamber was neither a dangerous cloister nor a mere way station before rejoining the clamorous world. Instead, there was a perfect poise: "Tumult seldom penetrates the walls of the interior castle which is, I find, in an ambiguous situation for, although it is very much *within* and I am very much the sole owner of it, the prospect it commands is of reality and of the world and of all the possibilities of experience which I had believed I had forsworn forever."

This public, confident optimism of the cured patient, ready to reenter the world, was in stark contrast to the private fears Stafford confided to her journal in the spring: "I have been here now seven months. Certainly I did not dream that I would see the leaves turn green when I saw them red in the fall. And even now, after all this time, I do not know where it will end nor how. I do not remember how one starts again and this is the hardest time of all, since I have left behind no life-lines." Death had evidently not been far from her mind. Returning to life was not going to be easy.

As SHE PREPARED to leave the hospital, Stafford sounded less certain in her letters about her readiness to face "the possibilities of experience" than she had in *Vogue*. Understandably enough, she was on the defensive. She was worried about money, burdened by medical bills she couldn't possibly pay and bitter about an estranged husband from whom she could expect next to no alimony (at that point Lowell had agreed to five thousand dollars over ten years). And she was anxious about the reception she could expect from her and Cal's friends. Supplanted by Gertrude Buckman (whom Lowell talked of marrying) and tainted by her psychological troubles, would she now be the woman everyone wanted to avoid? In a particularly distraught letter to Lowell, she put her predicament in extreme, general terms. She would be emerging "without money and without friends and this is harder for a woman than for a man," she wrote. She despaired of being able to pick up where she had left off: "A man who is called a scoundrel remains, to most people, attractive. . . . A woman who has spent nearly a year in a hospital with a sickness of the spirit has, with the people she has known before, an ineradicable black mark. Who would wish to know me? Because I am defeated and miserable, I cannot be appealing."

But she was leaving the hospital because her doctors judged her to have surmounted the worst of her defeat and misery, and in her more self-confident moments Stafford managed a quite different perspective on her situation. She announced that a break with that past was precisely the liberation she needed. Essential to her cure, she decided, was distance from the close-knit literary circles she and Lowell had been caught up in since their marriage. She had never felt comfortable as part of a literary cabal, as she now characterized both their friends from southern days and from the *Partisan Review* set. The competitive, claustrophobic spirit of those associations, she concluded, had played no small part in bringing on the troubles she was only now slowly recovering from. ("Bring a number of talented people together in a close area, and the neurotic tremors begin vibrating," William Barrett commented of the *PR* crowd. "Americans, who have less of a tradition of the salon or literary circle, fling themselves at the business with greater innocence—and violence.") In a letter to Peter Taylor over the summer, Stafford credited her new understanding of her unhappiness to her doctors. In fact, the revelation was not new. Long ago—in Baton Rouge—she had linked her fevers and her thirst for alcohol with too many intimidating friends who were obsessed with books and were brutal, or at least not gentle, with people. "I have been grateful, in this year, to be treated by my doctor as a human being and not as a writer and not as an outsider," she wrote to Taylor; "if I can only remember how wonderful this relationship has been, I think I shall be able to protect myself from those situations in which I become shy and suspicious that I am being battened on because I have a small reputation or in which I am tormented because I do not 'belong.'"

Not uncharacteristically, Stafford was overstating a transition in her life. To be a writer and an outsider had not simply been the destructive identity she suggested. On the contrary, it had been a mark of distinction. She had struggled for years to put her imagination and sense of alienation to creative use, and in her heady literary life with Lowell she had found a path that led not to the frustrated marginality she saw in her father but to an influential elitism. She had deliberately sought connection with Lowell's "very fabulous life," as she had confessed to Hightower; she herself had battened on associations that carried with them some reputation, social or literary. Once arrived, she had mostly wittily, sometimes anxiously, cultivated the acerbic profile of outsider.

The question facing her was how to follow the counsel that Peter Taylor had given her a year before, which fit with her own diagnosis—how to find "a community ... where people would care for [her] as a person not as a writer, [how] to develop an interest in a career other than writing ... to begin to make a life of [her] own." As she had acknowledged in her article for *Vogue,* her convalescent dependence on doctors had to end, or at least significantly diminish. She left Payne Whitney in November 1947 and moved to an apartment at 27 West Seventy-fifth Street, reassured that her sessions with Dr. Sherfey would continue, but unclear about what shape the rest of her life might take, whether she could control her drinking, whether she would write again. Lacking a new circle to turn to, she was immediately preoccupied with gingerly adjusting her relations to her old friends, determined to avoid her former role.

Cecile Starr was once again the loyal, nonliterary friend whom she counted on for help through a difficult transition, and who readily obliged. She had already been preparing the way before Stafford's release, holding a party for her in the spring. Stafford's poise had been precarious then and continued to be tenuous. She crumbled when Caroline Gordon unexpectedly appeared (her promised absence, Stafford claimed, had been what convinced her to venture out). Just how unsettling the encounter was for her was suggested by a letter about the gathering that Stafford wrote to Lowell, with whom she was still in frequent, but now much calmer, contact. "It was more than just seeing Caroline," she explained:

> it was realizing how you and I together, unable to grapple with the enormous complexity of our problems, took refuge from them in other people—and often it did not matter who the people were. We could not be blamed for that; the Tates, when we first knew them, were delightful company, they were wise critics, they were helpful, they seemed really fond of us, and I think that in a way, Caroline is still fond of us . . . and that her questioning me about where I lived was not altogether malicious. I remembered the anguish of the year in Tennessee and I was struck in a heap to think of how Caroline had always said she thought of us as her children, because we *were* children, we have been everyone's children.

Running into the Rahvs evoked comparably bad memories. When Stafford saw Natalie on the street one day, she had "a fit of trembling and terror," she wrote to Lowell. Meeting Philip on another occasion, she promptly wrote to Peter Taylor that the encounter "returned to me a whole world of tiresomeness, of a thousand and one nights of nothing wonderful but only the most sterile talk about writers and their private lives." They invited her to a party to meet Arthur Koestler, and she realized with great relief that there was no reason she had to go or feel guilty about not going; she could, and did, decline and counted it a major step in her development.

But the biggest step was cultivating another community. Out of the hospital, Stafford began going to Columbia to take science courses, which she explained in part as research for her Lucy novel, *In the Snowfall*—a refresher course on collegiate life to help her with her setting. But the new regimen seems mostly to have been a determined effort to sample the nonliterary life. "I am studying Botany and genetics and I enjoy it very much indeed," Stafford wrote to Lowell. "I find scientists much more interesting than writers and my favorite new word is 'skeptical.'" As she no doubt hoped, her preference roused Lowell to a defense of literature, but she was undaunted, and quite entertaining, in her newfound love of the laboratory: "I have never felt so liberated in all my life and some time I should like you to be introduced to the glories of my new study: you would see what I meant if you were to watch a great blob of plasmodium feeding upon a fungus." In fact, her studies didn't last very long. Toward the spring of 1948 she confessed to Lowell that the experiment hadn't really taken: "You will be as pleased as I am to know that I have had to give up the science. I was not understanding Whitehead and was feeling sick with guilt for not doing so (as I was always guilty for not reading Catholic apologetics even after you'd given up trying to improve my mind) so that I was getting no writing done."

More important was her friendship with Dr. Alfred Cohn, a cardiologist in his late sixties who was affiliated with the Rockefeller Institute. He knew several friends of hers—he had published a book with Robert Giroux and had been a teacher of Henry Murray, the doctor whom Stafford counted as "the first of [her] saviours" during the fall of 1946 (and whom she also saw several times after leaving the hospital). "Dr. Cohn," Stafford reported to Lowell, "is directing my scientific re-education," but the relationship was more lasting than her dabbling at Columbia. Cohn was smitten with Stafford, who in turn was flattered by the attentions of the older, elegant man, and the two of them took to having tea at the Plaza regularly. Owner of a great library (which he bequeathed to the Rockefeller Institute), Dr. Cohn was hardly an unliterary companion. But he was part of the medical world and he was a careful, unthreatening friend. He seems to have understood that Stafford didn't need yet another judgmental mentor—understood it better, in fact, than Stafford sometimes did, lapsing into her old insecure role. "Before we meet on Friday I must prepare you for the fact that I am a strict contender for your friendship," he wrote to her with the formality of a suitor, "but that I cannot accept the responsibility of being a superego—and so I am not for anything that betters you or interferes with the free play of your faculties."

Stafford was far from sure that she had found a haven to replace the hospital, and her confidence ebbed and flowed. "It has been rather rough and on the whole I hated the loss of all that calm and all that protection," she wrote to Lowell after being out of Payne Whitney for about a month. "Terribly slowly and terribly wonderfully, I am growing up. I have days of terror and on those days I talk only bombast to Dr. Sherfey (at last she has really used that word and said—but most compassionately—that my rhetoric frequently slows up the interviews). . . . But on the whole I am happy, or, at least, I know what happiness is." She resisted grand claims of recovery, recognizing that the year was a transition, not an arrival. She acknowledged that she was balanced uneasily between new friends and old ones. "I cannot truly feel that this life of being made over by men old enough to be my fathers and grandfathers is the right one, but it is a pleasant and a very *safe* stopgap," she wrote to Lowell, while admitting to Taylor that she hadn't left the old dangerous life behind: "Alas, I am still weak and foolish, and I still have a mortal fear of such people from the past as Allen and Caroline and all the cut-throats from Partisan Review."

STAFFORD'S REACTION to her insecurity was not, however, to retreat; she did not play the fragile convalescent that year. In fact, in the writing she immediately began doing, she took on precisely the difficult subjects she might have been expected to evade: her hospital experience and her ambivalence about her old friends and mentors. And she did it in settings that seemed least likely to put her at her ease. Right after emerging from Payne Whitney, she shared the podium with Lionel Trilling at Bard College's Conference on the Novel and delivered a lecture entitled "The Psychological Novel." She never liked speaking before the public. The critic's authority didn't come naturally to her even under the best of circumstances. Yet she ventured in front of an audience featuring some of those *Partisan Review* cutthroats to offer her views on a general subject— creativity and psychological instability—that not only was a live debate in that magazine's pages but also touched very close to home for Stafford. Trilling's "Art and Neurosis" had appeared in *PR* two years before, and William Barrett's "Writers and Madness" in the January-February issue of 1947. They were intimidating predecessors who had scrutinized Freud with a rigor she hadn't. Her claim to special expertise on the subject was a highly sensitive one: she was a writer who had just spent a year in Payne Whitney.

It was a traumatic reentry, Stafford wrote to Lowell: "I went to Bard to lecture and nearly died of terror (for no humane reason Mary Mc-Carthy and Bowdoin Broadwater [McCarthy's husband] came on and sat in the front row grinning like cats). . . . I hated it all and vowed never again to leave my red room for a public appearance." As she described it, McCarthy fulfilled her fears about the ruthless condescension of the "Rahv set." "Her one comment on my lecture, delivered with all her ignited ice, was 'your speech had a great deal of charm.' I wanted, almost, to reply that I was glad, that to be a charming woman was my principal ambition." Stafford's imagined reply was not simply sarcastic. In the wake of her collapse, she spoke up increasingly for civility and decorum, which seemed to her antithetical to the style of her old company. She wanted, as she wrote to Lowell at one point, to live henceforth at a "low pitch." Among her aims was to avoid the raw confrontation and scrutiny, and the intellectual intensity, that she had known all too well with the Tates and then the *PR* circle.

At the same time, she wasn't ready to be dismissed by them as merely charming, and worried about the reception of her lecture. She protectively played it down as a trifle, though clearly seeking approval. "[My lecture] is so foolish and unmeaning that I am ashamed to show it to anyone, but I am obliged to and I promised them that I would write and ask you if you would take a look at it," she wrote with overeffusive modesty to John Crowe Ransom, inquiring about the possibility of publishing it in the *Kenyon Review*. He accepted the piece, and she wrote to Lowell, obviously proud but still playing the apprehensive critical amateur: "Uncle Ransom is printing the lecture I gave at Bard and I am thoroughly unhappy about it because it is so awfully bad. . . . He wrote a very nice note on a penny postal saying it was 'belletristic if not academic.' I dread your reading it."

The lecture certainly made no pretense to rigorous argumentation. In it there were signs of the persona that was to acquire more caricatured proportions in Stafford's nonfiction writing later in life: the arch, opinionated commentator who took pleasure in bucking the contemporary tide, airing her old-fashioned views with vigor and humor. Stafford presented herself not as a professional critic prepared to make an erudite, abstract case, but simply as a writer who had briefly emerged from solitude to share some personal thoughts. But she was by no means interested in claiming creative-soul status for herself; she was a craftsman with down-to-earth advice and thoughts about her métier. And she was also a civilized reader in search of good literature and impatient with indulgent displays. With her characteristic blend of ornate and colloquial language, she managed at once to sound like a fusty older lady and a clear-eyed, unpretentious scout for the literate public.

Above all, what she didn't sound like was a neurotic writer—"loutishly well-adjusted," she referred to herself at one point—which was in itself a comment on her theme. The fact that novels deal in human psychology should not, she argued, mean that they become occasions for exposing personal perversities. "It is fashionable to be forthrightly and ungraciously autobiographical as if Freud had come as the emancipator of the skeleton in the closet," she chided. "It would be hard to count the novels of recent years which have been strip-tease acts in the psychiatric ward or on the psychoanalyst's couch." From that it followed (by way of a droll anecdote about a mailing she received requesting her to become a contributor to a new quarterly called *Neurotica*) that she had no truck with the assumption that writers are by definition animated by "the drive toward being a misfit" (one subject on which *Neurotica* proposed that she write). Thus Stafford obliquely entered the Trilling-Barrett debate and aligned herself with Trilling, who argued that the artist is unique not by virtue of his neurosis but

> in the respect of his relation to his neurosis. He is what he is by virtue of his successful objectification of his neurosis, by his shaping it and making it available to others in a way which has its effect upon their own egos in struggle. His genius, that is, may be defined in terms of his faculties of perception, representation, and realization, and in these terms alone.

Stafford's formulation was not so impersonal; she was not simply defining but prescribing, as much to herself as to her audience. Distance from one's psychological and spiritual unhappiness was essential, she proclaimed, urging "detachment from our characters' eccentricities and mis-adventures that prevents us from making them into improbable prodigies but that, on the contrary, enables us to be psychologically sound." Her own early fictional efforts (which Whit Burnett had de-nounced as a "pocket of exhibitionistic self-abuse," calling her characters "repulsively damned") no doubt lurked behind this advice, which she amplified: "We must be experts in the study of reality and cool judges of our own natures. . . . If we . . . are wanting in irony and are servants of our own pride and prejudice rather than of our sense and sensibility, we may bog down in self-pity or we may distort our personal misfortune into polemic or our idiosyncrasy into gospel."

Though she hastened to say that she didn't mean that fiction should be circumscribed and tame, Stafford emerged as a champion of civility—and of charm. "Naturally I go on the assumption that I am in the society of people who want to be charming and who want to be good," she said, sounding her gentlewoman's note. Just as she had counseled against per-sonal exhibitionism, so toward the end of her lecture she warned against zealous social engagement. The disorder both of psyches and of the times called for formalist discipline, not full expression:

> It is true that if we ignore the horrifying wounds of our society, we will be irresponsible, but we will be equally irresponsible if we do nothing but angrily probe them to make them hurt all the more. . . . As human beings, and therefore as writers, we are confronted by wars and the wickedness that makes them, and the famine and disease and spiritual mutilations that follow them, by the ship-wreck of our manners and our morality, by an almost universal sickness of heart. . . . Still, we are not entitled to be slovenly and hysterical because the world is a mess nor to be incoherent because governments do not make sense.

As Stafford recognized, her message to writers implied a message to readers as well: that a writer's work not be taken as autobiography. De-fending one of her models, Henry James, against the critic Clifton Fadi-man's reductive reading of "The Jolly Corner," she lamented that his interpretation "lowers the story from its great stature as an imagined and constructed work of literature to . . . a public exhibition of James's private life. I do not say that Fadiman is altogether wrong but that he is not precise."

It was a far from systematic aesthetic, but Stafford's lecture foreshadowed a shift in her literary associations, an artistic parting of the ways with Lowell. She was distancing herself from the milieu and some of the artistic ambitions they had shared during their marriage, and so was he, though moving in a very different direction. The outlines of the shift look stark. Toward the end of 1947, Stafford began her decade-long close association with *The New Yorker,* a world away in sensibility from the *Partisan Review* and the quarterlies. During the 1950s she wrote one more novel, *The Catherine Wheel,* a circumscribed exploration of mental and emotional isolation, but her specialty became meticulously crafted short stories, renowned for their stylistic and structural polish, for their mercilessly ironic, detached treatment of states of alienation. She was moving further and further from *Boston Adventure,* her sprawling debut. By the last third of the 1950s, she had encountered a block and all but stopped publishing fiction.

Meanwhile, Lowell was turning away from the formalist vision of Tate and toward the more flexible notions of style and content he found in a new mentor, William Carlos Williams. Lowell struggled with a block through the 1950s after the publication in 1951 of *The Mills of the Kavanaughs*, in which it was clear that his early, fiercely formal style and religious themes were no longer the source of inspiration they had once been. By 1957, when he suddenly began feverish work on *Life Studies,* he had discovered a radically different style and subject matter, breaking away from the prosodic restraints that had guided his early poetry and turning to undisguised autobiographical themes. "At forty I've written my first unmeasured verse," he wrote to Williams of the breakthrough. "I've only tried it in a few of these poems, those that are the most personal. It's great to have no hurdle of rhyme and scansion between yourself and what you want to say most forcibly."

It is easy to make the divergence sound too schematically symmetrical, as if to suggest that before their separation, Stafford and Lowell were in some sort of literary tandem, and that they faced comparable creative challenges in their development as writers after that. That couldn't of course be said of any two writers, let alone a poet and a writer of fiction. And it would mistakenly imply a marked swerve in Stafford's literary allegiances and intentions that year after she emerged from the hospital. She clearly was aiming to reorient her writing life, but her sense that she hadn't been in her element, that she needed a change of scene, was hardly new. Beneath the witty, poised writer who had so impressed young Lowell, there had always been the girl from Colorado who felt she wasn't suited to compete in the ruthless literary circles of the New Critics and the New York intellectuals. What was new was Stafford's attitude toward her own discomfiture. The old insecure defensiveness had subsided somewhat. She was readier to take the ironic offensive and expose what seemed to her the heartless egotism and maliciousness too often associated with the intellectual intensity of her friends. The claims of genius, Stafford suggested, should leave room for gentility, or at least civility. She was prepared to assert the simpler values and more modest tone of the clear-eyed rube.

It was at *The New Yorker* that Stafford found a new circle where the ambience and expectations were more congenial. In December she sold a story to the magazine and signed a first reader agreement, giving the editors right of first refusal of pieces for a year and Stafford 25 percent above their usual rates. When she began writing for it, the magazine had emerged from World War II a considerably more serious publication than it had been when Harold Ross founded it in 1925, though there were plenty—including a fair sampling of Stafford's friends—who criticized its abiding frivolity. In *The Years with Ross,* James Thurber described the sensibility Ross brought to the place, a spirit that lingered on long after him. Although Ross "secretly enjoyed being thought of as raconteur and man about town, [he] was scared to death of being mistaken for a connoisseur, or an aesthete, or a scholar, and his heavy ingenuous Colorado hand was often laid violently upon anything that struck him as 'intellectual.'" His favorite genre was the "casual," and as Thurber explained, "the word 'casual' indicated Ross's determination to give the magazine an offhand, chatty, informal quality. Nothing was to be labored or studied, arty, literary, or intellectual."

Yet Ross also understood that for the magazine to be suitably urbane (it was, its prospectus had declared, "not edited for the old lady in Dubuque"), it required a defter touch than his own. He found the more cultivated collaborators he needed in Katharine White and later William Shawn, who nudged the magazine beyond humor to more serious, and lengthy, reporting and fiction. (Under Ross, Shawn recalled, "for many years the word 'literary,' applied to some piece of writing—including fiction—was a house pejorative.") Still, Ross and his original conception of the magazine were far from overshadowed. The tone of ingenuous urbanity, of the quaintly innocent provincial in the big city, continued to exert real influence. Shawn acknowledged the anti-intellectual ambience in his obituary for Ross, characterizing the founder's shaping hand and describing a substance and style still recognizable in the magazine today: "Because Ross was suspicious of 'thinking,' the magazine that he founded and edited did not publish either essays or what are called articles of opinion. It was, fundamentally, a magazine of reporting, humor, fiction, and criticism. . . . Ross was an editor who doted on immaculate writing and on stylish writing, which is to say writing that had style."

Shawn and Thurber obviously admired and helped perpetuate the urbane qualities they described as Ross's legacy, and it is not hard to imagine the rapport that seems to have sprung up between Stafford and Ross, who still had five years of editorship ahead of him when she began writing for the magazine. Displaced Coloradans, they both relished the incongruous identity of colloquial hick and obsessive stylist, rube and sophisticated raconteur, and Ross appreciated her wit. But Stafford's most important relationship at the magazine was with Katharine White, whose Bostonian gentility exerted a very different appeal. In her, Stafford found a devoted editor and a mother of sorts; and in Stafford, White found "one of her best friends among the contributors"—and "a remarkable reviser. Stories would come in with very hopeful material that hadn't quite jelled; and . . . over and over again I [would] ask her to rewrite a story, and over again she [did] so successfully."

The association was more than merely professional, as it was for most *New Yorker* writers. It was familial in a peculiar way that suited Stafford well. *New Yorker* writers were treated as though they were shy recluses in need of cosseting—that is, as though they were close relatives of the quintessential *New Yorker* character ("a vague, little man helplessly confused by a menacing and complicated civilization," was the way Wolcott Gibbs, an editor, described the typical, Thurber-inspired protagonist in the magazine's stories). It was very different from the cutthroat literary company Stafford was used to. Ross considered writers an exotic breed, usually crazy and certainly oversensitive, who had to be indulged. Katharine White, herself one of the breed, specialized in commiserating. She and her husband were well acquainted with suffering, real and imagined: their psychosomatic travails were legendary, but they also always had time to hear about others' troubles. She and Stafford sometimes conferred as intently about ailments as they did about fiction. It was a friendship that seems to have offered Stafford just what she needed after her experience with Lowell and the tragic rebel school: the solicitude and approval of a well-bred Bostonian with taste.

But as Stafford was well aware, her new affiliation was greeted with skepticism among some of her friends. It wasn't a great surprise when the old intimations of philistinism and middlebrowism that had been in the air after the success of *Boston Adventure* surfaced again. *The New Yorker* came in for a good dose of condescension and criticism from the *Partisan Review* and the literary quarterly writers. To be sure, as an influential and comparatively lucrative outlet for writing, it was not entirely dismissed: plenty of writers crossed the line by the 1940s. But even they were often ready with scorn. Edmund Wilson, who was reviewing books regularly for the magazine, delivered an unvarnished assessment of its shortcomings at just about the time Stafford was signing on. In a letter to Katharine White in November of 1947, he was merciless in his judgment of her fiction department, dismissing "the pointless and inane little anecdotes that are turned out by *The New Yorker*'s processing mill and that the reader forgets two minutes after he has read them."

Delmore Schwartz gave a similar critique in an essay called "Smile and Grin, Relax and Collapse," which came out three years later in *Partisan Review*. "It's easy to make fun of *The New Yorker*," he began, "especially since *The New Yorker* has taught us how to make fun of anything and everything." But he intended more serious scrutiny: the magazine's effect on literature, he announced, was "powerful and pernicious." He echoed Wilson on style, lamenting that "in *The New Yorker* you are supposed to be chatty, relaxed, not very serious, and certainly never (God forbid!) intellectual"; the point is to "seem elegant, charming, sophisticated, full of good manners and good taste." His indictment of the content of the magazine's fiction specified what he saw as the source of the "anecdotal" wanness of the genre: "The chief recent tendency ... has been to break down the short story as such into some form of memoir, reminiscence, or anecdote, especially about childhood or about one's dear, foolish, pathetic, and comical elders," he observed, arguing that the impulse affected even the best writers: "When good writers write for *The New Yorker*, they adopt attitudes and mannerisms which are absent from their serious writing elsewhere. ... Most of these writers are striving in one guise or another—or none at all—to write their memoirs, although they are writers who in their writings elsewhere manage to distinguish very well between fiction and personal history." He was ready to acknowledge that autobiography couldn't be banished altogether: "It is probably needless to say that personal experience, memory, and conversation, are often the beginning of fiction. But in *The New Yorker* it is swiftly becoming the end of fiction, in more ways than one."

Schwartz cited Stafford as one of the writers so afflicted (he also cited Peter Taylor, Vladimir Nabokov, and Carson McCullers, among others), and he may well have had in mind her debut in the magazine, "Children Are Bored on Sunday" (actually the second story she submitted), which appeared in February 1948. The story seems to have had as its inspiration an episode in Stafford's personal history that involved him, and rough autobiographical contours are easy enough to discern. But Stafford's accomplishment was precisely to avoid confining her account to chatty memoir. It is true that its ingredients are among the most transparently autobiographical Stafford ever used. She wrote about literary people, which she did nowhere else in any detail except in "An Influx of Poets," and she alluded to her breakdown. Her theme was close to home. In her protagonist Emma, she described a young woman's wary reemergence into New York life after an unspecified trauma, convinced that a "rube" like her was always going to feel "in alien corn" among her former intellectual set.

Yet it was far from a therapeutic confession of insecurity, sensitive though the subject must have been for Stafford that fall. Instead she managed to make it the occasion for, among other things, a detached portrait of her place in a larger literary and social setting. Stafford welded anecdotal fragments into an ironically accurate sociology of the New York literary milieu that both Schwartz and she knew well. What Stafford demonstrated in her story was the peculiar power of her outsider status to liberate her even as it isolated her. Neither an authentic intellectual nor really a rube, she could pass for either but wasn't herself fooled by her poses (in her fiction, at least, she wasn't fooled) and so could capture the view from both sides. The tension between the rustic and the sophisticate, the colloquial and the refined, had been a theme of her fiction since *Boston Adventure* and continued to be. In "Children Are Bored on Sunday" she addressed it in more explicitly literary terms than she had before, at a time when her own literary direction and style were newly in question. Distinctly not a *New Yorker* staple, Stafford's story examined the intellectual insecurities that urbanity was designed to deny.

The factual source of her fiction was apparently to be found in the autumn of 1946, in a chance encounter with Delmore Schwartz on the day she entered Payne Whitney. As she wrote to Lowell, it crystallized her predicament perfectly and hauntingly:

> The day I came in here, I had gone out of my hotel to get a blouse from the cleaners and I ran into Delmore. I walked to Washington Square with him and we sat there for a little while. He tried to find out where I had been and what I was doing, but I would not tell him. Would I have dinner with him that night? I said I was going somewhere at four o'clock. He said, "Where are you going? Maybe you shouldn't go there. You have been among strangers for a long time." I looked at him (he looked dreadful) and it seemed to me that he was *the* stranger, he was the embodiment of all the strangers I had been with for years and years.

It was one of those events that seem too literary to belong to real life—and yet it did. Still, it was too literary for literature, as Stafford wisely saw. In the story she ended up writing, the portentous tone was gone, the event itself was stripped down and relegated to the last third of the story, and the moral was transmuted. The face of Alfred Eisenburg, the Delmore Schwartz character in the story, "the last familiar face she had seen before she had closed the door of her tomb," evoked more complicated reactions in Emma, her autobiographical protagonist, than melodramatic recoil.

Writing in a more explicitly comic vein than she had before, Stafford called on perfectly chosen details to convey Emma's fascinated estrangement from "Eisenburg's milieu . . . of composers, of painters, of writers who pronounced judgments, in their individual argot, on Hindemith, Ernst, Sartre, on Beethoven, Rubens, Baudelaire, on Stalin and Freud and Kierkegaard, on Toynbee, Frazer, Thoreau, Franco, Salazar, Roosevelt, Maimonides, Racine, Wallace, Picasso, Henry Luce, Monsignor Sheen, the Atomic Energy Commission, and the movie industry." Amid this intimidating company, Emma moved "shaky with apprehensions and martinis, and with the belligerence of a child who feels himself laughed at"—and she watched everything. Along with a child's belligerence, she had the childish innocence that Stafford had proclaimed was the key to irony and to a kind of naïvely devastating insight.

In the first of the story's three sections, Emma was the bemused observer, wandering one Sunday through the Metropolitan Museum of Art, where she unexpectedly caught sight of Alfred Eisenburg. An old friend, he had dropped from view for a long time, and now his presence thoroughly distracted her from the paintings. She was invaded by thoughts of him and his "cunning" set, "on their guard and highly civilized, learnedly disputing on aesthetic and political subjects"—just the people Emma had hoped to put out of her mind and her life. But on this day, though she was still shaky at even the thought of her old company, she was suddenly and newly detached, able to play anthropologist. In a central passage she dissected the main ritual of the clan—the cocktail party, at which merciless gossip and deadly drinks flowed, and all too often "the cream of the enlightened was horribly curdled, and an argument would end, quite literally, in a bloody nose." Emma missed nothing:

> These cocktail parties were a modus vivendi in themselves for which a new philosophy, a new ethic, and a new etiquette had had to be devised. They were neither work nor play, and yet they were not at all beside the point but were, on the contrary, quite indispensable to the spiritual life of the artists who went to them. It was possible for Emma to see these occasions objectively, after these many months of abstention from them, but it was still not possible to understand them, for they were so special a case, and so unlike any parties she had known at home.

The key to Emma's perspective was her origins, which emerged in the second section of the story, as Stafford took the sociology a step further. As Emma saw it, the fact that she had grown up in a house and played among lilacs instead of living in an apartment accounted for the chasm that divided her from the New York intellectuals. While she was innocently savoring the simple pleasures of experience, they were cultivating "opinions on everything political and artistic and metaphysical and scientific." Her insecurity had a satiric edge. The humble hick poked some fun at the New Yorkers' poses as she lamented her lack of them: "Her pretensions needed brushing; her ambiguities needed to be cleaned; her evasions would have to be completely overhauled before she could face

again the terrifying learning of someone like Alfred Eisenburg, a learning whose components cohered into a central personality that was called
'intellectual.' ... This being an intellectual was not the same thing as
dilettantism; it was a calling in itself."

But the real interest of the story was that Emma's perspective was not
simply that of the rustic innocent. As she acknowledged, "she was not
even a bona-fide rube," which explained her keen insight into her erstwhile company. More important, her uneasy sophistication explained her
identity crisis, and that was what, it turned out, this deceptively casual
story was about. She blamed her education, which though it "had never
dissuaded her from her convictions," had nonetheless "ruined the looks
of her mind—painted the poor thing up until it looked like a mean,
hypocritical, promiscuous malcontent, a craven and apologetic fancy
woman." Stafford summed up Emma's dilemma with comic poignancy,
mixing vernacular and formal styles:

> Neither staunchly primitive nor confidently *au courant,* she rarely
> knew where she was at. And this was her Achilles' heel: her iden-
> tity was always mistaken, and she was thought to be an intellectual
> who, however, had not made the grade. It was no use now to cry
> out that she was not, that she was a simon-pure rube; not a soul
> would believe her. She knew, deeply and with horror, that she was
> thought merely stupid.

In the final section Stafford revealed the depth of Emma's crisis, drawing on her own nightmarish autumn—"the months of spreading, can-
cerous distrust, of anger that made her seasick, of grief that shook her
like an influenza chill, of the physical afflictions by which the poor victimized spirit sought vainly to wreck the arrogantly healthy flesh"—and
on the encounter with Delmore. Emma had been suffering from psychological and spiritual woes far deeper than social insecurity—and so, she
suddenly realized, had Alfred, who had the telltale shaky look. She was
seized with the desire to commune with him, but Stafford was strict
about the limited terms of the rapprochement. Ravaged rube and intellectual could innocently share their loneliness over an afternoon drink,
but they shouldn't imagine that neurosis was the ground for some ennobling union: "If only it could take place—this honeymoon of the
cripples, this nuptial consummation of the abandoned—while drinking
the delicious amber whisky in a joint with a jukebox, a stout barkeep,

and a handful of tottering derelicts; if it could take place, would it be possible to prevent him from marring it all by talking of secondary matters? That is, of art and neurosis, art and politics, art and science, art and religion?"

Wary of weightiness, Stafford studiously aimed at lyrical irony to culminate her story: "To [Emma's] own heart, which was shaped exactly like a valentine, there came a winglike palpitation, a delicate exigency, and all the fragrance of all the flowery springtime love affairs that ever were seemed waiting for them in the whisky bottle." It was a tone, not unlike the style of her Bard lecture, that seemed on the surface designed to deflect expectations of ambition. In her talk, she was in effect saying, I'm not the *PR* kind of critic, and she was right, she wasn't. Her story was a more complicated case. She was not writing mere pallid memoir, as Schwartz accused her. Yet her larger social portrait looked like a case perhaps of even more explicit co-optation: it was as though she were offering up her credentials for joining the *New Yorker* family in the very theme of her first story for the magazine—the witty evocation of a charming, not crude, anti-intellectual sensibility.

But that is to overlook the extent of Stafford's irony, which was trained as much on Emma as on the intellectuals. And it is to miss a dark undercurrent beneath the playful, agile surface. In writing about social poses, Stafford was treating not mere antics but deep anxieties about identity. Emma "never knew where she was at," Stafford wrote with disarming casualness, and skimmed over the specific cause of her protagonist's "collapse." But it was precisely the understated tone that helped convey just how precarious Emma's situation was, how unsure she was "in the territory of despair" where the world and the self had become misaligned— and how comparably disoriented Alfred was, despite all his knowledge and confidence. Stafford's sociological tour de force unobtrusively proved to have spiritual implications. The same writer who showed herself acutely attuned to the subtlest social distinctions by which one claims one's place in the world also saw through them to the soul's abiding sense of homelessness. She looked into that darker realm in deceptively demure fashion—true to her Bard lecture's stricture against waxing "hysterical and slovenly" in the face of confusion.

But the story was summarily dismissed by more than Schwartz: Stafford's *New Yorker* debut created a stir, according to her report to Peter Taylor. The move to the magazine was treated as something of an apos-

tasy, as Taylor himself was to experience later. (At one point he responded firmly to Lowell's condescension: "If you think your snide
remarks about the New Yorker and its ruination of writers could affect
me you need to come home and refresh your memory of your friends. . . .
The trouble with most people is that they can't tell the difference between good and bad New Yorker writers.") Stafford's story seems to have
elicited an especially vehement reaction from John Berryman, and she
quavered some under the onslaught:

> John Berryman came to New York a few days after ["Children Are
> Bored on Sunday"] was published and spent one entire afternoon
> berating me for printing it. The cardinal sin was printing it in the
> New Yorker; it was, he said, the weakest story he had ever seen of
> mine; he said that I had no "right" to print so "lazy" a piece of
> work and that I should be perpetually ashamed of myself. It went
> on and on and on and as a result of it, I got terribly drunk. I
> thought, "He is right and I must allow myself to be judged only by
> my peers and the compliments I get from people who are not my
> peers are meaningless, foolish and inaccurate."

As for Schwartz, "he announced that this was proof positive that I was
going after middle-brow success and that presently I would turn into a
second Fannie Hurst." But Stafford was quickly bolstered by praise from
two other peers, Taylor and Randall Jarrell, and her confidence in her
independent course rallied—though she admitted that she wouldn't
mind a little of the old company in her new surroundings, urging Taylor
to submit work to *The New Yorker:* "Please consider it: it would comfort
me very much to have you as a co-author in the NYer and as an ally,
therefore, against my ex-friends and enemies like John Berryman."

CHAPTER II

Peace and Disappointment

U NEASILY yet eagerly launched among new company, Stafford had two larger projects in mind. She wanted to finish *In the Snowfall*— for which she had signed a contract with Harcourt, Brace in November 1947—and she wanted to remarry. She was starting over with the familiar foundations in view: a book, a husband, and a house. But she also had a new aspiration. From the Virgin Islands, where she went in late April 1948 to get divorced from Lowell, she wrote to him about immediate, practical arrangements (he was to sign papers allotting her $6,500, due in a single installment); and she also made a declaration about the more distant future. Her letter sounded breezily resilient (by this time, they were "good friends . . . and feel no bitterness toward each other, but only toward our bungling lawyers," Stafford claimed to her sister). First she broached the remarriage question—"I want us both to marry again, don't you?"—and then she announced her new attitude: "We'll be so much wiser and so much calmer. It is my ambition to live the rest of my life at a low pitch."

Compared with the eight years that had just ended, the next eight— from the end of the 1940s to the middle of the 1950s—were in fact relatively peaceful for Stafford as she moved from her early to her late thirties. That did not mean that she lived calmly by ordinary standards. Nor did it mean that she smoothly fulfilled her aims: both marriage and writing proved to be, once again, much more difficult enterprises than she had hoped. But she was consciously struggling against the pressure that had enticed and yet overwhelmed her with Lowell. And it was a struggle. No longer "part of Cal's very fabulous life," she was both let down and liberated. Her aim was now to usher in the time when, as she had predicted to Cecile Starr from her hospital bed, she would be "glad that [her] role was taken away." The implication was that a different Jean

Stafford—with a real, not a fabulous, life of her own—would have a chance to step forth. But Stafford knew herself too well to believe in such a simple transformation. As she wrote to her old Boulder friend Joe Chay in July, after her return from the Virgin Islands, "I am now divorced, at loose ends, trying as hard as I can to pull my life together into some sort of order, but it is a vast undertaking."

Through the spring and summer of 1948, Stafford went about the business of setting up at least the outlines of her post-Lowell life with energetic resourcefulness. Far from being in eclipse, she was happily reminded that she had her own reputation to rest on. She applied for a second Guggenheim to work on her novel, and she won it. She also received a National Press Club Award, presented by President Truman in Washington. Wittily, she described herself as being in a flurry about the trip to the capital, worried about city clothes and about the intimidating company (Rebecca West, Ingrid Bergman, to say nothing of the president and his wife), but she came back clearly pleased that the event had gone well. It "was a triumph in a way for me," she wrote to Mary Lee, "because I didn't get nervous and for the first time in my life I was able to eat soup in the presence of more than four people. . . . I liked Rebecca West and talked a good deal with her."

The divorce was mostly her burden to bear, and she did so gamely. Having decided with Lowell that six weeks for her in the Virgin Islands was the least disagreeable course, she did her best to write him jaunty letters and to entertain her other friends with corrosively humorous descriptions of the exotic scenery and the thoroughly unappealing company—the divorcées-to-be, the Rotarians, the unwholesome sybarites. And then through connections of Robert Giroux's, she met some completely congenial company, Nancy Flagg Gibney, who wrote for *Vogue*, and her husband, Robert. "For the three of us it was love and jokes at first sight," was the way Nancy Gibney remembered it. Stafford spent a happy weekend with them on St. John, the start of a lifelong friendship with Nancy. But beneath the surface cheer and wit, as she confessed to Dr. Sherfey, with whom she was in constant correspondence, Stafford was miserable. She had a fever, and she was drinking too much, which prompted some stern instructions from her doctor: "Pull yourself together and take it easy and say no to everybody. Live your life not theirs. Nothing is more important. I expect you to do it. Keep writing."

On her return, though she felt at "loose ends," she kept up the bustle of activity and the tone of jauntiness. She ran into Lowell and declared in a letter to Peter Taylor that the encounter had been therapeutic: "He is an altogether magnificent creature and I am so glad that I never have to see him again that I could dance." She was dating a man named Chris Merillat, an editor at *Time* whom she had met in the spring and whose picture she had taken with her to the Virgin Islands, though she seemed to know this wasn't really the match she had in mind. Her social life was active as she mixed with a new crowd at *Time* and saw her old friends, less insistent now on steering clear of her former company.

And her name was frequently in print. Her profile of Newport, originally written on assignment for *Life,* was accepted by *The New Yorker* and appeared in August. Two stories were published in the fall, "The Bleeding Heart" in *Partisan Review* and "A Summer Day" in *The New Yorker.* Both were tales of dislocation in which Stafford chose protagonists far removed from herself—a Mexican girl from the West transplanted to Concord, Massachusetts, and an eight-year-old Cherokee Indian sent from Missouri to Oklahoma—whose travails nonetheless struck close to home. They were stories of orphanhood, which was clearly on Stafford's mind, and the conclusions were bleak. Rose Fabrizio, who dreamed of being adopted by an elderly New England man, was profoundly disillusioned when she glimpsed his sordid life. Poor Jim Littlefield's arrival at a grim orphanage, full of sick children, was even more terrifying: dreaming of escape, he succumbed to a deathlike sleep in the heat.

Stafford herself was discouraged and disoriented, despite her efforts to forge ahead in her new life on her own. She wrote to her friend Bill Mock about a sense of frightening stasis. She was "stifled by the terrible rush of time," and by the feeling that she was getting older "without ever maturing." The past was very much on her mind, not least because she was wrestling with *In the Snowfall.* As she wrote to Joe Chay, who chided her about her reluctance to return to the West and her past, "Alas, alas, I live within it and if I *could* run away it could be ever so much better for me." She moved to a new apartment, at 32 East Sixty-eighth Street, hoping that quieter surroundings might help spur her stalled work along, but soon she decided that she really needed more distance from New York, a city of rootless souls among whom she saw herself fitting all too well. She began planning a trip to Europe, and *The New Yorker* was happy to commission some articles to make it possible.

But such a large step away from familiar surroundings suddenly seemed more than she could handle when her former life came back to haunt her. By the spring of 1949, the dark side of Lowell's "fabulous life" became starkly, clinically clear in a way that it had not been before, at least not to his friends, some of whom have wondered in retrospect at how long it took them to see Lowell's enthusiasms as a sign of real imbalance rather than mere zeal. After several months of increasingly strange behavior, Lowell suffered the first of his recurrent violent, manic attacks and was committed to the hospital. He was taken first to Baldpate in Massachusetts, then to Payne Whitney when he moved to New York with his new wife, Elizabeth Hardwick, whom he had gotten to know shortly before at Yaddo and had married on emerging from Baldpate.

Stafford was greatly shaken by the news of his troubles, though she was the rare intimate of Lowell's who had long suspected that "Cal is crazy," as she had told Eileen Simpson, remembering the fall in New York when he was in prison. But it was a suspicion that she had barely allowed to become conscious. That diagnosis had probably been meant to sound like her typical hyperbole. The truth was that she rarely knew for sure where the imbalances in their marriage began and ended, and she tended to play down the violence she knew firsthand. (Lowell's friend Frank Parker remembered her as remarkably cool as she recounted the "incident" in Maine.) With her own fears of going mad, and her final collapse, it was she who had assumed the role of radically unstable partner. Now suddenly there was external evidence that she was not alone, which doubtless prompted memories of precisely the high-pitched life she had vowed to escape. The saga of Lowell's breakdown, which Stafford apparently retold avidly, echoed some of the more manic moments in their life together. In the wound-up weeks that preceded Lowell's entry into the hospital, he abruptly became a zealous Catholic again, insisting that his marriage to Stafford was still valid. At a later stage, he confronted his father figure, Allen Tate, in a scene reminiscent of Stafford's battle with Caroline Gordon in Maine: he announced Tate's infidelities and bullied him, and Tate ended up calling the police.

At the same time, Stafford was deeply relieved by Lowell's collapse, strange though she knew that might sound, and she was even more intent on preserving her own precarious calm. She tried to explain the weight that was lifted from her with the revelation that the trials in their marriage had not been the work merely of her perverse will and mind. "Cal is in a sanitarium now, very ill, and while I grieve for him, I feel a kind of liberation at last in knowing we were both such emotional wrecks when we married we didn't have a prayer," she wrote to Paul and Dorothy Thompson in April. "It is an awful irony that perhaps out of this tragedy will come my happiness," she observed in a letter to her sister Mary Lee, and revealed how much she counted on her doctor for support: "I am going to stay here where Dr. Sherfey is and finally somehow liberate myself from my guilt over that poor boy."

The graphic evidence that she was not alone in her "sickness of the spirit" helped ease her fears that the "ineradicable, black mark" of the asylum inmate meant ostracism. The mark even sometimes beckoned as a sign of election. The mad artist theme was a familiar one, championed by Schwartz, taken up by Berryman and later by Lowell, who became the main mythologizer of the collective angst that distinguished their tragic generation, *Les Maudits,* as Lowell later labeled his poetic colleagues in "For John Berryman." Stafford was briefly tempted by the self-dramatizing identity herself, spurred by Berryman's anointment of her as a tormented soul in his poem "A Winter-Piece to a Friend Away," a meditation on the artist's ravaged lot prompted by her Payne Whitney stay. When Berryman sent her his new book, *The Dispossessed,* in 1948 she had singled out that poem for praise: "Is it wrong (Randall, at any rate, would say it was uncritical) of me especially to like, among my especial favorites, my own which makes my heart bleed for us all?" She was echoing Berryman's prediction about his creative friends elsewhere in *The Dispossessed:* "analysands all, and the rest ought to be." It was a prediction that Lowell confirmed many years later, in a letter to Theodore Roethke in 1963: "There's a strange fact about the poets of roughly our age.... It's this, that to write we seem to have to go at it with such single-minded intensity that we are always on the point of drowning." If the romanticizing tone was in any doubt, Lowell settled it by musing: "There must be a kind of glory to it that people coming later will wonder at. I can see us all being written up in some huge book of the age."

But for the most part Stafford's tone was quite different. She was determined to resist that romanticism as she set out on her life apart from the poets. Although she admitted a bleak comfort, and even a certain mystique, in knowing that she was not alone in her psychic fragility—especially in knowing that Lowell's intensity and violence transcended his involvement with her—she was disinclined to ennoble neurosis. As her Bard lecture had suggested, she shied away from elevating her ordeals as a sign of the artistic spirit, as the key to her gift. Noting the surge of unhappiness on all sides, she was caustic in a letter to the down-to-earth Thompsons. "It is not news to me that everyone is cracking up. I'm glad, since it was on the books for me to do so, that I cracked up this year instead of ten years from now," she had written to them from the hospital. "All my friends in the outside world are, most of them, entirely miserable and are all drinking themselves out of their minds and everyone is getting divorced and no one is getting any work done and they are all consumed with this universal rage that has swept the country."

DESPITE THE TURMOIL, by the summer Stafford was ready to leave the country, thanks to help from Dr. Sherfey and encouragement from *The New Yorker*. She set off for England, France, Germany, and Scotland, buoyed by the magazine's confidence in her as a nonfiction correspondent, not simply a fiction writer. Filing stories from abroad, she proved herself an able reporter and a prompt writer—and she had a very good time. She cabled a last-minute "Letter from Edinburgh" about the International Festival of Music and Drama, which was hurried into print. She also produced a more substantial "Letter from Germany" for a December issue that year, in which she sketched an acutely ironic portrait of the Allied occupation, drawing on her prewar memories for contrast. Her approach was clear-eyed observation and calm assessment: the ravaged country inspired pity, not rage. But her imagination was clearly roused at being back on formative ground, and the writing was metaphorically charged, beginning with the sinister image of a rat and closing with a monkey disappearing into the huge mouth of a rhinoceros.

The trip was a success, but it was also in a sense an evasion. Stafford had managed to find a style and to regain momentum working on nonfiction, which was a welcome change of pace. But as she admitted, she was turning away from the real challenge, which was to reestablish her creative writing life. Above all that meant tackling her novel. What kind of fiction writer Stafford would be seemed a newly open question during these "low pitch" years after she emerged from the hospital. In "The Psychological Novel" she had declared a decorous aesthetic, suggesting that her response to the chaos of her life would be increasing order in her work, an avoidance of exhibitionism. But in fact she was probing a new, more autobiographical direction in *In the Snowfall,* her large and finally unsuccessful project during the late 1940s. This was not the domesticated memoir genre Schwartz accused *The New Yorker* of encouraging, but a much more ambitious effort to write about a generation—students in the 1930s—and, more importantly, to confront the major demons of her past: Lucy McKee and John Stafford.

She described the toll that enterprise took on her in an essay, "Truth and the Novelist," which appeared in *Harper's Bazaar* in 1951. The account is not the definitive analysis of Stafford's difficulties during this time—she was not thoroughly baring her soul in the glossy magazine. But the article is a useful guide to her thoughts about writing during years that for her, as for Lowell, proved to be an important transition. In the late 1940s and early 1950s—after their marriage, their mental stability, and their faith had all come into question—both of them, in very different ways, faced a tension between the formalist lessons they had learned at the start of their careers and the experiences of their disorderly lives.

The essay reveals a struggle between Stafford's principles and her instincts. She had been taught, and she herself had preached, that writing should not be personal. Moreover, she had early on had arduous first-hand experience of the perils of intensely autobiographical writing. Her first published fiction reflected the lessons she had learned. In *Boston Adventure* her imagination had carried her far beyond her own experience, and in *The Mountain Lion* irony and a symbolizing impulse had transmuted powerful memories. But ever since her stay in Cambridge in the winter of 1945 to 1946, she had been brooding on two subjects that were much closer to her—and much closer to her earlier fictional efforts: her own adolescent turmoil, precisely what Sonie sublimated in her pilgrimage to Miss Pride and what Molly avoided by her death; and her father, the figure who quickly disappeared from *Boston Adventure* and who was dead from the start in *The Mountain Lion.* Writing in retrospect in "Truth and the Novelist," Stafford acknowledged that she had strayed from the advice given her by, among others, Ford Madox Ford, who had told her long ago that portraiture straight from life "is impolite and it's not fiction." Once again she adopted the tone of the critical amateur:

After years of attacking from ambush and throwing up smoke screens, I made the same tactical error I had made in the beginning, and did so unconsciously. It is my intention to tell you about this, a problem completely autobiographical. I am no teacher and I could not teach anyone the first thing about writing: the most I can do is to seek my own creed in the conclusions I hope to draw from this rather depressing and instructive story.

As Stafford told the story, it was the urging of "two poets" in 1946— Schwartz and Lowell (later joined by Berryman)—that convinced her to undertake her saga of "college life in the thirties and the shocking event that had altered the whole course of my existence and had loitered horridly as a nightmare for eleven years." She didn't exactly blame them for the advice that led to her writing troubles (she respected the "taste and wisdom of the poets," she said), but she made clear that their aesthetic concerns and hers diverged. The implication was that they failed to understand a fundamental requirement of fiction: the necessity of emotional distance. She did understand it, but misjudged her own objectivity, wrongly assuming that "the experience had sunk deeply enough to rise again as literary experience, and now that the immediacy was removed, I could examine its components judiciously and disclose its meanings." Instead she discovered that she was consumed all over again by the miseries of those years. She felt driven not to fictional creation, but to confession about past turmoil, and was sickened by her "ubiquitous self."

She turned to work for *The New Yorker* as a release from the large-scale ordeal of *In the Snowfall:* "Probably the most ingenious of my escapes was this: I declined an advance from my publisher and therefore, in order to live, I was obliged to write short stories and articles which naturally consumed my time and claimed my attention." In fact, she had received an advance from Harcourt, Brace, but there were still financial pressures to serve as a rationale for distraction from more ambitious, problematic fictional endeavors—as they did again and again in later years. Finally, in December 1950, her response was, she claimed, to burn the pounds of manuscript that she had accumulated during more than three and a half years of work—a reaffirmation of the aesthetic from which she had temporarily and disastrously strayed by being "more personally omnipresent than coolly omniscient." She concluded "Truth and the Novelist" in her old-fashioned, prim tone, reiterating the decorous standards she had announced in "The Psychological Novel": "There are times when I wish we might return to the reticence of my parents' era when people kept their secrets. . . . I dare say it was sometimes unkind to hide away relatives of unsound mind in upper bedrooms, but still that seems to me more becoming than to brag in public about the lunatic heritage that can explain our own misdeeds." And she announced a happy ending: she was now at work on a new novel, she said, which "deals with people I have never met and with a permutation of circumstances that has no counterpart in my own life."

Stafford's account in the essay was deceptively well rounded. The interlude of *In the Snowfall* was a major creative crisis and not so cleanly overcome as she suggested in her article. Her hopes for the novel were extremely high: it promised to be *her* book, her testament, the one in which she would "reveal the quintessence of [her] talent," achieve "the crystallization of what I, as a writer, want to say." And her fears, when she had trouble, were great. Almost in passing, she admitted that she worried that "whatever gift I once had had was gone forever." When she spoke up in favor of reticence, she was not simply being anachronistic but was addressing a real anxiety nowhere explicitly confronted in the article: that her experience of psychiatry was perhaps to blame for destroying her gift. She had spent months talking with her doctors, trying to exorcise the demons who were also her fictional subjects—Lucy and, even more important, that relative of "unsound mind," the source of her possible "lunatic heritage," her father (though she never named him in her article). Perhaps the constant exhuming of memories had undermined the role her imagination needed to play. Certainly plumbing the pain on the written page had no therapeutic benefits: "Take with a grain of salt the cliché that it is possible to rid oneself of a grief or a guilt or an ugly memory by writing of it," she counseled in her article. More important, the scrutiny bore no literary fruit.

Stafford was also skirting the truth when she said that she destroyed the manuscript, or when she said that the novel she then turned to (*The Catherine Wheel*) was progressing like a breeze. She saved drafts of *In the Snowfall*, which she kept returning to over the years, unable to admit complete defeat with the novel for which she had had such hopes. And *The Catherine Wheel*, though the writing of it progressed quickly enough during the spring and summer of 1951, proved to be a labor of another kind: Stafford had to work hard for a sense of passionate engagement with her material, precisely what had come all too readily with *In the Snowfall*.

Several letters shed more intimate light on the struggles Stafford publicly presented in "Truth and the Novelist." She had her moments of high expectation. In the spring of 1949 she wrote optimistically to Taylor about *In the Snowfall,* saying that she was "very hard at work. I have achieved the final tension because now at last I know what this book is about and I know how to write it. The plot has revealed itself and I can finish it in this last sitting. And I have *got* to finish it now because I am so sick of it, having lived with it for so very many years." But only a couple of months later, as she was about to leave on her European trip, she gave an entirely different report to Mary Lee, sounding distraught: "I feel that I have lost all energy, all courage, and, worst of all, all talent. . . . My book goes so badly that I am in despair half the time and my insomnia has returned in full force. There are times when I feel that it is psychiatry that has destroyed my gift, but perhaps the gift isn't gone yet, I don't know. If it has, God knows what will become of me because that is the only thing in the world I have."

It is clear that Stafford talked to Dr. Sherfey about her fear that, despite what she had said in "The Psychological Novel," her neurosis might well be the key to her gift, and that bringing her secrets to light in session after session might be the destruction of it. That same summer Dr. Sherfey wrote to her in Europe, reassuring her of the psychological and literary liberation that therapy should bring by enabling her imagination to take in not just the "hidden pathological tortures of man's soul," but also "those aspects of life which make it good." Sherfey emphasized that she wasn't invoking insipid wholesomeness: "You will never lose that capacity for remembering and experiencing the darknesses; it is a vital, moving part of you. You will but add to it the capacity to remember and experience the lightness." She acknowledged that the new capacity wouldn't come easily. But she was confident that she and Stafford together would succeed at "the job [which] is to make that capacity not a superficial part of you—so that writing about it *would* be frivolous—but a part as integral as the other. When that happens you will be quite 'well.' And I have no qualms nor concern about the kind of writer you'll be."

STAFFORD CLEARLY did have qualms, and on her return from Europe her response was to find distraction from her creative anxieties in energetic socializing. She was apparently no longer dating Chris Merillat, but at a party during the fall of 1949 she found a new beau, Oliver Jensen, a thirty-five-year-old editor at *Life*. He was a ruggedly attractive man, Yale educated, well paid, and gallantly solicitous of Stafford, then thirty-four, whose wit appealed to him and whose literary fame impressed him. Stafford in turn was thrilled to be wined and dined by a conventional man whose gracious wooing was such a welcome change (Alfred Kazin remembered her amazement, and gratitude, at being sent roses). Jensen arrived as the embodiment of the reliable protector she needed, the man with whom she might be able to live calmly. For it was a desire for security, rather than romantic longing, that inspired her eagerness for remarriage, which evidently peaked that winter. "I so terribly want to marry," she wrote to Peter Taylor in December. "I so desperately long for the orderliness and the security of marriage and the end of my intolerable loneliness."

Jensen belonged to a familiar journalistic set, and yet he was not one of the intense literary souls among whom Stafford had come of age and whom she had vowed to avoid. For both, that difference between them was part of the initial appeal. While in Europe traveling by himself late in the fall of 1949, Jensen evidently heard plenty about Stafford's creative gifts, which only increased her allure on his return. And while Jensen was away, Stafford went to Yaddo once again and was reminded of how anxious the place and the writers there made her. One of her fellow guests, psychopathic according to Stafford, completely lost control. Frightened, Stafford promptly got sick (insomnia, asthma), and in a letter to Jensen she reiterated her vow to avoid the miserable milieu. "When the whole thing dawned on me three years ago, I repudiated the company I had kept so long. I abandoned the enemies of serenity and the advocates of self-hatred . . . and I am cross as a patch that on my return to Life Among the Writers, there is immediately an incident."

She invited Jensen to come visit, welcoming him as an emissary from a much brighter, calmer world. His presence was just the proof she needed that "all of life is not hideous and that Yaddo doesn't constitute the world." Together they sneaked away from Yaddo, went back to New York, and hurriedly got married on January 28, 1950, in Christ Church. Dr. Sherfey counseled against it, and Blair Clark, who hosted the reception after the wedding, did so with a sinking heart. Harold Ross told the Whites that he knew the marriage wouldn't last. But for the start at least it was what Stafford had dreamed of. She had her first real honeymoon: they went to Haiti and Jamaica. And when they returned and settled in

Jensen's apartment, she played the part of the proper East Side wife. Along with wedding announcements, she sent out engraved cards informing acquaintances that "Mr. and Mrs. Oliver Jensen" were "At Home after the fifteenth of February [at] 222 East Seventy-first Street." By the summer, they were getting ready to move into another house, closer to Stafford's familiar vision. They rented a place in Wilton, Connecticut, while the old colonial house they had bought in Westport was being fixed up.

STAFFORD KNEW there was a price to be paid for her new sense of domestic comfort and stability, which she acknowledged was not as solid as it might have looked from the outside. And as she had admitted to Dr. Sherfey, she was worried about what might happen should "lightness" come to prevail in her writing, even as she was struggling with her dark novel, *In the Snowfall*. In "Truth and the Novelist" the tension between poised, formal detachment and autobiographical immersion seemed to be settled in favor of the former. But that was clearly an oversimplified account. Stafford never resolved the tension; her best fiction demonstrated the possibility of probing psychic confusions in unnervingly controlled prose, of commenting on the disorderliness of experience without succumbing to it. In fact, the tension between immersion and reflection was itself an underlying theme linking the stories she wrote during the late 1940s and early 1950s—years when she was also struggling with one novel, *In the Snowfall,* in which emotional proximity was the difficulty, and then with another, *The Catherine Wheel,* in which detachment was the problem. The result was a distinctive group of stories that, among their other accomplishments, indirectly raised questions about both the cool, Olympian style and the confessional, high-pitched approach.

Between her release from the hospital and her abandonment of *In the Snowfall* at the end of 1950, Stafford was writing quite steadily for *The New Yorker.* It seems that the stories came easily at first. During the winter, spring, and summer of 1949, three of Stafford's stories appeared in the magazine, variations on a common theme: a reclusive protagonist, trapped in unwelcome social relations, found himself both an ambivalent participant in and a merciless observer of social hypocrisies. Stafford set one of the stories, "The Cavalier," in Germany and introduced a character who was to reappear, an intensely shy American student who was confronted with more experience than he had bargained for. She called on more recent memories in the two other, more interesting stories. "A Modest Proposal" was set in the Virgin Islands and was a showpiece of Stafford's descriptive skills, much as her letters from there had been. Her protagonist, a divorcée-to-be serving out her appointed Caribbean exile, was profoundly aloof from the scene of which she was a part—a gathering of rejected wives on the veranda of a predatory, transplanted Dane. Despite the torpor that overcame her ("it was fitting, she concluded, that one come to such a place as this to repudiate struggle and to resume the earlier, easier indolence of lovelessness"), she succeeded in maintaining a withering distance from the decadence of the assembled company. But Stafford complicated the story by suggesting that the purer, isolated life guarded by her protagonist, freshly bereft of her husband, was a barren one.

In "Polite Conversation," Stafford took an earlier chapter of her marriage as the occasion for lighter social comedy and for experimentation with dialogue. Her protagonists were the Heaths, a young literary couple newly settled in Maine who struggled only half successfully to avoid the insistent social overtures of the local folk. As a letter several years earlier to Cecile Starr from Damariscotta Mills shows, Stafford was writing this one directly from life:

> To be quite frank, I have reached the age when I do not want to meet any new people. This appears quite hard for certain characters around here to believe and we are continually being summoned to swimming, dancing, cocktail and dinner parties and as you may well imagine, Cal is always extremely difficult and either makes me make up some horrendous lie or makes me go alone with an equally horrendous excuse for him.

The real interest of the story was Margaret Heath's ambivalence as she endured tea with the local ladies. She staunchly defended the reclusiveness of her husband, Tommy, yet there was also a part of her, as there was of Stafford, that agreed with her neighbor's exclamation: "I think Tommy is gravely mistaken if he thinks one can live by art alone. But I daresay he would call *me* bourgeois for posing that question!"

The choice between isolation and mingling posed in the stories was not clear-cut. On the one hand, retreat seemed to promise self-sufficient calm, whereas sociability involved self-compromising struggle. On the other hand, there was something ominous about the passivity implied by detachment—a sense that escape into the lonely psyche might well not offer peace or creativity. But Stafford kept these stories light, playing on the social ironies of her theme rather than exploring darker psychological implications. They apparently were not a struggle to write, and *The New Yorker* was pleased to print them.

Stafford began to have more trouble later in the fall of 1949 and in the course of 1950 as she and Jensen settled down together. Her ongoing struggles with *In the Snowfall* seemed to cast a shadow over all her work. Progress, which was always uneven at best, apparently slowed disastrously after a visit in the summer of 1950 from her sister Mary Lee. The intrusion of her past must have stirred her up. She felt exposed—it was the first time any member of her family had seen her with house and husband—and she felt judged: her sister came bearing tales of their father's increasingly sad straits. And though Stafford had held it against Lowell that he had had nothing to do with her family, Jensen's interest was perhaps threatening. He had initiated a correspondence with her father, who wrote back and even sent along a pair of deerskin gloves. At the same time, her relations with Jensen were becoming strained as she complained of his endless socializing with tedious friends and he hounded her about her drinking, which got worse as her writing difficulties mounted.

Starting in the fall of 1949 Stafford turned to the darker suggestions of her theme in four of her most notable stories. Two of them stood out as exceptions to *New Yorker* urbanity, as several critics remarked, and the other two were rejected by the magazine. Katharine White was unsettled by "A Country Love Story" (originally entitled "When the House Is Finished, Death Comes"), which appeared in the spring of 1950 (and won an O. Henry Award, her third). It is a "fascinating and poetic and puzzling piece of writing—not too personal I would think if certain things were done," she wrote to Stafford. "It fascinates me completely, but also bothers me." Inspired by "the incident" with Lowell during the spring of 1946 at Damariscotta Mills, the story was about the psychological dangers of submissive retreat. A couple living alone in the country grew increasingly estranged, the husband withdrawing into his work as he convalesced from a long illness, the wife sinking into depression when she was brutally rebuffed by him. Instead of finding peace in their solitude, they were caught up in a self-destructive drama. He accused her of infidelity and was consumed by jealous visions. She internalized the (false) charge and imagined herself adulterous and guilty, slipping into a fantasy world that was a source both of comfort—her imaginary lover was a solace in her isolation—and of fear. Was she going mad? "From every thought, she returned to her deep, bleeding injury. He had asked her if she were going mad."

Once again, Stafford set up a relation in which passivity invited mental tyranny, isolation invited enslavement. A curious diary entry reflecting on the role she played with Lowell, apparently written in the midst of work on *In the Snowfall,* suggests that in her story she was drawing on an interaction she knew firsthand. Her journal snippet was a cold self-diagnosis:

> Sometime, he said, I would lose my temper and stop letting people knock me about. "As you have always done?" I asked and he replied, "Yes, it's all that could be done with someone like you." But I did not know how to refuse to accept the mistreatment. If I fought back with anger, it only made things worse; yet my submissiveness maddened him. I apologized for everything; I had no center and therefore I had no self and therefore I did not lead a real life. His vanity and passionate self-devotion fascinated me evilly.

In "The Echo and the Nemesis" (originally entitled "The Nemesis"), which appeared in *The New Yorker* in December of 1950, Stafford pursued the theme of tyrannizing selves to a further extreme. It was another unusual story for the magazine, as Granville Hicks remarked in a review of Martha Foley's 1951 anthology of *Best American Short Stories,* where it was reprinted. "Jean Stafford's 'The Nemesis' on the other hand is a dark and sensitive study of psychological abnormality, not at all in the New Yorker vein," he wrote. Stafford took a step beyond "A Country Love Story," this time probing full-fledged mental illness. The trouble was essentially the same—the lack of a self, the inability to lead a real life—and at first the story seems merely a variation on a familiar subject.

The protagonist, Sue Ledbetter, was another agonizingly shy American student in Germany who half yearned to join the boisterous youthful crowds but who was drawn instead into a friendship with Ramona Dunn, an imperiously pedantic student of philology—and "fat to the point of parody." Ramona "did not seem to mind at all that she was so absurd to look at, and Sue, who was afire with ambitions and sick with conflict, admired her arrogant self-possession." Dr. Cohn wrote to Stafford admiringly of the story: "No doubt remains—your craftsmanship is superb. And so is your psychology." He rightly observed the device of doubling signaled by the story's title: "Sue and Ramona are mirror images, through a glass darkly, indeed very darkly, a dual person and so of course also one." But the story took a further turn, as Stafford carried the doubling one level deeper: fat Ramona, suffering from *adiposis dolorosa,* cultivated schizophrenic delusions in her unhappiness—an unhappiness, the story hinted, that had its origins in incest. She fantasized a thin, dead twin named Martha, who was in fact her old self.

There was nothing wan in Stafford's portrait of pathology as she unveiled layer after layer of Ramona's delusions in scenes so melodramatic they verged on dark comedy. In Ramona, Stafford vividly showed innocent Sue and her readers a more deranged version of the victim/tyrant relation than she ever had before. As Ramona announced to Sue at the end, " 'I am exceptionally ill.' She spoke with pride, as if she were really saying, 'I am exceptionally talented. . . .' " Her obsessional appetite—her vanity and passionate self-devotion, to borrow the terms from Stafford's diary—led to deep unhappiness, yet once again Stafford complicated her story by suggesting that Sue's unvoracious outlook on life, her inability to lead a real life on her own, was hardly an ideal alternative. "You have such a trivial little life, poor girl," Ramona told her, and the story confirmed the verdict. "It's not your fault. Most people do."

Ominous though the stories were, Stafford's protagonists were young and her endings, however bleak, did not rule out all hope. In "The Echo and the Nemesis" Sue—fleeing from a waiter who innocently asked her, "Are you afraid to get fat?"—perhaps had an independent life ahead of her. At the close of "A Country Love Story," the wife sat "with her hands locked tightly in her lap, rapidly wondering over and over again how she would live the rest of her life." Was there any escape from this vision of life as a divided self, at once tyrant and victim, at the mercy of an unappeasable hunger for love, or at least for some acknowledgment of one's existence? That was the question Stafford addressed in two other stories written around this time, both of them about the fate of older characters, neither of which made its way into *The New Yorker.* Her answers were far from heartening, as Katharine White's reaction to "Life Is No Abyss" (which eventually appeared in the *Sewanee Review* in the summer of 1952) suggested. White had clearly discussed the idea of the story—a girl's confrontation with two crones in a poorhouse—with Stafford before. "As you described your actual visit to me," White wrote, "your compassion, of course mixed with distaste and horror, came through strongly. If this compassion doesn't register somehow, one can't help wondering why the story was written."

But White failed to understand that precisely the point of the story was to convey spiritual terror at the loveless face of existence as revealed in the two old women. One of them had turned against her relatives in a rage of vengeful sadomasochism. The other, blind and witless, was cut off from the world and consumed by an "empty ecstasy." Stafford described that ecstasy in a passage reminiscent of William James's appalling image in *The Varieties of Religious Experience* of an epileptic idiot in an asylum, an image that overwhelmed him with "a horrible fear of my own existence." Stafford's old woman was equally, horrifyingly, vacant:

> In that hideous grin and that convulsive dance and that moan of bliss, she had demonstrated something sheer and inhuman and unnamable. . . . There had been no mistaking it: the look on the thinly covered skull had been one of white-hot transport, but what emotions had generated it? Hope? Gratitude for the heartening assurance that life was no abyss? A desire for love? Could there be in that travailing length of blue flesh and devious bone a longing . . . ?
> If there was, it was too terrible to contemplate.

And yet by comparison to the other crone, who was perversely settling her scores with the world, this abandoned soul "who can't take anything and can't give anything" seemed to inhabit a "state of grace," however terrifying. The only escape from the cruel complexity of passion, Stafford suggested, was a pure, detached irrationality.

Or else a pure, detached rationality, the alternative she explored in the ironically titled "I Love Someone," which ended up appearing in the *Colorado Quarterly* the same summer. It was the monologue of a middle-aged spinster surveying her own life after the shocking suicide of a friend. She described with a chilling calmness an existence devoted to the studious avoidance of any involvement beyond herself, of taking anything or giving anything. "The fact is there has been nothing in my life," she announced. "From childhood I have unfailingly taken all the detours around passion and dedication; or say it this way, I have been a pilgrim without faith, traveling in an anticipation of loss, certain that the grail will have been spirited away by the time I have reached my journey's end." Her state of grace, she acknowledged, was an empty accomplishment: "I, who never act on impulse, know nearly precisely the outcome of my always rational behavior. It makes me a woman without hope; but since there is no hope there is also no despair." She had paid a high price for her placidity and confessed to a curiosity to "penetrate at last the mysterious energy that animates everyone in the world"—except that she knew what it entailed: to venture forth in search of love was to encounter hate. Once more Stafford set out the alternatives of immersion and retreat, and granted retreat a victory at the same time that she revealed how hollow it was. "My friends and I have managed my life with the best of taste," Stafford's narrator declared in closing, "and all that is lacking at this banquet where the appointments are so elegant is something to eat."

STAFFORD WAS NOT, for the most part, writing autobiographically in the most direct, concrete sense. It is fruitless, for example, to plumb "A Modest Proposal" for her sentiments on the occasion of her final break with Lowell. "A Country Love Story" comes the closest to a confessional account of a traumatic personal experience, but here too Stafford pulled back. The husband's effort to strangle his wife that climaxed an early draft—which was apparently the actual, violent source of the story—was cut in the final version.

But in these stories, and in *The Catherine Wheel,* the novel she turned to when she abandoned *In the Snowfall,* Stafford was writing autobiographically in a thematic sense, as she worked through a transition in both her life and her writing. She was trying to find out whether living at a "low pitch" was a possibility for her, and what kind of price it might entail. Was she capable of sustaining a level of peace and detachment that could spare her the turmoil she had known during her marriage to Lowell? And she was trying to find out just how immediately from life she could draw her fictional material. How much could she afford to immerse herself in the drama of her past and of troubled personal relations, and how much did she need the distance and decorum of style to tame it? She addressed the dilemma in different forms in her fiction, where her inclination seemed increasingly to detachment.

In the early 1950s the dilemma was also surfacing with renewed intensity in her life, as the first year of relative calm in her marriage with

Jensen began to give way to trouble. The acclaimed writer he had married on very brief acquaintanceship was, he discovered, far unhappier than he had ever dreamed. Drinking heavily and plagued with medical troubles, Stafford was in and out of the hospital. And her past continued to haunt her with an intensity that Jensen, whose exposure to her father and Mary Lee had been entirely cordial, found difficult to fathom. Her sessions with Dr. Sherfey seemed to him counterproductive; at least her depression only increased. During a rare trip out to Mary Lee's ranch in Colorado in August of 1951, when her father was visiting as well, Stafford summoned up a bleak hope that she might be able to explain the torment of her past and perhaps overcome it. "I think maybe at last I shall be able to convey to Dr. Sherfey and to you exactly what this blight has been that has twisted and hallucinated me all my life and perhaps you, Oliver, will finally understand my unnatural feeling toward my father," she wrote to him as she was about to return to Westport. "Seeing him again I am amazed that all of us did not commit suicide in our cradles. Maybe at last I can get rid of some of the poison."

When she got back, she retreated to the hospital, thoroughly shaken by her visit with her father and clearly not eager to return to Jensen. "I don't want to go," she wrote to Mary Lee about the prospect of leaving the hospital, which was once again her asylum. "I never want to leave this simplicity and the utter freedom of this small space in which there is nothing superfluous." She did come home, and she managed to finish *The Catherine Wheel* that fall, but there was no real rapprochement between her and Jensen. They were a world apart, as had seemed so obvious to many of their friends when they married, and now the distance meant strife. Stafford was scathing about his middlebrow journalistic crowd. (He left *Life* soon after they married, and became associate editor at *American Heritage* in 1954.) Jensen was equally dismissive of her literary circle, convinced that the company was unhealthy; he was impatient with their eccentricities, their excessive drinking, and put off by all the backstabbing. The quarrels between the two of them—which usually began, Jensen remembered, with "the three big topics of our era: Communism, the Catholic Church, Psychiatry"—were fierce.

When Stafford went out West again in the summer of 1952, invited by the Writers' Conference in Boulder to deliver the keynote lecture (the speech she had heard Ford Madox Ford give fifteen years earlier), she took advantage of the geographic distance to initiate a separation from

Jensen. Thus her second marriage unraveled where the first had in a sense begun, in her encounter with Lowell at the Writers' Conference in 1937—and her literary career arrived at a plateau at the site where she had started the climb upward. Her letters to Jensen from Boulder were letters of retreat. She had no more energy for involvement, she wrote to him, echoing her passionless protagonists: "I feel a desperate fatigue and I should think you would too—a fatigue that comes from an expenditure of emotion. We cannot do that anymore." In a letter a week later, she tried to explain her resigned embrace of loneliness, which she both dreaded and yet needed:

> I cannot give you the kind of help that a wife should give a husband. . . . [I]t is useless for me to say, the fault is mine and I will correct it. I cannot correct it because it goes so deep and is bound up with my writing which I cannot in any way relinquish. A woman so isolated by nature as I am, so terrified of possessiveness, cheats when she marries and I shall not soon forgive myself even though I did not mean to cheat.

At the same time, Stafford delivered a lecture of retreat in Boulder. The conference, at which she was expected to talk to prospective writers and read their work, as well as give the main speech, was precisely the kind of spotlight she was eager to avoid. Her reluctance apparently showed in her bearing, as she mumbled and stood or sat hunched in front of her classes (the students had been primed by Stafford's friends to ask questions, to spare her mortifying silences). And her address was devoted, paradoxically, to the theme that writers should be read and not seen or heard. Once again, to an even greater extent than in "The Psychological Novel" and "Truth and the Novelist," she adopted the anecdotal style of the amateur—and, as if to emphasize her fusty approach, called her talk "An Etiquette for Writers." Boulder disarmed her with nostalgia, she explained, and she "concluded at last it would be impossible for me to speak here with academic detachment of the art of the novel, or the state of the novel, or the future of the novel, or the novelist and society, or the novelist and psychoanalysis. I knew that I should be able to do little more than peregrinate amongst personal meanders."

Her theme was familiar: that a decorous distance ought to be maintained between art and life. Where she had previously argued against exhibitionism, she now took commercialism to task. Her target was the transformation of the writer into a huckster for the big business of publishing. She disapproved of "the private-made-public life" of authors, this time not within their own pages but on the promotion circuit that had become a routine part of publication. She spoke as a disillusioned innocent, who had started out with visions of writing not as a profession but as a pure end in itself, and had been rudely awakened to the book business by her first publishing experience.

It was hardly an original indictment, though Stafford's version was charming enough and gave her an opportunity to do some reminiscing about her college days. But it is possible to read the talk in a more personal light, as a comment on the state of her own career as much as on the state of the publishing business. Especially in hindsight, her reflections seem to betray a sense that she, the once much-hyped writer, was entering a phase in which she hoped (and feared) that the pressure would be off. She sounded as though she was somehow trying to prepare the way for a second act considerably less celebrated than her first had been. She was being lionized by her hometown, and her latest book, *The Catherine Wheel,* was selling quite well, but she was determined to downplay her stature and her future. The burden of reputation was heavy, she told her audience, and though she wasn't speaking directly of her own experience, her anecdote spoke prophetically, and poignantly, to what lay ahead for her:

> In recent years we have seen the birth and flourishing of literary reputations months and sometimes even years before the writers to whom they belong ever appear in print. They have acquired a solid status on the strength of their intention, on their charm and their wit and their presentableness at dinner parties. . . . I know of a man who has been called a writer all his life—and he is nearing sixty— who has, nevertheless, published nothing except an excerpt from his "forthcoming novel" in an obscure and ephemeral magazine. . . . It is a full-time job to be a non-practicing writer and I suppose that it is an honorable enough profession but it should get itself a new name.

Of course Stafford's reputation had been founded on a truly unusual book. But she had felt the burden of reputation nonetheless, and from two sides: she had known not only the pressures of publishers, but also the disdain of her poetic friends and colleagues for the mass success and celebrity she had enjoyed. At the same time, even among that company, cultivating a literary persona was part of the game—an especially intimidating part. As she well knew, her charm and wit, her conversational virtuosity, her "presentableness at dinner parties," had played a role in establishing key connections for her fifteen years earlier when she had so impressed the visiting faculty at the Writers' Conference, and those social gifts had been part of her public literary profile ever since. She felt increasingly ambivalent about that—an ambivalence perfectly embodied in her speech. Certainly the role of author on the dais ill suited her; she wasn't just being modest when she complained in her speech that she was not very good at it. And yet here she was, relying on precisely the superficial qualities she had impugned—giving a charming, witty, afterdinner sort of speech. Stafford may have disdained the public performance that she was called upon to give (in particular now that she had dedicated herself to her "low pitch," post-Lowell life), but even more she dreaded anything that approached real personal disclosure. The anecdotal charm was her defense against confessional revelation—especially now that her writing was not going as smoothly as it once had.

She alluded to her troubles in one sentence that stands out in her speech as a revelation, however oblique. It was Stafford's declaration of privacy:

> Writing is a private, an almost secret enterprise carried on within the heart and mind in a room whose doors are closed; the shock is staggering when the doors are flung open and the eyes of strangers are trained on the naked and the newborn; one's doubts and misgivings and fears should be allowed to rest in sick-room quiet for a while.

Stafford was drawing both on a universal metaphor—linking literary creativity and birth—and on her own, idiosyncratic chamber imagery. The result was a rather unsettling portrait of the writing process, a striking contrast to the pure youthful zeal for expression that she had recalled earlier in the talk. The progression she described here could hardly be further from the conventional birth sequence: mysterious gestation followed by miraculous arrival in the world and a proud presentation by parents. Stafford evoked an unnatural, almost sinister gestation, followed by an exposure that seemed above all to entail shame. She emphasized doubt and fear, rather than relief and joy. Stafford's imagery conveyed a sense of failure, or at least trepidation, not just about her future as a writer but also about her fate as a woman. There was no vision of fruitful procreation, literary or biological. Instead she came close to accusing herself of a kind of perversity.

Back from the conference, Stafford stayed in Westport for a couple of months, working up her resolve to leave, which she did in the fall of 1952, having prepared Jensen for it in a series of self-accusatory letters from Boulder. "I am all you say, a liar, a breaker of promises, an alcoholic, an incompetent . . . a hypochondriac. Do you imagine that knowing this and knowing it full well—I can also love myself and wish to go on living, making your life an incessant disappointment?" One day in early November she called a friend to drive her to the train, and she went to New York, where she disappeared in another nightmarish week of solitary hotel living and drinking. In a letter to her sister Mary Lee after her flight, Jensen confirmed Stafford's own bleak reading of her fate as a woman. Whatever possibilities literature still held for her, her life looked unhealthy and barren, and he acknowledged that he was not a husband who could help:

> Her pessimism, catholic and profound, and her memory, which is photographic only, alas, in respect of unhappy things, hold her in thrall. She believes in diseases but not in cures. She is convinced she cannot live with me and also write. . . . What in God's name is to happen to Jean, Mary Lee? I wish she could find some joy in life, some mode of existence sans all the violence, sickness, and mental self-torture. I can't provide them. Cal Lowell couldn't. Psychiatry, and it is not all nonsense whatever Jean thinks I believe, hasn't done much for her in six years. Catholicism couldn't help. She is 37 but the road is dark and the destination obscure.

Jensen had by then discovered that Stafford had ruled out one avenue of creativity. Not long after she arrived in New York, she retreated to her familiar asylum, the hospital, to tend to the uterine fibroid tumors she had been diagnosed as having. While she was there, she told her doctor to go ahead and perform an unnecessarily drastic treatment—a hysterectomy.

It was as though Stafford needed to make a dramatic statement of disillusionment with the ordinary, domestic plans with which she had begun her post-Lowell life. On emerging from Payne Whitney in 1947,

she had written to Cal of her hopes that "I will soon be loved and married so that I can have a child before it is too late." Now she was ready to
be divorced again (before she left Westport she had already written to
the Gibneys about a return trip to the Virgin Islands), and she was explicitly acknowledging what she had implicitly realized long before: that
she could not imagine a life stable enough to have children.

Her assessment of her literary life during the early 1950s tended to be
bleak as well. At least that was her judgment of the two longer pieces of
writing she did then, after she had abandoned *In the Snowfall,* the biggest disappointment of all. (Her short stories, by contrast, kept coming
and mostly escaped her ruthless self-condemnation.) Of *The Catherine
Wheel,* which appeared in early 1952, she wrote disparagingly to Mary
Lee: "All I ask you, when you read it, is to remember that this is only the
present book, and I will write a better one." She urged Caroline Gordon,
with whom she was briefly back in touch, not to read it at all: "Please do
not read my new one coming out in January. It is no good."

And she was dismissive of her novella, *A Winter's Tale*—which she
had reworked from a story that in turn harked all the way back to *Autumn Festival* and to the sequel, featuring a monk named Dom Paternus,
that she had once envisaged for *Boston Adventure.* "I only refurbished the
dull thing to help Mary Lou [Aswell, at *Harper's Bazaar*] get a collection
together [it appeared in *New Short Novels* in 1954], since it's far from my
favorite story," she wrote to Jensen, who had praised it. And to Lowell,
who had evidently mentioned hearing about something she had written,
she was even more self-effacing (after saying how proud she was of Peter
Taylor and Randall Jarrell for their recent successes): "I don't know what
new novel you mean unless it's a nasty little rent-payer in a paper back.
I'm not going to send you a copy because I don't want you or anybody
else to read it." By the time she wrote that, toward the middle of the
decade, she had reason to wonder whether her promise to Mary Lee that
she would write a better novel had been in vain.

WHEN STAFFORD HAD BEGUN *The Catherine Wheel*—at least as she
told it in "Truth and the Novelist"—she had had high hopes. Her re-
nunciation of autobiography was a liberation, she claimed. As she described it, her project sounded like a confident effort to follow Dr.
Sherfey's prescription, to exercise a new "capacity to remember and experience lightness" and to avoid the ordeals she had encountered with *In*

the Snowfall. She wrote of her new novel that "It deals with people I have never met and with a permutation of circumstances that has no counterpart in my own life, and it is set in a part of the world that bewitches me. (I had always quarreled with the landscape of the other.)" And she emphasized what relief that distance had brought: "I am not required to resuscitate any black humors and therefore to suffer again; and because my protagonist is not myself, I am kindly and uninhibited."

The first half of her statement was true enough. The setting of *The Catherine Wheel* was New England, a town called Hawthorne that Stafford modeled more or less on Damariscotta Mills and that, as an exotic commingling of locals and summer intruders from Boston, was also a kind of inland, upscale Chichester, Sonie's birthplace. The characters were not based on friends or relatives. As in many of the stories she had been writing, Stafford drew only thematically, not explicitly, from her own life. In fact, *The Catherine Wheel* blended essentially the themes of those stories in its two interwoven plots.

In the portrait of the summer agony of shy, twelve-year-old Andrew Shipley, who was tormented by the sudden indifference of his erstwhile best and only friend, Victor Smithwick, Stafford found a new incarnation of the alienated youth who yearned to participate in the world but was instead overwhelmed by it. The counterbalancing portrait of Andrew's spinster cousin, Katharine Congreve, a generation older than he, was perhaps Stafford's most polished tale of an ossified heart. Katharine's usual passionless calm had been disturbed when Andrew's father, who two decades earlier had betrayed her to marry her orphan cousin Maeve instead, suddenly declared his love anew. Depositing his three children with her and setting off on a summer cruise with Maeve, he pleaded with her to marry him on his return.

During the summer spanned by the novel, which passed slowly on Katharine's graceful Hawthorne estate, Andrew's and Katharine's preoccupations undermined what had for years been a special sympathy between them. In fact, suffering side by side, each was made only more miserable by intimations of the other's unhappiness. While Andrew guiltily dreamed of killing Victor's brother, Charles (to whom Victor now devoted all of his attention), Katharine guiltily nursed resentments of Maeve—and their guilt was compounded by the conviction that the other had somehow glimpsed their secret, shameful desires. Both were visited by the fear Stafford evoked so well. They were convinced that the mind could all too easily tyrannize the world (their evil wishes had for them the status of murderous deeds), and yet they were also convinced that the mind could be all too easily tyrannized by other minds. Katharine "was looking right through the back of his head," Andrew was sure, "reading everything written there."

As that summary suggests, Stafford had not been quite accurate when she implied that it was a novel of airiness and light. To be sure, she wasn't plunging into the black humors of her own past, but she was again writing about the ravages of gentility and about the masochism of the mind, about social and psychological entrapment. At the same time, as in some of her stories about the perils of experience and the allure of detachment, the novel also encourages a self-reflexive reading. This all but plotless, painstakingly crafted book is an illustration of literary entrapment, of the encroachments of style on substance. But it is harder to tell how consciously Stafford had fashioned a mannered, static book to reflect the lives within it. To judge by her own comments on the novel, she hadn't started out intending such a detached and coolly wrought book, even if she was aiming to avoid the immediacy of *In the Snowfall*.

Stafford may well have conceived of this novel as the fulfillment of the aim she announced in an interview not long after it was published. Her ultimate goal, she said, was to "fuse the two manners" of her first two very different novels—that is, to blend the "leisurely ... embroidered, contemplative, old-fashioned" style of *Boston Adventure* and the more symbolic approach of *The Mountain Lion*. On the surface she did just that. Stafford's serpentinely introspective prose, which had become even more elaborate than in her first novel, wound its way to a symbolic ending, which was even more freighted than Molly's end in *The Mountain Lion*. The refined diction of the elegant Katharine, more arch than the Bostonian argot, was juxtaposed with the almost caricatured rustic talk of the local folk. Andrew's first scene, for example, included this "leisurely ... embroidered" evocation of his mood: "He waited, in the larger chambers of his being, for the world to right itself and to become as it had been in all the other summers here, at Congreve House in Hawthorne, far north, when he had gathered the full, free days like honey and had kept his hoard against the famine of the formal city winter when he was trammeled and smothered by school and a pedagogical governess and parents whom he barely knew and certainly did not understand." By contrast Victor, the local boy, inspired a colloquial turn:

"Once Andrew had seen a green worm in [Victor's hair] and when he reached up to brush it off, Victor said, 'Leave um be. I put um there. He's measuring me a hat.'"

The characters, too, alluded back to her earlier novels. Andrew, cut off from his twittering twin sisters, was a cross between the young Ralph and Molly, less brilliantly strange than she was, more uncommon and unmasculine than he. (The boy's sexual ambivalence, hinted at, was more explicitly suggested in some of Stafford's earlier drafts.) Miss Pride lurked not too far behind Katharine, whose family physiognomy could almost be lifted from the earlier book. The Congreve portraiture hanging on the walls of the grand summer house in Hawthorne would look fine in Pinckney Street:

> These fine long faces were civilized. They were the faces of people so endowed with control and tact and insight and second sight that the feelings that might in secret ravage the spirit could never take the battlements of the flesh; no undue passion would ever show in those prudent eyes or on those discreet and handsome lips. For these was no doubt here, no self-contempt, but only the imposing courage of sterling good looks and the protecting lucidity of charm.

But rather than achieving a successful synthesis of the two manners, or a conjunction of the characters, Stafford ended up succumbing to style. The description of the Congreve gallery could almost apply to her own portraiture, for given the absence of real plot, portraiture was what the book essentially consisted of: alternating tableaux of her two protagonists. The poses that her lapidary prose allowed them to take were stiff, and their passions seemed artificial. Andrew in particular never emerged as remotely the riveting soul that poor Molly immediately was; he seemed to occupy a central place in the novel for reasons more of symmetry than sympathy. In earlier drafts, Stafford had made him an older boy and complicated his unhappiness, with mixed success, by suggesting at once an incestuous fascination with his cousin and effeminate leanings that enraged his father, and by implying a potentially artistic nature. In her final version, Stafford had retreated, deciding to hang the whole of his spiritual malaise on a summer breach with a friend. But Andrew's circumstances and his crisis inevitably seemed disproportionate, and lengthy abstract introspection only accentuated the difficulty. Since Stafford told so much more than she showed about this boy—slumped in a

hammock for most of the summer, Andrew offered little opportunity for
action—he threatened to become what so few of her children are: an
adult's idea of a child. The ritualistic, timeless world of childhood that
Stafford had captured so well before often seemed simply static here.

Katharine, who "in her rarefied world . . . countenanced no change"—
she drove around in a brougham, among other quaint habits—was a
more interesting figure, a social specimen Stafford had limned in *Boston
Adventure* and a psychological type she had sketched in her stories. Katharine was the hypertrophied Puritan, the Bostonian as seen from, in a
sense, the southern perspective: she was cut off from all vital sense of the
past and from feeling, but was fanatically devoted instead to desiccated
notions of history and humanity. And she was the frigid woman, who
had sacrificed a life of substance for an existence of appearances. Unlike
her Brahmin relatives in the earlier novel but like her aloof predecessor
in "I Love Someone," she saw her chilling predicament: "It struck her
. . . that . . . she would never participate, that she would read astutely and
never write, observe wholeheartedly and never paint, not teach, not
marry God. Untalented and uncompromising, she would not commit
herself." But her self-knowledge did not liberate her; in fact, it only
added to her resigned complacency.

Stafford had set herself a real challenge in trying to create a changeless
yet compelling protagonist. She had demonstrated that she could sustain
such a figure, almost fablelike in frozen detachment, over the course of a
story, but in her novel, her sense of distance collapsed. The fact that the
whole tone and style of the book were so close to Katharine's tone and
style introduced a central problem. In place of the old controlled irony
there was a recurring confusion: How much was in fact meant as irony,
and how much was romanticization? To what extent was Katharine intended to be a charming anachronism and to what extent an exemplar of
petrification? In earlier drafts, Stafford had included episodes to suggest
a truly sinister sterility at work: Katharine had wreaked real havoc in the
Shipleys' lives, encouraging Andrew's deep distraction and actually driving one of his sisters mad.

But by the final version, she was a considerably tamer figure. There
was a deeply unhappy woman beneath the unruffled surface—Stafford
referred throughout to the image of Katharine's Catherine wheel of torture—but her tribulations didn't live up to the metaphor. When Stafford
played out the St. Catherine symbolism in Katharine's end (she was

burned to death by a misfired Catherine wheel in a fireworks display at a grand party on her estate), the very melodrama of the conclusion called attention to the absence of real drama until that point. The only resolution for this disengaged life was a final, fantastic flight. Stafford's epigraph from Eliot's *Murder in the Cathedral* stood as a kind of endorsement of her protagonist's rarefied detachment—and a justification of her own slow, oddly hollow novel:

> Man's life is a cheat and a disappointment;
> All things are unreal,
> Unreal or disappointing:
> The Catherine wheel, the pantomime cat,
> The prizes given at the children's party,
> The prize awarded for the English Essay,
> The scholar's degree, the statesmen's decoration.
> All things become less real, man passes
> From unreality to unreality.

Although the book sold quite well (it even made it onto the bottom of the *New York Times* best-seller list), the critical reception was distinctly cool, and the emphasis was the same: the masterful formalist had abandoned life. In *The New Yorker,* the reviewer Anthony West was disappointed in the novel's preciosity: "At other times, the curse of the catalogue, which Flaubert laid upon the novel, descends, and the characters are held frozen while the oversensitive eye travels slowly over the materials of their clothing, the furniture, the bric-a-brac, the curtains, the wallpaper, and the creepers tapping at the windows." To be sure, her technique was stunning, but the trouble was that it was too stunning. "Miss Stafford's prose is so fine and frequently so winning," Irving Howe wrote in the *Kenyon Review,* "that it finally becomes a source of fascination in itself, undermining the matter it is supposed to reveal."

Oddly enough, Stafford herself seemed to offer a similar indictment in her interview with Harvey Breit in the *New York Times* when the novel appeared. At least it is possible to read her criticisms of current trends as a comment on herself: "You need to get back to even the confusions you had, which all help. I think the self-consciousness today, the over-editing, is a mistake," she told Breit. "The writer today is competent. The English writer can't write a bad sentence, but too often it doesn't add up. Writers have been directing their talents to tiny things.

There's a fear of making a mistake, of sticking your neck out, there is a finicking."

Stafford's great "gifts for language and for details" were, as Peter Taylor rightly saw, "one and the same gift and ... inseparable," and there was real brilliance in the carefully crafted surface: "For me," Taylor wrote, "the genius shines forth in the selection and use of all the paraphernalia." But here she seemed to be relying more heavily than ever before on style, and she was using her virtuosic skills less to dramatize than to elaborate abstractly on her characters' anxieties, which were in any case wan compared with the raw unhappiness in her earlier novels. It was as though, as her own earlier story had predicted, she had laid out an exquisite banquet at which there was nothing to eat.

She was at a crossroads after her troubles with *In the Snowfall,* and there was an uncanny correspondence between Stafford's novel and the long title poem Lowell published the year before in *The Mills of the Kavanaughs* at a broadly comparable stage of uncertainty. His poem and *The Catherine Wheel* shared the Damariscotta Mills setting, and there was an underlying thematic similarity in the stories both of them told, about fraught love, betrayal, and the threat of madness in an aristocratic New England clan: at shaky midcareer, both recovering from breakdowns, they reached back to the theme of New England decay that had launched their careers, not sure where else to turn. The two works represented transitional efforts for both of them and suggested the very different courses they were embarked on. Lowell was struggling to introduce autobiographical elements and a more direct, dramatic voice into his still formal poetic style. (At the end of her life, Stafford indicated to Robert Giroux that she felt intimately, inwardly, familiar with Lowell's poem, in which there were clearly echoes of their troubled marriage.) By contrast, Stafford was refining an increasingly oblique approach; she was in search of some way to escape the confessional pressures that had sabotaged *In the Snowfall.* The result for both of them was oddly analogous: lifeless subject matter and a mannered style. But the creative future that lay ahead for each could hardly have been less similar.

AT THE CLOSE of 1952, the year *The Catherine Wheel* appeared, Stafford was back in the Virgin Islands, this time ending her marriage to Oliver Jensen. She was in terrible physical shape. A doctor who saw her at the Gibneys' thought she should be hurried back to New York for medical care, which is exactly where she ended up when her requisite stay in the tropics was over. After subletting an apartment in New York, she decided to go back to Connecticut, despite her derision of the bourgeois bohemianism there. She rented rooms on the top floor at 24 Elm Avenue in Westport, and after a run of illness and discomfort, which she recounted in a letter to the Gibneys in her usual comic, hyperbolic style, she settled in and claimed she was feeling very content.

As Stafford described it, her new existence was the culmination of her retreat. It was a new role—reclusive spinsterhood—that she, echoing her character Katharine, took self-conscious satisfaction in cultivating. In a droll letter to Peter Taylor, she presented herself as a caricature, drawing attention to the continuity between her life and her fiction. Or perhaps more accurately, between her fiction and her life, for the relation once again seemed reversed: Stafford's own existence imitated her art, rather than the other way around. "I'm very happy. Have you ever heard me say that before? You couldn't have because I've never said it. I am living the life I was destined for: I am a single woman with a cat and when I am not writing crabbed stories of frustration, I am hard at work on needlepoint."

She was not always so cheerful, but at the outset, even in her darker moods, she continued to emphasize self-sufficiency. Her greater aloofness was not for lack of invitations. Blair and Holly Clark urged her to join them in Europe, assuring her it could be a quiet life of concentration, but she was not persuaded. She was far from totally isolated (she counted on Westport friends to keep her company, sometimes at ungodly hours), but she liked to be able to escape when she wanted. She aimed to avoid the literary-social distractions to which she knew she was so unhappily susceptible, and which inevitably made her feel compromised and insecure. "I see almost no one, really—the P.R. boys are really beyond the pale with their machinations," she wrote to the Clarks. "Everyone seems to be crumbling away into false positions and inertia—but maybe they're all having the time of their lives and it's only I who sit out here glooming away, reminded distressfully of my rooming house in Concord by this establishment."

She exaggerated her isolation, especially as time went on, when she made periodic trips to New York to see her friends, often staying and entertaining at the Cosmopolitan Club, of which she was very pleased to be a member. Still, she obviously valued her "spinsterish, rural life," as she called it, even if the old insecurity was still there. The Concord parallel was a revealing one. Then she had been convalescing after the car accident and feeling ambivalent about the attentions of Hightower and Lowell: the woman who had declared her desire to be loved was wondering if she was after all simply a cheat—of herself, and of others—unable to love. And she had been busily writing, turning out pages of *Autumn Festival* for Archie Ogden. In Westport, to judge by a diary entry from the spring of 1953, she was in a sense convalescing again, from a depression that seemed to stem from a version of the old fear of frigidity. She was ruefully aware, like her character Katharine, of the self-imprisonment that her remoteness brought:

> The depression has commenced to lift a little and possibly I know why. (I am too doctoring and too diagnostic when I begin to heal and my pretentiousness sickens me more than the depression.) My ailment is that I cannot be overtly loved. (Oh, Dr. Sherfey knows that. And if I were to die tonight and this were the only scrap of paper I left it would not be news to her. Probably not to anyone.) I mean: Oliver was worshipful and I was scornful. . . . Now at the moment of release for which I longed, I see the loss of what I needed.

This time, too, she was "writing like crazy," working on (among other things) *A Winter's Tale.* As Mary Louise Aswell noted in her introduction to the collection of *New Short Novels* in which the novella first appeared, it was "an example of emotion recollected in tranquillity, a supreme example." That was the plot and structure of *A Winter's Tale:* a middle-aged woman reflecting back on a youthful love affair in Heidelberg from the vantage point of a barren life in Boston. But the emergence of the novella was itself also an example of retrospective revision: Stafford was turning back to a piece of youthful fiction, *Autumn Festival,* in which she had been unable to establish the right distance, and she was trying to tame it in her reworking of the material. On both levels, the result was not a Wordsworthian synthesis of passion and reason, but rather an unsettling display of a deep tension between the two.

A Winter's Tale started out as another of Stafford's portraits in petrifaction. Her infinitely resigned first-person narrator, Fanny, sounded like a close relative of the narrator of "I Love Someone" as she introduced herself in the framing episode that opened the story. Though this wan woman was married and a mother, she was as isolated as a spinster: "I am at peace with my beyondness and the melancholy that it implies . . . but there do come moments when I wonder if ever again I will prefer the sun of summer to this weary light." It seemed at first as though recollecting her passionate past would help cure her detachment and reconcile her to her present. But the story did not turn out to be such a conventional tale of middle-aged accommodation. It was a bleak account of disenchantment at the core, as the narrator turned to face the sources of her cynical aloofness.

The love story Fanny conjured up was far from a happy, healthy affair. Though Stafford had seen to it that young Fanny was not the extreme self-hating specimen Gretchen Marburg was, once again Germany served as the setting for a punishing mixture of decadence and discipline. Instead of the religious conversion that she planned in the original Dom Paternus story, Stafford staged a revelation in human faithlessness. An unfocused college girl whose loneliness had lately been assuaged by lots of beaux and whiskey, Fanny had been sent by her widower father, "an ascetic Boston Irishman," to Germany for a term to be supervised by an ex-Bostonian and zealous Catholic convert named Persis Galt—a woman who, it turned out, was having an affair with a young Nazi, Max Rössler. They were a loveless pair, Max long since disillusioned but still entrapped, fearing exposure by Persis, who knew he was a Jew. Fascinated by Max, Fanny was drawn into a secret affair with him, not exactly the careless fling she had planned for her year. "It was not love; it was another thing. I don't know what," Fanny reflected, as she and Max tormented themselves before he ultimately left on maneuvers in Spain, only to die on the way.

Compared with the subdued suffering in *The Catherine Wheel, A Winter's Tale* is high historical drama. Yet the prose was in the cool style of Stafford's maturity, far from the fervent overwriting of her first German effort. It showed how she had modulated the paired themes of the sadistic tyrant and the masochistic outsider, desperate to belong and seeking in vain for real love. Frau Galt was a portrait in twisted power lust, with "a lack of talent which she had deceived herself into thinking was a talent for writing poetry or painting water colors or marrying a Bostonian but was really a lack of talent for being good. In the absence of goodness, she had to have power." She was Miss Pride, with an admixture of Hopestill, yet the old imposing fire was gone.

Fanny and Max, the lost souls, were similarly dampened; there was a world-weariness to their alienated agony. "I haven't any politics and I haven't any ideals," Max told Fanny, and then outlined the barrenness of his life with unsettling resignation: "It would be wonderful to be a Christian or entirely to love one's country. Entirely loving oneself would be the best of all." The young Fanny made the motions of rebelling against his fatalism, but as recounted by her older self, her protestations of hope and love rang hollow. When he died, she studiously insulated herself against any real feeling: "There had always been the danger that I would mourn Max, that I would miss him, would become inward about him. It had been necessary to get back to America to return to the exterior."

It was a bloodless portrait in disengagement, and yet Stafford ostensibly granted the middle-aged Fanny a kind of liberation in the novella's conclusion, which returned to the framing story. Her survey of memory accomplished, the past was erased—and Fanny announced: "I am exalted; I believe that I am altogether purged." Yet it was an eerie purgation, which left a woman who still seemed detached from her present detached now from her past as well. At least that Heidelberg memory had once kept alive a sense of conflict in her life. As Fanny and her husband looked forward to a trip to Bermuda, that "sun of summer" she was escaping to seemed as bleached as the "weary light" she claimed she had escaped from.

The novella suggested that for Stafford, too, the resurrection of that German memory and plot was not the creative inspiration she might have hoped. Doubtless she was pleased to be encouraged by Mary Louise Aswell, but a sense of her own disengagement pervades the story. Though rewritten into the first person, it was studiously constructed so that the narrator was as aloof as possible. And though Stafford had clearly worked at including more dramatized action, the scenes in *A Winter's Tale* were stagy rather than immediately moving. Finally, she had expanded the original story, but it was evident from the result how far Stafford was from a theme and characters adequate to a novel, which was once again the challenge facing her.

IN THE SPRING of 1953 Stafford's first collection of short stories, *Children Are Bored on Sunday,* was published to general acclaim, and after a dispute with Harcourt, Brace (over foreign rights), she signed a contract with Random House in the fall of 1953 for another book of stories. The contract also called for a novel, due by the beginning of May 1955, only slightly more than a year and a half away. But Stafford had trouble getting down to work on the book. Practical considerations, she emphasized, had something to do with her evasion of the novel. She was more worried than ever about money, which had been a preoccupation since she had emerged from Payne Whitney. Her recourse, now as then, was to turn out stories for *The New Yorker,* along with occasional articles for women's magazines. Sickness, too, made sustained work on a large undertaking more difficult. Among many other complaints, Stafford contracted hepatitis in the fall of 1955. (It was in Westport that she acquired one of her treasured possessions, a hospital bed.) Those were the explanations she gave her editor, Albert Erskine, when she failed to meet her deadline, but she knew the trouble went deeper: "It's mainly indolence, stupidity and a fundamental lack of talent," she wrote to him, full of self-recrimination.

It was a typically hyperbolic catalog of indictments, but it suggested a crisis of confidence not unlike her experience with *In the Snowfall,* when she also had trouble facing her daunting project and worried that her talent had deserted her. As for her "stupidity," she might have been alluding to the fact that she found herself doing again what she had vowed, in "Truth and the Novelist," not to do. It is clear from the manuscript fragments that remain that she was trying to write a novel based quite closely on her own life, focusing on her fate in the East but also ranging back to her Colorado childhood. "I'll tell you this much," she revealed to an interviewer two decades later when the book was still unfinished, "it is my first autobiographical novel. It's about Mommy and Daddy and Missouri and Colorado and Massachusetts and New York, all places where I've lived. A well-known American poet, with whom I was once closely associated, is petrified. And well he should be! I'm cutting up the poets to a fare-thee-well."

Her jaunty confidence in that interview was not at all characteristic. It was a pose put on for precisely the public relations machinery that she detested and that she had eerily predicted in "An Etiquette for Writers" would come to hound her during fallow times. Already in the 1950s, when the novel was not yet the albatross it later became, she was worried about its future, as she confessed to her intimates. Katharine White was especially sympathetic and encouraging, sending Stafford reassurances in the summer of 1955 (shortly after the Random House deadline had come and gone): "I do hope the novel gets going. Don't worry about it, though, for if you would just write some short stories that would start you off."

It was a natural suggestion, for until then, Stafford had been fruitfully turning out short stories. Before Christmas of 1954 (which she spent in the hospital with pneumonia), she had been "absolutely on top of the world, so healthy, so happy, so productive," she wrote to the Thompsons. Her short stories, unlike her novella or her novels, were a real source of satisfaction. But they did not serve to start her off on the novel. Rather than catalysts, the stories represented another recourse altogether, an alternate way of dealing with the substantive and stylistic challenges she faced in the novel. In the group of western stories she had been producing, she found a very different route around the troublesome autobiographical terrain. Shifting to a comic tone and making childhood her subject, she discovered that she could return to her home ground without succumbing to memories that overwhelmed her imagination. And a newly confident ironic distance enabled her to revisit other parts of her past as well in the nonwestern stories she continued to write.

Her strategy in the Colorado stories is a stark contrast to *The Catherine Wheel.* Where her baroque manner predominated in that book in almost exaggerated form, she drew on her *Mountain Lion* style for the central group of stories she wrote during the 1950s. In fact, in these stories, set in a town called Adams, a fictionalized Boulder, she looked even more explicitly to Twain as a model than she had in her earlier novel. Here she overcame the "quarrel with the landscape" of the West that had partly stymied *In the Snowfall,* and she also dealt successfully with people she had met, in fact with her own kin (who had also stymied that novel). It was a strictly literary breakthrough, for her actual relations with her Colorado past had become, if anything, more strained. She had ended up in the hospital after her reunion with her father at her sister's ranch in the summer of 1951. And as she wrote to the Thompsons in 1954 when they urged her to come for a visit, her father and his increasingly hopeless predicament remained an insurmountable reason for avoiding the West: "I'm still no better able to face it than before," she confessed. To Blair Clark and his wife she was more vehement, after a visit in the fall of 1954 from her sister Mary Lee, who came bearing more tales of her father's misery: "I have never had an encounter with my family that did not fetch me up in the hospital with one thing or another. I *hate* them."

Of course it was not that simple. She stayed as far away as she could, but not without guilt for her negligence. "I dreamed that I never visited my parents although they lived in Westport and I went often to other friends," Stafford had written in her journal in 1947. "I woke to lie an hour in a torment of guilt and then, as if my dream had been prophetic, there was a letter from my father in the mail, heartbreaking, relentlessly pitiful. He is inconsolably lonely, but he will live on and on, the sad, senile child." During the 1950s, her father wrote more frequently, two-to-three-page letters in which the full extent of his eccentricity was on display in a style strangely reminiscent of Stafford's own epistolary manner. In long, ornate sentences sprinkled with colloquialisms and exaggerations, he described one harebrained scheme after another (including plans for an outlandish novel about a prehistoric modern civilization) and vented his spleen on some of his favorite topics, such as the degradation of the American public, the national debt, and the virtues of the country over the city.

There was an undercurrent of irony throughout, as though he were drawing on an old comic homespun parlance he had shared with his daughter during her youth, and yet also acknowledging the great distance that now loomed between them. "Jean, why the Sam Hill don't you jump a plane some day and come out here for at least a few days," he wrote to her in 1955. "You and I could have a good visit, reminiscent of our great summer at Mrs. Meyer's house in El Dora." It was an invitation that made Stafford cringe and stay East (in real life), and yet it helps explain her ability to make the trip back in her fiction. John Stafford was recalling a retreat to the mountains that the two literary Staffords, father and daughter, had made in the 1930s, both of them full of plans to write.

It was the trip that Jean had commemorated as a child in her story "Fame Is Sweet to the Foolish Man," in which she good-humoredly mocked both herself and him: "But each knew that the other was weakening—that his thoughts were turning from the philosophy of the short story and the movement of the drama to the extraordinarily inviting snow-capped peaks and cool shaded lakes." They had been united in a Twainian world of well-intentioned delinquency, and the delight was doubled because here the father, far from an authority figure, was a companion in dereliction. Together they had escaped ordinary society for independent adventure, which they conceived in solitary, high literary terms. They planned to spin out their imaginative fantasies on paper amid the peaks. But distracted by each other and by their surroundings, they had settled for more mundane experience—in the end, the experience of failing to find the perfect creative retreat. That was not a great frustration, as Stafford told it. Instead, it was an ironic comeuppance that both of them were able to take in stride.

During the 1950s, Stafford found herself able again to draw on that mocking comic treatment of the anticlimactic Colorado adventures of her childhood, adventures that otherwise seemed to overwhelm her. It was as though she had discovered a way imaginatively to recover the spirit of her childhood before she had felt her father's shadow everywhere. Stafford wasn't writing purely autobiographically by any means (in several of the Adams stories, the father was the stolid manager of Safeway, an ironic inversion if there ever was one). But she was staking a claim to her western heritage, and indirectly addressing enchantments and disenchantments from her past. On the surface, it was a significant departure from her *New Yorker*-style stories, with their sophisticated manner and comparatively enervated characters. In the central group of Adams stories, Stafford was writing about rambunctious children, and like Twain, she was definitely not writing for genteel grown-ups. Her aim was, like his, "to try to pleasantly remind adults of what they once were themselves, and of how they felt and thought and talked, and what queer enterprises they sometimes engaged in," as he put it in his preface to *Tom Sawyer*. Despite the stylistic novelty, Stafford's underlying theme drew on her persistent preoccupation—the impossible dream of escape, which expressed itself contradictorily in a desire for solitude and a dread of loneliness. The notable difference was that in these stories, as in "Fame Is Sweet to the Foolish Man," the failure really to flee, either oneself or society, was not a psychic crisis but a comic adventure.

"The Healthiest Girl in Town" (1951), Stafford's first Adams story, signaled the shift in tone in an outspoken way. Its very title suggested that she had in mind an ironic commentary on herself and her neurasthenic reputation as well as on her fiction. (After all, Stafford was well known as one of the least healthy girls in town. Describing the literary crowd at a New York party in the late 1940s, the eclectic writer and artist Weldon Kees gave her a starring invalid role: among the guests were "people you thought were permanently settled in sanataria, like Jean Stafford, looking more ravaged and nervous than you had thought possible.") She hadn't yet introduced the protagonist who regularly appeared in subsequent stories, Emily Vanderpool. But young Jessie, who told the story in the first person—a rarity for Stafford—was Emily's forerunner, a tomboyish girl who stood out for her vigor in a town heavily populated by tuberculars.

In the story Stafford reversed the usual pose of alienation. This time it was the sturdy exiled from the weak. Arrived in Adams with her mother, a nurse, Jessie felt left out among "the ailing citizenry." And the drama took the opposite turn. Rather than retreating to resigned isolation, Jessie in the end triumphantly asserted her independence and affirmed the energetic pursuit of experience: she was healthy and happy to be that way. But she was not granted her zest without first suffering the familiar insecure desire to belong, which Stafford played for all its comic potential. She satirically portrayed illness as an elite social category and developed her character's class anxiety in clever episodes that also perfectly captured the cadences of childhood—and were very funny. Jessie made an incongruous aspiring invalid. She was ridiculed by the spindly, sickly Butler girls (from Boston), who vaunted their invalidism in a succession of well-paced scenes:

> I do not think that Laura and Ada [Butler] despised me more than they did anyone else, but I was the only one they could force to come home with them. "Who wants to be healthy if being healthy means being a cow?" said Ada one day, looking at me as I reached for a third insipid cooky. I withdrew my hand and blushed so hotly in my humiliation that Laura screamed with laughter and cried, "The friendly cow all red and white, we give her biscuits with all our might."

There was obvious self-mockery involved in the story. After all, Stafford, unlike Jessie, did in a sense succumb to the romantic allure of illness to escape her hickness—and she ended up in a different kind of sanitarium. (Young Jessie, like Stafford from childhood on, pored over medical tomes, studying symptoms in hopes of developing them; but whereas Jessie got over the fixation, Stafford didn't.)

Emily Vanderpool was a still more autobiographical protagonist, whose salient characteristic was not her health but her "awful tongue." Stafford explicitly admitted her affiliation in her introduction to her second story collection, *Bad Characters* (1964):

> Emily Vanderpool . . . who acknowledges that she has a bad character, is someone I knew well as a child; indeed, I often occupied her skin and, looking back, I think that while she was notional and stubborn and a trial to her kin, her talent for iniquity was feeble— she wanted to be a road-agent but she hadn't a chance. Her troubles stemmed from the low company she kept, but she didn't seek these parties out: they found her. It is a widespread human experience.

Emily was the good-hearted "bad" girl with a susceptibility to dubious associations, which led her into adventures that discomfited the conventional world—and that backfired on her. She was at once a rebel and a show-off, eager to stir up her family and the townsfolk, but also dying to be a star; she was alternately "possessed with a passion to be by myself"—which was when her malicious tongue came into play, antagonizing all those nearby—and desperate for companionship. But this girl Tom Sawyer had no Huck to escape with. ("Tom was like the rest of the respectable boys, in that he envied Huckleberry his gaudy outcast condition, and was under strict orders not to play with him. So he played with him every time he got a chance.") Instead, as Stafford depicted her predicament in the two best Vanderpool stories, "Bad Characters" (1954) and "A Reading Problem" (1956), Emily stumbled on inadequate substitutes—outcasts who were indeed gaudy, but who were not the seriously subversive influence that Huck was.

Emily's brushes with the unwashed—in "Bad Characters" she got mixed up with Lottie Jump, an eleven-year-old shoplifter from the wrong side of the tracks; in "A Reading Problem," she crossed paths with a preacher con man and his scrawny daughter—introduced excitement into her life, but they didn't really threaten her connection with the "respectable" world of Adams and her family (a far more conventional clan than the real-life Staffords). The willful girl whose taste for solitude had gotten her into trouble ended up somewhat chastened and more sociable. In fact, the ironic moral of the stories was that it was Emily's very antisociability that made her a good citizen: a high-spirited, independent girl could prosper in dull Adams after all. Not that she was going to stay there: "Yes, sir, Emily, you're going to go places," the local sheriff told her admiringly in "A Reading Problem." But in the meantime, she could happily settle for escapades instead of true escape—as Stafford had done with her father in the mountains.

As in her youthful fictional efforts, Stafford was busy experimenting with dialects, again in Twainian style. In "Bad Characters," it was Lottie Jump's tongue that especially enthralled Emily: "I had never heard such gaudy, cynical talk and was trying to memorize it all." Equally enthralled herself, Stafford devoted a great deal of attention to capturing accurately the telltale vernacular of her low characters. In "A Reading Problem" Evangelist Gerlash and his daughter Opal spent twelve pages trying to talk Emily out of some money or food in a comical hybrid of stentorian sermonizing, huckster talk, and backwoods slang. Occasionally a hokey, inauthentic note crept in, but Stafford managed to make much of the humor—and pathos—of the stories ride on the dialogue, coupled with her flair for the perfectly placed detail.

The Vanderpool stories painted a surprisingly cheery picture of childhood in Adams, and the grown-up Emily who narrated the stories seemed to have turned out to be a very witty character with a wholesome perspective on her past. There was no hint of the real trauma of Stafford's youth, or at least what she later came to see as the trauma: her strange father, whom she saw in a different light after a period of childish adulation—as a version of Huck Finn's pap, the man who kept his family forever on the margins of respectability. He was the figure who made escape imperative and yet also impossible, the character she tried to limn in *In the Snowfall*. Stafford had real trouble writing about him, though she did allude, however indirectly, to problematic paternal influence in her one other collected story (aside from "The Darkening Moon") about young children, "Cops and Robbers." Published in 1953, "Cops and Robbers" was a story notably *not* set in Adams but in Westport, and the tone was completely different from the spirit of her western stories. She drew on an incident from her own childhood that loomed large years later, at least in the memory of her sister Marjorie. In his penury, John Stafford had started cutting his family's hair himself, to the mortification of his youngest daughter, who once rebelled midway through and sported a ragged look for months. In her story, young Hannah's golden locks— which were just like her mother's extravagantly admired hair—were shorn by a barber at the instruction of her father, who was wreaking indirect revenge on his wife. It was a devastating portrait of a child's fall from innocent security into loveless anonymity: "She felt that she was already shrinking and fading, that all her rights of being seen and listened to and caressed were ebbing away. Chilled and exposed as she was, she was becoming, nonetheless, invisible."

In two very different Adams stories that appeared the same year as "Cops and Robbers," sandwiched in among her Vanderpool tales, Stafford again alluded, again indirectly, to that darker version of her past. Here the "children" were grown-up, and the stories she told were of entrapment. They shared the vernacular vigor of Stafford's sunnier Adams stories but reversed the Vanderpool plot line of progress toward healthy maturation. She avoided fathers altogether, making her characters orphans. The narrator of "In the Zoo" and Polly Bay, the protagonist of "The Liberation" (both published in 1953), could hardly have been less like resilient Emily, who prospered rebelliously in Adams and then presumably moved on, well prepared for abandoning her provincial past. Here Stafford portrayed an insidious destruction of spirit that rendered her characters, when they finally did manage to leave, anxious souls ill equipped to face the world.

In the antipastoral Adams stories, Stafford's protagonists were passive creatures who couldn't fight back against the influences that oppressed them but could only try to flee. In "In the Zoo" two middle-aged sisters, meeting in Denver, were suddenly overcome by memories of the dismal past they had spent fifty miles north in Adams, where their view of the world and of themselves had been eroded by Mrs. Placer, their foster mother. A Dickensian figure, she ran a boardinghouse and dedicated herself to proselytizing a view that echoed John Stafford's bleaker attitude, that "life was essentially a matter of being done in, let down, and swindled." Polly Bay in the ironically titled "The Liberation" finally worked up the courage to escape the tyrannical provincialism of Adams to marry an Easterner, only to learn, just as she was ready to depart, that her fiancé was dead. Bravely, she set off anyway, but Stafford deftly conveyed the naïveté of her valor in the concluding sentences of the story: "How lonely I have been, she thought. And then, not fully knowing what she meant by it but believing in it faithfully, she said half aloud, 'I am not lonely now.'"

What was striking in Stafford's Adams stories was the distance she established from the troublesome landscape of her past, which not so long before had frustrated her efforts on *In the Snowfall*. With her roguish girls, she had discovered a comic voice that was a welcome counterweight to the highly wrought prose of *The Catherine Wheel.* Even in the darker stories about older "children"—the intimidated orphans—Stafford managed to convey psychological suffocation without getting caught in the tortuous narrative of introspection that had tangled her third novel. Instead, she found a tragicomic approach that worked. She turned to drama and above all to dialogue, direct and indirect, as the external clues to casts of mind. Her virtuosic style was ideally suited to capturing the nuances of speech, and in these stories she found a way to make language itself one of her main subjects, without succumbing to mere surface preoccupation with style.

A similar comic distance liberated Stafford to conquer other terrain that had proved difficult in the past. In two of her lighter non-Adams stories of these years, "Maggie Meriwether's Rich Experience" (1955) and "Caveat Emptor" (originally published as "The Matchmakers" in *Mademoiselle* in 1956), she turned to themes that she had tried to treat in, respectively, *Autumn Festival* and her Neville novel. Now she had the satiric perspective that she had lacked then, and she was able to draw on two ironic genres—the tale of the innocent American abroad and the campus spoof—in putting resistant autobiographical material to fictional use. In fact, Stafford demonstrated a kind of double distance: at the same time that she drew on the conventions of the genres, she stood back and satirized them.

Admittedly, Stafford's comic approach meant domesticating the themes that had overwhelmed her novelistic efforts years before. Nashvillian Maggie Meriwether's mortifying afternoon among decadent European aristocrats was an echo of Gretchen Marburg's ordeal among the Germans. But Maggie's identity crisis was a mere superficial episode, where Gretchen's disorientation led to a radical convulsion of consciousness. That was precisely Stafford's point: the richness of Maggie's experience was not really in the experience itself, but in the telling of it. For in this verbally acrobatic story, the central subject was language. High-spirited Maggie, off on a European lark, was unexpectedly "bamboozled into muteness by the language of France," which rendered her an embarrassed outsider among the voluble guests gathered at M. le Baron's manor house. But the story's happy ending declared Maggie's alienation on this outlandish afternoon to be the perfect source for lighthearted storytelling, once "the most sophisticated, the most cosmopolitan, the prettiest raconteur of middle Tennessee" was back among her fellow Americans and in command of her tongue. By then Stafford had already shown how to tell the tale with a display of her stylistic repertoire. She mocked the varieties of vacuous chatter, relishing the occasion for exotic words, serpentine sentences (she opened with a ten-line extravaganza), colloquialisms, and daringly manipulated similes and metaphors.

Stafford called on the same tone and technique in "Caveat Emptor," turning what had been a heavy-handed diatribe against Neville into a deft satire of Alma Hettrick College for Girls—and of two scholarly misfits there, new members of the faculty, who were appalled by the silly school. Standing back from earnest Malcolm and Victoria (whose thesis—*Some Late Borrowings from Provençal* fin amour *in Elizabethan Miscellanies and Songbooks*—recalled Stafford's own on thirteenth-century love motifs), she identified the problem in her first attempt at a takeoff. "They were far too young and their principles were far too vernal for them to rise above their circumstance," she observed of her characters and implicitly of her youthful self; "their laughter was not very mirthful but was, really, reflexive." This time Stafford had no trouble rising above the circumstance. Appropriating details from her abandoned Neville manuscript, she shaped another comic drama about clashing vocabularies and values, as her two high-minded teachers rebelled against their banal surroundings.

Stafford relished incongruity in these stories, turning it into comedy that was mirthful precisely because it wasn't reflexive. She had the distance to make the most of juxtapositions and tensions that had once seemed threatening. And in writing about language, she was in a sense commenting on her own stylistic experiments, her efforts to intermix the polished and the colloquial, to avoid precious refinement in the first and facile contrivance in the second. Her stories reflect an appreciation of the ways in which style can betray its supposed masters. Pretensions don't last long: appearances can be deceiving, but the way people sound tells more than they may want others to know—or than others may want to know.

The frightening, rather than amusing, implications of that theme emerged in two roughly contemporaneous but radically different stories, "Beatrice Trueblood's Story" (1955) and "The End of a Career" (1956). The farcical tone that marked so many of Stafford's stories of the 1950s was gone here, and so was any trace of her own past experience. Instead,

Stafford seemed to be drawing on the conventions of fable in these stories, which both had a prophetic cast. "The End of a Career" reads like a parable about the future of Stafford's own art. "Beatrice Trueblood's Story" can't help looking in retrospect like an uncanny foreshadowing of her personal fate.

Both were, once again, stories of retreat. "When Beatrice Trueblood was in her middle thirties and on the very eve of her second marriage, to a rich and reliable man—when, that is, she was in the prime of life and on the threshold of a rosier phase of it than she had ever known before," Stafford began, and then gave the conventional opening the twist of a dark fable, "she overnight was stricken with total deafness." Beatrice's affliction, it became clear, was psychosomatic: she desperately wanted to shut out the "whole menagerie of passions—fire-breathing dragons and bone-crushing serpents and sabertoothed tigers" that seethed within marriages. Stafford once again called on the imagery of St. Teresa's besieged castle: Beatrice, the ever-patient listener haunted by the "humiliating, disrobing displays" that she witnessed between her parents and endured with her first husband, did what Pansy Vanneman in "The Interior Castle" in the end denied herself—sought escape into that inner chamber by willing deafness. But then Beatrice found herself trapped. "She had not bargained for banishment, she said; she had only wanted a holiday. . . . And now," she explained, "I'm sorry because I'm so lonely here, inside my skull. Not hearing makes one helplessly egocentric."

Stafford was explicit here as nowhere else about the nature of psychosomatic travails, though the mind's struggle with matter and with other minds was the preoccupation of most of her stories. The whole point of the fable was to look behind fate to find psychological forces working with an incredible, fairy-tale–like potency. Wishes were granted, and the wisher was overwhelmed. Stafford expertly balanced psychological realism and a sense of the mind's fantastic powers. "My God," Beatrice exclaimed, incredulous that she had actually chosen deafness, "the mind is diabolical! . . . Even in someone as simple as I."

Stafford seems to have had similar trouble putting much stock in psychosomatic explanations in life—despite her brilliant exploration of them in fiction. "I have had two rather good days during which I felt that I was on the verge of a revelation: what Sherfey was trying to get across to me was the meaning of 'psychosomatic' and there have been moments when I've almost understood," she once wrote to a friend, "but I listen to everything she says with no more than the skin of my mind." She acknowledged the inconsistency of her skepticism in a letter in the spring of 1956 to another friend, Nancy Flagg Gibney, about a conversation with her "groper." They were discussing the possible psychological causes of a tearing eye that began after her trip to the Virgin Islands to divorce Jensen, when she had been enchanted by Gibney's baby:

> If one can accept the premises [*sic*] that the trouble is psychogenic (and it's very hard for me to do so; she said, "You wrote a story about psychological deafness so why can't you accept this?" and my reply, the only possible one, was "Yes, but I don't believe it,") things fit neatly into place—the hysterectomy and immediately afterward my first experience with a baby. But it's too neat and even if we've found the cause, how can the symptoms be removed?

Twenty years later, Jean Stafford's story took a turn not unlike Beatrice's: overnight she, the virtuosic talker, was suddenly struck dumb. Too neat though it may seem, it is hard not to be reminded by this story (which was originally entitled "Patterns") of Stafford's eerie guidance to a biographical reading of her work in her sketch years before: "She was terrified by the patterns of her life, . . .by the fact that she had imagined and had written much that had happened later."

The silencing of Stafford's speech was still decades away. It was her writing that was worrying her during the mid-1950s. In December of 1955, Stafford confessed to Katharine White that she was having trouble producing stories, never mind the novel. It was not a confession she was making widely (on the contrary, an item in the *Writer's Newsletter* in the spring of 1956 announced that she was finishing up her new novel in Westport). But the admission lurked within a story that she had sent to *The New Yorker* earlier in the fall and that was published in January of 1956. True to the story's title—"The End of a Career"—it turned out to be the last year her fiction appeared with any regularity in the magazine. Only two stories, neither of which she included in her *Collected Stories,* appeared the next year, and then more than a decade passed before "The Philosophy Lesson," drawn from *In the Snowfall,* was published in 1968 and another decade before "An Influx of Poets" appeared in 1978.

"The End of a Career," Katharine White wrote to Stafford, "is done in such an interesting style.... Everything is meant to be somewhat larger than life, I take it, since this is a sort of fable in hyperbole." It was the story of fifty-year-old Angelica Early, "one of the most beautiful women in the world's history," and the demise of her career dedicated to the preservation of that beauty. A variation on "I Love Someone," the story was about the allure and the ultimate hollowness of striving for a life of perfect surfaces. Stafford encouraged an analogy between Angelica's enterprise and the artist's vocation:

> Perhaps, like an artist, [Angelica] was not always grateful for this talent of beauty that destiny had imposed upon her without asking leave, but, like the artist, she knew where her duty lay; the languishing and death of her genius would be the languishing and death of herself, and suicide, though it is often understandable, is almost never moral.... If my talent goes, I'm done for, says the artist, and Angelica said, if I lose my looks, I'm lost.

Of course Angelica did lose her looks as she aged, despite all the craftsmanship that she devoted to preserving herself. In this fairy tale, there was no fountain of youth, no salvation—except for love, as a wise doctor tried to explain to her: " 'There is an aesthetic principle,' he pursued, 'that says beauty is the objectification of love. To be loved is to be beautiful, but to be beautiful is not necessarily to be loved.... Go and find a lover and obfuscate his senses.' " It was a version of the principle that Stafford the artist had poignantly declared to Lowell years before: that literary talent for her held second place to the talent he had cruelly told her she lacked—the talent of loving and being loved. The principle had been a recipe for pain then, when she was lonely and her talent was in full flower, and it was even harder to live by now, when she was leading the solitary spinster life and doubting her gift. (She was also doubting that craftsmanship could compensate—though she tried: White proposed a plot to her, which Stafford turned into "The Mountain Day," not one of her better stories.) The words that she had written to her sister five years earlier at another creative impasse lurk behind Angelica's: "If [my gift] has [gone], God knows what will become of me because that is the only thing in the world I have."

Though not consciously confronting the end of her career, Stafford was less sure of her gift at this point. She had produced an impressive group of stories, but they didn't seem to help spur on the novel. She had found a way to write about Colorado, Europe, and Stephens by stepping back and scaling down. Short stories are of course not necessarily minor,

but Stafford was quite consciously shaping hers as circumscribed tales—
and she was quite consciously counting on producing something longer.
Her projected novel, however, apparently loomed as a loose and baggy
monster—more on the *Boston Adventure* model than her other carefully
tailored novels. And as the years went by it seemed to get even looser
and baggier as she groped among the different, mostly dark episodes of
her life for a plot to propel it, for perspective on her all-too-familiar
protagonist.

When Peter Taylor's story about their youthful aspirations, "1939,"
came out in *The New Yorker* in 1955, Stafford was vividly reminded of
the early years of making her literary way. Taylor dared her to counter
his portrait of her as a young artist with her own version: "If any little
detail in it makes you cross, I hope—no I challenge you to write a story
giving some impressions of your own of that part of our lives." To Nancy
Flagg Gibney she admitted that the story had made her cross, but Taylor's challenge was just what posed problems for Stafford, and her poignant reply to him helped explain why: "I thought the story fine and
very sad," she told him, "—at least it was for me because I don't see much
difference in myself from those gauche days although I do dress better.
What alarmed me the most, I suppose, was that all of it seemed like
yesterday and nearly as important as it was then: so that, on your part, is
genius."

Stafford was still too close in spirit to that past to turn her impressions
into successful fiction. Back then, in 1939, full of insecurity and ambition,
she had been anxiously attempting to launch her career; now as her career approached an awkward midpoint, she knew she hadn't escaped the
insecurity. She feared that her peak might be behind her, and a certain
ambivalence seemed to have edged out ambition. As she looked ahead,
wondering how to make a living, those early, fabulous days cast a
shadow. "I'm quite sure [grant applications] will never work in a million
years," she wrote dispiritedly to the Thompsons as she set about applying
for them anyway. "It might if I were still married to Cal and were still
best friends with the Tates but now there's scarcely a prayer."

CHAPTER 12

Isle of Arran
and Samothrace

S TAFFORD ENDED UP taking a trip to London in the summer of 1956, and her spirits were low. The spring in America had been dismal, to judge from a letter that Katharine White sent her soon after she arrived in England. "Your last letter was wonderfully funny," White wrote, "in spite of the hell you must have been going through, what with the heat, the getting off, the telephone calls from 'Cal'—if I can refer to him so to you—and your present dissatisfaction with the novel." She went on to offer encouraging advice on both counts, emotional and literary. She reassured Stafford that she was dealing maturely with Lowell: "That marriage [between Lowell and Elizabeth Hardwick] is amazing but even more the fact that he is out of the sanitarium. I am distressed that you had to be stirred up all over again and think you were right to tell him not to write or call you direct." More importantly, she expressed breezy confidence about Stafford's book: "I'm sure the book is not as inchoate as you think now and that when you come back it will fall into place to please you."

The key was distance. Stafford needed to detach herself from disturbing reminders of Lowell, who had suffered another breakdown after his mother's death in 1954, and she needed a respite, too, from her uncooperative novel. A London visit the summer before had been therapeutic, though cut short by financial worries. This time the trip was shaping up as a disaster. Stafford was sick with bronchitis after a grueling boat crossing, and her rented flat at 20 Chesham Place faced a noisy construction site—not an ideal convalescent spot. Despite her health, she socialized with energy (and with well-connected company: George Orwell's widow, Freud's grandson, and Walker Evans one night; Dorothy Parker's husband, Alan Campbell, on several other occasions). As was her habit when she was unhappy and convivial, she was drinking too much, with the usual bad results: her frame of mind was hardly better than the state of her body. Her physical and psychological trials were oppressively familiar, as Stafford lamented in a letter to her friend Ann Honeycutt:

> I have eaten nothing since I arrived. . . . I have started with a psychiatrist, but I don't intend to deliver this intelligence to anyone but you. . . . I think maybe it'll work, except that I am so sick of telling the same dreary story and having to stop and control the disgusting tears and feeling that nothing I can possibly say ever can convey what it's like to be inside this particular skull.

Once again, the past all too easily engulfed her. Looking ahead, she confessed that her hope of somehow mastering that "dreary story," with a doctor or on paper, was fading. And as she wrote to another friend, at forty-one the energy to plunge into the present eluded her: "After the age of 22, the search for experience is narrowing and harrowing."

But her trip took a welcome turn when she met A. J. Liebling, a fellow *New Yorker* writer who was also in London and who looked her up at Mrs. White's urging. He couldn't rescue her from her past, nor did he succeed in reinspiring her about her literary future. What he did do, though a decade older than she and not as energetic as he had once been, was to show her how the search for experience could be very different from anything she was used to. Attend to your appetites and avoid literary intellectuals were among the first principles of this voracious eater and prodigious journalist, who wrote about the war, New York City lowlife, food, the races, boxing, politics, the press, and anything else that struck his wide interest. His precepts were hardly familiar ones for Stafford.

Let me take care of you was Joe Liebling's dominant tone with her, which was equally unfamiliar. The invitation was one she was thoroughly ready to accept, as was clear from a letter Stafford wrote to Honeycutt with further news of her London psychiatrist and her state of mind. The letter offers perhaps the best insight into the seemingly odd but immediate bond between huge, prolific Liebling and Stafford, the "problem feeder" and now problem writer. So often the defensive victim, Stafford described a new willingness to acknowledge her vulnerability, and an unapologetic desire to depend on someone. That someone could not, obviously, continue to be her doctor, though she had seized on to him as her temporary guardian. Her new psychiatrist, she wrote to Honeycutt,

> is so much more articulate than any of the others I've ever seen, and it's a new and extremely good and astringent experience for me to be with a man. . . . I think I am in love with him. . . . I don't know his status, whether single or married, but I want him to adopt me. . . . On the whole, I'm more for adoption than marriage. . . . I think he thinks I'm losing my mind and I'm with him there. It's the food (absence of) and drink (superabundance of) syndrome that inspires him to this drastic move [he advised her to spend a week in a nursing home]. . . . When I told him at one point that I was indestructible, he said, "Balderdash, have you ever tried a .45 Colt?" I said no, what I meant was that I'd been told I was indestructible and he said, then why hadn't I said I was really fragile and wanted to be taken care of. . . . I do honestly think he could set my feet on a safe path.

Liebling, in his gallant, gluttonous way, knew how to court fragile women (his first wife, Ann McGinn, turned out to be schizophrenic), and Stafford was ready to be scooped up: he was an ideal emissary from *The New Yorker,* for which she had such strong familial feelings. The fantasy of adoption was not a new one; orphans surfaced in her fiction, and in "The Bleeding Heart" she had spun out a young woman's delusory fixation on a father figure. (In a letter to Nancy Flagg Gibney, Stafford tried to explain her sense of needy estrangement: "I have looked on myself all my life as an orphan who had siblings and living parents . . . and have spent a great many of my years being involved in some aspect of rejection: dying a thousand deaths over being rejected or dying a million over rejecting.")

Nor was the reality of finding refuge with protective men new—Dr. Cohn, and Jensen even, had played that role. But where Stafford had always been acutely aware of the dangers of dependence (father figures in her world were not to be relied upon—rejection always lurked around the corner), with Liebling there was romantic fondness as well and hope for a "safe path." It was a well-grounded hope. Liebling was a notably clear-eyed rescuer, confident in his reassuring powers but never overconfident or condescending. He sized himself up in a letter during a moment of trouble for Stafford while they were apart:

As to the word waif, please don't take it away, I'd be speechless without it. Since 1945 ... I've been using it to describe the only kind of women I attract, and that attract me. I am a Symbol of Security, but I have feet of clay with broken arches. Still, since I love waifs, I try to live up to their ridiculous misapprehension of my characteristics. I am really just a he-waif, what never had no mammy. . . .

If you were near me and let out a wail like that, I'd either yell that I had troubles enough of my own, or, much more probably, cuddle you and soothe you and reassure you, and it would be all over in an hour either way. . . . I want to be needed, but by God I need you.

That summer Liebling was more than a year into a trial separation from his demanding second wife, Lucille Spectorsky. It had been her idea, after years of difficult relations between them, and though Liebling hadn't quite made an explicit break, he was clearly in need of company, physical and emotional. While he waited on Lucille's whims, he pursued women, many of them much younger than he, with what one of them, Nora Sayre, the daughter of a *New Yorker* writer, described as "the abrupt lunge of a man who rather expects to be rejected." Stafford, another *New Yorker* daughter, was a different case. When he called into the magazine's London office from his rooms at Dukes Hotel to check on a piece and found Stafford there, picking up her mail, he invited a woman to tea who promised to be more than an acolyte likely to rebuff him before too long. She was a colleague, a writer whom he had long admired and who, he had reason to know from the Whites, admired him. And he doubtless also knew from them that she was lonely.

For Liebling, their first meeting over drinks at Dukes was probably a tantalizing glimpse of Stafford's uneasy mix of fragility and toughness, as the raffish, hard-drinking side of the impeccable prose stylist emerged. Appropriately enough, the two of them broke the ice by making fun of their matchmakers, the valetudinarian Whites. They took to each other right away, and the courtship proceeded in high style. In England, Liebling swept her up into his life—escorting her in a hired Rolls-Royce to the races, entertaining her in pubs and at plentiful meals. At some point she paid a solo visit to Heidelberg, and she arranged her own side trip to Brussels for a congress of poets (not Liebling's kind of event). The active summer was exactly what Stafford needed, as she wrote to her agent, James Oliver Brown: "I've been having far too good a time and never want to come home or work or do a blessed thing except to be pleased in just the way I'm being pleased."

But Stafford did sail home in October, and Liebling set off traveling for *The New Yorker*—continuing to woo her attentively during the year they were apart. His letters reveal how fascinated, and curiously intimidated, he was by her dramatically literary life, for all of his commanding, confident style. Above all, he was full of praise for her writing, which he was reading and rereading as he traveled to Italy and the Middle East on assignment. "I seem to have held a very great lady in my arms at all those race meetings," he wrote to her just after she had gone. "It was a very great honor! I've been reading 'Children Are Bored on Sunday,' and really you are a better writer than almost anybody I know."

But he also admitted to quick jealousy about her emotional past, which for him was entangled with her literary history. Her life among the literary quarterly writers elicited what was for him a habitual defensive mockery of a cultural milieu so different from his own. In two decades at *The New Yorker*, he had distinguished himself as an artful stylist and a journalistic innovator, but his loyalties and temperament allied him with the newspapermen among whom he had begun his career; "intellectual" for Liebling was a term of scorn. His reading of *Boston Adventure* gave him an occasion to stake his claim against those wan men in Stafford's high literary past: "All through the last 100 pages I was wondering who was going to get Sonie . . . prepared to be jealous of any one of them. You can see how impersonally I take literature, and how completely I detach fictional characters from reality," he wrote to her from Naples, mixing flirtation and criticism. "You couldn't fool me for a minute with the black hair. When the book ended with Sonie uninvaded, I wanted to go back and beat up all three of them for passing up such an enchanting bet."

It was a flattering combativeness, but Liebling warned Stafford that he was prone to carry it too far:

I began to write you a letter about that book, The Good Soldier [which Stafford evidently had urged him to read]. . . . I tore up the letter because I found I was using the book as an excuse to tease you about literary people, as I used to tease Lucy about Southerners. In time this becomes damn wearisome. The chain of causation is flattering enough, but it is necessary for the woman to understand it from the beginning. I'm jealous of the people who have been around her before she met me. So I belittle them (especially in contrast to myself). There's nothing rational about it—I don't really despise men of letters, or Southerners, or doctors, except when I'm in love with a writer, or a Southern woman, or a lady doctor (that has happened, too). The dame, *eprise de moi,* pretends to agree completely and then when she gets fed up with the badinage she feels it would be inconsistent to speak up, until she *blows* up. Don't let me pull your tail, Jeanie, ever. (This is like a boy who has had bad luck keeping rabbits, which die on him one after another. He decides to take the next rabbit into his confidence. God knows what good it will do.)

Most of the time, Stafford didn't mind having her tail pulled about her past. As Wilfrid Sheed, the son of her former employers, the Catholic publishers Frank and Maisie Sheed, observed, "Liebling and his set had supplemented the back-biting of the poets with the jaunty irreverence of the sports press box and Jean absorbed this too, and I think felt very American about it."

Still, both of them clearly were aware of a tension between Stafford's highbrow, *PR* pedigree and the lowlife reporter tastes that Liebling liked to cultivate. He faced it head-on and with fond praise always encouraged Stafford's literary course. At the same time, he seems to have disarmed her physically. His wholehearted embrace of her was more than figurative, and despite Stafford's long-standing fears of sexual aloofness, she welcomed him in bed. They enthusiastically overlooked the incongruities between them—not the least of which was the almost comical physical contrast, well-rounded Liebling and well-worn, angular Stafford. "I want you to write because you're a great woman, and I love what you write, and because you'll never be happy—for more than one afternoon or one night at a time—unless you do yourself justice," Liebling saluted her, and then got down to more concrete details. "I'll not give you up, and I'll combine things to have you together with me as soon as possible, and I'll make love to you as much as I want, which is certainly as much as you'll want, and we'll see wonderful things together and mortise our minds like the rest of us."

In fact, what was more notable than the disparities between them, at least from the outside and at the outset, was this mortising of their minds. There was a convergence in the broad direction of their literary course at this stage of their lives, when middle age was clearly weighing heavily on them: they were both drawn to nostalgic efforts at memoir. It was also the enterprise on which Lowell, the literary man they both made a show of disparaging, had embarked. They took early note of his explorations, which were quickly to acquire a kind of representative significance for a literary generation, as Lowell's personal agonies became the archetypal ordeal of the artist, the social outcast.

Liebling and Stafford watched the emergence of Lowell's *Life Studies* with, it seems fair to say, at least a preliminary sense of identification. No sooner had Liebling confessed his jealousy of the *PR* circle in early 1957 than he reported to Stafford (whom he often fondly addressed as "Cat") that he had found an issue of the magazine in his hotel in Israel, immediately delved into it, and actually liked a piece by his rival:

> The bookstore in the hotel had a copy of Partisan Review, Fall Number, on display. The lead story was a part of 91 Revere Street, Lowell's autobiography, so I bought the PR and sat down in the lobby to see if he had anything to say about Cat. . . . The installment got him only about as far as the age of ten, but most of it was about his father and mother, and I must say that I liked it. . . . But you've probably read it. The rest of PR was outrageously funny as ever.

When Stafford read "91 Revere Street," she complained to Giroux that Lowell had deliberately parodied her own writing. Although there was nothing about her in it, there was more than a faint trace of her own literary style and voice. *Boston Adventure* lurked behind the cadences and texture of Lowell's prose and the mythographic scale of his portraiture— or perhaps it was the other way around: here were versions of stories that Lowell must have told Stafford back in the days when she was at work on her own Boston tableau. Certainly the young Lowell looking "forward to the night when my bedroom walls would once again vibrate, when I would awake with rapture to the rhythm of my parents arguing, arguing one another to exhaustion" recalled Sonie on her pallet in Chichester, listening to the storm between her similarly beleaguered father and resentful mother. The echoes between that novel and Lowell's almost surreal narrative reverberated back and forth in his images and in his sentences, crammed with detail and alliteration: "On the joint Mason-Myers bookplate, there are two merry and naked mermaids," he wrote, and then let his tongue chase his observant eye in extravagant Stafford-esque style as he described them, "lovely marshmallowy, boneless, Rubenesque butterballs, all burlesque-show bosoms and Flemish smiles. . . ."

In a letter to Peter Taylor after his autobiographical story "1939" appeared, Lowell characterized his own radically new effort at memoir. Taylor's portrait had wounded him, he confessed, but also deeply impressed and influenced him: he was ready to mine his own past overtly. Stafford and Liebling would have recognized the lure of melding truth and fiction:

> Well, I stand off, hat in hand, and thank you with grudging bewildered incomprehension. But were we really quite such monsters? Seriously, though, the whole thing fascinates me—I have been trying to do the same sort of thing myself with scenes from my childhood. . . . I want to invent and forget a lot but at the same time have the historian's wonderful advantage—the reader must always be forced to say, "This is tops, but even if it weren't it's true." I think you've done the trick.

The struggle to find a creative balance between inventing and forgetting was one that Stafford knew all too well after years of trying to transform her life into a novel. So did Liebling, who had been impatient with the simplistic journalistic distinctions between objectivity and subjectivity since the start of his career. Both of them, not unlike Lowell, were ready to try a new strategy, which meant turning more explicitly to autobiographical memories than they ever had before.

FOLLOWING UP on his fond courtship by correspondence, Liebling came back briefly to the United States at the beginning of 1957 for a visit with Stafford, who was in the process of leaving Westport and setting up house in an apartment at 18 East Eightieth Street. ("I was moving so that the confusion was perpetual but, on the whole, sweet," she wrote to a friend.) He also came back to sign a contract with Simon and Schuster for a book, *Normandy Revisited,* in which he made his present and past self the subject of his reporting. He agilely shifted between his tour of France as a well-seasoned writer in the mid-1950s and his earlier visits as a student and war correspondent. Digressive in the extreme (Liebling alluded to the great meanderer Laurence Sterne, one of his favorite writers, in his subtitle, *A Sentimental Journey*), he was ironic about himself as the aging tourist in calm times and nostalgic about the younger intrepid Liebling. The project was the natural culmination of his experiments in more ruminative journalism, as his biographer, Raymond Sokolov, has emphasized. Liebling was still the objective reporter, but he was on new subjective terrain as he probed his memories and juxtaposed versions of himself.

Stafford was having less luck with her obstinate autobiographical novel, and back in New York, she made the most of the distractions, attending plenty of parties, going to the opera with Robert Giroux, being escorted to dinner by various men. During the spring, feeling frustrated by how little she had accomplished, she evidently wrote to Liebling that she might not join him in Europe in the summer of 1957 as they had planned. Liebling sympathized with her troubles: "The book's the thing to think about," he agreed. With his usual directness, he addressed her fears of what companionship might mean for their work; he was evidently thinking beyond a summer rendezvous to longer-term arrangements, and he had some worries about productivity himself. He was willing to go slowly, and put work first. "It may be all for the best," he wrote to her in early spring, "if we don't constrain each other to depart from our respective courses—we're stars of such fiery portent and Roman-candlescent magnitude—and if I make you come to Europe when you want to be writing in Eightieth Street, or if you woo me to the Gideon Putnam Hotel when I want to be in Djerba, the one who concedes may catch with a slow burn difficult to extinguish." It was revealing imagery—ostensibly celebratory of their careers, but in fact clearly anxious: the stars risked falling, the Roman candles might sputter. In a similar half-facetious but frank tone, Liebling touched on their other worry besides work—health. He had had bouts of renal colic, and Stafford had been in the hospital again with a series of complaints: "I don't understand why you are sick all the time. Maybe you are a hypochondriac? Did you ever hear of them? They are like a Christian Scientist in reverse...."

But in early August, though Stafford still hadn't made it to Europe, they both had work published in *The New Yorker,* and Liebling took it as an auspicious portent: "The New Yorker married us again in the August 3 number ...; a big story by you, then a long fact piece by me. As you have it, we complement each other, and it makes a fine New Yorker, but I wonder whether it's pure coincidence, or matchmaking." Whatever the Whites had in mind, Stafford did finally head for England not long after the issue appeared, to enjoy two months of unproductive pleasure, only somewhat marred by a severe bout of Asiatic flu for Liebling. When he was up to it, he wined her and dined her and kept her entertained (he met her at Southampton in a Rolls, took her to Paris to the races at Longchamp). When they returned home together in November, they took separate rooms at the Fifth Avenue Hotel, though they were clearly a couple. A concrete obstacle to marriage remained, since Liebling's second wife kept stalling on a divorce.

Even when the divorce came through, they didn't get married for another year and a half, both evidently hesitant about the prospect—though that wasn't what they said. Stafford claimed they "kept getting too busy to get married," and their life certainly was rarely dull. Stafford enjoyed the unfamiliar ambience of Liebling's crowd, especially Walt Kelly and John Lardner of the self-described "The Formerly Club," who gathered at Bleeck's (once the Artists and Writers Club, the New York *Herald Tribune* hangout). Perhaps it was the lack of bustle in their literary lives that gave them pause. Stafford wasn't writing much, only a few articles and a weak story, and Liebling's *Normandy Revisited* didn't sell well when it came out in 1958. But they finally got married, on April 3, 1959, and they launched their wedded life in Liebling's well-known style: the reception was held in his favorite haunt, Tim Costello's bar, and they moved into an elegant apartment at 43 Fifth Avenue.

The question of how to balance work and life in each other's company had by no means disappeared. In fact, Liebling and Stafford were headed for comparatively dry stretches in their careers. Companionship, at least during the first years they were married, was an exhilarating distraction. Liebling was avid and eclectic in his interests and in his friends—he loved the curious corners of New York, he adored France. He was devoted to his friend Jean Riboud, whom he had gotten to know in New York, where Riboud had come after emerging from Buchenwald and where he had since become a great success as an investment banker (and later became president of Schlumberger); and Liebling was devoted to his bar cronies. The couple was energetically social, eating out often, serving elaborate feasts in their apartment (Liebling had a loyal housekeeper, Madella, to help), keeping up with Liebling's cast of eccentrics—

and Stafford fell for the combination of high style and low living. She had always yearned to be drawn out of herself, and he succeeded in keeping her entertained and extroverted as no one else had.

For the monumentally productive Liebling, his literary output in the late 1950s and early 1960s was still impressive: along with piecework for *The New Yorker,* though somewhat less of it, he wrote two more books. Most of *Between Meals,* another nostalgic memoir, this time of his youthful appetites, ran in *The New Yorker* during 1959 and the whole appeared in 1962. In 1961 he published *The Earl of Louisiana,* a book about Earl Long, the governor of Louisiana, which had been prompted by a suggestion from Stafford, who had been intrigued by the place and its peculiar natives ever since she lived there with Lowell. For Stafford, the record for writing was bleak. She wrote some book reviews, none of them major pieces; a few articles, the most substantial of which, "Souvenirs of Survival," was a chatty memoir of coming of age during the 1930s; and several movie reviews for *Horizon* in 1961. In 1962 Farrar, Straus and Cudahy published *Elephi: The Cat with the High IQ,* an engaging children's story that sometimes verged on whimsy. Stafford also retold two tales from the Arabian Nights for a Macmillan series, another less-than-full-scale fictional effort for her.

Only two more stories appeared during this time, neither of them in *The New Yorker.* Her exile from its pages coincided with the retirement of Katharine White, her longtime patron and champion at the magazine, but the stories—"The Children's Game" and "The Scarlet Letter"— were both weaker than her best (as White herself frankly told her about the first, which was based loosely on her Brussels trip). Even "A Reasonable Facsimile," the story that had appeared along with Liebling's piece in the August 1957 *New Yorker,* showed a certain strain as Stafford groped for material, skirting autobiography. Set in Colorado, it was an unusual story, about an old professor whose peace was destroyed by a predatory acolyte who invaded his life. It was far from her Vanderpool vein, and she explained to the Thompsons that it was pointless to mine it for personal clues: the model was not a teacher from her alma mater— or, for that matter, one of her subsequent mentors. The story was born of more detached inspiration: she had been reading the correspondence between Harold Laski and Oliver Wendell Holmes.

In retrospect, Stafford tentatively traced her creative block to contentment: "During our marriage, which was short, I was *extremely* unproductive. It was a source of woe to Joe. I could never figure out why it happened. Perhaps it's too simple an explanation, but I was happy for the first time in my life. He thought that if I wasn't writing, it meant I was unhappy with him." Years before, during her sessions with Dr. Sherfey, she had tried out the same analysis: that suffering was the source of her inspiration, that a "cure" might mean the end of creativity. But she had also expressed skepticism about the portrait of the artist as neurotic, and she knew that happiness was not her imagination's only enemy by any means. Some literary strain may have lurked between Stafford and Liebling. She told Blair Clark that she feared her own writing might inhibit Liebling's productivity, which can't help sounding farfetched, but perhaps served as a partial excuse for silence.

What is more plausible is that Liebling's productivity daunted her; certainly with Lowell, she had known the frustrating rhythm of fallow times for herself during his fertile stretches. But above all now it was more mundane, domestic distractions that slowed her down. These had always exerted a powerful lure, and her bustling life with Liebling gave her plenty of pretexts for avoiding her typewriter. Drinking, which Liebling alone of her husbands did little to discourage (he was hardly in a position to police appetites), now plainly encroached on her work—both as a source of her troubles with writing and as a solace in the face of them.

Another source of her creative block was, however, literary. Her difficulties, after all, had begun long before she met Liebling—and they were not very different from troubles she had had with another, much earlier novel, *In the Snowfall*. She herself had offered a revealing analysis of that struggle: her material had consisted of memories too powerful to work with. Back then, she had acknowledged what was plain from her unfinished pages, that Lucy McKee frustrated all her efforts at imaginative distance. Stafford hadn't quite faced up to her father as an even more unmanageable figure lurking in the background of her story. But he clearly was an unwieldy presence—begging to be reshaped in her fantasies, yet stubbornly resisting it—and he continued to be unwieldy a decade and a half later as she floundered on her fourth novel. Lowell seems to have presented similar problems.

The surviving manuscript of her attempt at a novel is a tangle, encompassing several different drafts—or, rather, abortive starts of drafts, the same opening chapters rewritten again and again. In a version that was envisaged as a sequel to *Boston Adventure,* usually titled *The Parliament of Women* or *The Dream of the Red Room,* she struggled to transform her life with Lowell into Sonie's pilgrimage toward a terrifyingly empty maturity and to mix social satire of suburbia (modeled on Westport) and spiritual tragedy. In a draft labeled *The State of Grace,* generally subtitled *Varieties of Religious Experience,* Stafford was evidently trying a broader autobiographical novel. She had abandoned *Boston Adventure* as her base and was instead building on her Colorado past, opening with fiercely caricatured scenes of life among characters inspired by her Stafford and McKillop grandparents.

Making chronological sense of the jumble of pages is difficult, but it was apparently during her years with Liebling that Stafford shifted from efforts to build on *Boston Adventure* to an attempt to shape her book around a more explicit family memoir. It meant turning from comparatively recent memories—of her marriage to Lowell—to the more distant past. That may have made the enterprise seem safer, though it was still an unnerving psychological step: she was testing her aesthetic strictures against personal exposure and was clearly ambivalent. Watching Lowell at work in *Life Studies,* dramatically flouting the principles of impersonality, stirred her up. She wrote to Peter Taylor in early 1958 that she was appalled at the direction in which Lowell's work was heading: "You will have read Cal's new poems in *Partisan Review.* I cannot think why they were published. He has been sick again and I dare say you know this too. I feel terribly sorry for Elizabeth. . . . The poems made me really very angry, not only with Cal but with all the people that further this obscene egocentricity in him—and, of course, angry with myself for being even now affected by recollections of him."

It was no surprise that the *PR* sampler of Lowell's poems agitated her. The grand proportions of his autobiographical project were clear, and so were its intimate sources. In two of the poems, "Memories of West Street and Lepke," inspired by his prison term back in 1944, and "To Delmore Schwartz," a portrait of the winter of 1945 to 1946 in Cambridge, Lowell revealed how high he was prepared to elevate his own experiences; he raised two episodes during his life with Stafford to emblematic historical status. In two more of them, "Man and Wife" and "To Speak of Woe That Is in Marriage," he showed how close to the heart he was prepared to probe. The declamatory confessional style went against all of Stafford's instincts, but her denunciation perhaps also masked a certain defensiveness. After all, she was notably absent from all the poems, near though they came to her life.

Whether or not Stafford's reaction to Lowell's poems directly affected her own work, it seems to have been around this time that she abandoned, at least for a while, her efforts to draw on her past with him for her novel. In turning to her family instead, she was embarking on a project that was grandiose in its own strange way. Her inspiration came in the form of a dream that she took surprisingly seriously. It was as though she hoped that by following half-conscious associations she might find a pathway into terrain that had so far resisted more direct exploration. Stafford had long made a habit of scribbling down fragments of her dreams in stray notebooks and on scraps of paper. More recently she had become a devotee of the Ouija board, entranced by the game of coaxing testimony from unplumbed depths of the mind, a pastime she took quite seriously. Among certain friends, she would pull out the board when she had been drinking, and together they would summon voices, everyone hoping that Liebling wouldn't intrude, since he firmly disapproved of the séances. Her brother's name often materialized on the board, his spirit trying to make contact, Stafford was certain. Similarly, the dream that suddenly inspired her new literary project was a quest for her kin. "On a winter night, I dreamed these words," she jotted down: " 'Look anywhere and you will find roots. Samothrace. Gadopolis.' It was then revealed to me, through an intelligence existing outside me in the upper air, rather like a disembodied history professor, that my Scotch ancestors had arrived at the Isle of Arran in the Firth of Clyde only in the seventeenth century and that they had come there by a circuitous route from Samothrace."

Stafford seized on this strange message as a guide for her next project, which she aimed to pursue alongside her novel. "My dreams are . . . rarely so instructive as this one or, indeed, so autobiographical," she explained in some notes. "I was pleased that after years of serving me nothing but travesty and tomfoolery my unconscious mind had at last yielded up something I could cogitate and, conceivably, check." She knew it all sounded outlandish and took pleasure in the oddity of her enterprise. Her literary goal was as counterintuitive as her inspiration: "I am going to put this material to two uses: the provable and factual aspects of it I am incorporating into a novel; the mythical, the fictitious parts of it will comprise a work of non-fiction." In the end, her curious investigations blurred into her continuing efforts to reshape her novel. Her mythological memoir never fully materialized, though some friends saw tantalizing pieces.

Before she was ready to write anything, however, she had research to do. The dream led her first to amateur genealogical sleuthing, something this would-be orphan had never imagined herself doing. She wrote letters to relatives, asking for information and memories of the McKillop and Stafford clans before and after they had come to America. Her inquiries didn't bear much fruit, but what news she received she used to buttress her long-standing archetypes of her ancestors: the adventurous Staffords, the deadly prim McKillops, "plain, thrifty, law-loving United Presbyterians who went to church all day on Sunday and read Foxe's *Book of Martyrs* with outraged pleasure."

Stafford then moved on to slightly more scholarly investigations, dabbling in the archaeological findings of Phyllis Williams Lehmann and Karl Lehmann, director of the excavations on Samothrace. Again her method relied on intuitive associations rather than rigorous study. With her eyes closed, she opened *Samothrace, the Ancient Literary Sources,* the first volume in a series about the dig, and came upon a discussion of exporting rites involving Demetore and Core to an island near Britain. "Why shouldn't the island have been Arran?" Stafford asked, undaunted by the unprovability of her hypothesis. She plunged ahead, making other tenuous connections. Excitedly she linked Core, the goddess, and Corrie, a village on Arran, and Chora, the main village on Samothrace. Her reaction when that thread snapped was calmly to acknowledge the preposterousness of all her speculation, and then to carry on with it anyway: "I learned to my disappointment that Core simply means 'maiden,' Corrie means 'cauldron,' and Chora is no more than the word for 'village.' No matter, I was by now deep in my myth and so, indeed, was my husband."

When Liebling left for Europe in the fall of 1959 to cover the British elections, Stafford was ready to go with him and follow her fantasy even further. The plan was for her to go to Scotland by herself first and then head for mainland Greece and Samothrace with Liebling. On the eve of their departure, she got a letter from Karl Lehmann that helped put the adventure in a perspective that suited Stafford's own inchoate but obviously high expectations for her bizarre project. "As an old student of Greek mythology, I am much amused with your ancestral dream," Leh-

mann wrote in answer to a letter in which Stafford had evidently described her quest. "I have often wondered how long it takes for a legend
deriving mortals from divine or heroic ancestry to form itself, and what
the processes involved are. I now see that dreams, poetic imagination,
and adventurous travels all play their part in it, and that it might just
happen within one person's lifetime." Taking that somewhat jocular
comment as the imprimatur of expertise, Stafford noted down that she
"felt now that I had been issued a legal hunting license."

Traveling was, as usual for Stafford, an ordeal—especially a grim boat
ride to the Isle of Arran in the early morning. But once there, she was
greeted by shocks of recognition, which were really what she had come
to find: she had transformed the search for a home from the metaphorical theme it was in so much of her fiction into an actual undertaking. On
a stroll through the main village, she was taken aback by the sight of a
nine- or ten-year-old girl tying her shoelaces. "I was at the castle gates
before I knew who she was: she was the replica of myself as I had been
in grammar school and she and I were one, pausing in the early autumn
sun to re-do the shoelace that presently would come undone again and
catapult us to our knees to wound us freshly." It was a freighted image of
vulnerable childhood, and Stafford was excited but also unnerved by the
exposure of her identity as she stumbled upon so many familiar faces:

> In the next few days, I was to meet my skeleton and its integument
> many more times, sometimes as they had been and sometimes as
> they were to become. One off-islander, a salty old topper in the
> public room of the Corrie hotel, observed to me that I looked a true
> Arranite. The hallucination, though interesting and exciting, was
> unseating: it was like coming face to face with the ghost of a still-
> born twin of whom I had never heard.

She then rejoined Liebling, and they flew to Athens and from there
sailed for Samothrace, where they seem to have had a very good time,
guided around the island by a young Greek with whom they became
friends. After her Arran adventure, Stafford wrote a letter to her agent,
James Oliver Brown, brimming with an optimism she hadn't felt in a
long time: "The trip was fantastically, thrillingly fruitful. . . . If I don't
get a story out of this, I'm not and never have been a writer."

She and Liebling came back inspired to write, only to be disappointed.
The early 1960s turned out to be less fruitful, certainly for Stafford, and

they could no longer claim that distracting companionship was the main obstacle to work. They were drifting apart somewhat, but not into solitary productivity. Liebling was discouraged by the comparatively poor sales of his books, worried about money, and felt less and less well as kidney troubles and gout took their toll. In the summer of 1960 he went by himself to do more work on *Between Meals* at the house in East Hampton, Long Island, that he had bought with his second wife.

That same summer Stafford headed out to Reno on an assignment for *Horizon* to write about the filming of *The Misfits,* and she stopped for a visit with her sister Mary Lee in Hayden. That was a calm reunion, and Stafford's analysis of why it went smoothly perhaps sheds some light on her literary struggles. "My weekend in the bosom of my family wasn't really bad at all," she wrote to Nancy Flagg Gibney. "I like my sister in her own house but can't stand her in mine—I can slip back into my western girlhood with no trouble at all, but she is completely irrelevant to my eastern adulthood." It was linking her past and her present that posed the real problems, and as she was leaving she sounded anxious about her still-unfinished work: "Really, when I come back, I'd like to settle down to Samothrace and the novel and not interrupt these two projects until I'm finished."

Such purposeful declarations were common (and often well publicized: in 1960 a magazine called the *Griffin* announced that Stafford's novel, billed as a sequel to *Boston Adventure,* was due out the following spring). She had reason to hope she might face fewer distractions from her work. She was spending less time gallivanting with Liebling and his friends, and in a letter to Peter Taylor, she emphasized her sense of estrangement from her old literary circle: "It's been so long since I've seen any specifically literary people. To be sure I hear about them—hear about Cal all the time and how Philip Rahv and Allen and everybody else has taken a new lease on life now that he's got a new girl and he and Elizabeth for the dozenth time are talking divorce." But the truth was that Stafford was not close to done with her novel or with her Samothrace project. As in the past, comparative peace was not as conducive to work as she had hoped.

Instead, she seemed to feel dispirited by her isolation, and by her own sense of inertia. As if to compensate, in 1962 she stirred up unhelpful commotion with her publishers: she decided to break with her editor at Random House, Albert Erskine, whom she had owed a manuscript for seven years, and to sign up with Robert Giroux at Farrar, Straus and Cudahy. Erskine was an old friend from *Southern Review* days, and it was clear from the drama of the rift that Stafford was projecting her sense of failed promise onto him. She explained in a letter that she wanted to be released from her contract "for a number of reasons," and went on to say that "the only one that needs to be stated is that, in spite of all our making a joke of it, I have an eccentric but ineradicable sense of being still your not very competent secretary, subject to scolding and I hate being scolded. . . . Nor can I help feeling very strongly that this has contributed to my block." It was all rather implausible, as she half acknowledged in this letter (but forgot as their correspondence heated up): Erskine had in fact been a studiously unaggressive editor. In bitterly recalling her secretary days, she was really lamenting her stalled career, not his scoldings.

Later that spring she signed a contract with Farrar, Straus and Cudahy for twelve thousand dollars, seven thousand dollars to buy her way out of her Random House contract, five thousand dollars for new work. The deadline for her novel was now set in January 1965; a collection of short stories, to be titled *Bad Characters,* was due in 1964. There was also talk of her Samothrace project, but her new publishers were less excited about it than she. "Robert [Giroux] is very worried about the Greek-Scotland book (this is very much off the record)," James Oliver Brown wrote to her. "They want a novel and it is a novel for which they are gambling." Gambling was an accurate though not very kind way to put it: hopes, Stafford's included, were hedged. She kept a low literary profile over the next several years, though she gave a very visible boost to another career, convincing the jury of the National Book Awards on which she served in 1962 that a novel called *The Moviegoer* by an unknown novelist named Walker Percy in Louisiana should win the prize. The unexpected award caused a stir, including the charge that it was all really Liebling's, not Stafford's, doing. It was true that Liebling had alerted her to the book, but the novel proved to be one she too was ready to champion—a case of collaborative enthusiasm not unlike the fascination, first Stafford's and then her husband's, that had inspired Liebling's book about that other Louisianan, Earl Long.

Two pieces of Stafford's own fiction were on their way into print in the early 1960s, but neither was a sign of newfound inspiration. Both were stories that she had done earlier, a weak one called "The Ordeal of Conrad Pardee," which appeared in *Ladies' Home Journal,* and "The Tea Time of Stouthearted Ladies," a sketch that kept finding a place in various unfinished manuscripts, from *In the Snowfall* to *Parliament of Women.* Stafford quietly unearthed it to contribute to a commemorative issue of the *Kenyon Review,* in honor of John Crowe Ransom, and it was a telling revisiting of her past. The story drew quite directly from her life. It was a rare portrait based on Stafford's mother, the self-deluding optimist, whose refusal to face the dismal facts of her family's pinched, provincial life inspired the protagonist, her daughter, to dreams of escape from Colorado, "from the spectacle of her eaten father and from her mother's bright-eyed lies, from all the maniacal respectability with which the landladies strait-jacketed the life of the town." A tour de force of descriptive detail and colloquial dialogue, the story showed Stafford at a distance from her autobiographical character, leavening her brutal bitterness with comedy. Stafford downplayed the resuscitation of her story, neglecting even to mention it to her agent, perhaps because it was an all-too-vivid reminder of her failures with her larger project—and because its publication was presided over by the spirit of Ransom, who had predicted great things for her.

By the spring of 1963 Liebling too, increasingly ill, had sunk into a depression and was having trouble with his writing. They had moved to a much smaller apartment on West Tenth Street (rent on their grand Fifth Avenue apartment had gotten too steep), and life was not the whirl it had been. "For the first time in his life," Stafford told his biographer, Sokolov, Liebling "developed a real block. Depression was new to him. Looking back on it, I wasn't sufficiently sympathetic because I had always had depression with me." Liebling did his best to rally, visiting fight-training camps, despite painful, advanced gout, and then flying to Algeria, planning a "North Africa revisited" piece and pondering an essay on Camus. While there, he wrote to Stafford in the old gallant vein, proposing another European trip together, but acknowledging in his comically direct way that they would hardly be traveling in vigorous style: "I can show you how beautiful and amusing France is," he promised her, and then continued: "Your letter indicated that I'd find you more of a wreck than I am. Well, we'll collapse in each other's arms."

The summer trip to Europe was a memorializing tour. Liebling retraced his steps through France, and Stafford searched for her brother's grave, and they spent some time with Jean Riboud at his spectacular château near Lyons. They returned home in the fall, and Liebling's depression didn't lift, though he went into the *New Yorker* and tried to work. He had in mind a "Wayward Press" column about Kennedy's assassination, which had shaken them both profoundly. (The Thompsons in Boulder received a long, late-night call of mourning from Stafford.) Intimations of death were clearly very much with Liebling, though he was only fifty-nine, and with Stafford as she watched his decline. On December 21, 1963, he went into the hospital, suffering from pneumonia.

Stafford apparently informed her family, and her father responded with a peculiar letter of sympathy, commenting on his own longevity, not Liebling's frailty. He said what his daughter had said for years—that his lease on life was perversely long:

> Jean, I am now in my 90th year. I ought to be dead but am on the contrary indestructible and hard as nails. My mother your Grandmother Stafford often told me "John you are too ornery to live and too ornery to die a natural death. You will have to be shot or hanged. Either is too good for you." She was a woman of discernment, Jean.... Well, my dear, this isn't the sort of letter a man should be writing his daughter when her troubles may be too great and too real to be borne.

The letter must have been extremely unsettling. It echoed not only Jean's death wish for him, but also her own fear about herself, which she had confessed to her doctors: that she too was perversely indestructible. The reminder of her inescapably bleak heritage could hardly have come at a worse time: the letter arrived shortly after her husband died on December 28, and she was left alone in life yet again.

Her father seemed to sense what a disturbing message he had sent, for he wrote again right after Liebling's death. It was another confession of his failings, but in this letter real distress replaced the stylized self-indictment:

> Please forgive me in what I now know that letter inflicted. However that is a large order. Forgiving a man like me calls for more than can be asked of anyone. All my life I have been a pain and a disappointment to all those who had every right to expect every thoughtfulness on my part.
>
> I have been a shock to everyone: in a word the Laughing Jackass. Until lately I couldn't even suspect it. Now the truth comes home

to me like a thousand [*sic*] of brick. So don't anyone feel sorry for me. I freely chose my way. But know this Jean, and this for sure:—

This is a good life anyhow, no matter what we may have made of it or imagine we have made of it. We go our separate ways. A few of us are wise enough to choose wisely, most of us are wise enough to let Fortune to be our guide, only a few bone heads like myself deliberately do go the way prescribed for the Idiots from the Dawn of Time and choose it more or less knowingly.

Well enough of this:—

Without Joe you will be lost for a while at least.

In a postscript, he added, "My dear Jean: know that we would all like to help you if only we knew how. Forgive us our ignorance." A certain reproach perhaps lurked there, a puzzled unhappiness about his unresponsive daughter, who impatiently resisted all such gestures from her kin. But there was also a palpable desire to play the comforting father for once. And he knew what obstacles he had to overcome; that was clear from his awkward efforts to lift at least one burden from his daughter, the burden of her guilt and resentment toward him. In his pre-deathbed confession, he took responsibility for the course of his life, and yet also stood by it, a spirited Stafford to the end. It was probably the most compelling image of himself that he could hope to bequeath: the ancient man acknowledging his folly, but valiantly denying the role of victim and implicitly urging his daughter to do the same.

STAFFORD was beyond fond comforting and cheering in the months after Liebling's death. As she had once written wittily and prophetically to her friend Ann Honeycutt, "You and I might as well make up our minds that we are going through the rest of our lives—or part of it— buttressed up by doctors, and I know of no better buttressers. We certainly want no family buttressing in on *their* terms—and that is the only way they would do it—and the friends we admire are largely of such collapsible material themselves they can't be counted on for any sustained work. Further, they are all amateurs, and when we blow, we need the pros in. . . ." True to her own prescriptions, Stafford summoned her doctor, Dr. Thomas Roberts, who admitted her to New York Hospital in early January 1964, just after Liebling's death. She hadn't blown dramatically, but he described her as "drinking, run-down, and depressed" and listed plenty of problems: a benign gastric ulcer, chronic malnutrition, bronchitis, "reactive depression with excessive alcohol intake," and fibrocystic disease in one breast. James Oliver Brown wrote to her full of relief that she was in medical hands: "I'm so very glad you are going into hospital. You are worn out. You must get a rest and get out from under this strain or you are going to crack." Her treatment was hardly high-tech medicine; for sixteen days she dried out and was served real meals in the protective confines of the hospital, which must have seemed even more protective than usual, given the emptiness that awaited her in the world outside.

When she was released, she was well equipped with medicine and well supervised by Dr. Roberts: she was on a regimen of Antabuse (an antialcohol drug) and had tranquilizers to help her sleep and antidepressants to raise her spirits. But she was ill equipped with plans and energy. She had to move from the Tenth Street apartment but didn't know where she would go. February and March were grim months, and on April 5 while she was having lunch at the Cosmopolitan Club, she was seized "like a bear" by a pain that ran through her upper body. Now she had truly blown: it was mild heart failure, and she was taken by ambulance back to New York Hospital, where she stayed for five weeks.

Feeling thoroughly bereft, Stafford seemed more than half ready to follow Liebling. Months after the worst of her ordeals was over, she wrote to Hightower and itemized her physical travails: along with the heart attack, she had suffered a gallbladder attack and been stricken with pancreatitis, which reanimated an old ulcer—and all this had happened only two days after she emerged from the Hospital for Special Surgery, where she had a tumor removed from her foot and a calcium deposit from her wrist. But the real trauma, she told him, had taken place in the soul. "It was interesting," she said in the calm of retrospect, "and I learned one thing: the spirit gives up easy as pie, it's the flesh that fights. I have always suspected this and now I know for sure." It was evidently a formulation she used with another old friend, for it surfaced more than a decade later in Lowell's poem "Jean Stafford, a Letter," in *Day by Day* (1977); "we learn the spirit is very willing to give up," he wrote, echoing his ex-wife's revelation, "but the body is not weak and will not die."

Stafford was well versed in the complexity of the drama between flesh and spirit. The disenchanted mind, this practiced hypochondriac knew, had the power to undermine the body; but in its turn the body, with its demands and desires, could stubbornly distract the mind from its dreams of escape. That contest had been the theme of perhaps her best story, "The Interior Castle," and it returned as the theme that preoccupied her during her illness and recovery. Among her many visits to hospitals, this one seems to have stood out as a formative and strangely inspiring interlude—not unlike her painful stay in Mount Auburn Hospital in Cambridge after her car crash with Lowell, and her retreat to Payne Whitney after the collapse of their marriage.

She was indeed "lost for a while," as her father had predicted, but she was clearly struggling to find some new ways of putting her disorientation into prose. Though it is hard to tell when the work was actually done, much of the labor on the different versions of her novel, alternately called *The Parliament of Women* and *The State of Grace,* seems to reflect what she took to be a brush with death during the spring after Liebling died. Her drafts show her trying to give some objective form to terrifying subjective experience, as her body and spirit resisted but also courted defeat.

In the remnants of *The Parliament of Women,* Stafford continually circled around a struggle either to accept or escape the world, a struggle in which the mind and body were now uneasy allies, now enemies. Picking up with Miss Pride's death, she focused on Sonie's dilemma as she faced a future without her oppressive patron, searching in the dark for some sense of home: "In the spring I lived in a nebulous atmosphere of homesickness, the more distracted and the more saddened because I had never known, in all my life, what was the home I was sick with longing for, or whose were the faces and the voices that my nostalgia craved to redeem." Here Stafford experimented with different versions of the "red room" image that had emerged in *Boston Adventure,* for that was the closest Sonie could come to comfort. Not so secretly, she desired oblivion, suffering from a disease that Stafford described as both physical and mental: "My disappointment was second nature," the passive girl confessed, "an incurable and bothersome disease that didn't hurt but so sapped my strength that I had not the energy to change my life." Her lethargic body accommodated her drifting mind, and she retreated into her comfortably insulated chamber. "What commended [the room] so dearly to me was the quiet and the red of the dusk that imbued it. . . . Here I was not required to emulate or compete or to contribute."

Shifting to the saga of Sonie's troubled courtship with and then mar-

riage to Philip, Stafford aimed for more social vividness and sketched in
a claustrophobic community clearly modeled on Westport, which she
called Lymington, Connecticut. She also introduced a more concrete,
material source for Sonie's spiritual disorientation: alcohol, Sonie's vice
as well as the plague of all her friends, a "distressful secret" that she at
first tried to hide from Philip. Stafford interwove the strands of two stories, Philip's increasing interest in a neighbor named Daisy, and Sonie's
increasing passivity—stories that eventually coalesced in "An Influx of
Poets"—but she couldn't shape a larger tapestry from them. Instead,
some of the most interesting, though always fragmentary, writing returned again and again to the interior of Sonie's head, which Stafford
evoked as a scene of suffocating terror. In one of those passages, Stafford
managed to sum up vividly not only Sonie's hell but also her own literary
entrapment. The speaker was Sonie, but her haunted monologue could
be Stafford's description of her own endless, futile attempts to find some
way to illuminate her pain in prose:

> I tried to recite the Psalms I knew and the Shakespeare sonnets. . . .
> But I could not remember anything and could not extricate myself
> from the absorbing bear-hug of egocentricity. I wrestled weakly
> against it, half-suffocated, fevering, unable, in the engrossing
> struggle, to imagine anything beyond this present pain. . . . I began,
> amid the lowering mountains of the night, to yield to the addiction
> of the sick at heart, that dogged hunt for the wrong turning, that
> tedious, tireless retracing of the erratic, stumbling footsteps that
> have brought us to the bottom of our world. Began to marshall my
> draggled ranks of gnashing guilts and bilious wraths, beginning
> from the beginning of the history of my woe which, in the amnesia
> that obliterated all memory of joy, became my whole history. The
> smithereens of my smashed self lay in a bleeding heap inside my
> skull, past mending, past miracle. How fantastic was the instinct to
> preserve these ugly, unworthy ruins. But it was an instinct so bru-
> tish and so crafty that I had no power against it; if I had been able
> to destroy them once and for all, this rubble pile of myriad and
> miserable selves, it would have been through accident. I could not
> kill myself; I wished to be dead but I did not wish to die, I was
> afraid. . .

It was an echo of the diagnosis Stafford had made long before in "Truth and the Novelist": she was trapped by the bitter facts of her life and seduced by the illusion that somehow writing could be therapeutic. But the lesson of that first failed, raw autobiographical novel, *Which No Vicissitude,* still held, all too tenaciously: the "bear-hug of egocentricity" doomed her imagination.

She didn't give up. *The State of Grace* drafts suggest desperation on the one hand and potentially fruitful experimentation on the other. It seems clear that the two were not far apart for Stafford as she floundered in search of direction. The disparate pieces of the manuscript show her dipping back into the Boulder material she had struggled with in *In the Snowfall,* as if she couldn't relinquish the effort to inscribe the ordeal of her childhood in Colorado. Some of the research she had done in the course of her Samothrace project showed through in her portraiture of her family, and above all in the prominent place her father now occupied. Earlier he had loomed over her Lucy story from the periphery, but now a surreal caricature of him was at the center. At the same time, Stafford also drew from her much more recent experience in the hospital after her heart attack. The setting was clear: "I was a sick middle-aged woman and Sam had widowed me in December during the holidays." She gave Sam the surname Gottlieb, as close as she dared come to Liebling.

Much as she had done before in Sonie's ruthless introspective monologues of despair, here she tried again to give shape to her pain. Her prose was a wild variation on the metaphoric description she had tried in "The Interior Castle"; she even called on some of the same imagery of the besieged mansion. She was, her first-person narrator explained, "absorbed with the mythological terrain of my body," and Stafford let loose with language that mixed the baroque convolution of her earliest style and the intense, symbolic concreteness of her later prose:

> Within such cul de sacs does the mind rummage when hurricanes or wars or plagues assail the castle. It finds some juiceless scar, some desiccated bone or shrivelled rind, and with perseverance worries it, getting by heart each minuscule fissure and node and maggot-tunnel. Though the labor is monotonous and tiring and exasperating, it offers asylum from the responsibilities of pain. Industrious

within my blind and private alley, I had no time, I had no need, I had no *obligation* to discover why I was so sick (or was I hurt?) or when there would be an end to this mysterious dilemma. . . . The pain presented [fear] to me in an amazing number of guises, and the whole of my anatomy was as clear as a contour map. . . . It was a violent landscape, a mise-en-scene for the corybantics [*sic*] of evil spirits; they burned me, these incubi and bogeymen, they pinched me, harrowed me with colic. But for each perfidious roughneck, there was a deputy of my own, tutoring me patiently in how to ride with the waves and how to fall with the blows.

Aware that such virtuosic rummaging in the mind could lead her far from the world and from the suspenseful investigation of "this mysterious dilemma"—why was her autobiographical protagonist so sick, or hurt?—Stafford tried a radically new maneuver. She took advantage of the surreal landscape she had entered upon and proceeded to visit hallucinations on her character in order to transport her from her present pain back into her past memories. In one sense, it was a facile device for linking the disparate pieces of Stafford's intransigently fragmentary novel. But it was perhaps also an experiment that could have saved her from retreating into ever more claustrophobic corners of the self. This shifting focus was, after all, perfectly suited to the presiding theme of her undertaking: disorientation.

That Stafford saw this is clear from the comments on the hallucinatory shifts between inside and out, between present and past, that she incorporated into her story. Her protagonist gave a name to her strange power of schizophrenic perspective, calling it "bilocation." It offered a potential answer to Stafford's nightmare of the isolated consciousness, a way of mediating the hidden internal world and the threatening external world. But it also implied a dangerous indeterminacy, as Stafford acknowledged in a subsequent, important passage. "This is not bilocation, I thought (or perhaps said)," her protagonist realized. "It's dislocation. Every blessed part of me has swapped places and nothing fits anymore. For a quarter of a second I fell asleep and this is what I dreamed: There is a child who knows where an oyster is that has a pearl inside and the pearl will open like an oyster and inside it is a thistle." It was Stafford's consummate image of disenchantment: the child's magical search crowned with painful disappointment. It was her final, desolate variation on St. Teresa's image of the jewel that awaits the spiritual pilgrim in the ultimate, inner chamber.

STAFFORD LEFT the hospital in early May of 1964 and moved to Liebling's place in the Springs in East Hampton, a brown shingle house with modestly sized rooms and ample land extending out to the back. The house, which he had loved and which she had tended with increasing care during the time they spent there together (so much care that Liebling sighed to neighbors about his wife spending all her time on the house rather than on her book), was just about all that he left her and really the only place she had to go. It was a time of mixed hopes and fears, as convalescences usually were for her. The prospect of a fresh start beckoned, but life and the future seemed precarious. Certainly the drafts of her novel that centered on her ordeals suggested that the sense of dislocation was not easily shaken. A letter to her sister during the summer showed Stafford battling the same old demons, entrapped by her past. "I wish, as I have wished all my life," she wrote impatiently, "that you would stop worrying when you don't hear from me. When I am sick, I know how to get help, when I am low in mind I want above all to be left alone, when I am working well I dare not interrupt myself." And then she turned to the most sensitive point and was promptly caught up in the old fury, which she made no effort to hide from her sister: "I've not written him [her father] . . . at all. Each time I contemplate a letter I feel so sick and sad that I find something else to do. That so preposterous a life should be so endlessly prolonged is an unfathomable mystery."

Yet she was prepared to take a more merciful perspective on another part of her past as she surfaced from her descent into disorientation. Her revival took an unexpected form: a renewal, of sorts, of ties with her old life. Lowell had apparently been in touch, and full of solicitude, and Stafford was eager to reciprocate. She wrote him a letter from the hospital that couldn't have been a greater contrast to the messages that she had sent him from the hospital decades earlier, or to the resentment with which she had greeted most of his intrusions into her life since then (and with which she was to greet subsequent ones): "There's no possible way of thanking you for your concern, for your lovely letters, for the books, the beautiful unpronounceable blue flowers . . . and for this new splendid gift which I feel I shouldn't accept but am doing so with all the thanks in the world." Then, in return for whatever his splendid gift had been, she offered the gift of forgiveness for the pains of the past, about which Lowell had evidently been agonizing. It was Stafford in her most lyrical vein, completely sincere for the moment yet with a hint of precariousness not far from the surface: "My dear, please never castigate yourself for what you call blindness—how blind we both were, how green we were, how countless were our individual torments we didn't know the names of. All we can do is forgive ourselves and now be good friends—how I should cherish that."

Lowell was more than ready to lend a hand, and set about helping to arrange a fellowship for her at Wesleyan University. She reported with some trepidation to Peter Taylor that plans were well under way: "Cal is at work on something for me at Wesleyan but that sounds very scary because there are intellectuals up there. Geographically it would be lovely, half way between Boston and New York, but I don't know how I'd attend to Edmund Wilson and Dick Wilbur." It was an ironic end to a stage in her life that had begun with her fatalistic letter to her friends the Thompsons about how hopeless her quest for a fellowship was, now that she was no longer in the Lowell-Tate orbit. Then she had gone to London and met Liebling. This time the fellowship did come through, and she put her fear of intellectuals aside and welcomed this new way station in an unclear future: "All is well," she wrote to Taylor in the early summer. "Thanks to Cal and Bob Giroux I have been made a fellow at Wesleyan and I'm as pleased as anything."

CHAPTER 13

Long Island

As Stafford prepared to make the shift to a radically new life, she sounded more apprehensive. She wrote to Lowell in the midst of moving from the Cosmopolitan Club, where she had been staying, to East Hampton, before heading for Wesleyan in the summer of 1964: "I'm well and restless and haunted but I think a reunion with my house and my cat will dull my keen desire to be gathered to Abraham's bosom which probably isn't as comfy as it's made out." The tone was typical: Stafford opened with the standard modernist lament—like everyone, she was restless and haunted—and then switched to her old-fashioned, colloquial style. It was a curious self-portrait that dramatized her unhappiness and at the same time domesticated it: she was dreaming of her cozy house, but she was also dreaming of cold death. The tension was there throughout the remaining decade and a half of her life, as Stafford continued to be restless and haunted—and became increasingly sick. What writing she managed to produce was a testament to that tension. She kept on struggling, or at least she talked about struggling, toward a novel about her sense of dislocation, apparently willing to experiment with less structured prose. Stalled as ever on that project, she lapsed into her colloquial style and perfected a quaintly anachronistic, often curmudgeonly perspective in an assortment of quite modest nonfiction pieces. The manner recalled the provincial tone that she had cultivated early on, only now with an often dyspeptic edge. That domesticated rage, like her raging domesticity in her beloved Springs house, preoccupied her, but neither was a match for her lurking desire to be done with life.

Stafford anticipated a year of productivity at Wesleyan. "I should be forced to work as I have not done for many years," she wrote to her sister Mary Lee on leaving for Middletown, Connecticut. "The faculty is bound to be sophisticated and the boys are bound to be bright." She knew she needed goading to start writing again, and she was probably remembering how she had responded to the pressures of academia the last time she had been there, at Iowa and LSU during the late 1930s and early 1940s. The company (mostly "boys" back then, too) had been intimidating, but for all of her insecurity she had been spurred to write. Her colleagues this time were certainly a far cry from the Liebling crowd, amid whom she had written little: Paul Horgan, the head of the Center for Advanced Studies at Wesleyan and an old friend of Robert Giroux's, and Edmund Wilson and Father D'Arcy, whom she had known before, as well as a larger group of scholars, including Herbert Butterfield, René Dubos, Moses Hadas, and others. And there were few official burdens. The fellows were mostly left alone, except for a weekly gathering and a light load of student conferences.

Yet when Stafford left Wesleyan in the spring of 1965, she confessed to her friend Nancy Flagg Gibney that during that year she had written "not a word except reviews." And she told a newspaper interviewer, "There's something inimical to me about an academic atmosphere—I can't work at all." She left Wesleyan briefly to be on a panel at a writers' conference at the University of North Carolina in Greensboro, which was as usual an anxiety-inducing experience. The discovery that Randall Jarrell was deeply depressed didn't make it any easier; it was the last time she saw him before his death (possibly a suicide) the following fall.

Back at Wesleyan she apparently kept quiet about her novel, and when her turn came to present some work-in-progress to the fellows, she read from her Samothrace manuscript. Her one larger-scale effort was an assignment from Barbara Lawrence, an editor at *McCall's,* to write an article about Lee Harvey Oswald's mother, Marguerite Oswald. Launching the piece was no small achievement, since it meant travel, which Stafford dreaded; she left Wesleyan for a trip to Dallas in May and spent several days interviewing Mrs. Oswald. But she tended to disparage the project and sounded a little apprehensive about actually completing the writing. In a letter to Allen Tate that spring, she cast her assignment in thoroughly pragmatic terms, describing it as a hedge against the future: she was writing, she confided, "for a magazine whose name I am ashamed to write down, but for one so rich that if I can get the story done I won't be too badly let down if the Rockefeller grant doesn't come through."

Rather than settling down to work, Stafford found plenty of diversions at Wesleyan. She ran a social hour every afternoon, drinking and talking with the less academic fellows, often mocking the donnish life. It was her familiar anti-intellectual pose, except this time she seemed to feel less of the defensiveness that had roused her to productivity in the past. She had an ideal companion in Edmund Wilson, who was notoriously scathing about the academy and who was happy to spend long cocktail hours with her. And as always, an appreciative audience soon gathered to hear her witty, acerbic talk.

Given all the distractions and all the previous difficulties she had had with writing, it is perhaps hardly a surprise that Stafford made no progress on fiction that year. The fallow period was easily overlooked, thanks to the publication and warm reception of *Bad Characters,* a collection of nine of her stories and the longer "A Winter's Tale," in the fall of 1964 while she was at Wesleyan. Most of the notices, like the one in the *New York Times Book Review,* were an encouraging combination of praise and implicit expectation of more fine fiction to come: "Jean Stafford is surely one of our best writers. She makes the English language a weapon or a wand."

But the fiction wasn't in fact under way just then, and though she made an energetic foray into journalism and so could claim some productivity for the first time in several years, it seems quite clear that Stafford's literary trouble was essentially the same: the unwieldy truth, in particular autobiographical truth, continued to draw and to deter her. If she had ever entertained much expectation that the role of critic might open new nonfictional terrain to her, she made no real effort to develop a serious voice in the regular column she started writing for *Vogue* that year. Her monthly book reviews were brief (seven hundred words or so), largely devoted to summary, with some display of her distinctive prose, but not much sign of a unifying perspective or analytic intent. Many of the reviews were positive, and the praise was largely predictable (she liked Walker Percy, Saul Bellow, William Trevor, V. S. Pritchett). Although her subject was usually fiction, she showed little interest in working out any of her confusions about the direction of her own work in her discussions of other people's writing.

In an article called "Truth in Fiction," published in 1966 in *Library Journal,* Stafford did face her difficulties, but she had plainly come to no new conclusions. It was a rehash of "Truth and the Novelist," written fifteen years before when she was having trouble with *In the Snowfall,* the novel about Lucy McKee and her college days, and the gist was exactly the same: "While autobiography is inevitable, we must winnow carefully and add a good portion of lies, the bigger the better." Ostensibly, the occasion for the reflections was also the same. Almost verbatim, Stafford detailed her ordeal with the Lucy novel, now cast as an episode long behind her.

But she then very abruptly shifted to talk about her more recent writing life in the only fresh section of the essay, a discussion of her experience with Marguerite Oswald: "Let me change my tack now and tell you about a time more recently when telling the truth and nothing but the truth was the job I had to do." That creaky transition perhaps suggests the real impetus for resurrecting her essay. In writing about her previous block with her autobiographical novel, she was indirectly writing about her current block, from which the Oswald interview was a kind of an escape.

The journalistic project was quite a different tactic for overcoming obstacles than the one she had resorted to earlier. Then she had turned to more purely imagined material, and in *The Catherine Wheel* ended up writing a novel comparatively free of autobiographical fact and memory. This time she turned to more purely factual material. If subjectivity was the problem, she was ready to try objectivity and see where that led her. As "Truth in Fiction" went on to reveal, Liebling's spirit presided over her Oswald project. The subject was close to his heart. Before his death, he had been collecting clippings for a "Wayward Press" column—never written—about Kennedy's assassination. More important, the reportorial technique Stafford aspired to was modeled on her late husband's methods, which she had seen in action when she accompanied him to New Orleans to talk to Earl Long. "What I wanted to do was report exactly what I heard and saw, not what I felt," Stafford explained. "And the hardest job I had, when I started the writing, was to edit without editorializing." She admiringly described Liebling's oblique way of winning the crazy governor's trust and then admitted that she had never managed to establish any rapport with the assassin's peculiar mother, who was all but oblivious to Stafford throughout her long, addled monologue in defense of her son.

Still, Stafford thought she had succeeded in her journalistic pilgrimage, even if readers were less sure about what to make of her profoundly unsympathetic portrait of Mrs. Oswald. "It seemed to me and it seemed to the editors I worked with, and it seemed to my friends," she wrote in "Truth in Fiction," "that I had presented the case of Mrs. Oswald without slant or analysis, and that the irony derived from the facts rather than from any commentary." But there was a note of defensiveness in her claim. In fact, the book showed her succumbing to a version of the same trouble that dogged her in her novel: she couldn't seem to get her sensibility out of the picture. If the problem in her fiction was that self-loathing deadened her imagination as she tried to conjure with characters too close to herself, here the problem was her obvious loathing of a woman with whom she had nothing in common. Hardly impartial or invisible, Stafford could not resist the opportunity to comment witheringly on her hapless subject and to bemoan her own deep fatigue ("I was tired and headachy") during her nine-hour ordeal.

It was an unfortunate pose. Rather than letting Mrs. Oswald's tape-recorded outpouring speak for itself, Stafford constantly interrupted the bizarre monologue to add snobbish visual detail and heavy-handed ridicule of the malapropisms, grammatical lapses, and other embarrassments and inanities of Mrs. Oswald's homely efforts at high rhetoric on behalf of her son. The woman's often incoherent harangue was plainly outlandish: "they" in Washington had decided that her son was the sole, evil assassin, Marguerite Oswald claimed, but if only they would listen to her, she would reveal the "truths" to set the story straight: "I'll write a book and the title of it will be *One and One Make Two* or *This and That*. Oh, I could write three books or five books! I could write books and *books* on what I know and what I have researched." Out of the haze of misinformation and non sequiturs, Mrs. Oswald's case came down to a pathetically bizarre defense, which made for unsettling comic reading:

> Now maybe Lee Harvey Oswald was the assassin. . . . But does that make him a louse? No, no! Killing does not necessarily mean badness. You find killing in some very fine homes for one reason or another. And as we all know, President Kennedy was a dying man. So I say it is possible that my son was chosen to shoot him in a mercy killing for the security of the country. And if this is true, it was a fine thing to do and my son is a hero.

Stafford's piece was finally a cruel portrait, executed pitilessly. As if Mrs. Oswald's own deranged self-exposure were not damning enough, Stafford insisted on intruding in the role of merciless judge. As Martha

Gelhorn suggested in her review of *A Mother in History,* Stafford seemed under pressure to proclaim her own eminently sensible perspective in the face of Mrs. Oswald's megalomaniacal persecution complex: "Perhaps Miss Stafford puts herself in the picture too often, as if to remind herself that she is still there, still sane; and this is a journalistic error."

The heartless mockery of a misguided mother is a curious permutation of Stafford's youthful plan, sketched out in letters to Hightower decades before, to transcribe the damning evidence of her parents' benighted vision of life. She had been avid to ridicule her own mother's clichéd expressions and hopelessly banal, optimistic outlook, much as she made fun of Mrs. Oswald's refusal to face the facts; and she had listened intently to plenty of her father's long accounts of conspiratorial persecution by "them." As she had half admitted to Hightower back then, fear lurked behind her ruthless project—fear that there were deep bonds and similarities linking her to the pathetic parents she desperately hoped to escape. In her Oswald piece, she expressed the same apprehensive curiosity about the ineradicable traces of kinship. The quest for the roots of character, she explained, was the motive for the profile:

> I had come to Texas to see Mrs. Oswald because she is, as she was frequently to tell me, "a mother in history," and while she remains peripheral to the immediate events of the Dallas killings, she is inherent to the evolution of the reasons for them. She is inherent, that is, if we accept (as I do) the premise that her son had something to do with the assassination and accept the further premise that the child is father of the man: we need to know the influences and accidents and loves and antipathies and idiosyncrasies that were the ingredients in making up the final compound.
>
> ... Relatives are often (perhaps more often than not) the last people on earth to know anything about each other. Still, there was the possibility, and I had come down from Connecticut to explore it.

A version of the same quest motivated the novel she was having such trouble writing. Where did she come from, what had been the influences and accidents and loves and antipathies and idiosyncrasies that had helped to shape her? What secrets might those ignorant relatives, especially her father, hold? To ask the questions in a radically different context, for the Oswald article, was perhaps a relief of sorts. The writing of the piece apparently proceeded smoothly and promptly, and Stafford also expeditiously enlarged it into a short book *A Mother in History,* which Farrar, Straus & Giroux was happy to publish in 1966, even if it wasn't the work they were waiting for.

STAFFORD HAD BEEN BACK in East Hampton for half a year, settling into a new, rustic life (her Rockefeller grant in hand), when her father died in January of 1966. It was the liberation she had been impatiently awaiting for years, as she had bluntly told even her loyal sisters, who had been shouldering most of the burden of caring for him. But not surprisingly, her reaction to his death was not the simple sense of release she had hoped for. Distance had never been as easy to establish as she liked to pretend. She had resisted her sisters' pressure to visit him and found every excuse not to write to him, but he was clearly very much on her mind, not least perhaps because she had set herself the task of writing *about* him. She had begun to help contribute to his support when he was moved, unwillingly, into a nursing home near Marjorie in Oregon, where his health deteriorated quite rapidly. (He apparently suffered several strokes and started rambling incoherently toward the end, and bronchitis made breathing difficult.)

Stafford didn't go to his funeral, and she proceeded to be the thoroughly recalcitrant daughter and sister. Confronted with the overwhelming fact of her father's death, she seemed to feel compelled, out of guilt and a fear of facing the loss straight on, to stir up a petty family squabble as a pretext for severing ties. A letter to Peter Taylor, written "in a winter mope" shortly after John Stafford's death, offers a glimpse of the extent of her guilty conscience and of her ambivalence about the bonds of kinship:

My father died about a week ago. He was an old, old man and in the last month or so, he'd been uncomfortable to the point of awful pain. Up until that time he'd been as peppery as ever and his letters were still crotchety, semi-learned, blasphemous little glades of Mark Twainish kind of wit. He died in Oregon and my Colorado sister was out there with my Oregon sister. If I've never told you anything about those two, this is all you need to know: they called collect to tell me that my father had died. . . . They are wanting in some terribly important human quality. It scares me to death to think that I am too. But now I'm through with both of them. To calculate, at such a time, a toll charge of perhaps $1.75.

It is queer and unproductive to live this completely alone.

The question of the heritability of inhumanity had been the theme guiding her investigations of Mrs. Oswald: Was her discovery of the mother's chilling absence of empathy a clue to the son's act? Here Stafford almost ludicrously trivialized the fear of being "wanting in some terribly important human quality" by linking it to her sisters' reversal of telephone charges, but in fact it was a fear that had haunted her relations with her father for a long time. That was evident in her ruminations in *In the Snowfall* on Joyce Bartholomew's father, his misanthropic bitterness as a man and his coldness as a father, and on Joyce's fears of her own profound detachment. In her letter to Taylor, apparently without any sense of irony, she offered an almost pathetic instance of her susceptibility to precisely the traits she least admired. She abstractly admitted the possibility that she was as coldhearted and petty minded as her sisters, but she seemed unaware of her own actual display of just those qualities. If it was astounding that they, "at such a time," should have called collect, it was hardly less notable that she should have magnified that lapse into cause for a complete rupture. And no sooner had she celebrated the break than she acknowledged the barren isolation she had created for herself.

Stafford was alone in a more profound way than she had been for a long time. She was right that living so completely on her own, as she continued to do in East Hampton, didn't turn out to be productive, and she was right to characterize her existence as "queer." But the oddity of it was not entirely new. More than a decade earlier, after her divorce from Oliver Jensen, she had set up house alone in Westport and cultivated the role of the spinsterish literary lady. It had been an old-fashioned pose that covered up a reality that was not in fact so cozy: then Stafford had been quite sick and often drunk. Her style this time was similarly fusty, though a new fierceness began to surface. Her stylized eccentricity looked less like an entertaining act and more like an effort at symbolic caricature of the kind she had once undertaken in her fiction.

The fact that she was no longer successfully writing fiction seems to have meant that Stafford became more absorbed than ever before in crafting a protective persona. The reclusive spinster role in the 1950s had served as a playful deflection from her personal troubles, while she was hard at work writing her way out of her literary troubles. She had been more than ready to drop the pose, as her susceptibility to Liebling showed. Now the role was more central to her life, more firmly established every year. And for all of her steadfast rejection of the claims of kinship, avoiding her father's funeral and feuding with her sisters, the alternately crotchety and demure provincial style that Stafford perfected after Liebling's death looked like a belated embrace of her "hick" origins. It was as though she was trying to work out some of the themes that thwarted her in her fiction, to find some accommodation with her Colorado past.

A curious loyalty to the memory of her reclusive, embittered father is reflected in her retreat to her Springs house and in much of the indignant writing that emerged from her downstairs study, where, she said, "I wear pants and boots and a green visor and I turn into a journalist." That was an echo of her descriptions of her father the cowboy freelancer, pounding away at his old typewriter. Describing her attachment to her haven in the article "East Hampton from the Catbird Seat," she acknowledged that she, "a Westerner," was hardly a native, but then spent most of the piece demonstrating that her heart was with the locals and with the other curious characters who had come not to find the chic parties but to flee the ordeals of contemporary urban life. It was an evocation of an eccentric agrarian life not unlike the existence she sometimes described her father aspiring to. Among its great virtues was, she claimed, freedom from conventional sociability. "I can be a grasshopper for two weeks running and then I can be a mole for the next three months. I am not obliged to see anybody who bores me or anybody who disapproves of me and nobody whom I bore and nobody of whom I disapprove is required to keep my company."

Similarly, when Stafford took off her visor and became a bustling lady of the house, her allegiance to her mother's domesticity showed through. She was happily preoccupied with homey pastimes like making potpourri and doing needlepoint. She admitted that "I'm a compulsive housekeeper. I even go into corners with Q-tips"—an echo of Shura Marburg's obsessive poking with hairpins at the dust on the Hotel Barstow furniture. Though Stafford acknowledged that these "explosions of orderliness" were signs of the doldrums, she played down the dark side: "They're better than staring-into-space depressions." She was unabashedly house-proud once again, as she had been in Maine: "I give presents to my house—gave it a cedar-closet last year, gave it a new study this year—and when the workmen have finished for the day, we cut up a few touches over a Bud." Much of Stafford's renovation entailed gradually turning extra bedrooms in her house into studies to avoid having guests, whereas her mother had been forever looking for more room to sleep another boarder. The effect, ironically, was not so different: whirlwinds of domestic energy, yet no real family hearth. And there were plenty of studies, yet next to no work was getting done in them.

To keep her company in her house, she resurrected an imaginary alter ego, named Henrietta Stackpole after Henry James's feisty journalist in *The Portrait of a Lady,* whom she had originally invented when she lived in Westport. Her role then, as Stafford explained Miss Stackpole's inception, was to be an intermediary with a vulgar world that too often and rudely intruded on her treasured, civilized retreat. This fictional character played the role of secretary, sending out letters under her own name for her refined companion. Stafford pretended that the name had fortuitously sprung to mind, but in fact her amanuensis was more carefully chosen and helps shed light on the persona and perspective that Stafford cultivated during the last decade and a half of her life.

The juxtaposition of Jean Stafford and Henrietta Stackpole showed Stafford at work borrowing from her literary mentors in fashioning a style, this time for her life rather than for her fiction. In appropriating Miss Stackpole as her secretary/alter ego, Stafford was invoking James, but she had picked his most Twain-like character. James himself, in his preface, apologetically explained the uncharacteristic Henrietta as his effort at "the cultivation of the lively," to counteract the danger of "thinness" in the rest of the refined novel. James's heroine Isabel Archer gave a fuller account of her blunt friend, whom she appreciated as an exemplar of American virtues for which she felt a real nostalgia. It's not hard to see why Stafford kindled to Isabel's portrait of the less-than-ladylike Henrietta Stackpole. "I know enough to feel that she's a kind of emanation of the great democracy—of the continent, the country, the nation," Isabel said, defending Henrietta to her cousin Ralph Touchett, who had fled his native ground for England:

I don't say that she sums it all up, that would be too much to ask of her. But she suggests it; she vividly figures it. . . . I like the great country stretching away beyond the rivers and across the prairies, blooming and smiling and spreading till it stops at the green Pacific! A strong, sweet, fresh odour seems to rise from it, and Henrietta—pardon my similes—has something of that odour in her garments.

Settled in comparative solitude on the eastern tip of Long Island, Stafford was eager to welcome the West back under her roof. As a pair, Stafford and her invented companion encompassed the tensions that had long animated her distinctive style. In the drama that Stafford scripted between the two of them, she juxtaposed the established lady and the combative journalist and played on the contrasts entailed by that paleface-redskin dualism—between refined and colloquial, elitist and populist, retiring and "lively." The letters that the loyal Miss Stackpole penned for her employer carried Stafford's own idiosyncratic, indignant voice to extremes, ridiculing the stupidity of her correspondents in a vein that John Stafford would have appreciated.

Yet "Miss Stafford," who stood behind this blunt amanuensis, was no less outraged by the world, only more detached and polished. The tone of their collaboration—and their common sensibility—is captured in a withering letter Henrietta wrote to a poor young man who had happened to write Stafford for advice about his love life. After a dose of contempt, Miss Stackpole informed him that her employer might find his letter "sufficiently outré to include in her Dunciad which she has been compiling over the past 25 years." Sent a sexually frank novel by some hapless and apparently none-too-talented writer, with a request to write a blurb for it, Miss Stafford had her secretary respond fiercely; her employer, Miss Stackpole explained, "would undergo a most grievous curdling of the blood" at the prospect. Apparently Stafford was amused enough by the correspondence to send it to several friends, including Ann Honeycutt, who wrote a note back to Stackpole, making fun of her purer-than-thou employer:

Thank God you are there to protect Miss Stafford. Had that book and title and portrait of the author fallen into those fine, unsullied, but too delicate hands of hers, she might well have swooned away for her last time on this earth and be by now in heaven. I often think—and frequently say—that Miss Stafford is on loan to us poor mortals here below from the saints on high.

The merciless disdain of Misses Stackpole and Stafford is reminiscent of the young Stafford, scathing about Babbitt-infested America in her letters to Hightower soon after she had returned from Germany. But a significant transformation had occurred. Then she had been full of impatience toward her philistine country and family and had dreamed of modernist adventure. Now Stafford was still inveterately opposed to philistinism, but she was more inclined to associate it with the disorder of "this so-called 20th Century" (one of her favorite Waugh phrases) and especially, as she confronted the 1960s, with contemporary turmoil.

As 1967 OPENED , Stafford sent her agent a dramatically bleak letter: "Things grow grimmer and grimmer. Anger alone keeps me alive." Settling down in her Springs house the year before had not been a cozy retreat. She had had plenty of physical ailments (including pinched nerves, which meant an immovable arm), and she had done little writing. She was very upset at her doctor's instructions to quit smoking, and then at her utter failure to buck the habit, which was clearly dangerous in more ways than one: dropped cigarettes had already set two fires in her bedroom. Judging her acutely depressed, Dr. Roberts advised her to see a psychiatrist, Dr. Jacques M. Quen, and though the sessions didn't last very long, his impressions of her state of mind are revealing. His general diagnosis echoed those of countless doctors before him, and of Stafford herself: "There is a markedly passive, perhaps even a masochistic element prominent in her personality structure." But in a report back to Dr. Roberts, he went on to remark on the unexpected high-spiritedness she also conveyed: "I am intrigued by a sense of vitality and energy which she transmits, despite the severity of her depression."

It was thanks to that energy that she ventured out into the world in 1967. She managed to be quite funny about one brief emergence into the limelight that summer, a passing appearance in a *Time* cover story about Lowell, in which—to her surprise—she found little to get angry about. (She had been "intense, beautiful, a gifted writer of fiction" when he met her.) Far from betraying any pangs at the gulf that loomed between them, she wittily played the part of the scrounging ex-wife of the famous poet in a letter to Peter Taylor about the article:

> I was, to tell the truth, quite sorry that I came off so well; I had partly hoped that they'd be so scurrilous about me that I could sue them for huge sums. (There seemed to me a note of reproof in the statement that we wrote in separate rooms. How else is it done?) I counted nine factual errors just in the part I figured in.

Stafford's real entry back into the literary bustle and city life came in the fall, and it was not so diverting. No huge sums forthcoming from anywhere, she had agreed to teach creative writing in the master of fine arts program that had just been founded at Columbia, and she had rented an apartment on East Eighty-seventh Street for the year. She was evidently more than a little ambivalent about what lay ahead, as she wrote to her agent at the start of September:

> It has been a most monstrous summer (including for me a savage attack of peripheral neuritis thought to have been brought on by arsenic poisoning from sprayed fruits or vegetables—I ended up in the local hospital sobbing). . . . I dread Columbia and in certain ways I dread New York. In others I greatly look forward to being back. Lately I have been trying out my city shoes, changing them every hour; my wig is extremely successful, but I've nothing at all to put on myself between my feet and my head.

She was the rural lady in a dither about going to town. ("I am so rustic," she wrote to Nancy Flagg Gibney, "that when I go into town once in a blue moon my feet hurt and I am afraid of the traffic and my clothes look as if I'd snatched them off my cleaning woman.") It was a manner that could hardly have been less in step with the times. Prim in her city shoes and gloves, she was an almost comic contrast to her Columbia colleague Edward Dahlberg, who, though not young, had a much more fashionable reputation: an eccentric writer admired by the Beats, he had been described by *Esquire* in the early 1960s as one of the heroes of the American literary underground. It was quickly clear that Stafford and her students were confronting each other across an enormous divide, and though she listened with her typical curiosity to the cadences of their complaints, she couldn't begin to imagine responding to them. She wryly recalled her experience several years later:

"I have nothing to say about 'A Rose for Emily,' " said Y one day. "I read two paragraphs, and it didn't turn me on. I don't dig Faulkner." And a few weeks later, X said, "Of course I didn't read *Heart of Darkness.* Do you seriously think I'd read anything by a pig who wrote a book titled *The Nigger of the Narcissus?*"

I was stopped in my tracks: I could be neither collaborator nor disputant, and my role of teacher was canceled out, as were Y's and X's roles of students. I was a servant who had not divined what services I was to render.

In the calmest of times, Stafford had not found teaching easy, and now her ordeals in the classroom were a sign of more than professional unease. They captured her broader sense of alienation from the surrounding culture. When students staged a sit-in during the spring of 1968, the turmoil roused Stafford to some general reflections on the state of society that revealed her growing cultural conservatism. It was part of her curmudgeonly style to strike reactionary poses, but her declarations were usually more rhetorical than substantive. Now, in a letter to Peter Taylor, she made a more serious effort to gather her thoughts, and the result was a surprising, sweeping defense of the institution of the family. "I am out of my element in a debate like this one, primarily because I believe our society is an utterly decadent one," she began, meaning the society in convulsions around her:

And I believe so because I believe any society is decadent in which the family is not the basic unit—the basic moral, social, economic unit.... In opposition to this idea is that of individual freedom. The rights of the individual must be put before everything else! But the family is just as organic as the individual, say I,—more so—and its rights should be put first. How can one speak of the brotherhood of man if one does not really know what a brother is? Of course families cause us great pain, but unless we are decadent we must be willing to suffer for principles. Today more than ever before, we can know what a permanent relationship is only through our families.... We have abandoned the ideal of the family, which *is* humanity, for the ideal of the individual, which is not quite human.... It is not enough to think of a man or a woman simply as a lover. A man must also be a son, a brother, a father. A woman must be also a daughter, a sister, a mother. Otherwise, we are all either enemies or lovers, and I don't believe that. I won't have life so simple minded.

It was an analysis that she elaborated a couple of years later in an article for *McCall's* about Charles Manson and his followers, whom she took as an extreme specimen of the anomie to which society had succumbed. "It is not entirely surprising that the girls in California drifted into Manson's community, out of the instinctive (though often inadmissible) need to belong to someone and to own someone, to have brothers and sisters and, above all, a father—to have, in short, kinsmen under the skin if not by blood," she wrote in "Love Among the Rattlesnakes." "The horrendous perversion of the moral code and of the traditions of protectiveness, guidance, and support that accrued to Manson as pater-familias was not just a cry for love but a desperate shriek in the wilderness." Here she made clearer that in appealing to the traditional family, she did not intend to romanticize it, but simply to claim it as the best available civilizing force: "The structure of the family, of whom the woman is the architect, has been weakened to the point of debility, and in our waifdom, our orphanhood, we sue total strangers—we sue, indeed, our enemies—to be our teachers and our protectors. Nothing obliges us to love our parents or our cousins; and, so far as I know, no authority has ever proposed we *like* them; but, plainly, the individual must be nurtured within an edifice, within a form."

Stafford defending the family as a source of stability and strength is a long way from the young Stafford battling against her clan, and a long way from the novelist struggling to explore the darker side of kinship. There is a strange undercurrent of self-denunciation in Stafford's indictment of rebellious youth for overthrowing the family. After all, she had abandoned her own family and championed a ruthless individuality in the face of their persistent efforts to claim some kind of permanent relationship with her. She had spent much of her life chafing at the roles of daughter and sister, and motherhood had never been a very serious prospect for her; her bond with her brother had not been as continuously close as she suggested in retrospect. In her concluding assessment of the dire implications of the sixties ethos in her letter to Taylor, she was perhaps alluding to her own decisive youthful break with her family: "The direct appeal to youth for youth's sake will always be the making of just so many little Hitlers," she wrote. "They love nobody but themselves and their cry is *I* want *mine!*" Years before, Stafford had escaped from home to Hitlerian Germany, where—to judge by the ordeals she arranged for her autobiographical character Gretchen Marburg in *Autumn Festival*— she had been trapped by egocentric desires and, though appalled by Nazi youth in Heidelberg, had been profoundly adrift herself.

Now Stafford was adamant about sticking to her own, anachronistic cause. The student rebellion at Columbia in the spring of 1968, however disorienting, did little to intimidate her into playing along. On the contrary, as she contemplated returning to teach in the fall, she was emphatically uncompromising, as she explained in a letter to Frank McShane, the director of the creative writing program:

> Peter Taylor and I talked the other night . . . and, as I understand it, you have asked him to meet with the students before his talk so that the students can tell him what they want him to talk about. . . . This policy of appeasement is, to me, intolerable and I will have no part of it. I intend to talk to my students about the short stories of Chekhov, Henry James, Stephen Crane, Kafka and so on. I intend to make absolutely no reference to the troubles. . . . If I find a switch-blade at my jugular, if my ears are assailed by rude language, if, in short, I find myself in the eye of a storm irrelevant to education, to writing, to civilization, and to my life and my work, then I shall have no choice but to quit the premises.

That letter made clear the underlying consistency of Stafford's emergence as a cultural conservative in the scattered journalism that by now eclipsed her fiction. Though her traditionalist discontentment with contemporary culture consorted somewhat uneasily with her own rebellious, bohemian youth, and though her defense of conventional decorum looked a little odd in light of her own psychological turmoil, there had been a steady allegiance at work. From the outset Stafford had felt the need to embrace order in the struggle with unruly experience, and to buck the tide of majority opinion—however much tension was entailed.

As usual, there was plenty of tension. When her first year at Columbia was over in the spring, she didn't feel much relief. She returned to East Hampton only to face more physical ordeals (further trouble with pinched nerves) and to continue to vent her spleen at the state of the world. A letter she wrote that summer to the local newspaper, the *East Hampton Star,* is a typical example of the humorously peevish journalistic manner she increasingly adopted and the arch populism it expressed. (It was the sort of letter she often had Miss Stackpole pen for Miss Stafford.) In it, a sampling of her characteristic crotchets was on display:

> I have it in for all public utilities, for all businesses, for all businesses that use computers, for all petitioners for all causes who come to my door, have the unconscionable brass to call me on the telephone, and fill my letter box with their matter. I am down on Mark Rudd, John Wayne, Cassius Clay, modern inconveniences, the United States postal service, The New York Times with its interminable essays which I believe are called "think pieces," and its whole-hearted participation in the debasement of the English language.

While she was cultivating her out-of-date image—often wittily, sometimes more indignantly—she was also keeping track of Lowell, who was energetically abreast of the times. It was easy enough to follow him during the late 1960s when, as his biographer has put it, his "public persona achieved its remarkable apotheosis." He had been protesting prominently—refusing to accept an invitation to the White House from President Johnson, marching on the Pentagon—and now he plunged into electoral politics, campaigning with Eugene McCarthy. Though he must have seemed to be on the other side of the barricades most of the time, Stafford was for the most part fondly humorous, and sarcastic, about Lowell's high profile. "It is a little hard to keep up with R. T. S. L., Jr. these days," she wrote to Taylor in the spring of 1968, "but I'll try to run this clipping service as efficiently as possible. I like the image of a president-maker lolling about with his loafers off (you can imagine what condition they're in) and fetching up with that definition of acedia." It all seemed outlandish, but in a half-familiar way. "The whole business sounds like the mythology of the Wuberts," she commented, remembering Lowell's role as Arms of the Law, the sheriff-like bear who scripted elaborate parts for all of his friends in the game of "berts" that Lowell and Stafford had played during their marriage.

Amid all the turmoil, there was one interlude of peace, when her friend Jean Riboud spirited her away for a visit to his château in France. There she escaped the rude modern world for a brief taste of old-fashioned gentility. As she wrote in an article several years later, "Why I

Don't Get Around Much Anymore," an amusing catalog of her horrifying travails every time she set forth from her beloved house, her visit to
France was her last trip abroad. It had been so uncharacteristically painless that she took it as an omen not to press her luck: "I doubt that I will
ever go abroad again, unwilling to challenge that record and come a
mighty cropper."

As she went on to say in the article, she was occasionally tempted
against her better judgment to venture out in her own country. Invited
to participate on some panel or other, "compulsively I accept because, I
tell myself, I will see a part of the country hitherto unknown to me; the
fee is attractive; the date is so far in the future that it will never come."
Instead, she found the experiences yet more rude confrontations with an
uncongenial world. "Far from broadening, travel in this unenlightened
age has narrowed my mind to a hairsbreadth. Chatty seatmates on
planes, trains and buses have made me misanthropic; motels and hotels
with no or with lackadaisical service have made me undemocratic." Her
experiences at Columbia were her most extended exposure to the unenlightened age, and on her return to teaching in the fall of 1968, she found
herself even more out of her element than she had felt the year before.
Eager to be back in East Hampton, she arranged to have another writer
take her place for the spring term.

Stafford's retreat roughly coincided with the sudden emergence of her
fiction in print. Her story "The Philosophy Lesson" appeared in *The
New Yorker* in November of 1968. It was apparently drawn from work
she had done long before on *In the Snowfall,* which had since then mi-
grated into the autobiographical novel that was still giving her so much
trouble. The story was set at a university clearly modeled on her alma
mater, and its plot also linked it to *In the Snowfall,* though Joyce had been
renamed Cora Savage. Like the protagonist of *The Parliament of Women,*
she confronted a familiar, Lucy McKee–inspired trauma: while posing
for an art class, Cora heard the news of a fellow student's suicide. In
exploring Cora's consciousness as she meditated on the death and
watched the snow start to fall, Stafford included a moment reminiscent
of the bilocation that she was experimenting with in her new novel—the
disorienting shift between vivid present and dreamlike past. But in this
version, rather than aiming for unsettling disjunction, she smoothed it
into a relatively tame moment of memory. Looking out at the snow, Cora
was suddenly transported back to her childhood in Adams by thoughts

of the danger she had associated with winter when the sleds came out: "Once Cora lost control and went hurtling into a barbed-wire fence. It seemed to her, on reflection, that she had slowly revolved on her head, like a top, for a long time before the impact. Then, too frightened to move lest she find she could not, she had lain there waiting for her brother.... Afterward she had been afraid of the ski jumps...." The vision of cold loneliness haunted her again as she found herself all too able to imagine what had driven her fellow student to death. "A darkness beat her like the wings of an enormous bird and frantic terror of the ultimate hopelessness shook her until the staff she held slipped and her heart seemed for a moment to fail." This story about the terrors of an isolated consciousness within an alienating body was a carefully shaped work, whose very artfulness served to underscore the dangers of disintegration.

Stafford's appearance in *The New Yorker* after so long was soon followed by an announcement in *Time* of a forthcoming novel ("her first ... in seventeen years"), a misleading report, though her public revival did continue. *The Parliament of Women* was nowhere in sight, but in February of 1969 her *Collected Stories* was published. Here, too, Stafford was obviously riding on old work: almost all of the stories had been published at least a decade earlier. It was a consolidation of her career that clearly meant a lot to her, though it was also a potentially difficult reemergence. She hadn't managed to produce much since those stories, and meanwhile literary tastes had moved significantly beyond the sensibilities and standards that informed much of her work. But Stafford betrayed no apprehension, in fact took the occasion to emphasize her nonconformist, out-of-date literary allegiances. Studiously resisting any "relevant" packaging of her reentry into a literary scene that she disparaged as undecorous, she paid homage to Twain and James in the author's note, borrowed from those unfashionable mentors for the section titles of the collection, featured the elegant *New Yorker* in a cover collage of the magazine's pages, and dedicated the book to Katharine White.

Her confidence was well rewarded. However unenlightened she judged the times, she herself was judged very favorably. Enthusiastic reviews appeared promptly and prominently. The daily *New York Times* declared, "Everything that we desire from a collection of short stories, from the art of fiction, in fact, can be found in this gathering of Jean Stafford's work"; Guy Davenport in the Sunday *Book Review* heralded it as "an event in our literature," and others followed suit. Early in 1970 Stafford was at last elected to the National Institute of Arts and Letters, after years of not quite making it. When the most unexpected recognition of all, a Pulitzer Prize, was announced that spring, Stafford was taken by surprise, and so, apparently, was the *New York Times*. The newspaper's editorial about the awards—after saluting Seymour Hersh's prize for reporting on the My Lai massacre and noting that "in the arts and letters section, the judges appeared to be aware of what's new"— was caught up short by the anachronistic air of the fiction prize winner. "And if Jean Stafford's stories are more traditional than adventuresome," the editorialist rather lamely observed, "they are surely among the best of their kind being written today." Stafford herself commented in an interview on the incongruous timing of her elevation. "I find it awfully heartening that a writer as traditional as I can be recognized," she said— and then took the opportunity to vent her typical impatience with the prevailing aesthetic: "Do we really need a poem about a banana that is set in type to form the shape of a banana?"

Stafford's sudden prominence pleased her, though true to her retiring rural-lady style, she liked to play down her success, treating the fanfare as a rude intrusion into her life. "For a few days my privacy was outrageously invaded by telephone calls," she wrote to Mary Lee, "but now everything has quieted down." In fact, the flurry over the award did subside relatively quickly, and if she was disappointed, Stafford could also claim she was not at all surprised. Before the Pulitzer she had written caustically to Allen Tate about the complaints of her less sympathetic readers: "I'm now getting very snippy reviews—I'm not 'relevant,' I'm not involved with issues, I'm not a Jew and I'm not a Negro, I deal only with the human heart and that has been transplanted." After the prize, she was invited to be a writer-in-residence briefly at the University of Pennsylvania and was similarly under no illusion about her relevance: "None of them [her students] had ever heard of me and certainly had not read me, but this was understandable enough since neither had their teachers."

As those declarations suggest, Stafford's sense of marginality inspired indignation and resignation, depending on her mood and depending on her audience. In the 1970s, in the journalism that now constituted her literary output, she mostly kept her disgruntlement within decorous bounds. "I could wish that the 1970s came to be known as the Age of

Order," she wrote in *McCall's* as the decade began, and the demure tone and glossy venue were typical. "I would like to see government once again informed by statecraft and education dignified by humanism; I would like to see a straightening up of the language and the removal of rubbishy jargon and solecisms." Rather than veering into extreme bitterness, she seemed almost consciously to be holding herself in check, carefully taming her personal turmoils, present and past, and curbing her critique of public disarray. Of course, the style was partly the product of the places she was writing for—women's magazines, for the most part, where she had a hope of making some money. But the gentility of her rage perhaps reflected deeper constraints as well. Stafford knew all too well the direction in which old rural recluses could incline: she had written about addled isolates, and she had known her father.

It was in five lectures that she was invited to give at Barnard in the early spring of 1971 that Stafford gathered up her ruminations on the state of the times. Her ambition was not to work up a systematic discussion. As always, the prospect of the podium inspired real nervousness, and she skirted all pretenses to being anything but an amateur proud of her colloquial touch. The material was derivative of earlier work; she plundered freely from previous journalism (and later she plundered freely from the lectures, reprinting versions of them as articles and spinning off new pieces on the same themes). She gave the series an imposing title, "Tradition and Dissent," and located a unifying preoccupation in her opening comments: "For the next two weeks I'm going to be talking on a number of subjects, although as I look back on what I've written, they all seem to be variations on the same subject: the upheaval of our traditions." But the titles of her individual lectures are a better clue to the more informal, quaintly old-fashioned cast of her undertaking: "The Felicities of Formal Education," "The Present Afflictions of the American Language," "The Teaching of Writing," "Sense and Sensibility," and "The Snows of Yesteryear."

As she had done in the past, beginning with her first public-speaking effort, "The Psychological Novel," Stafford pursued her themes in an anecdotal, autobiographical manner—all the while shying away from confession. It was sometimes a curious tactic, as it had been in that youthful lecture: she would approach painful truths (back then, psychological breakdown), only to round them out in a resolutely conventional perspective (years earlier, her message was that fiction writers should avoid baring their psyches). Here she explicitly invoked the memory of her father and his curmudgeonly complaints against the times, only to declare her independence from him. He was a "man embattled from his bassinet," convinced "the world was going to hell in a handbasket." She professed much more optimism.

Although Stafford did not in fact have very much hopeful to say, she was evidently taken aback when a student who interviewed her for the *Barnard Bulletin* halfway through the series commented on how bleak the lectures sounded. Stafford hadn't intended a screed, told the student she feared she had "muffed" the lectures, and spent the interview speaking as a very approachable if unfashionable lady of letters, the edge all but gone from her tone. "The lectures almost seemed a harking back to the nineteenth century," her interviewer observed, and Stafford replied serenely: "Well, what I'd like to call myself is not a conservative, but a conservationist. I want to preserve everything that is good, dignified, and that is an adornment to the country, including the language." She emphasized that she was feeling far from fierce: "I don't feel bitter, I feel satiric," she explained. "I felt much bitterer when I was younger, but now I'm mellowing. No, that isn't true. I've no way to test myself, because I've retired to a sort of hermit's life, and I get awfully cross when I read the *New York Times,* but I live such a pastoral life. . . ." In "Sense and Sensibility" she made the same point, turning it into an implicit critique of the current reverence for youth, a familiar theme: "I look back upon the years of my own young life with a certain admiration and with a certain embarrassment and with no desire whatever to live them over again. I am glad that I was once obliged to be intransigent, but I am even more glad that I am now mollified and slowed down by the obliquities of old age."

Stafford also did her best to assure her interviewer that her views on the women's movement were mellower than the student had surmised. She declared that she was "all for equal opportunity. I think it's shameful that women with the same credentials and the same ability get smaller wages," said she could not "think that I've ever suffered from discrimination by being a woman," and concluded by emphasizing that it was the style of the debate as much as anything that she objected to: "I, well, I hate noise, and I think this great brouhaha between, who is it, Mailer and Kate Millett . . . the awful mudslinging . . . it's just an ill mannered, bad public performance."

Of considerably more concern to Stafford was a clarification of her views on language. She hastened to explain to her interviewer that she was "not opposed by any means to the vernacular, the living language, the colloquial language. It's something that I love and honor, and I use it all the time. I would be lost in my own writing without the vernacular. What I object to is the jargon of such things as 'meaningful dialogue.'" The full extent of Stafford's love of and alarm about language was clear in an article derived from her lecture, in which she declared one of her main missions to be vigilance on its behalf. Her carefully chosen figures of speech suggest how important this cause was for her. It was a tribute to her past, a continuation of the work she had once done in her fiction: "Who will carry on the rich oral traditions of New England and the South and the West?" she asked, and her answer invoked her own stories, the bad characters in Adams: "I reckon that convicts and children, who have the most time on their hands, will go on contriving slang and jokes, and, God willing, the wellspring will not be polluted and will not go dry, and hillbillies and pickpockets and able-bodied seamen and timbercruisers and Southern politicians will go on sweetening the pot."

At the same time, her worries about the state of the language were an extension of her fears about her own future, about her frailty amid contemporary barbarities. Here she invoked the metaphor of an ailing body to describe the ordeals of language, much as she had once used that same figure in writing about her deep attachment to her house. In both cases, her psychological and physical health were intimately tied to those two important refuges, her houses and her words:

Besides the neologisms that are splashed all over the body of the American language like the daubings of a chimpanzee turned loose with finger paints, the poor thing has had its parts of speech broken to smithereens: Setting the fractures and dislocations has been undertaken by tinkers with tin ears they have fashioned for themselves out of old applesauce cans ... ; and upon its stooped and aching back it carries an astounding burden of lumber piled on by the sociologists and the psychologists and the sociopsychologists and the psychosociologists, the Pentagon, the admen.... The prognosis for the ailing language is not good. I predict that it will not die in my lifetime, but I fear that it will be assailed by countless cerebral accidents and massive strokes and gross insults to the brain and finally will no longer be able to sit up in bed and take nourishment by mouth.

Her fears for the "ailing language" were an eerie prediction of her own fate, though for the moment Stafford claimed that she was feeling quite hale. In concluding her talks, Stafford announced that she had found this particular encounter with the wide, wild world much less bruising than she had expected. In "The Snows of Yesteryear," she played the role of rural recluse to the hilt. She was the quiet lady ready to go home, but surprisingly pleased to have ventured forth:

> I came here in fear and trembling because in these last years when I have been living in the country, I have turned into such a slowpoke hayseed that I expected every sentence I uttered to be greeted with a Bronx cheer. . . . But you have been amiable and generous. . . . You have cheered me. I feel far less acerb. I can't pretend I want to stay on—in truth I can't wait to get back home to my own bed and my own cat (and my own work) and to see if there are any signs of buds on the lilac bushes.

BACK IN EAST HAMPTON during the summer, Stafford was less cheerful. That certainly didn't mean unremitting grimness, as Wilfrid Sheed emphasized. He and his wife were her "share-croppers" in her little bungalow out back that year, and they knew what good company their sharp-tongued landlady could be. During long evenings spent drinking together, they indulged in "manic flights of humor, all gone, alas, by the next day":

> She was cruelly funny [and] . . . she interwove this with a rare gift for affectionate complicity: you felt just for now that you were the only two people remotely capable of understanding how silly it all was. "Let's merely see each other every day for the rest of our lives," she said one morning at five o'clock. It was a handsome exaggeration, definitely not to be acted on. Yet it was always the understanding on which she celebrated: that we could seize a little permanence, a moment of immortality and if it wasn't art, it would have to do.

It wasn't art, however, and Stafford wasn't quite prepared to reconcile herself to that. She wrote to her sister Mary Lee, with whom she was intermittently feuding and confiding, that she was ailing and her work was suffering. It was a familiar complaint, she acknowledged, and it became an ever more recurrent refrain:

> Once again back in my orthopedic corset and cervical collar and elastic stocking and excoriating the driver of that automobile that mucked me up 33 years ago, one of my pleasures these days ... I am not so much depressed as vexed. I had counted on an enormously productive summer but the weaknesses of the skeleton invade the brain and make it listless. . . . I'd meant to get the Barnard lectures in shape; I'd meant to write a good many small essays on manners and the works of departed friends; I'd hoped to finish my novel. Now I am immobilized so many hours of each day that I don't know what I'll get done.

The plans that Stafford outlined help to put her last years into perspective. Notably, she relegated her novel to last on her list of endeavors and admitted less certainty about it: she merely "hoped" rather than "meant" to have that behind her. She was proved right in her skepticism. Her other projects were considerably more modest and backward looking, and they weren't fulfilled in the form she probably had in mind. She did eventually get a couple of the lectures in shape to publish, but in less than prestigious places (such as *Saturday Review World* and *Confrontation*). And instead of the tidy tribute to the past implied by her plans to write about manners and departed friends, the scattered journalism that she ended up producing over the next five years (under pressure, as Peter Taylor said, of some "real or imagined need of money") can be read as a curious revisionist accounting of her life.

Her themes were for the most part familiar. She did write about manners in assorted pieces on etiquette for women's magazines. She continued to write about language and commented intermittently on the women's movement. (Her most celebrated pieces were a little diatribe against the use of "Ms." for the *New York Times* and an article for the same paper entitled "Women as Chattels, Men as Chumps," in which she declared that "the fustian and the hollering ... the strident jokelessness attendant on the movement are woefully unpropitious because they obfuscate a good many justified grievances," such as unequal pay.) She reviewed books, and she tried her hand at several profiles, mostly for

Vogue. And she wrote letters, increasingly full of complaints and despair about the world. As Taylor commented in his tribute to Stafford after her death, a spirit of disappointment infused these miscellaneous writings: "She wrote numbers of book reviews and articles, of course, but frequently with tongue in cheek and always seemingly in a terrible rage, a rage against a life that had contrived to place her in such a ridiculous situation." This was not what her literary career was supposed to lead to, and the different pieces, though chatty on the surface, suggest that some darker sublimation was at work. There was a good deal of denial and domestication of the real trials of Stafford's life in the journalistic exercises that consumed her.

Various assignments prompted her indirectly to rewrite her past, taming the creative tumult that she had known. Thus in a review for the *New York Review of Books* she was condescendingly dismissive of Thomas Wolfe, claiming that she had been disaffected long before she had in fact outgrown her early imitation of him. Her characterization of Wolfe echoed the merciless reactions that her own prose had elicited from her first readers: "The man revealed [in the letters] is infuriating and pathetic, so deformed by self-absorption and self-indulgence, so macerated by his warm bath of self-pity, so worshipful of the physical appetites he deified that he was incapable of deep friendship or deep love." In another piece for the magazine, commenting on Robert McAlmon and Kay Boyle's *Being Geniuses Together,* a memoir of expatriate life in the 1920s and early 1930s, she found an occasion to be less than kind about another of her mentors during her early, confusing years— Evelyn Scott, whom Stafford backhandedly rescued from McAlmon's dismissal this way: "He's not above taking pot-shots at sitting birds or of being as cheaply cruel as a bad, bright child: of Evelyn Scott he says, 'She'd be more restful if she would just admit her mediocrity.' " If Stafford thought McAlmon's tone was wounding, she evidently was not inclined to challenge the substance of his assessment.

On other occasions, she wrote with a notable lack of sympathy about women whose troubles were not entirely foreign to her, sometimes adopting an oddly judgmental tone. In a piece about Isak Dinesen, for example, she described an eccentric woman who was often cruel about her husband, cold in her writing, uninterested in food, plagued by ill health, and given to donning unusual masks—a portrait quite close to home, which Stafford concluded with a warning that was perhaps meant for herself: "Such whims (the hat, the kohl), such personal theatricals are to be applauded unless they become too important, unless the personage takes over the personality."

Stafford's etiquette pieces, mostly cast in the form of advice columns, were similarly peremptory on subjects that were in fact sources of pain and confusion. She emerged as a crotchety expert on sociability (in such pieces as "Suffering Summering Houseguests" and "Some Advice to Hostesses from a Well-Tempered Guest," both for *Vogue*), making a gimmick out of her reclusive tendencies. Her temperamental aversion to company allowed her to be the unillusioned guide to the burdens of conviviality. And her old-fashioned approval of formality made her a stern critic of the vogue of immediate intimacy. Sent by *Horizon* magazine to cover a course in encounter-group techniques, Stafford was so appalled by the rudeness that her article "My (Ugh!) Sensitivity Training" was all about why she simply had to quit going.

The truth was, her solitary streak was not quite the quaint eccentricity she liked to suggest in her slight pieces. While she was telling others how to endure their guests, she was arranging her house so that no one would come stay with her. It was the old, deep lure of isolation and, it seems clear, a desire to hide the life she lived—to escape the drinking she did in company, to obscure the drinking she did alone, to elude advice about her unhealthy habits in general. In "Don't Send Me Gladiolus," she gave tips on social protocol with hospital patients, a trivializing treatment of a troubling, chronic subject in her life—sickness, and the vulnerability it entailed. "Cherish but do not pamper me. Treat me as if I were a grown-up temporarily under the weather," she wrote, and her complicated dependence on doctors and on bouts of invalidism was reduced to a glib maxim well suited to the pages of *Vogue*.

The profiles Stafford wrote, which fall into roughly two categories—grandes dames and alarming eccentrics—can also be read in an autobiographical light. They reflected, as the editors who assigned them must have felt, two contrasting impulses obviously central to her self-conception. Miss Prides, in more or less intimidating versions, had long figured in Stafford's life, in her aspirations to a sense of social connection. At the same time, her fascination with propriety never obscured her iconoclastic inclinations. Both are easy to trace to her past, to the ambivalence she felt about her provincial roots and her colorful father. But her magazine articles are notable for glossing over any confused allegiances.

Stafford gushed shamelessly over the aristocratic ladies (Katharine Graham, publisher of the *Washington Post;* Lally Weymouth, her daughter; Millicent Fenwick; Mrs. Warren G. Topping, founder of the Hampton Day School), adopting the tone of a refined woman appreciating another rare specimen in a crass, democratic world. In a letter to Nancy Flagg Gibney, Stafford complained that "the Fenwick caper did me in as the Katherine Graham one did last year" and swore that she would never write for *Vogue* again. Still, she proved herself remarkably adept at producing the fawning pieces, and the result was reminiscent of Sonie Marburg's blind infatuation with her starchy mentor. The end of the piece on Mrs. Graham, a long digression on the theme of family loyalty inspired by a reunion of the wellborn clan at Christmas, suggested Stafford's lurking preoccupation with her own family origins, so different from the patrician Grahams'. As in her previous defenses of the family, she seemed notably unhindered by the irony of her own situation—she was a woman who hated Christmas, and who kept her relatives at a distance:

> Christmas has come to be . . . a ritual to honor or, at any rate, to *recognize* the family, the household; . . . and while there may be schisms within the order . . . there should be a truce at least once a year to remind the fractious fractions of the integer from which they derived. We can transplant ourselves from home and native ground, but our bloodroot cannot be extirpated. Whether we're glad or sick at heart about the matter, we were *born* and we were born by some woman and to some man. Our feeling about these two and any other creatures they may have created can be as various and as shifting as the sands and as fragile or tough, or lovely or teratoid as the shells upon the seashore. But not a blessed thing can alter the fact of our origin.

Stafford was closer to her familiar, acerbically witty self in her treatments of eccentrics (Mrs. Oswald, the filming of *The Misfits,* Martha Mitchell, the pathological Charles Manson), though as her portrait of Mrs. Oswald showed, her articles often lapsed too quickly into condescension toward her curious subjects. It was her own idiosyncrasies that she seemed to take more seriously, devoting increasing energy to a form

of self-portraiture that had a lineage in her family: the outraged, beleaguered, peeved, appalled letter or short piece, which her father had specialized in toward the end of his life as well. As she admitted in an article
in *Esquire,* "Somebody Out There Hates Me," "the venting of spleen and
bile is relieving and, if it offends and is sourly returned, perversely delicious." In the diatribes she clearly relished, she mostly defended the unfashionable views that often riled her readers, and elaborated her fusty
persona, complaining about miniskirts, illiteracy, malapropisms, and
other offenses of the undecorous times—often in a less-than-decorous
way. Or, as in a long battle with Con Ed over an erroneous bill, she
adopted the pose of the aggrieved little person—often in an arch, less-
than-populist way. The first and longest of the letters she exchanged with
the electric company, and later wrote about, was a seven-page document
of manic name-dropping, itemizing the famous people with whom she
had socialized over the course of a month (proof that she had not been at
home using electricity). There were moments of real amusement in the
epic self-mockery, but the energy she devoted to it seemed bizarre:

> I find that on April 28th I dined at Le Pavillon (dreadfully over-
> rated) with M. Jean Riboud, the distinguished president of Schlum-
> berger, Ltd and went with him to the opening of the Royal Ballet.
> (The dancing engaged us—up to a point—but oh, Good God, that
> opera house. Those chandeliers—lighted, of course, by Con Ed—
> could be, were they flesh and blood, haled into court and charged
> with criminal vulgarity.) On the 29th, I dined at Gino's (excellent
> food but much too noisy) with Stephen Greene, the celebrated
> painter.... On the 30th and the 1st, I dined with slightly less (but
> only *slightly* less) luminous friends. . . .

More poignant were the letters to her editors in which she complained
about the treatment that her pieces had received at their hands. Once
more she was the defender of the language and of her own history of
stylistic polish, and it was clear how much was at stake for her even in
her less substantial journalism: she cursed it as hackwork and then, as if
in compensation, became the imperious author. "Digression is integral to
my style. Parenthesis is my middle name," she lectured Shana Alexander
at *McCall's.* "I have been assiduously at work on my style for a great
many years. Style is the morality of language, and I look upon myself as

a moral writer." Describing another editing ordeal, this time at *Cosmopolitan,* she invoked the by now familiar metaphor of the body to describe her sense of linguistic violation: "I knew they would [greatly cut] but I was nevertheless sickened to see all the flesh stripped from the bones and the bones, in general, dislocated."

There was an exception to the journalistic constriction that Stafford courted and yet chafed under. For six years, from 1970 through 1975, she wrote the Christmas roundup of children's books for her old patron, *The New Yorker.* Not that it was a thoroughly liberating, fulfilling project by any means. She dreaded the arrival of the holiday season, when the books that had been steadily accumulating finally had to be tended to, and she was far from impressed by the caliber of the writing she was commenting on. But appearing in *The New Yorker* was a welcome return to the ground of her earlier success, and writing about children's books offered a way to tap into an otherwise daunting past. Much as her Adams stories had opened a door onto her childhood, in these reviews she could and did write as an adult enlightened rather than entrapped by her vivid memories of the state of innocence, its fears and its exhilarations. She began her first review with a declaration of her critical perspective and standards, which was also one of her best statements of her own imaginative debt to her childhood:

> Writers of books intended to be read by children can be placed in two general categories. There are those who took childhood seriously as they lived through it (the jokes and the razzmatazz together with the terrors, the mysteries with the disenchantments, the profits with the losses) and respected themselves as children, so as adults they can remember the early ways they took through experience. Some of these ways were plain and sunlit, others were bosky, and some were harsh and tangled and ominous, but all of them, travelled for the first time, were surprising and important. These writers remember how they collected and inspected information and why they were gluttonous for certain kinds and stupefied by others. Above all, they remember the books that pleased them and the writers whose worlds they could inhabit with full franchise and without embarrassment. As children, they were devout and incessant readers. . . . They savored unexpected words like *truncheon* and *blunderbuss, cohort* and *constable, samite, brougham,*

comfit, curmudgeon. They can recall the emotions of childhood and the sensations, the cabals of it and the ethics. Childhood is not a tolerant time of life, but it is governed by a rather grand and reckless integrity: the child goes headlong to the root of the matter—if he is not deflected—although he has not yet discovered the heart of it. This first group of writers maintain a tact, a courtliness of address to their audience, no matter how colloquial or extravagant or absurd or soberly instructive their performance may be. They are good writers.

The others are bad. They seem to have gone through childhood so swiftly and heedlessly that they had no time to master the runes of the language (which cannot be picked up later on) or to record the weathers and landscapes of their Hells and Utopias.

Stafford's past was very much on her mind as the 1970s progressed and her health declined, but she was rarely able to maintain that kind of poise about it. Although a visit to her alma mater in the spring of 1972 to receive an honorary degree went very well, and although her survey of her career in her lecture "Miss McKeehan's Pocketbook" sounded satisfied (she even talked of collecting her miscellaneous nonfiction writing), it was clear that the sense of accomplishment and equilibrium she conveyed was more than a little fragile. Just how fraught the prospect of a return to Colorado was for Stafford is suggested by a letter she wrote to Mary Lee, who had evidently expressed interest in seeing her when she came West. In it the youngest, bitter sister spoke as though still a defensive adolescent, as though her lifetime away had brought no distance:

> Come if you like: I can't imagine it would give you any pleasure. And if you do come, do not expect any long private talks. If it gratifies you to know that you still exert over me the most remarkable power, rest assured that since our conversation I have not slept, eaten, or done a tap of work. And, as very often in my long and troubled life, I have wondered why in the name of God I did not, once I got to Germany, change my name and establish for myself a brand new identity.

Unfortunately, Stafford's failures to eat, to sleep, and to work were far from a merely passing fit occasioned by her sister. Several years later, Stafford was ready to acknowledge that she had arrived at a disheartening turning point. Despite regular free-lance work (she took over Malcolm Muggeridge's slot reviewing for *Esquire* in 1975) and intermittently hopeful mentions of her novel, the truth was that her writing was not going well. In 1975 she wrote a dismal, prophetic letter to her agent James Oliver Brown, suggesting that she leave him: "I am so unproductive (I've had a miserable and long siege of bronchitis with the asthma that goes with it and just before Christmas I was in the Hospital for Special Surgery for treatment of the arthritis with which I will be stuck for the rest of my life) that I can't think I will ever bring you anything but small, unprofitable nuisances. The novel is still miles and miles in the future." It was the first time she had been so explicitly hopeless about the book.

She turned to Lowell for help, and though the tone of her letters was jaunty, her mission must have been uncomfortable: she was asking him to autograph some of his books for her to sell. If part of her enjoyed playing the importunate ex-wife, part of her clearly didn't. "Do you loathe me for this? Do I wound you?" she asked him, questions probably half directed at herself. "If you do, tell me and I'll stop," she said, though she admitted her desperation for some money with which to buy time. "I do *so* want to finish my novel. I do *so* hate to have to interrupt it to write reviews and articles. I wasn't put on the earth to be a journalist. I'm *sure* I wasn't."

As she went on to confess to Lowell, she was leading an even more reclusive life, and if she lied to him about drinking alone only "occasionally," her general description of her ambivalently antisocial life was painfully true:

> One of the principal reasons I have become so reclusive is that I don't want to drink, and I find that I can't not drink when I'm with people—I use booze as insulation against boredom and impatience, or to exalt my feeling of camaraderie to the point of mania. Moreover, it makes my stomach ache and brings on monstrous insomnia. If I drink alone—and sometimes I do occasionally—I fall down and break something—either an irreplaceable piece of something breakable or one of my bones. And on those occasions, my solitude becomes loneliness and I may plan a dinner party and telephone invitations. And then I have to cancel it with some heavily documented excuse, the details of which I can never remember.

In a mock memo several years before, sent from Henrietta Stackpole to Dr. Roberts, Stafford had been even more forthright about the central place that alcohol played in her increasing unhappiness. The colloquial, lighthearted style of her confession only added to its poignancy:

> Old though she is, and outstandingly wise, she is as tough as a mule and my sorrowful prognosis is: Extensive Longevity. . . . If she stays away from John Barleycorn, she is, in our opinion, an OK kid, and to tell you the honest truth, I think JB is basically the root of her problem . . . who, in conjunction with J. Calvin and J. Knox, have mucked up this poor woman to a fare-thee-well. . . . We wouldn't mind (after all, we're not strait-laced) if she and Barleycorn stole a few kisses from time to time. It's this going all the way that causes so much trouble.

The metaphor was all too accurate. That dominant attachment, along with her many troubles, took its toll on Stafford's other relationships. A demanding friend at the best of times, she became increasingly unpredictable and difficult as her health worsened. She went into New York Hospital in 1975 shortly before her sixtieth birthday with heart trouble and chronic lung disease and left it with all the accoutrements of a perpetual invalid (but none of the improved habits: she continued to smoke and to drink). She had to clear out her lungs regularly with a machine, and she was dependent on supplementary oxygen, which tethered her to a tank of air several times a day.

Her predicament tested her ties with her friends, of whom she had a large circle in East Hampton—the artist Saul Steinberg; the *New Yorker* writer Berton Roueché and his wife; Wilfrid Sheed and Miriam Ungerer; the poet Richard Howard and Sanford Friedman; Eleanor Hempstead across the road and the Guedenets, friends of Liebling's, not far down it; Craig Claiborne; the comedian Dick Cavett and his wife, Carrie Nye; Ralph Carpentier, a local sculptor, and his wife, Hortense; Jeannette Rattray, the publisher of the *East Hampton Star,* and her son Everett, the editor, and his wife, Helen; a retinue of locals, including her housekeeper, Josephine Monsell, and handymen, the taxi driver, and many others. She also had plenty of friends in other places, who had gotten used to her late-night calls, which were often long and not always totally lucid.

Now those calls became longer and more of an ordeal, and Stafford clearly felt ever more ambivalent about actual visits, as she acknowledged in a letter to Hightower, who was still teaching at Harvard and with whom she had been in intermittent touch. She rebuffed an invitation from him with a moving mixture of deluded optimism about her work and undeluded realism about her life. "All of this valetudinarianism has its advantages: the [health] regimen (not as time-consuming as it may sound) has driven me into work as an escape from the nuisance of it and I am at work almost altogether on my novel," she told him, and then elaborated her reasons for staying home: "Even if I could bring all my gear with me, even if I were not so well at work, you would find me no fun: I am too egocentric, too preoccupied with my disorders and my novel." Wittily she explained that she couldn't sit by an open fire, due to her oxygen tank, couldn't laugh because of her heart—so how would they have fun? "Ten million thanks, ten million apologies for being as mindlessly quixotic as the day I was born."

Often her quixotic dealings with friends and the world had a more desperate tone. Soon after her humble proposal to leave James Oliver Brown, she turned on her agent, accusing him of failing her time and again, complaining of his "peevishness, . . . irascibility, . . . paranoia." A late relationship she formed with a young East Hampton couple, Kenneth and Maria Robbins, was perhaps the most dramatically problematic, and it suggests how her mounting dependence and egocentricity skewed her social life. When Stafford first met Maria Robbins, a children's book writer, in 1975 during a ride on the East Hampton jitney, she was thoroughly enamored of her and quickly took up the couple as her special intimates. Such infatuations were Stafford's style: one of her friends described her as a queen at court, who collected suitors with zeal. But her favors were fickle, as she herself knew, and it was ambivalence about her reliance on her courtiers that seemed to underlie her disorientingly unstable affections.

When she gave the Robbinses an acre behind her house in 1976, she saw the deal quite clearly. They had become her tacit caretakers, tending to her and her house, to say nothing of offering companionship—all of which she knew she needed. Her aim was to make an offering in return, one that would ensure assistance without undue intrusion. But she also knew that however clear the terms of the relationship, she was bound to feel intruded upon at some point: when she urged the land upon them,

Kenneth Robbins remembered, she warned that they should hurry up and take it before she had a turn of heart. And indeed she did, when her dignity and privacy seemed to her violated. Perhaps the most degrading exposure came when Robbins found her, bloodied, at the bottom of the stairs in her house one night, and insisted on sending her to the hospital, against her protestations. Helpless to fend off unwanted help, she felt deeply betrayed. The Robbinses were abruptly and absolutely exiled from her graces, a fate visited upon one set of friends after another in her last years.

On November 8, 1976, Stafford's health took a drastic turn for the worse, following the bleak course that her doctors had warned her of—and a revised version of the course that she had outlined for her character Beatrice Trueblood years before. Stafford had a stroke, which was the physical blow she feared most. Where Beatrice Trueblood, the expert listener, lost her hearing, Stafford, the virtuosic talker, lost her speech. Her note to her sister Mary Lee about the catastrophe must be the most linguistically acrobatic announcement of aphasia ever composed. "Since my speech is gone altogether now I have to write you," she explained to her in May of 1977. "My fine labials and lenes are lean, disabled." It is tempting (not least in light of such feats as that) to extend Stafford's own psychosomatic analysis of Beatrice Trueblood to herself. Her close friend Nancy Flagg Gibney gave it a try during her last visit to East Hampton in 1977 and described the occasion in a short reminiscence of Stafford:

> The last time I saw her ... I said, "Come clean, sister. I'm on to your game. It's Beatrice Trueblood's story again. Okay, so you didn't believe it—you wrote it, and now you've done it. You can't speak because you find everything unspeakable. You can't talk because you see no one fit to talk to."
>
> She nodded her wonderful ravaged head and laughed. Her laughter was eloquent and unimpaired.

As Stafford acknowledged, at least in her imaginative writing, the mind and the body worked on each other in ways sometimes too uncanny to be believed. Certainly she had been a prime candidate for a stroke on physical grounds, but the mental terrain had been prepared as well. She had come close to prophesying her affliction in her story, a fable about the ironically fitting fates that the head can visit upon the flesh. And she had clearly been poised to retreat before it ever happened. A

month before her stroke, in her last review for *Esquire,* a pan of Mary
Hemingway's autobiography, *How It Was,* she announced an impending
silence: "This is the last review I shall write for Esquire—through circumstance and not through disagreement; and we part in peace. It may
be the last review I will write ever."

There was cruel irony in the fate of this woman who had counted on
language as her salvation, and her aphasia was clearly a source of great
pain and further rage. Her stuttering efforts to bring forth words were
agonizing for her and for her friends. (One of her speech therapists—
toward whom she exhibited "passive hostility," according to a speech pathology report—remarked that Stafford made little attempt to ease her
ordeal: "Marked speech frustration experienced by patient along with
marked inclination to search . . . for polysyllabic word rather than common colloquial word which is easily within patient's linguistic grasp.")
But in another sense, as Gibney suggested, it was an all too fittingly
scripted fate for a woman who had come to feel that there was nothing
very good to say about the world. Or, perhaps even more to the point, for
a woman who was full of frustrated anger at her inability to find imaginative verbal form for her vision, full of disappointment at her lapse into
disgruntled commentary—and, who knows, full of terror at hearing the
echoes of her poor father in that decline. Perhaps it was not so much that
Stafford saw no one fit to talk to as that she felt herself unfit to talk;
silence was better than the speech she had been reduced to. She had long
known the allure of isolation.

Yet, as Stafford knew, retreat was not easily accomplished. A succession of women hired to help her were dismissed, usually in dramatic
fashion; therapists were hardly more welcome. Her East Hampton
friends drew back, daunted by the difficulty of any dealings with her
(though they and others rallied with financial help, and Stafford sold
roughly thirty acres of land to ease her dire straits). At the same time,
her past, though she had tacitly abandoned hope of mastering it in fiction, was not to be banished. This time it was Lowell, rather than her
family, who loomed large. Only a couple of months before her stroke
(and a year before his death), he wrote her a letter from England, in
which he waxed fondly nostalgic about their life together long ago:

> 1940. Remember Chimes Street and Baton Rouge . . . ? I got a letter
> last month from Vanderbuilt [*sic*] to write for Red's [Robert Penn

Warren's] 70th festschrift. After struggling with a laborious prose compliment, I dropped it for a poem, more of the tone, the humidity, less critique. A hundred unusable things came back to me—the arrival of Gaga's chairs, Peter's earplug falling out at bridge ... , Peter and I in pajamas sick over taking out Cinina's [Warren's wife's] cat-shit, waiting still in pajamas outrageously for you to return from the office to get our lunch, Christmas with Red staring long at a sheep that looked like Cinina and saying it reminded [him] of someone he couldn't place. You could toss up fifty times as much in the same number of words. How can I thank you?

Time, but we must call it age, they are so inextricably married, is really full of novelty, and even wisdom, never quite enough to say we have repaired our losses or smoothed our distortions. Do you see I am trying to thank you for the past? ... Once we thought we could potentially imagine everything, or anything. But I couldn't have imagined these "mellow" days, and gentle as they are—what a mercy.

Intimations of mortality were clearly very much with Lowell, as they were with Stafford, but his elegiac perspective was distinguished by an almost exultant tone. The same day he sent that note to her, he proclaimed in a letter to his friend and fellow poet Frank Bidart: "I think the ambition of art, the feeding on one's soul, memory, mind, etc. gives a mixture of glory and exhaustion." There is no record of how Stafford reacted to his gesture of gratitude, but she was clearly feeling that exhaustion, not glory, was the legacy of her ambitions.

A month after her stroke, Lowell gave a reading at the 92nd Street Y, in which he again paid tribute to her, and this time her response survived. He read "The Old Flame" from *For the Union Dead* (1964), a poem about revisiting their Damariscotta Mills house, which expressed a mixture of relief and of loss at the passing of that chapter of life:

> Everything's changed for the best—
> how quivering and fierce we were,
> there snowbound together,
> simmering like wasps
> in our tent of books!
>
> Poor ghost, old love, speak
> with your old voice

of flaming insight
that kept us awake all night.

Lowell also read a poem shortly to appear in *Day by Day,* "Jean Stafford, a Letter," which he prefaced with a rather double-edged comment to the audience: "Men may be superior to women, but women always do better in college, I think, and are much more precocious. . . . She could punctuate, and do all sorts of things. . . . She is one of our best writers, and her talent developed early."

That curious tone of condescension culminating in praise was reflected in the poem as well. It began by twitting Stafford about her affected German pronunciation (a cruel joke, given Stafford's mortification about her bad German) and proceeded backhandedly to credit her linguistic skills (she wrote "outlines for novels more salable than my poems," and "*Roget's* synonyms studded your spoken and written word"—not exactly praise for her high artistry). And then it closed with two stanzas in which Lowell suggested a convergence at the end of life between the precocious novelist and himself, the more ponderous poet, and at last declared her words worth listening to:

Tortoise and hare
cross the same finishing line—
we learn the spirit is very willing to give up,
but the body is not weak and will not die.

You have spoken so many words and well,
being a woman and you . . . someone must still hear
whatever I have forgotten
or never heard, being a man.

Stafford's reaction, when Giroux described the reading during a visit to her in the hospital, was fury, though her friend the *New Yorker* writer Joseph Mitchell, who had come to see her too, thought he perhaps detected a glimmer of inadmissible pride. Not long after she cursed Lowell in her halting speech, exclaiming, "Why doesn't he leave me alone?" she wanted to talk about the poem. Years earlier, after one of the phone calls from Lowell that she both dreaded and awaited, she had jotted down a fuller version of the same exclamation on a scrap of paper, as if recording a vow she knew she would break: "I who have less reason to tolerate that

man than anybody else—legally, legally, divorced him—have been obli-
gated by his unquenchable vanity to remain a part of him. Now I'm
finished and done with him." As she doubtless knew then, and still knew,
she wasn't really done with Lowell. That refrain, which had punctuated
their long and complicated relationship ever since their separation, conveyed both her deep desire for escape and her own unshakable preoccupation with him.

Lowell was in fact the subject of the last piece of writing that appeared
before her death, her story "An Influx of Poets," which Robert Giroux
carefully excised from the unfinished manuscript of *The Parliament of
Women,* laboriously working over it with Stafford, conversing with her
in the form of questions to which she could manage simple answers. She
did what Lowell had urged in his poem: in her story, which appeared a
year after he died, others heard what he had "forgotten or never heard,
being a man"—and being Lowell. It was her belated answer to Peter
Taylor's challenge years before, to tell her side of the story. She crafted
her version of her marriage to Lowell and its collapse and produced the
first story in which she had come quite so close to her own personal
history. In the ordeal of transforming autobiography into fiction, she
managed to confront one of the most devastating episodes in her life and
turn it into a distinctive mix of social satire and psychological revelation.
The story was not a therapeutic self-exculpation, not a thinly veiled brief
against the famous poet. Its unexpected, perfectly tuned comic edge—
the detachment from her younger self, the ruthless eye for ironic details—rescued the story from the bitterness that constantly threatened to
overwhelm Stafford's imagination. In fact, it was precisely the hard-won,
tenuous balance between clear-eyed irony and corrosive grievance that
gave the story its power.

Sustaining that feat of imaginative poise was now beyond Stafford.
Not only did the rest of her autobiographical novel keep escaping her
control, but the publication of "An Influx of Poets" in *The New Yorker* in
November of 1978 seemed to throw her completely off balance. To acknowledge that this was almost certainly her last published piece of writing, that her long-awaited novel had come to this story and no more, was
too much to bear. She in a sense turned deaf as well as speechless, claiming that she had heard no response to her story, though in fact her friends
had been quick with their congratulations. She became disoriented in

her bitterness: Giroux and her friends were cast as her betrayers, and she wrote them off one by one as ingrates and enemies—much as Molly in *The Mountain Lion,* in her frantic unhappiness, had compiled her list of unforgivable fat people.

Stafford was to live another four months, mostly reclusive but every so often rallying in her typical style. In a reminiscence, her friend Dorothea Straus, a writer and the wife of Roger Straus of Farrar, Straus & Giroux, described visiting her in the New York City club where she was staying toward the end. The Strauses watched her emerge from the library in scarlet pumps, with a bag to match, and listened to her say, with great effort, that she had decided to sell the Springs house, move to New York, and see all her old friends. Discovering that the bar was no longer open to entertain these particular old friends, she promptly made the long trip back to her room for a bottle of whiskey, a gesture not just of need but of desire for the old conviviality. Yet the defiantly sociable style was usually fleeting. During those same last weeks, she told her friend Joseph Mitchell at dinner one night that she was half in love with easeful death, and it was clear to him that she had made her choice.

Not long after that evening she was taken to New York Hospital, clearly failing, and was soon transferred to the Burke Rehabilitation Center, where she lasted a week. At her bedside when she died were two volumes of Twain and Lowell's *Mills of the Kavanaughs,* which she had annotated. Reading the title poem, she had paused over various details to give her version of the autobiographical facts behind them. Her jottings look like yet one more effort to settle scores, this time in an almost childlike way. She noted down Lowell's debts—she had typed for him, taught him solitaire, showed him flowers: "He saw nothing of the natural world—*nothing!!*" She defended his father, and herself, at the poem's first mention of the figure clearly modeled on the senior Robert Lowell: "Poor old Mr. Bob Lowell, bossed by Charlotte, & despised, despised & patronized by his son. He did, I know he did, love me—he thought I was a regular fella & he also thought I was a pretty girl." But then, in a surge of literary appreciation, she left off her crabbed scribbling and exclaimed beside one passage, "How marvelous this is. It's the kind of writing that reminds me why I married him." Lowell's lines clearly spoke to her own vision of precarious innocence, so central to her imagination. And behind them, she perhaps heard a commemoration of a youthful marriage that had overwhelmed them both, but also inspired them:

> ... Here bubbles filled
> Their basin, and the children splashed. They died
> In Adam, while the grass snake slid appalled
> To summer, while Jehovah's grass-green lyre
> Was rustling all about them in the leaves
> That gurgled by them turning upside down;
> The time of marriage!—worming on all fours
> Up slag and deadfall, while the torrent pours
> Down, down, down, down ...

THE SHADOW of Stafford's fiction, which dappled her life all along, seemed to loom over it at the end. Like Katharine Congreve in *The Catherine Wheel,* she had her tombstone ready well before her death, ordered from a stone carver in Newport (along with one for Liebling) and engraved with a snowflake, the emblem of her early unfinished novel, *In the Snowfall.* Shortly after "An Influx of Poets" appeared, she rewrote her frequently revised will for the last time, and as many of her friends remarked—some with appreciation and some with exasperation—her change of heart was the kind of end one might expect from her fiction.

The spirit of Sonie Marburg lurks in the peculiar abandonment of the literary world that Stafford's final will represents. Before her stroke she had asked Everett Rattray to be Liebling's literary executor and Robert Giroux to be her own. A New York lawyer had drawn up her will accordingly—only to be fired by his client after a dispute about his bill. Without a word to her friends, in November 1978 Stafford hired an East Hampton lawyer for the last revision of the will. In it, no literary executors were appointed. Instead she named as heir to her estate Josephine Monsell, her housekeeper, a middle-aged local East Hampton woman who had always been there when Stafford needed her but had never been intrusive—who never seemed to cast judgment, perhaps because (as Monsell was the first to admit) she didn't begin to comprehend her often mercurial employer. It was as though Stafford were settling the long tension between her identity as a woman and as a writer by declaring her allegiance to domesticity. The most important material legacy to Monsell was the house that Stafford had once thought of turning into a library. Presiding over the earlier plan had been the spirit of Emily Vanderpool, the indomitable rebel who was always looking for a quiet place to read— and happily finding it in the least likely of places. But it was Sonie, the troubled daughter who never found a home for herself, who spoke up in the end. Behind Josephine Monsell stood Shura Marburg, a cleaning woman herself, behind whom stood Stafford's own mother, the keeper of boardinghouses. Stafford never managed to write the sequel to *Boston Adventure,* but at the end of that novel she had pointed toward a future claim on Sonie's conscience. Sonie had banished Shura, much as Stafford had banished her own mother, but she knew that the exile was not forever for either of them. "For the time being, I had walled up my mother into the farthest recess of my mind, knowing that the time would come when I must let her out again."

Acknowledgments

I owe many thanks to many people and institutions for their help and encouragement in the course of my work on this book. None of it would have been possible without those who made Jean Stafford's unpublished words available for quotation. I have reprinted excerpts from her letters, manuscripts, notebooks, journals, and other writings by permission of Russell & Volkening, Inc., as agents for the Estate of Jean Stafford. Most of that material is located in the Jean Stafford Collection of the Norlin Library, at the University of Colorado in Boulder. My visits there and my subsequent long-distance research were immensely aided by the efforts of Nora Quinlan and Kris McCusker. For permission to use material housed elsewhere, I would like to thank Blair Clark; Andrew Cooke; Eleanor Gibney; James Robert Hightower; Oliver Jensen; William B. T. Mock; Cecile Starr; Peter Taylor; Paul and Dorothy Thompson; Stuart Wright; the Robert Lowell Papers, Houghton Library, Harvard University; Harry Ransom Humanities Research Center, the University of Texas at Austin; Department of Rare Books, Olin Library, Cornell University; the John Berryman Papers, Manuscript Division, University of Minnesota Libraries, Minneapolis; the James Oliver Brown Papers and the Random House Papers, Rare Book and Manuscript Library, Columbia University; the Peter Taylor Papers, Jean and Alexander Heard Library, Special Collections, Vanderbilt University; the *Story* Magazine Archives (Box 50), the Caroline Gordon Papers (Box 37), and the Allen Tate Papers (Box 8), Princeton University Library; Dartmouth College Library; Greenslade Special Collections of Olin and Chalmers Libraries at Kenyon College.

I owe a large debt to the following relatives, friends, and acquaintances of Stafford, who agreed to interviews and patiently unearthed their memories of her: Louis Auchincloss, Pearl Bell, Elaine Benson,

James Oliver Brown, Vivian Cadden, Hortense Carpentier, Ralph Carpentier, Edward Joseph Chay, Craig Claiborne, Blair Clark, William Cole, Andrew Cooke, Peter Davison, Anatole Ehrenburg, Sanford Friedman, Brendan Gill, Robert Giroux, Steven Hahn, Elizabeth Hardwick, Ihab Hassan, James Robert Hightower, Howard Higman, Eleanor Hempstead, Ann Honeycutt, Maureen Howard, Richard Howard, Oliver Jensen, Joe Kaufman, Alfred Kazin, Barbara Lawrence, Frances Lindley, Robie Macauley, Janet Malcolm, William McPherson, Frank McShane, Joseph Mitchell, William B. T. Mock, Josephine Monsell, Howard Moss, Frank Parker, Marjorie Stafford Pinkham, Helen Rattray, Kenneth Robbins, Berton and Kay Roueche, Wilfrid Sheed, Eileen Simpson, Raymond Sokolov, Cecile Starr, John Stonehill, Dorothea Straus, Peter and Eleanor Taylor, Paul and Dorothy Thompson, Diana Trilling, Miriam Ungerer, Marie and Alex Warner, Dan Wickenden.

I am grateful for permission to quote from the correspondence of Stafford's friends and family, as follows: James Oliver Brown; Whit Burnett (by permission of Whitney Burnett Vass); Lambert Davis; Nancy Flagg Gibney (by permission of Eleanor Gibney); Robert Giroux, Copyright © 1992 by Robert Giroux (courtesy of Houghton Library, Harvard University); Caroline Gordon (by permission of Nancy Tate Wood, courtesy of The University of Tulsa, McFarlin Library, Department of Special Collections); James Robert Hightower; Ann Honeycutt (by permission of Robert MacMillan and Joseph Mitchell); Oliver Jensen; Karl Lehmann (by permission of Phyllis Williams Lehmann); A. J. Liebling (by permission of Russell & Volkening, Inc., as agents for the author, copyright © 1991 by Norma Liebling Stonehill; courtesy of the Department of Rare Books, Olin Library, Cornell University); Robert Lowell and Charlotte Lowell (by permission of Frank Bidart, courtesy of Houghton Library, Harvard University); A. G. Ogden (by permission of the Atlantic Monthly Company); Dr. Jacques Quen (by permission of Dr. Thomas N. Roberts); Philip Rahv (by permission of Betty T. Rahv); Dr. Thomas N. Roberts; Delmore Schwartz (by permission of Robert Phillips); Evelyn Scott (by permission of Paula Scott); Mary Jane Sherfey (by permission of William E. Sherfey); John Stafford (by permission of Marjorie Stafford Pinkham); Allen Tate (by permission of Helen H. Tate, courtesy of Princeton Library and McFarlin Library, The University of Tulsa); Peter Taylor (courtesy of Houghton Library, Harvard University);

Paul and Dorothy Thompson; Edward Weeks (by permission of Phoebe-Lou Weeks); Katharine S. White (by permission of Roger Angell).

Soon after I began my research, I discovered that two other biographers were also at work. My aims have been different from theirs, but I have benefited from the ground covered and the information uncovered by David Roberts in *Jean Stafford: A Life* (Little, Brown) and Charlotte Margolis Goodman in *Jean Stafford: The Savage Heart* (University of Texas Press). Ian Hamilton's *Robert Lowell: A Biography* (Random House) and Raymond Sokolov's *Wayward Reporter: The Life of A. J. Liebling* (Harper & Row), the fullest biographical accounts of two of Stafford's husbands, were also valuable resources.

Finally, I would like to thank the National Endowment for the Humanities for a fellowship in support of my work. But above all, I am grateful to my friends and family, without whom this book would have been unimaginable. Martin Peretz, the editor-in-chief of *The New Republic,* didn't hesitate for a moment when I asked for a year's leave to get started. Leon Wieseltier, my colleague in the magazine's "back of the book," urged me on, shouldering various burdens during my absence and sharing his thoughts about literature and criticism all along; those conversations have left their mark on the book. Scooter Libby gave me helpful legal advice. Mary Jo Salter was the first to see the manuscript, and as always, she was my ideal reader; the book's final shape owes a great deal to her comments, large and small. Luke Menand, who stood in for me at *The New Republic* during my sabbatical year, helped me early on to refine my thoughts about what literary biography could and should be; four years later I relied once more on his advice. Dorothy Wickenden was yet again an acute and rigorous editor. Brad Leithauser, Jay Tolson, and Janet Hook gave me very useful suggestions in the last stages of my work. Many thanks also to my agent, Rafe Sagalyn, and to my endlessly patient and perceptive editor, Ann Close.

This book owes more than I can say to my husband, Steve Sestanovich. Over the past five years, he has seen me through not only its writing but the arrival of our children, Ben and Clare. I could not have wished for wiser help or more love.

Notes

INTRODUCTION

p. ix: "I am so sick": JS to Ann Honeycutt, June 25, 1956, Jean Stafford Collection, Special Collections Dept., University of Colorado at Boulder Libraries.

p. ix: "predilection for masks": Howard Moss, "Jean: Some Fragments," *Shenandoah* 30, no. 3 (1979), p. 78.

p. ix: "Lowell-to-Liebling": Wilfrid Sheed, "Miss Jean Stafford," Ibid., p. 98.

p. x: "reporter's moll" to "the Widow Liebling": Ibid., p. 95.

p. x: "Although it often may": Peter Taylor, "A Commemorative Tribute to Jean Stafford," Ibid., p. 57.

p. xi: "Actually, what she was like" to "she was always seeking": Ibid., p. 59.

p. xii: "Yet really we had the same life": "For John Berryman," Robert Lowell, *Day by Day* (New York: Farrar, Straus & Giroux, 1977), p. 27.

p. xiii: "What do I care": JS to Robert Lowell, n.d., Houghton Library, Harvard University.

p. xiv: "The esthetic distance": Guy Davenport, review of *The Collected Stories of Jean Stafford, The New York Times Book Review,* Feb. 16, 1969, p. 40.

p. xv: "the poets to a fare-thee-well": Alden Whitman, "Jean Stafford and Her Secretary 'Harvey' Reigning in Hamptons," *The New York Times,* Aug. 26, 1973, p. 78.

p. xv: "You have spoken": "Jean Stafford, a Letter," Lowell, *Day by Day,* p. 29.

PART I: *Cowboys and Indians and Magic Mountains, 1915–1936*

CHAPTER I: *California and Colorado*

p. 3: "If I have that dream again": Sheed, "Miss Jean Stafford," p. 96.

p. 3: "By the time I knew him": JS, *The Collected Stories of Jean Stafford* (New York: Farrar, Straus & Giroux, 1969), author's note.

p. 4: "whose life-long interest": John R. Stafford, *When Cattle Kingdom Fell* (New York: B. W. Dodge and Co., 1910), dedication.

p. 4: she was fond of citing: Eileen Simpson, *Poets in Their Youth: A Memoir* (New York: Random House, 1982), p. 122.

p. 4: "as soon as I could" to "they won't go back": JS, *Collected Stories,* author's note.

p. 5: *"When Cattle Kingdom Fell* is back": JS to Mary Lee Frichtel, postmarked Aug. 19, 1969, JS Collection, U. of Co.

p. 5: In 1920 her father's: JS to James Robert Hightower, n.d. (probably May 1940), JS Collection, U. of Co.

p. 5: Richard Stafford's land and money: JS notes, Samothrace folder, JS Collection, U. of Co.

p. 5: John Stafford and Ethel McKillop's meeting, marriage, early married life: Marjorie Pinkham to author, Apr. 20, 1987; and Charlotte Margolis Goodman, *Jean Stafford: The Savage Heart* (Austin: University of Texas Press, 1990), p. 9.

p. 6: Malcolm McKillop and family: JS notes, Samothrace folder, JS Collection, U. of Co.

p. 6: John Stafford's career: obituary from JS Collection, U. of Co.; Marjorie Pinkham letter to author; John Stafford letter to JS, Dec. 21, 1951, JS Collection, U. of Co.

p. 6: "get down to what": John Stafford to JS, Dec. 21, 1950, JS Collection, U. of Co.

p. 7: At the Covina ranch: Marjorie Stafford Pinkham, "Jean," *Antaeus,* no. 52 (Spring 1984), pp. 11–13.

p. 7: "Our days on the ranch": Ibid., p. 11.

p. 7: "She's all right": Ibid., p. 9.

p. 8: "On the lippia lawn": from a speech JS was to deliver at California State University at Northridge, quoted in William Leary, "Native Daughter: Jean Stafford's California," in *Western American Literature* 21, no. 3 (November 1986), p. 198.

p. 8: "There is drama": JS childhood MS, JS Collection, U. of Co.

p. 8: In 1920 John Stafford sold: Pinkham, "Jean," pp. 15, 18–21.

p. 9: "The Rocky Mountains were": JS, "Enchanted Island," *Mademoiselle* 29, May 1950, p. 140.

p. 9: "in truth [she] would": JS, *In the Snowfall* MS, JS Collection, U. of Co.

p. 10: "My father . . . cursed": JS notes, JS Collection, U. of Co.

p. 10: "his mind was": Pinkham, "Jean," p. 14.

p. 10: "She was nearly" to "not a man": JS, *In the Snowfall* MS, JS Collection, U. of Co.

p. 11: "problem feeder": JS, "On My Mind," *Vogue* 162 (Nov. 1973), p. 200.

p. 11: "The Stafford-McKillop predilection": JS to Marjorie Pinkham, n.d., JS Collection, U. of Co.

p. 11: When Grandmother Stafford: David Roberts, *Jean Stafford* (Boston: Little, Brown and Co., 1988), p. 43.

p. 12: As for Dick: Pinkham, "Jean," p. 20; and Marjorie Pinkham to author.

p. 12: "Jean was a quiet child": Pinkham, "Jean," p. 15.

p. 12: "pledged allegiance to the English language": JS, "An Etiquette for Writers," lecture at 1952 Writers' Conference in the Rocky Mountains, University of Colorado, p. 3.

p. 12: "Sometimes when my eye": JS to Marjorie Pinkham, Dec. 21, 1974, JS Collection, U. of Co.

p. 13: "I typed it": JS, "An Etiquette for Writers," p. 3.

p. 13: a friend, Howard Higman: Howard Higman interview with author, Dec. 18, 1986.

p. 14: Anyone who walked with her: Mary Davidson McConahay, "Heidelberry Braids and Yankee *Politesse:* Jean Stafford and Robert Lowell Reconsidered," *Virginia Quarterly Review* 62 (Spring 1986), p. 219; and Edward Joseph Chay interview with author, Dec. 23, 1986, reminiscing about college.

p. 14: "a race of social-climbing": JS, "Vox Populi" column, *Prep Owl,* Apr. 24, 1931.

p. 15: "It wasn't everyone" to "so stupidly serious": JS childhood MS, JS Collection, U. of Co.

p. 15: "before August" to "cool shaded lakes": JS, "Fame Is Sweet to the Foolish Man," childhood MS, JS Collection, U. of Co.

p. 15: "pounding out 'shorts'": JS, "Smith Saga," childhood MS, JS Collection, U. of Co.

p. 15: "with only the true passion": JS, "Our Latin Teacher," childhood MS, JS Collection, U. of Co.

p. 16: "the most imaginative": JS, "Miss Lucy," childhood MS, JS Collection, U. of Co.

p. 16: "I am sending you": John Stafford to Oliver Jensen, Nov. 13, 1950, JS Collection, U. of Co.

p. 17: *Roughing It* (one of the books at Stafford's bedside): Joseph Mitchell interview with author, Jan. 30, 1987.

p. 17: "Pretty soon he would be": Mark Twain, *Innocents Abroad; Roughing It* (New York: Library of America, distributed by Viking Press, 1984), p. 541.

p. 17: "The Reo was packed": JS, "Disenchantment," JS Collection, U. of Co.

p. 18: "How we suffered": Twain, *Innocents Abroad; Roughing It*, p. 546.

p. 18: "Our beautiful dreams were shattered": JS, "Disenchantment," JS Collection, U. of Co.

p. 18: "years of tiresome": Twain, *Innocents Abroad; Roughing It*, p. 548.

p. 18 "We were dismayed" to "celestial spirited": JS, "Disenchantment," JS Collection, U. of Co.

p. 19: "After his schooling": JS, *In the Snowfall* MS, JS Collection, U. of Co.

p. 19: "I will rigidly eschew": Justin Kaplan, *Mr. Clemens and Mark Twain* (New York: Simon and Schuster/Touchstone, 1984), p. 67.

p. 20: "Some persons may ask": JS, "Some Advice to Hostesses from a Well-Tempered Guest," *Vogue* 164 (Sept. 1974), p. 296.

p. 20: "frustrated spirit" to "spiritual valetudinarian": Van Wyck Brooks, *The Ordeal of Mark Twain* (New York: E. P. Dutton and Co., Inc., 1933), pp. 40–41.

p. 21: "Of course there's no market": John Stafford to JS, June 3, 1963, JS Collection, U. of Co.

p. 21: "Only a few people have": John Stafford to JS, Feb. 26, 1950, JS Collection, U. of Co.

p. 22: "There was a photograph": JS, "Woden's Day," *Shenandoah* 30, no. 3 (1979), p. 13.

p. 23: "Dan's bilious moods": Ibid., p. 16.

p. 23: "laughter strangled him": Ibid., p. 18.

p. 24: "figure, this replica": JS, *In the Snowfall* MS, JS Collection, U. of Co.

p. 24: "He got up at dawn": Ibid.

p. 24: "Much of Joyce's tragedy": Ibid.

CHAPTER 2: *The University*

p. 27: "restless, plunging into work": JS to Robert Lowell, n.d., Houghton Library, Harvard University.

p. 27: Joseph Cohen: Howard Higman interview with author, Dec. 18, 1986.

p. 27: "In my chronic inability": JS, *In the Snowfall* MS, JS Collection, U. of Co.

p. 27: Stafford encountered psychology: Roberts, *Jean Stafford*, p. 61.

p. 28: "the splendor of [Dr. Rosen's] intellect": JS, *In the Snowfall* MS, JS Collection, U. of Co.

p. 28: "Miss Irene Pettit McKeehan": JS, "Miss McKeehan's Pocketbook," *Colorado Quarterly* 24 (Spring 1976), p. 408.

p. 28: "equipment as useless as any": JS, "Souvenirs of Survival," *Mademoiselle* 50 (Feb. 1960), p. 175.

p. 29: "express [her]self": JS to Robert Lowell, n.d., Houghton Library, Harvard University.

p. 29: "democrat of the" to "gangs": JS, "Vox Populi" column, *Prep Owl,* April 24, 1931.

p. 29: "my mother spared his feelings": JS notes, JS Collection, U. of Co.

pp. 29–30: " 'Culture' was a word" to "disrupts her plans": JS, *In the Snowfall* MS, JS Collection, U. of Co.

p. 30: She wore jeans: Alex and Marie Warner interview with author, Dec. 17, 1986.

p. 31: "Then she wandered about": JS, "The Philosophy Lesson," in *Collected Stories,* p. 362.

p. 31: "She concluded": Ibid., p. 365.

p. 31: "In my last year": JS, "An Etiquette for Writers," p. 5.

p. 32: "She did not really listen": JS, *In the Snowfall* MS, JS Collection, U. of Co.

p. 33: "All of [the intelligentsia]": Ibid.

p. 33: "the red-haired queen": Anatole Ehrenburg to author, Jan. 31, 1987.

p. 33: "It was the fashion": JS, *In the Snowfall* MS, JS Collection, U. of Co.

p. 33: "We would have been shocked": JS, "An Etiquette for Writers," p. 6.

p. 33: "limp, disreputable entourage" to "terrifying modus vivendi": JS to Edward Joseph Chay, July 3, 1948, JS Collection, U. of Co.

p. 33: Lucy's and JS's relations: tape from Andrew Cooke, May 1987.

p. 34: Stafford was mesmerized: Ibid.

p. 34: leaving the local boardinghouse: Roberts, *Jean Stafford,* p. 66.

p. 34: Her enthrallment: tape from Andrew Cooke, May 1987.

p. 34: according to another friend: James Robert Hightower interview with author, Oct. 20, 1986.

p. 34: Just how entangled: tape from Andrew Cooke, May 1987.

p. 35: Lucy's suicide: "Girl Student Shot Herself Late Saturday," *Boulder Daily Camera,* Nov. 11, 1935.

p. 35: "explanation of myself": JS, "Truth and the Novelist," *Harper's Bazaar* 85 (Aug. 1951), p. 189.

p. 35: "Most of them": Sinclair Lewis, quoted in *After the Genteel Tradition: American Writers, 1910–30,* ed. Malcolm Cowley (Carbondale: Southern Illinois University Press, 1964), p. 174.

p. 36: "the aroma of Bohemianism" to "nine months": Maurice Zolotow, "Bohemianism on the Campus," *American Mercury* (Dec. 1939), quoted in James Atlas, *Delmore Schwartz* (New York: Farrar, Straus & Giroux, 1977), p. 35.

p. 36: "Maisie herself was a symbol" to "imitate their ways": JS, *In the Snowfall* MS, JS Collection, U. of Co.

pp. 37–38: "My own morality" to "they existed in hers": Ibid.

p. 38: But it was not, it seems: tape from Andrew Cooke, May 1987.

p. 38: "badly lived life" to "most precious thing you have": lectures and plays file, JS Collection, U. of Co.

p. 39: "Too bad I failed" to "for the lonely man": Ibid.

p. 39: "She believed herself": JS, *In the Snowfall* MS, JS Collection, U. of Co.

p. 39: "I think you had left Boulder": JS letter to Edward Joseph Chay, Oct. 12, 1944, JS Collection, U. of Co.

p. 39: "undisciplined eating arrangements": Paul and Dorothy Thompson interview with author, Sept. 3, 1986; and Paul Thompson's transcription of his diary, Feb. 16, 1935, courtesy of Paul Thompson.

p. 40 "We both like her": Paul Thompson's transcription of his diary, March 1, 1935, courtesy of Paul Thompson.

p. 40: "Landlocked, penniless, ragtag": JS, "Souvenirs of Survival," p. 175.

p. 40: Lucy's parents evidently agreed: tape from Andrew Cooke, May 1987; and JS to James Robert Hightower.

p. 41: Hightower and Fairchild had both met Stafford: James Robert Hightower interview with author, Oct. 20, 1986.

p. 41: merely "physical": JS to James Robert Hightower, June 28, 1938, JS Collection, U. of Co.

p. 41: The affinity between Stafford and Hightower: James Robert Hightower interview with author, Oct. 20, 1986.

p. 42: her parents (who had temporarily moved to Denver): Marjorie Pinkham to author, Apr. 20, 1987.

PART II: *The Innocents Abroad, 1936–1938*

CHAPTER 3: *Mentors*

p. 45: "In Heidelberg, tongue-tied": JS, "Miss McKeehan's Pocketbook," p. 410.

p. 46: "Radcliffe or Bryn Mawr" to "impossibly silly daydream": Ibid., pp. 410–411.

p. 46: Initially a favorite: James Robert Hightower interview with author, Oct. 20, 1986.

p. 47: "In a foreign country": JS, "It's Good to Be Back," *Mademoiselle* 34 (July 1952), p. 26.

p. 48: "the helmets and the masks": JS, "An Etiquette for Writers," p. 1.

p. 48: Stafford's arrival in Heidelberg: James Robert Hightower interview with author, Oct. 20, 1986.

p. 48: "The great engines of war": David Donald, *Look Homeward: A Life of Thomas Wolfe* (Boston: Little, Brown and Co., 1987), p. 387.

p. 48: "a nation of madmen": JS to Andrew Cooke, Oct. 28, 1936, courtesy of Andrew Cooke.

p. 49: "It was a grand, operatic, declamatory display": JS notes for "Sense and Sensibility," Barnard Lectures, unpublished MS, JS Collection, U. of Co.

p. 50: "It is with reluctance" to "very important work": Martha Foley to JS, Jan. 25, 1937, Archives of *Story* Magazine and Story Press, Princeton University Library.

p. 50: "This was the first time": JS to Martha Foley, Feb. 5, 1937, Archives of *Story* Magazine and Story Press, Princeton University Library.

p. 50: "I'm at work": Ibid.

p. 50: McKees' loan: JS to James Robert Hightower and Robert Berueffy, n.d., JS Collection, U. of Co.

p. 51: after a difficult December: Roberts, *Jean Stafford,* p. 111.

p. 51: "When I think": JS to James Robert Hightower, Jan. 13, 1938, JS Collection, U. of Co.

p. 51: a declaration of his isolation: Donald, *Look Homeward,* p. 353.

p. 52: "It's *female trouble*": JS to James Robert Hightower and Robert Berueffy, n.d., JS Collection, U. of Co.

p. 52: he argued that in fact it was likely syphilis: Roberts, *Jean Stafford,* p. 117.

p. 52: she later told a friend: Roberts, *Jean Stafford,* p. 111.

p. 53: "It's hideous": JS to James Robert Hightower, n.d., JS Collection, U. of Co.

p. 53: "revolting body": JS to James Robert Hightower, n.d., JS Collection, U. of Co.

p. 53: "Having had to be conscious": JS to James Robert Hightower, n.d., JS Collection, U. of Co.

p. 53: "I am afraid of following in my pa's footsteps": JS to James Robert Hightower, n.d., JS Collection, U. of Co.

p. 53: "When I knew Ford in America": *Robert Lowell: Collected Prose* (New York: Farrar, Straus & Giroux, 1987), p. 3.

pp. 54–55: "This John Crowe Ransom (poet) is swell" to "will become great writer": JS to James Robert Hightower, n.d., JS Collection, U. of Co.

p. 55: "says she'll browbeat Scribner's": JS to James Robert Hightower, n.d., JS Collection, U. of Co.

p. 55: "Have not embellished": JS to James Robert Hightower, n.d., JS Collection, U. of Co.

p. 55: "I watched an audience": *Robert Lowell: Collected Prose,* p. 4.

p. 56: " '*Towmahss Mahnn*'": Robert Lowell, "Jean Stafford: a Letter," in *Day by Day,* p. 29, and Ian Hamilton, *Robert Lowell: A Biography* (New York: Random House, 1982), p. 51.

p. 56: "butterfly existence": *Robert Lowell: Collected Prose,* p. 37.

p. 56: "had nothing to do with" to "strained and terrific": Ibid., p. 59.

p. 56: "The only man" to " 'tricks of the trade' ": Allen Tate, "Techniques of Fiction," in *Essays of Four Decades* (Chicago: Swallow Press, 1968), p. 129.

p. 56: "As he is a very great master": Hamilton, *Robert Lowell,* p. 52.

p. 57: "charm school" to "was the Reader's Digest.": JS, "What Does Martha Mitchell Know?" *McCall's* 100 (Oct. 1972), p. 31.

p. 57: apparently Lowell kept: Hamilton, *Robert Lowell,* p. 60.

p. 57: "I don't know": JS to James Robert Hightower, Jan. 3, 1938, JS Collection, U. of Co.

p. 58: "The sanest and most charming" to "in both lines": John Crowe Ransom letter to Allen Tate, Jan. 1, 1938, in *The Selected Letters of John Crowe Ransom,* ed. Thomas Daniel Young and George Core (Baton Rouge: Louisiana State University Press, 1985), pp. 236–237.

p. 58: "Ford is a big man": JS to James Robert Hightower, Mar. 3, 1938, JS Collection, U. of Co.

p. 58: "voluminous notes": JS to Ford Madox Ford, Feb. 1, 1938, Dept. of Rare Books, Olin Library, Cornell University.

p. 58: "Not long ago": Ibid.

p. 59: "something from a poem": Ibid.

p. 59: "I have done some good writing" to "half of the tapestry": JS to James Robert Hightower, Nov. 13, 1937, JS Collection, U. of Co.

p. 59: "Well, I don't know" to "pristine as Hemingway": JS to James Robert Hightower, Dec. 1, 1937, JS Collection, U. of Co.

p. 59: "With the generosity": JS, "Truth and the Novelist," p. 187.

p. 60: "When I wrote them": JS to James Robert Hightower, Dec. 6, 1937, JS Collection, U. of Co.

p. 60: "Which of the three": JS to James Robert Hightower, Dec. 6, 1937, JS Collection, U. of Co.

p. 61: "I read Wolfe's": JS to James Robert Hightower, Jan. 1938, JS Collection, U. of Co.

p. 61: "a Gargantuan creature": Lewis, quoted in *After the Genteel Tradition,* ed. Cowley, p. 174.

p. 61: "The book that I was writing": Thomas Wolfe, *The Story of a Novel* (New York: Charles Scribner's Sons, 1936), p. 8.

p. 61: "Whoever is impressed": Donald, *Look Homeward,* p. 77.

p. 62: "whirling vortex" to "formal structure": Wolfe, *The Story of a Novel,* p. 36.

p. 62: "I was not": Ibid., p. 86.

p. 62: "each poem he finished": *Robert Lowell: Collected Prose,* p. 59.

p. 62: "did harm to" to "artistic intelligence": Donald, *Look Homeward,* p. 362.

p. 62: "The force of Wolfe's talents": *Collected Essays of John Peale Bishop,* ed. by Edmund Wilson (New York: Charles Scribner's Sons, 1948), p. 131.

p. 62: "Incarcerated in his own" to "but be morbid": Ibid., pp. 132–133.

p. 62: "the characterizations": JS to Whit Burnett, Jan. 3, 1938, Princeton University Library.

p. 63: "Parts of it": Ibid.

p. 63: "I do not think this book": Whit Burnett to JS, Feb. 28, 1938, Princeton University Library.

p. 64: "Yes, I know": JS to Whit Burnett, n.d., Princeton University Library.

p. 64: "He, as well as": JS to Whit Burnett, Jan. 3, 1938, Princeton University Library.

p. 64: Stephens episode: JS to James Robert Hightower, Apr. 20, 1938, JS Collection, U. of Co.

p. 65: "Davidson's [*sic*] certainly right" to "in some degree": Evelyn Scott to JS, July 10, 1938, JS Collection, U. of Co.

p. 66: "to cultivate their own": Evelyn Scott to JS, n.d., JS Collection, U. of Co.

p. 66: "Your depth of insight" to "education of years": Evelyn Scott to JS, Nov. 21, 1937, JS Collection, U. of Co.

CHAPTER 4: *Men*

p. 67: "The crucifix of the artist": Evelyn Scott to JS, n.d., JS Collection, U. of Co.

p. 67: "The more perfect the artist": T. S. Eliot, "Tradition and the Individual Talent," in *The Selected Essays of T. S. Eliot* (New York: Harcourt, Brace & World, Inc., 1964), pp. 7–8.

p. 67: "Poetry is not": Ibid., p. 11.

p. 68: "each poem he": *Robert Lowell: Collected Prose,* p. 59.

p. 68: "We claimed": Hamilton, *Robert Lowell,* p. 85.

p. 68: For all the antiromanticism: Louis Menand, *Discovering Modernism* (Oxford and New York: Oxford University Press, 1987), pp. 140–142.

p. 68: "the worst summer of my life": JS unpublished memoir, courtesy of Oliver Jensen.

p. 68: Trip out West with Hightower: James Robert Hightower interview with author, Oct. 20, 1986.

p. 69: "I started loving you": JS to James Robert Hightower, June 21, 1938, JS Collection, U. of Co.

p. 69: During a stopover in Boulder: JS to William Mock, postmarked June 23, 1938, Dartmouth College Library.

p. 69: the Thompsons remarked: Paul Thompson's diary, June 19, 1938, courtesy of Paul Thompson.

p. 69: "I have a desk": JS to James Robert Hightower, postmarked July 5, 1938, JS Collection, U. of Co.

pp. 69–70: "I am doing" to "not an artist": JS to James Robert Hightower, July 2, 1938, JS Collection, U. of Co.

p. 70: "A rather nice gent" to "with his hands": JS to James Robert Hightower, Aug. 31, 1938, JS Collection, U. of Co.

p. 71: "poor benighted father" to "in league against him": JS to James Robert Hightower, July 2, 1938, JS Collection, U. of Co.

p. 71: "He sits in a corner": JS to James Robert Hightower, June 25, 1938, JS Collection, U. of Co.

pp. 71–72: "I wish to keep" to "how will I ever forget them": JS to James Robert Hightower, Aug. 1, 1938, JS Collection, U. of Co.

p. 72: "I don't laugh" to "I was writing": JS to James Robert Hightower, July 21, 1938, JS Collection, U. of Co.

p. 73: "Today Mother said": JS to James Robert Hightower, July 2, 1938, JS Collection, U. of Co.

p. 73: "bright solid color": JS, "And Lots of Solid Color," *American Prefaces* 5 (Nov. 1939), p. 25.

p. 73: "Well, we'll be riding" to "all his life": Ibid., p. 23.

p. 74: "beautiful friends": Ibid., p. 24.

p. 74: "wooed her something fierce": Hamilton, *Robert Lowell,* p. 60.

p. 74: "Whenever you uncover": Ibid., p. 61.

p. 75: "Always I will": JS to James Robert Hightower, June 25, 1938, JS Collection, U. of Co.

p. 76: "Really, I don't mind": JS to James Robert Hightower, July 7, 1938, JS Collection, U. of Co.

p. 76: "It is not": JS to James Robert Hightower, July 5, 1938, JS Collection, U. of Co.

p. 76: "I will put it": JS to James Robert Hightower, July 7, 1938, JS Collection, U. of Co.

p. 77: "And the comparative ambition": Evelyn Scott to JS, n.d., JS Collection, U. of Co.

p. 78: "That's the place": JS to James Robert Hightower, July 7, 1938, JS Collection, U. of Co.

p. 78: "I hate all this": JS to James Robert Hightower, Sept. 30, 1938, JS Collection, U. of Co.

p. 78: "Darling (oh, hell)": Ibid.

p. 79: "the sickness of my soul": Ibid.

p. 79: "I want to be a woman": Ibid.

p. 79: "if you have told": James Robert Hightower to JS, first week of Oct. 1939, JS Collection, U. of Co.

pp. 79–80: "sick . . . of *not* being sentimental" to "as my husband": JS to James Robert Hightower, Oct. 3, 1938, JS Collection, U. of Co.

p. 80: "I have not read": James Robert Hightower to JS, Oct. 7, 1938, JS Collection, U. of Co.

p. 81: "My love for you": James Robert Hightower to JS, Oct. 10, 1938, JS Collection, U. of Co.

p. 81: "I want to be impetuous" to "the sake of my book": JS to James Robert Hightower, Oct. 1938, JS Collection, U. of Co.

p. 82: "I wrote him": JS to William Mock, postmarked Nov. 27, 1938, Dartmouth College Library.

p. 82: "some rather scary days": Robert Giroux, "Hard Years and 'Scary Days': Remembering Jean Stafford," *The New York Times Book Review,* June 10, 1984, p. 3.

p. 82: "There is nothing": Evelyn Scott to JS, Nov. 12, 1938, JS Collection, U. of Co.

PART III: *The Bostonians and Other Manifestations of the American Scene, 1938–1946*

CHAPTER 5: *Boston*

p. 87: "frail agrarian mailbox post" to "an abolitionist": *Robert Lowell: Collected Prose,* pp. 58–59; and Hamilton, *Robert Lowell,* p. 44.

p. 87: "massive head injuries": Blair Clark, quoted in Hamilton, *Robert Lowell,* p. 62.

p. 87: The disastrous car ride: James Robert Hightower interview with author, Oct. 20, 1986.

p. 88: "he got savage" to "psychopathic murderer-poet": JS to William Mock, postmarked Nov. 27, 1938, Dartmouth College Library.

p. 89: "I will say nothing": JS to James Robert Hightower, Jan. 10, 1939, JS Collection, U. of Co.

p. 89: "I want children": JS to James Robert Hightower, Jan. 25, 1939, JS Collection, U. of Co.

p. 89: "About Boston": Hamilton, *Robert Lowell,* p. 72.

p. 89: "she can handle": report on JS novel, Atlantic Monthly Press correspondence file, n.d.

p. 90: "ironic, heartless story" to "seems to lack": Edward Weeks letter, Dec. 1, 1938, Atlantic Monthly Press correspondence file.

p. 90: "sizable portion": A. G. Ogden to JS, Dec. 9, 1938, Atlantic Monthly Press correspondence file.

p. 90: "there is too much": JS to Edward Weeks, June 27, 1938, Atlantic Monthly Press correspondence file.

p. 91: "no further thought": A. G. Ogden to JS, Dec. 22, 1938, Atlantic Monthly Press correspondence file.

p. 91: solitary drinking: JS to William Mock, Feb. 1, 1939, Dartmouth College Library.

p. 91: "I have taken": JS to James Robert Hightower, June 27, 1939, JS Collection, U. of Co.

p. 91: he tracked her down: Goodman, *Jean Stafford: The Savage Heart,* p. 97.

p. 91: "convinced that Cal Lowell": JS to A. G. Ogden, n.d. (probably late Mar. or early Apr. 1939), Atlantic Monthly Press correspondence file.

p. 91: "completely metamorphosed": JS to William Mock, postmarked April 18, 1939, Dartmouth College Library.

p. 92: Incensed by : Blair Clark interview with author, Jan. 13, 1987.

p. 92: "Part II is going": JS to A. G. Ogden, early May, Atlantic Monthly Press correspondence file.

p. 92: "Jollying the sight": Robert Lowell, "On a Young Lady Convalescing from a Brain-Injury but Unable to write a novel in Concord, Mass.," Houghton Library, Harvard University.

p. 93: "fast worker": A. G. Ogden to Mr. McIntyre, Jan. 10, 1939, Atlantic Monthly Press correspondence file.

p. 93: "Verbally I think": Whit Burnett to JS, Feb. 14, 1938, Archives of *Story* Magazine and Story Press, Princeton University Library.

p. 94: "is impressed": A. G. Ogden to JS, May 12, 1939, Atlantic Monthly Press correspondence file.

pp. 94–95: "There was never a time" to "flirting with strangers": JS, *Autumn Festival* MS, JS Collection, U. of Co.

p. 95: "I will not write": JS to James Robert Hightower, July 7, 1938, JS Collection, U. of Co.

p. 96: "I like Gretchen Marburg": JS to James Robert Hightower, n.d., JS Collection, U. of Co.

p. 96: "You could anaesthetize": JS, *Autumn Festival* MS, JS Collection, U. of Co.

p. 96: "is so completely negative" editorial report, n.d., Atlantic Monthly Press correspondence file.

p. 97: "proud and sensitive": James Joyce, *A Portrait of the Artist as a Young Man* (New York: Viking Press, 1976), p. 91.

p. 97: "a priest of eternal imagination": Ibid., p. 221.

p. 97: "It was the same" to "a beautifully twisting river": JS, *Autumn Festival* MS, JS Collection, U. of Co.

p. 98: "curiously tortured story": A. G. Ogden memo on JS's revision of *Autumn Festival,* Atlantic Monthly Press correspondence file.

p. 98: "doctrine of futility": JS to James Robert Hightower, July 7, 1938, JS Collection, U. of Co.

p. 98: "The war came along": Mary Darlington Taylor, "Jean Stafford's Novel—'a Superb Literary Accomplishment,'" *Bridgeport Sunday Post,* Jan. 13, 1952, quoted in Mary Ellen Williams Walsh, *Jean Stafford* (Boston: Twayne Publishers, 1985), p. 55.

p. 98: "I am engaged": JS to James Robert Hightower, Dec. 19, 1938, JS Collection, U. of Co.

p. 99: "It is full": Peter Taylor to JS, Dec. 24, 1954, JS Collection, U. of Co.

p. 100: "Those two nice boys": Peter Taylor to Robert Lowell, May 1, 1955, Houghton Library, Harvard University.

p. 100: "mature and adult experience": "1939," Peter Taylor, *The Collected Stories of Peter Taylor* (New York: Farrar, Straus & Giroux, 1979), p. 337.

p. 100: "'critical' and 'objective'": Ibid., p. 338.

p. 100: "When we were": Ibid., p. 345.

p. 101: "Poor Carol Crawford!" to "*so* naive, *so* undergraduate": Ibid., p. 351.

p. 102: "I am confident" to "than by eccentricity": Robert Lowell to Merrill Moore, n.d., Houghton Library, Harvard University, quoted in Hamilton, *Robert Lowell,* p. 65.

p. 103: Lowell also had guilt: Hamilton, *Robert Lowell,* p. 64.

p. 103: "glorious affair": JS interview with Joan Cuyler Stillman, 1952, quoted in Roberts, *Jean Stafford,* p. 198.

p. 103: Ransom obliged: Hamilton, *Robert Lowell,* p. 65.

p. 103: "Lowell is more": Ibid.

p. 104: "should not have left" to "my natural days": JS to James Robert Hightower, March 31, 1940, JS Collection, U. of Co.

p. 104: "I am beginning" to "he will have with me": JS to James Robert Hightower, Apr. 4, 1940, JS Collection, U. of Co.

p. 105: "It was an absolutely" to "to the bone": JS to James Robert Hightower, n.d., JS Collection, U. of Co.

p. 105: "Gossip that is said": JS to James Robert Hightower, Apr. 23, 1940, JS Collection, U. of Co.

p. 105: "You may enjoy": Robert Lowell to Charlotte Lowell, n.d., Houghton Library, Harvard University, quoted in Hamilton, *Robert Lowell,* p. 73.

p. 105: "Customs are not": Orations in the state contest of the Ohio Inter-Collegiate Oratory Association, 1940, Ibid., p. 68.

p. 106: "dualism, division": William K. Wimsatt and Cleanth Brooks, *Literary Criticism: A Short History* (Chicago: University of Chicago Press, 1957), p. 743.

p. 106: "Cambridge ladies" to "comfortable minds": e. e. cummings, *Complete Poems 1913–1962* (New York: Harcourt Brace Jovanovich, 1972), p. 70.

p. 106: "The tale is dismal": Evelyn Scott to JS, Apr. 30, 1940, J.S. Collection, U. of Co.

p. 107: "[live] for love" to "an intellectualized woman": John Crowe Ransom, *The World's Body* (New York: Charles Scribner's Sons, 1938), p. 77.

p. 107: "ornament" to "shining talent": JS to James Robert Hightower, Apr. 26, 1940, JS Collection, U. of Co.

p. 107: "I'm a bitch": JS to James Robert Hightower, n.d., JS Collection, U. of Co.

p. 108: "Thank God": JS to James Robert Hightower, Apr. 4, 1940, JS Collection, U. of Co.

CHAPTER 6: *Catholicism*

p. 109: "we spent": Caroline Gordon to JS, n.d., McFarlin Library, University of Tulsa.

p. 109: "I told [the president of LSU]": John Crowe Ransom to Allen Tate, spring 1940, in *Selected Letters of John Crowe Ransom,* p. 270.

p. 110: "Louisiana, on the whole": JS to James Robert Hightower, Mar. 4, 1941, JS Collection, U. of Co.

p. 110: "owes his first duty": Allen Tate, *The Collected Essays of Allen Tate* (Chicago: Swallow Press, 1959), p. 71.

p. 110: Their Agrarian goal: Grant Webster, *The Republic of Letters: A History of Postwar American Literary Opinion* (Baltimore: Johns Hopkins University Press, 1979), p. 74.

p. 111: "unification of sensibility": *The Selected Essays of T. S. Eliot,* p. 248.

p. 111: In fact, it was: JS to James Robert Hightower, late spring 1940, JS Collection, U. of Co.

p. 111: "I feel exiled": JS to James Robert Hightower, June 6, 1940, JS Collection, U. of Co.

p. 112: "This place, Robert" to "nothing more": JS to James Robert Hightower, June 26, 1940, JS Collection, U. of Co.

p. 112: "The place is": JS to James Robert Hightower, postmarked June 21, 1940, JS Collection, U. of Co.

p. 112: "I am not looking": Robert Lowell to his grandmother Mrs. Arthur Winslow, n.d., Houghton Library, Harvard University, quoted in Hamilton, *Robert Lowell,* p. 75.

p. 113: "About LSU I have" to "liberal English majors": Robert Lowell to Robie Macauley, 1940, quoted in Hamilton, *Robert Lowell,* p. 75.

p. 113: "The opposite of the professional": T. S. Eliot, "Professional, Or ," *Egoist* (Apr. 1918), quoted in Menand, *Discovering Modernism,* p. 125.

p. 114: "My life seems annually": JS to James Robert Hightower, June 26, 1940, JS Collection, U. of Co.

p. 114: "To be intellectual" to "men are trained": Ransom, *The World's Body,* pp. 101, 103.

p. 114: "because they are not": Ibid., p. 103.

p. 115: "It will probably": Ransom, *The World's Body,* p. 228.

p. 115: "a great gauche lummox" to "wants a brain": JS to James Robert Hightower, Oct. 31, 1940, JS Collection, U. of Co.

p. 115: There was an obvious: Robie Macauley interview with author, Oct. 1986.

p. 115: "Peter & I got": JS to James Robert Hightower, Oct. 31, 1940. JS Collection, U. of Co.

p. 115: "berts": Hamilton, *Robert Lowell,* pp. 55–56.

p. 116: plowing through Étienne Gilson's: Ibid., p. 78.

p. 116: "The religious mind": W. K. Wimsatt, *Hateful Contraries: Studies in Literature and Criticism* (University of Kentucky Press, 1965), p. 48.

p. 116: "the vision of suffering": Wimsatt and Brooks, *Literary Criticism: A Short History,* p. 746.

p. 116: "his mind was heavy": Steven Gould Axelrod, *Robert Lowell: Life and Art* (Princeton: Princeton University Press, 1978), p. 16.

p. 116: new order and direction: JS letters to James Robert Hightower, JS Collection, U. of Co.

p. 117: "My mission had not": JS, "An Influx of Poets," *The New Yorker* 54 (Nov. 6, 1978), p. 49.

p. 117: "Like Father Strittmater" to "which was blind": Ibid.

117: "Cal is to make": JS to James Robert Hightower, Oct. 31, 1940, JS Collection, U. of Co.

p. 118: "I can't bear": Evelyn Scott to JS, Sept. 1, 1940, JS Collection, U. of Co.

p. 118: "As for myself": JS to James Robert Hightower, Oct. 31, 1940, JS Collection, U. of Co.

p. 119: twenty-seven-page manuscript: JS, untitled MS, JS Collection, U. of Co.

p. 119: "Theron once told me": JS, "An Influx of Poets," p. 49.

p. 120: "It would be" to "no one can stop": from *The Way of Perfection,* quoted in Teresa of Avila, *The Interior Castle* (New York: Paulist Press, 1979), p. 14.

p. 120: "To judge by": *Ascent of Mount Carmel,* vol. 1 of *Complete Works of St. John of the Cross,* trans. and ed. E. Allison Peers (London: Burns and Oates, 1964), p. 317.

p. 120: "our soul to be": from *The Way of Perfection,* quoted in Teresa of Avila, *The Interior Castle,* p. 20.

p. 121: "the expert of experts": William James, *The Varieties of Religious Experience* (New York: New American Library, 1958), p. 313.

p. 121: "I refer to": Ibid., p. 297.

p. 122: "a gifted woman" to "while retaining sanity": Ibid., pp. 301–302.

p. 122: "Time was passing": JS, *Autumn Festival* MS, JS Collection, U. of Co.

p. 123: On a trip to New Orleans: Hamilton, *Robert Lowell;* Blair Clark interview with author, Jan. 30, 1987; Frank Parker interview with author, Nov. 23, 1990.

p. 123: "She fancied the consummation": JS, untitled MS, JS Collection, U. of Co., p. 5.

p. 124: "The room was": Ibid., p. 8.

p. 124: "tranquil mortal melancholy" to "This she knew": Ibid., pp. 10, 12.

p. 125: "made on her": Ibid., p. 13.

p. 125: "Though the room": Ibid., p. 12.

p. 125: "Doing our own will": Teresa of Avila, *The Interior Castle,* p. 65.

p. 125: "Because her nose": JS, untitled MS, JS Collection, U. of Co., p. 19.

p. 126: "Her solitude was pyramidal": Ibid., p. 25.

p. 126: "Her solitude was a sustained shriek": Ibid., p. 26.

p. 126: "She was so loving": Ibid., p. 27.

p. 126: "Now she lay": Ibid.

p. 128: "essential aspect of fiction" to "his own self-division": Cleanth Brooks and Robert Penn Warren, *Understanding Fiction,* rev. ed. (New York: F. S. Crofts and Co., 1943), p. xvi.

p. 128: "The steadfast plant": JS, untitled MS, JS Collection, U. of Co., p. 2.

p. 129: "As the unworldly creature": Ibid., p. 24.

p. 129: "The surgical second" to "precipitate of section two": Evelyn Scott to JS, Jan. 19, 1941, JS Collection, U. of Co.

p. 130: "My life has": JS to James Robert Hightower, Nov. 15, 1940, JS Collection, U. of Co.

p. 130: "Cal is becoming": JS to James Robert Hightower, Feb. 10, 1941, JS Collection, U. of Co.

p. 131: "My particular brand" to "great compensations": JS to James Robert Hightower, Mar. 4, 1941, JS Collection, U. of Co.

p. 131: With customary hyperbole: JS to James Robert Hightower, Aug. 6, 1941, JS Collection, U. of Co.

p. 132: "I have some new opinions": JS to James Robert Hightower, Mar. 4, 1941, JS Collection, U. of Co.

p. 132: "turnabout as this may sound": JS to James Robert Hightower, Apr. 9, 1941, JS Collection, U. of Co.

p. 132: "State some plan": JS to James Robert Hightower, Apr. 17, 1941, JS Collection, U. of Co.

p. 132: "I never, of course": JS to James Robert Hightower, May 4, 1941, JS Collection, U. of Co.

p. 132: "I think I can": JS to James Robert Hightower, May 12, 1941, JS Collection, U. of Co.

p. 133: "Oh Lord . . . I cannot" to "always be in alien corn": JS to James Robert Hightower, Aug. 6, 1941, JS Collection, U. of Co.

p. 134: "You would not recognize": JS to James Robert Hightower, Mar. 4, 1941, JS Collection, U. of Co.

p. 134: "which is religious": JS to James Robert Hightower, Apr. 9, 1941, JS Collection, U. of Co.

p. 134: Lowell's short list: Hamilton, *Robert Lowell*, p. 79.

p. 134: "Proust outstrips everyone" to "a comparison between them is precarious": JS to James Robert Hightower, Mar. 4, 1941, JS Collection, U. of Co.

p. 135: "Having been reading" to "much admire him": JS to James Robert Hightower, Aug. 6, 1941, JS Collection, U. of Co.

p. 135: "It has been a dreadful": Ibid.

p. 136: "We must avoid": JS to Paul and Dorothy Thompson, July 30, 1941, courtesy of the Thompsons.

p. 136: "I came to feel": Irving Howe, *A Margin of Hope* (New York: Harcourt Brace Jovanovich, 1982), p. 181.

p. 137: "We are both excited": JS to James Robert Hightower, Sept. 9, 1941, JS Collection, U. of Co.

p. 137: Allen had been hired: Ann Waldron, *Close Connections: Caroline Gordon and the Southern Renaissance* (New York: G. P. Putnam's Sons, 1987), p. 184.

p. 137: "both of whom are": JS to Peter Taylor, Oct. 1941, reprinted in *Shenandoah* 30, no. 3 (1979), p. 33.

p. 137: "nothing but ideas": Howe, *Margin of Hope*, p. 130.

p. 137: "Your poetic style": Allen Tate to Delmore Schwartz, Jan. 5, 1939, quoted in Atlas, *Delmore Schwartz*, p. 129.

p. 137: Frank Sheed, the founding editor: Wilfrid Sheed, *Frank and Maisie: A Memoir with Parents* (New York: Simon and Schuster, 1985), p. 135.

p. 138: "I should tell you": JS to Peter Taylor, Oct. 1941, reprinted in *Shenandoah* 30, no. 3 (1979), p. 30.

p. 138: "We went to look": JS, *In the Snowfall* MS, JS Collection, U. of Co.

p. 139: "I remember the translation": JS notes, JS Collection, U. of Co.

p. 139: "a rather exhausting joy" to "kind of fun": JS to Peter Taylor, Oct. 1941, reprinted in *Shenandoah* 30, no. 3 (1979), p. 33.

p. 139: "We met Blackmur": Ibid., p. 29.

p. 140: "said it came": Ibid., p. 32.

p. 140: "It's a conscious imitation": JS to James Robert Hightower, Sept. 9, 1941, JS Collection, U. of Co.

p. 140: "It is well written": Robert Giroux, "Hard Years and 'Scary Days': Remembering Jean Stafford," p. 29.

p. 141: "not the twaddle": JS to Paul and Dorothy Thompson, June 10, 1942, courtesy of the Thompsons.

p. 141: two hundred and fifty dollars on signing: Harcourt, Brace and Co. contract for *The Outskirts,* Apr. 30, 1942, JS Collection, U. of Co.

CHAPTER 7: *The Tates*

p. 142: "We always start working": Caroline Gordon to Léonie Adams, n.d., quoted in Waldron, *Close Connections,* p. 208.

p. 142: "We will just hole up": Caroline Gordon to Malcolm Cowley, n.d., Ibid., p. 206.

p. 142: "the winter of four books": Robert Lowell's diary, 1974, quoted in Hamilton, *Robert Lowell,* p. 82.

pp. 142–143: "formal, difficult poems" to "achieve such a life": Axelrod, *Robert Lowell,* pp. 36–37. See also Robert Lowell, "After Enjoying Six or Seven Essays on Me," *Salmagundi* no. 37 (Spring 1977), p. 113.

p. 143: "Consorting with the Tates": Hamilton, *Robert Lowell,* p. 50.

p. 143: "how often we": Caroline Gordon to JS, n.d., McFarlin Library, University of Tulsa.

p. 143: "for the millionth time": JS to Peter Taylor, Nov. 1942, Vanderbilt University Library.

pp. 143–144: "Cal was very right" to "grossness of their lives": Peter Taylor to JS, Aug. 29, 1944, JS Collection, U. of Co.

p. 144: "There is not": R. P. Blackmur, *Kenyon Review* 7 (Spring 1945), p. 348.

p. 144: "much more interested": Axelrod, *Robert Lowell: Life and Art,* p. 46.

p. 145: "abstract-minded, sharp-witted": Allen Tate, "Remarks on the Southern Religion," in *I'll Take My Stand: The South and the Agrarian Tradition* (Baton Rouge: Louisiana State University Press, 1980), p. 170.

p. 146: "Thank God for being": Caroline Gordon to Dorothy van Doren, April 6, 1937, quoted in Waldron, *Close Connections,* p. 170.

p. 146: "We had this statement": JS to Peter Taylor, Mar. 1943, reprinted in *Shenandoah* 30, no. 3 (1979), p. 37.

p. 147: "passionate pilgrim" to "worldly world": Philip Rahv, *Essays on Literature & Politics, 1932–1972,* ed. Arabel J. Porter and Andrew J. Dvosin (Boston: Houghton Mifflin, 1978), p. 46.

p. 147: "On a clear morning": JS, *Boston Adventure* (New York: Harcourt Brace Jovanovich/A Harvest Book, 1971), p. 3.

p. 147: "With its first page": Alfred Kazin, "Art and Resistance," *The New Republic,* 111 (Oct. 23, 1944), p. 539.

p. 148: "become the master": copy of Harcourt, Brace editorial report on *Boston Adventure* MS, JS Collection, U. of Co.

p. 149: "all are sick": Edmund Wilson, *Axel's Castle: A Study in the Imaginative Literature of 1870–1930* (New York: Norton, 1984), p. 134.

p. 149: "My mother believed": JS, *Boston Adventure,* p. 28.

p. 149: "infamous beyond pardon" to "utterly improbable": Ibid., p. 77.

p. 149: "so fantastic that": Ibid., p. 7.

p. 150: "I looked upon my mother": Ibid., p. 164.

p. 150: "My father was not" to "could stand alone": Ibid., p. 172.

p. 150: "Then he put": Ibid., pp. 48–49.

p. 151: "that I might": Ibid., p. 3.

p. 151: "It was not until then": Ibid., p. 4.

p. 152: "I had not read": Ibid., pp. 119–120.

p. 153: "Between these two": Ibid., p. 181.

p. 154: "I think he writes": Ibid., p. 180.

p. 154: "Boston was something": Ibid., p. 285.

p. 155: "It takes an outlander": Ibid., p. 374.

p. 155: "I read him constantly" to "all the triumphs": Ibid., p. 259.

p. 157: "literary convention" to "romantically wayward": Elizabeth Hardwick, "Poor Little Rich Girls," *Partisan Review* 12, no. 3 (Summer 1945), p. 420.

p. 157: "Hopestill in my book": JS to Edward Joseph Chay, Feb. 27, 1946, JS Collection, U. of Co.

p. 158: "The eyes": JS, *Boston Adventure*, p. 505.

p. 159: "I cannot say": Ibid., p. 425.

p. 159: "It was a sanctuary": Ibid., p. 449.

p. 159: "the fear of my own mind": Ibid., p. 459.

p. 159: "looked again": Ibid., p. 538.

p. 160: "Four of us": Caroline Gordon to Katherine Anne Porter, quoted in Veronica A. Makowsky, *Caroline Gordon: A Biography* (New York: Oxford University Press, 1989), p. 124.

p. 160: "the larger part": T. S. Eliot, *Selected Essays of T. S. Eliot,* p. 18.

p. 160: "poetry . . . must be": *Robert Lowell: Collected Prose*, p. 60.

p. 161: "There must be many": Allen Tate, *Essays of Four Decades,* pp. 124, 126.

p. 161: "I am so sorry": Caroline Gordon to JS, n.d., McFarlin Library, University of Tulsa.

p. 162: "I have decided": Caroline Gordon to JS, n.d., McFarlin Library, University of Tulsa.

p. 162: "I have not ever forgiven him": JS to Peter Taylor, Dec. 13, 1946, Vanderbilt University Library.

p. 162: "effort to deduce": Philip Rahv, *Literature and the Sixth Sense* (Boston: Houghton Mifflin, 1969), p. 225.

p. 162: "solidity of specification": Ibid., p. 231.

p. 162: "world of utility" to "actual being": John Crowe Ransom, "The Understanding of Fiction," *Kenyon Review* 12, no. 2, (Spring 1950), p. 201.

p. 162: "I wished . . . to make": Allen Tate, *The Fathers* (Denver: Alan Swallow, 1960), p. ix–x.

p. 164: "I guess it wasn't": JS to Peter Taylor, Apr. 1943, Vanderbilt University Library.

p. 165: "a little guilty" to "married to someone else": Caroline Gordon to Katherine Anne Porter, quoted in Waldron, *Close Connections,* p. 209.

p. 165: "He really has no interest": Caroline Gordon to Josephine Herbst, n.d., Ibid., p. 76.

p. 165: "I wonder if Caroline's": John Peale Bishop to Allen Tate, Ibid., p. 146.

p. 165: "He has commenced": JS to Peter Taylor, Nov. 1942, Vanderbilt University Library.

p. 165: "We are hoping": JS to Peter Taylor, Feb. 1943, Vanderbilt University Library.

p. 165: "I have intended all week": JS to Peter Taylor, Apr. 1943, reprinted in *Shenandoah* 30, no. 3 (1979), pp. 36–37.

p. 166: "When [Cal] asked": JS to Peter Taylor, Nov. 1942, Vanderbilt University Library.

p. 166: "constant criticism": Waldron, *Close Connections,* p. 208.

p. 167: "Imagine the Bean Bert": JS to Peter Taylor, July 10, 1943, reprinted in *Shenandoah* 30, no. 3 (1979), p. 40.

p. 167: "Either a tubercular": JS to Peter Taylor, July 20, 1943, Vanderbilt University Library.

p. 167: "nervous exhaustion": JS to Peter Taylor, Aug. 3, 1943, Vanderbilt University Library.

p. 167: "is by no means": JS to Peter Taylor, July 10, 1943, reprinted in *Shenandoah* 30, no. 3 (1979), p. 38.

p. 167: "Mrs. Ames": Ibid., p. 39.

p. 167: "I could stay here": JS to Peter Taylor, Aug. 3, 1943, Vanderbilt University Library.

p. 167: "As the taxi brought me": JS diary, Dec. 27, 1949, JS Collection, U. of Co.

p. 168: "is doing something" to "too deep for words": Caroline Gordon to JS, n.d., McFarlin Library, University of Tulsa.

p. 168: "I wrote [Mrs. Ames]": Caroline Gordon to JS, n.d., McFarlin Library, University of Tulsa.

p. 168: "I wrote Mrs. Lowell": Caroline Gordon to JS, n.d. McFarlin Library, University of Tulsa.

p. 169: army employment questionnaire: Hamilton, *Robert Lowell,* p. 86.

p. 169: "declaration of personal responsibility" to "propaganda and violence": typescript in Houghton Library, Harvard University, quoted in Hamilton, *Robert Lowell,* p. 89.

p. 169: "You know more": Robert Lowell to his grandmother Mrs. Arthur Winslow, n.d., Houghton Library, quoted in Hamilton, *Robert Lowell,* p. 90.

p. 169: "carried through to unconditional surrender": typescript in Houghton Library, Harvard University, quoted in Hamilton, *Robert Lowell,* p. 89.

p. 170: "You know, Jean": Allen Tate to JS, Nov. 19, 1943, McFarlin Library, University of Tulsa.

p. 170: "the most decisive thing": Hamilton, *Robert Lowell,* p. 86.

p. 170: "poetic temperament": article from Boston *Post,* Sept. 10, 1943, quoted in Hamilton, *Robert Lowell,* p. 90.

pp. 171–172: "whole man" to "aggressive stance": Ibid., p. 85.

p. 171: "I have not started": JS to Peter and Eleanor Taylor, Oct. 10, 1943, Vanderbilt University Library.

p. 171: "It was a rather bad winter": JS to Paul and Dorothy Thompson, Oct. 12, 1944, courtesy of the Thompsons.

p. 171: Two of her closest friends: Cecile Starr interview with author, Dec. 4, 1986.

pp. 172–173: "He is the most attractive" to "presently they left": JS to Eleanor and Peter Taylor, Nov. 1943, reprinted in *Shenandoah* 30, no. 3 (1979), pp. 46–47.

p. 173: "This morning": Ibid., pp. 47–48.

p. 173: "Charlotte Hideous": Ibid., p. 48.

pp. 173–174: "Bobby" to "integrity of purpose": Mrs. Charlotte Lowell to JS, Nov. 10, 1943, courtesy of Blair Clark.

p. 174: "great trouble with": JS unpublished memoir, courtesy of Oliver Jensen.

p. 174: "more Catholic than the church": Hamilton, *Robert Lowell,* p. 96.

p. 174: "crazy": Simpson, *Poets in Their Youth,* p. 145.

p. 174: "It is not right": JS to Peter Taylor, Feb. 11, 1944, quoted in Hamilton, *Robert Lowell,* p. 96.

CHAPTER 8: *Connecticut*

p. 176: "I myself have nothing": JS to Cecile Starr, n.d., courtesy of Cecile Starr.

p. 177: "Our dreams are probably" to "unattractively materialistic": JS to Eleanor Taylor, June 29, 1944, Vanderbilt University Library.

p. 177: He had looked forward: Hamilton, *Robert Lowell,* p. 97.

p. 178: "Cal . . . is working": JS to Peter Taylor, July 26, 1944, Vanderbilt University Library.

p. 178: "Cal has started writing" to "I spend my time": JS to Eleanor Taylor, July 31, 1944, Vanderbilt University Library.

p. 178: "Despite the ugliness": JS to Peter Taylor, July 12, 1944, Vanderbilt University Library.

p. 178: "Actually I think few things": JS to Eleanor Taylor, June 29, 1944, Vanderbilt University Library.

p. 180: "It was as though": JS, "The Lippia Lawn," *Collected Stories,* p. 177.

p. 180: "It's a crime" to "now detested": Ibid., p. 178.

p. 181: "There ain't nothing": JS, "The Darkening Moon," *Collected Stories,* p. 254.

p. 181: "swarmed slimily" to "reptilian odor": Ibid., p. 261.

p. 182: Her novel did very well: Harcourt, Brace royalty statements for *Boston Adventure,* JS Collection, U. of Co.

p. 182: "Your book struck me" to "first title best": Philip Rahv to JS, n.d., JS Collection, U. of Co.

p. 182: "Cal's book": JS to Paul and Dorothy Thompson, Oct. 12, 1944, courtesy of the Thompsons.

p. 182: "The success of this book": JS to James Robert Hightower, Sept. 8, 1944, JS Collection, U. of Co.

p. 183: "It looks as if": Caroline Gordon to JS, n.d., McFarlin Library, University of Tulsa.

p. 183: "I hope it's going": JS to James Robert Hightower, Sept. 8, 1944, JS Collection, U. of Co.

p. 183: "we are neither respectable nor rich": Hamilton, *Robert Lowell,* p. 101.

p. 183: "I am so glad": JS to Mary Lee Frichtel, Oct. 1944, JS Collection, U. of Co.

p. 184: "The shock was": JS to Peter Taylor, Nov. 16, 1944, Vanderbilt University Library.

p. 184: "image of a modest schoolteacher": Pinkham, "Jean," p. 28.

p. 184: "It was not a very good trip": JS to Cecile Starr, May 5, 1945, courtesy of Cecile Starr.

p. 185: "I have bad nerves": JS to Edward Joseph Chay, Dec. 22, 1944, JS Collection, U. of Co.

p. 185: "The book on James" to "nothing but the symbol": JS to Peter Taylor, Dec. 14, 1944, Vanderbilt University Library.

p. 185: "something completely new": JS to James Robert Hightower, Mar. 21, 1945, JS Collection, U. of Co.

p. 185: "My new novel is": JS to Edward Joseph Chay, Feb. 4, 1945, JS Collection, U. of Co.

p. 186: "BETWEEN THE PORCH AND THE ALTAR" to "only at your best": Allen Tate to JS, Aug. 5, 1944, McFarlin Library, University of Tulsa.

p. 187: "She was not assured": JS, "Between the Porch and the Altar," *Collected Stories,* p. 412.

p. 187: "leaving herself alone": Ibid., p. 413.

p. 187: one critic observed: Albert Gelpi, "The Reign of the Kingfisher: Robert Lowell's Prophetic Poetry," in *Robert Lowell: Essays on the Poetry,* ed. Steven Gould Axelrod and Helen Deese (Cambridge: Cambridge University Press, 1986), p. 60.

p. 187: "my heart": Robert Lowell, "Colloquy at Black Rock," in *Lord Weary's Castle* and *The*

Mills of the Kavanaughs (San Diego, New York, London: Harcourt Brace/A Harvest Book, 1974), p. 11.

p. 187: "quite clearly Lowell": Hamilton, *Robert Lowell*, p. 97.

p. 188: "second prize-winning novelette": *Partisan Review* 12 (Spring 1945), p. 149.

p. 188: "Anything happening": Randall Jarrell to Robert Lowell, Aug. 1945, in *Randall Jarrell's Letters*, ed. Mary Jarrell (Boston: Houghton Mifflin Co., 1985), p. 128.

p. 188: "Since I like": Allen Tate to JS, Aug. 9, 1945, McFarlin Library, University of Tulsa.

p. 189: "The ivory tower": JS, "The Captain's Gift," *Collected Stories*, p. 439.

p. 189: "You have concentrated": Caroline Gordon to JS, n.d., McFarlin Library, University of Tulsa.

p. 189: "cut off cleanly": JS, "The Captain's Gift," *Collected Stories*, p. 445.

p. 189: "What I am trying": Caroline Gordon to JS, n.d., McFarlin Library, University of Tulsa.

p. 190: "*ideas* tested by": Allen Tate, quoted in Axelrod, *Robert Lowell: Life and Art*, p. 39.

p. 190: Lowell too was seduced: Ibid., p. 40.

p. 190: "richer in immediate experience": Ibid., p. 44.

CHAPTER 9: *Maine*

p. 191: roughly twenty thousand dollars: Harcourt, Brace royalty statement for *Boston Adventure*, JS Collection, U. of Co.

p. 191: "It is about": JS to Cecile Starr, Aug. 23, 1945, courtesy of Cecile Starr.

p. 191: "I imagine it": JS to Paul and Dorothy Thompson, Aug. 23, 1945, courtesy of the Thompsons.

p. 192: "Two families living": Caroline Gordon to JS, n.d., McFarlin Library, University of Tulsa.

p. 192: In December of 1945: Hamilton, *Robert Lowell*, p. 108.

p. 192: Stafford meanwhile: Robert Giroux to author, May 6, 1991.

p. 192: "Everything crashed": JS to Cecile Starr, Nov. 27, 1945, courtesy of Cecile Starr.

p. 193: "I shouldn't tell": JS to Mary Lee Frichtel, Nov. 27, 1945, JS Collection, U. of Co.

p. 193: "One might think": Delmore Schwartz to Helen Blackmur, quoted in Atlas, *Delmore Schwartz*, p. 263.

p. 193: "Underseas fellows": "To Delmore Schwartz," Robert Lowell, in *Life Studies and For the Union Dead* (New York: Noonday Press, Farrar, Straus & Giroux, 1977), p. 53.

p. 193: "You said": #152, John Berryman, in *The Dream Songs* (New York: Farrar, Straus & Giroux, 1969), p. 171.

p. 194: "to 'express'": Atlas, *Delmore Schwartz*, p. 231.

p. 194: "No matter where": Ibid., p. 235.

p. 194: "suicide that had come" to "by the New Deal": JS, "Truth and the Novelist," p. 187.

p. 194: "my friends said": Ibid., p. 188.

p. 194: "circulating malicious rumors": Atlas, *Delmore Schwartz*, p. 265.

p. 194: His gossip was: Roberts, *Jean Stafford*, p. 237; and Frank Parker interview with author, Nov. 23, 1990.

p. 195: "We shall probably": JS to Cecile Starr, Mar. 11, 1946, courtesy of Cecile Starr.

p. 195: "house of ingratitude" to "house He built": John Berryman, "Lowell, Thomas &c," *Partisan Review* 14, no. 1 (Winter 1947), p. 76.

p. 195: "Death comes": Axelrod, *Robert Lowell: Life and Art,* p. 52.

p. 196: "When he came": JS to Peter Taylor, Dec. 19, 1946, quoted in Hamilton, *Robert Lowell,* p. 111.

p. 196: "We have had a taste": JS to Allen Tate, Jan. 4, 1946, quoted in Hamilton, *Robert Lowell,* p. 108.

p. 197: "They were entirely different" to "to fuse the two manners": Harvey Breit, "Talk with Jean Stafford," *The New York Times Book Review,* Jan. 20, 1952, p. 18.

p. 197: "less inclined": Lambert Davis to JS, Dec. 21, 1945, JS Collection, U. of Co.

p. 199: "Your major change": Robert Giroux to JS, n.d., Houghton Library, Harvard University.

p. 199: "creature of funny precocity": Robert Fitzgerald, "The Children," *The Nation* 164 (Apr. 5, 1947), p. 400.

p. 200: "Gradually I became Molly": JS to Robert Lowell, n.d., Houghton Library, Harvard University.

p. 200: "double bildungsroman": Charlotte Goodman, "The Lost Brother/The Twin: Women Novelists and the Male-Female Double Bildungsroman," *Novel: A Forum on Fiction* 17 (Fall 1983), pp. 28–43.

p. 201: "He looked at": JS, *The Mountain Lion* (New York: E. P. Dutton/Obelisk, 1983), p. 116.

p. 201: "this scrawny" to "satiric nature": Ibid., p. 143.

p. 201: Bonney merchants and the Kenyon men: Ibid., p. 114.

p. 202: "sissy life": Ibid., p. 79.

p. 202: "unseemly second marriage": Ibid., p. 22.

p. 202: "half legendary": Ibid., p. 55.

p. 202: "massive, slow-footed bear": Ibid., p. 33.

p. 203: a reconsideration of the novel: Blanche H. Gelfant, "Reconsideration," *The New Republic* 172 (May 10, 1975), pp. 22–25.

p. 203: "virile opacity": JS, *The Mountain Lion,* p. 168.

p. 203: She was a symbolic element: Gelfant, "Reconsideration," p. 22, for example.

p. 203: "always smoldering": JS, *The Mountain Lion,* p. 98.

pp. 203–204: "list of unforgivable" people to "were all fat": Ibid., pp. 178–179.

p. 204: "She burst into tears": Ibid., p. 217.

p. 204: "bereft in an unadulterated": Maureen Ryan, *Innocence and Estrangement in the Fiction of Jean Stafford* (Baton Rouge: Louisiana State University Press, 1987), p. 55.

p. 204: "Ralph was troubled": JS, *The Mountain Lion,* p. 186.

p. 204: "Because his own": Ibid., p. 168.

p. 205: "If he did not become": Ibid., p. 186.

p. 205: " 'My literature is": Ibid., p. 95.

p. 205: "Gravel, gravel": Ibid., p. 31.

p. 205: "Everyone said she had": Ibid., p. 144.

p. 206: "though there was nothing" to "to have tuberculosis": Ibid., p. 182.

p. 207: "The pain was not": Ibid., p. 131.

p. 207: "For the most part": Ibid., p. 177.

pp. 207–208: "In some respects" to "uses of literary expression": Philip Rahv to JS, Feb. 8, 1947, JS Collection, U. of Co.

p. 208: "My theory about children": Alice Dixon Bond, "Fascination with Words Started Jean Stafford on Writing Career," *Boston Sunday Herald,* Jan. 27, 1957.

p. 208: "I know I'm ugly" to "got a home": JS, *The Mountain Lion,* pp. 139–140.

p. 209: "For ages": JS to Robert Lowell, n.d., Houghton Library, Harvard University.

p. 210: "I felt perpetually": JS to Paul and Dorothy Thompson, Apr. 3, 1947, courtesy of the Thompsons.

p. 210: "Come as soon as you can" to "pleasure and profit": JS to Peter and Eleanor Taylor, Apr. 5, 1946, Vanderbilt University Library.

p. 210: "That awful summer!": JS, "An Influx of Poets," p. 43.

p. 211: "last summer of innocence": Simpson, *Poets in Their Youth,* p. 134.

p. 211: "It has been the most confused": JS to Cecile Starr, n.d., courtesy of Cecile Starr.

p. 211: She called it "the incident": Oliver Jensen interview with author, Dec. 1, 1986.

p. 212: "as if it were their": JS, "A Country Love Story," *Collected Stories,* p. 138.

p. 212: "it seemed to her": Ibid., p. 138.

p. 212: "seized with the terror": JS to Robert Lowell, n.d., Houghton Library, Harvard University.

p. 212: "nest of ex-Communists": JS unpublished memoir, courtesy of Oliver Jensen.

p. 213: "tongue of an adder": JS, "Influx of Poets," p. 52.

p. 213: "There was an influx": Ibid., p. 48.

p. 213: "Theron the poet's": Ibid., p. 47.

p. 214: "I helped in every way": Ibid., p. 56.

p. 214: "Mine! Remember": Ibid., p. 46.

p. 214: "God almighty": Ibid., p. 51.

pp. 214–215: "baby bards" to "drink didn't help": Ibid., p. 43.

p. 215: "listening to the poets": Ibid.

p. 215: "all poets' wives": Atlas, *Delmore Schwartz,* p. 223.

p. 215: "the prodigal poet": Marjorie Perloff, "*Poètes Maudits* of the Genteel Tradition," in *Robert Lowell: Essays on the Poetry,* ed. Axelrod and Deese, p. 109.

p. 216: "I knew—although": JS, "An Influx of Poets," p. 43.

p. 216: "But great as you are": Nancy Flagg Gibney to JS, Jan. 29, 1979, JS Collection, U. of Co.

p. 217: "somber mood": Simpson, *Poets in Their Youth,* p. 135.

p. 217: "Everything is going" to "houses with servants": JS to Mary Lee Frichtel, June 13, 1946, JS Collection, U. of Co.

p. 218: "I don't care": Robert Lowell to Peter Taylor, Aug. 13, 1946, quoted in Hamilton, *Robert Lowell,* p. 115.

p. 218: "There has been such": JS to Cecile Starr, n.d., courtesy of Cecile Starr.

p. 219: "I have wanted to write": JS to Peter Taylor, Aug. 28, 1946, Vanderbilt University Library.

PART IV: *Manhattan and Other Islands, 1946–1979*

CHAPTER 10: *Patterns*

p. 224: "There was something" to "can protect me": JS to Peter Taylor, Nov. 20, 1946, Vanderbilt University Library.

p. 224: "He was, despite": JS, "An Influx of Poets," p. 44.

p. 224: "If it had not been": JS to Robert Lowell, n.d., Houghton Library, Harvard University.

p. 225: "I have finally": JS to Mary Lee Frichtel, Sept. 23, 1946, JS Collection, U. of Co.

p. 225: "my marvelous man": JS to Mary Lee Frichtel, Oct. 26, 1946, JS Collection, U. of Co.

p. 226: Cecile Starr thought of her: Cecile Starr interview with author, Dec. 4, 1986.

p. 227: "Boston Adventure was the product" to "finished the book": JS to Robert Lowell, n.d., Houghton Library, Harvard University.

p. 227: "almost more than": JS, "A Personal Story" MS, JS Collection, U. of Co.

p. 228: "Still, the torment": Ibid.

p. 228: "So ignorant and sheeplike": JS, "An Influx of Poets," p. 55.

p. 229: "All I can feel now": JS to Peter Taylor, Dec. 31, 1946, quoted in Hamilton, *Robert Lowell,* p. 122.

p. 229: "not go any further": JS to Robert Lowell, n.d., Houghton Library, Harvard University.

p. 230: "If only I could sleep": JS to Peter Taylor, Nov. 20, 1946, Vanderbilt University Library.

p. 230: "safe between innumerable": JS to Mary Lee Frichtel, Dec. 21, 1946, JS Collection, U. of Co.

p. 230: "Luna Park": Simpson, *Poets in Their Youth,* p. 150.

p. 231: "I think the stumbling block": JS diary, June 9, 1947, JS Collection, U. of Co.

p. 231: "I warn you": JS to Peter Taylor, Jan. 6, 1947, Vanderbilt University Library.

p. 232: "I have had many very": JS to Peter Taylor, n.d., Vanderbilt University Library.

p. 232: "to get yourself": Peter Taylor to JS, Nov. 12, 1946, JS Collection, U. of Co.

p. 232: "a symbol to me": JS to Peter Taylor, Mar. 31, 1947, Vanderbilt University Library.

p. 232: "I must be believed in": JS to Robert Lowell, n.d., Houghton Library, Harvard University.

p. 233: "Once again I have": JS to Peter Taylor, Mar. 31, 1947, Vanderbilt University Library.

p. 233: "appearing in the Nation": JS to Robert Lowell, n.d., Houghton Library, Harvard University.

p. 233: "Cal, let me point": JS to Robert Lowell, n.d., Houghton Library, Harvard University.

p. 233: "last year's authors": Cyril Connolly, "Introduction," *Horizon* 93–94 (Oct. 1947) p. 5, quoted in Roberts, *Jean Stafford,* pp. 265–266.

p. 234: "I am only": JS to Cecile Starr, n.d., courtesy of Cecile Starr.

p. 234: "I have never": JS to Robert Lowell, n.d., Houghton Library, Harvard University.

p. 234: "What do I care" to "being a writer": JS to Robert Lowell, n.d., Houghton Library, Harvard University.

p. 234: "incapable of being loved": JS to Peter Taylor, Dec. 19, 1946, Vanderbilt University Library.

p. 234: "Jean has suffered": Peter Taylor to Robert Lowell, Nov. 19, 1946, Houghton Library, Harvard University.

p. 235: "I love children": JS, "Sisterhood," an unfinished essay, JS Collection, U. of Co.

p. 235: "I have never": JS biographical fragments, JS Collection, U. of Co.

p. 235: "Partly because I was born": JS to Mary Lou Aswell, n.d., JS Collection, U. of Co.

p. 236: "My mother's death": JS miscellaneous notes and drafts, JS Collection, U. of Co.

p. 236: "I received": JS to Robert Lowell, n.d., Houghton Library, Harvard University.

p. 236: "I grieve that": JS to Peter Taylor, Feb. 5, 1947, Vanderbilt University Library.

p. 236: "I try to see" to "presently be kidnapped": JS diary, JS Collection, U. of Co.

p. 237: "Deep-rooted as it all is": JS to Peter Taylor, Dec. 25, 1946.

pp. 237–238: "There are no pictures": JS diary, JS Collection, U. of Co.

p. 238: "I felt awful" to "without drinking": JS to Mary Lee Frichtel, Feb. 11, 1947, JS Collection, U. of Co.

p. 238: "mutilated with woe" JS to Peter Taylor, June 2, 1947, Vanderbilt University Library.

p. 238: "Faced with its loveliness": JS to Cecile Starr, n.d., courtesy of Cecile Starr.

p. 238: awarded a Pulitzer: Hamilton, *Robert Lowell,* p. 124.

p. 238: "The pictures of him": JS to Peter Taylor, June 2, 1947, Vanderbilt University Library.

p. 239: "I went alone": JS to Mary Lee Frichtel, postmarked May 19, 1947, JS Collection, U. of Co.

p. 239: "It would be": JS to Robert Lowell, n.d., Houghton Library, Harvard University.

p. 240: "What Pansy thought": JS, "The Interior Castle," *Collected Stories,* pp. 182–183.

p. 241: "the time would come" to "rosy luster": Ibid., p. 192.

p. 241: "never had the quiet" to "treasureless head": Ibid., p. 193.

p. 242: "And now that": JS, " 'My Sleep Grew Shy of Me' " *Vogue* 110 (Oct. 15, 1947), p. 135.

p. 242: "I honored the good practice": Ibid., p. 171.

pp. 242–243: "convalescence, the charming" to "had forsworn forever": Ibid., p. 174.

p. 243: "I have been here": JS hospital diary, May 30, 1947, JS Collection, U. of Co.

p. 243: at that point Lowell had agreed: JS to Robert Lowell, n.d., Houghton Library, Harvard University.

p. 243: "without money" to "cannot be appealing": JS to Robert Lowell, n.d., Houghton Library, Harvard University.

p. 244: "Bring a number": Atlas, *Delmore Schwartz,* p. 253.

p. 244: "I have been grateful": JS to Peter Taylor, Aug. 4, 1947, Vanderbilt University Library.

p. 245: "It was more": JS to Robert Lowell, n.d., Houghton Library, Harvard University.

p. 245: "a fit of trembling": JS to Robert Lowell, n.d., Houghton Library, Harvard University.

p. 245: "returned to me": JS to Peter Taylor, Apr. 27, 1947, Vanderbilt University Library.

p. 246: "I am studying" to "feeding upon a fungus": JS to Robert Lowell, n.d., Houghton Library, Harvard University.

p. 246: "You will be": JS to Robert Lowell, n.d., Houghton Library, Harvard University.

p. 246: "the first of [her] saviours": JS to Robert Lowell, n.d., Houghton Library, Harvard University.

p. 246: "Dr. Cohn": JS to Robert Lowell, n.d., Houghton Library, Harvard University.

p. 247: "Before we meet": Dr. Alfred Cohn to JS, Mar. 25, 1948, JS Collection, U. of Co.

p. 247: "It has been rather rough" to "what happiness is": JS to Robert Lowell, n.d., Houghton Library, Harvard University.

p. 247: "I cannot truly": JS to Robert Lowell, n.d., Houghton Library, Harvard University.

p. 247: "Alas, I am": JS to Peter Taylor, Dec. 17, 1947, Vanderbilt University Library.

p. 248: "I went to Bard" to "my principal ambition": JS to Robert Lowell, n.d., Houghton Library, Harvard University.

p. 248: "low pitch": JS to Robert Lowell, n.d., Houghton Library, Harvard University.

p. 248: "[My lecture] is so foolish": JS to John Crowe Ransom, n.d., courtesy of the Greenslade Special Collections of Olin and Chalmers Libraries at Kenyon College.

p. 248: "Uncle Ransom": JS to Robert Lowell, n.d., Houghton Library, Harvard University.

p. 249: "loutishly well-adjusted": JS, "The Psychological Novel," *Kenyon Review* 10 (Spring 1948), p. 218.

p. 249: "It is fashionable": Ibid., p. 215.

p. 249: "drive toward being": Ibid., p. 220.

p. 249: "in the respect": Lionel Trilling, "Art and Neurosis," in *The Liberal Imagination,* (New York: Harcourt Brace Jovanovich, 1978), p. 170.

p. 250: "detachment from our characters'": JS, "The Psychological Novel," p. 220.

p. 250: "We must be experts": Ibid., p. 221.

p. 250: "Naturally I go" to "do not make sense": Ibid., pp. 223–224.

p. 250: "lowers the story": Ibid., p. 217.

p. 251: "At forty I've written": Robert Lowell to William Carlos Williams, Dec. 3, 1957, quoted in Axelrod, *Robert Lowell: Life and Art,* p. 91.

p. 252: In December she sold: Roberts, *Jean Stafford,* p. 275.

p. 252: "secretly enjoyed": James Thurber, *The Years with Ross* (Boston: Atlantic Monthly Press Book, Little, Brown and Co., 1959), p. 97.

p. 252: "the word 'casual'": Ibid., p. 13.

p. 252: "not edited for the old lady in Dubuque": Ibid., p. 85.

pp. 252–253: "for many years" to "that had style": Brendan Gill, *Here at The New Yorker* (New York: Random House, 1975), p. 390.

p. 253: "one of her best friends": Linda H. David, *Onward and Upward: A Biography of Katharine S. White* (New York: Harper & Row, 1987), p. 152.

p. 253: "a remarkable reviser": Ibid., p. 154.

p. 253: "a vague, little man": Thurber, *The Years with Ross,* p. 131.

p. 254: "the pointless and inane": Edmund Wilson to Katharine White, Nov. 12, 1947, quoted in Edmund Wilson, *Letters on Literature and Politics, 1912–1972,* ed. Elena Wilson (New York: Farrar, Straus & Giroux, 1977), p. 410.

p. 254: "It's easy to": Delmore Schwartz, "Smile and Grin, Relax and Collapse," in *Selected Essays of Delmore Schwartz,* ed. Donald A. Dike and David H. Zuckor (Chicago: University of Chicago Press, 1970), p. 416.

p. 254: "powerful and pernicious": Ibid., p. 412.

p. 254: "in *The New Yorker*": Ibid., p. 416.

pp. 254–255: "The chief recent tendency" to "fiction and personal history": Ibid., p. 413.

p. 255: "It is probably needless": Ibid., p. 414.

p. 256: "The day I came": JS to Robert Lowell, n.d., Houghton Library, Harvard University.

p. 256: "the last familiar face": JS, "Children Are Bored on Sunday," *Collected Stories,* p. 379.

p. 256: "Eisenburg's milieu" to "laughed at": Ibid., p. 374.

p. 257: "cunning" set, "on their guard": Ibid., p. 373.

p. 257: "the cream of the enlightened": Ibid., p. 375.

p. 257: "These cocktail parties": Ibid., pp. 374–375.

pp. 257–258: "opinions on everything" to "calling in itself": Ibid., p. 377.

p. 258: "she was not even": Ibid., p. 378.

p. 258: "had never dissuaded her" to "apologetic fancy woman": Ibid., p. 379.

p. 258: "Neither staunchly primitive": Ibid., p. 378.

pp. 258–259: "the months of spreading" to "art and religion": Ibid., p. 381.

p. 259: "To [Emma's] own heart": Ibid., p. 383.

p. 259: "never knew where": Ibid., p. 378.

p. 259: "in the territory of despair": Ibid., p. 382.

p. 260: "If you think your snide remarks": Peter Taylor to Robert Lowell, May 1, 1952, Houghton Library, Harvard University.

p. 260: "John Berryman came": JS to Peter Taylor, Mar. 8, 1948, Vanderbilt University Library.

p. 260: "he announced that": JS to Peter Taylor, Jan. 17, 1950, Vanderbilt University Library.

p. 260: "Please consider it": JS to Peter Taylor, Mar. 8, 1948, Vanderbilt University Library.

CHAPTER 11: *Peace and Disappointment*

p. 261: signed a contract: memo on *In the Snowfall,* Nov. 28, 1947, Harcourt, Brace, JS Collection, U. of Co.

p. 261: allotting her $6,500: JS and Robert Lowell, divorce decree, March 1948, Houghton Library, Harvard University.

p. 261: "good friends": JS to Mary Lee Frichtel, Apr. 10, 1948, JS Collection, U. of Co.

p. 261: "I want us both" to "at a low pitch": JS to Robert Lowell, n.d., Houghton Library, Harvard University.

p. 262: "I am now divorced": JS to Edward Joseph Chay, July 3, 1948, JS Collection, U. of Co.

p. 262: "was a triumph": JS to Mary Lee Frichtel, April 10, 1948, JS Collection, U. of Co.

p. 262: "For the three": Nancy Flagg Gibney, "People to Stay," *Shenandoah* 30, no. 3 (1979), p. 67.

p. 262: "Pull yourself together": Dr. Mary Jane Sherfey to JS, Apr. 28, 1948, JS Collection, U. of Co.

p. 263: "He is an altogether": JS to Peter Taylor, June 28, 1948, quoted in Hamilton, *Robert Lowell,* p. 133.

p. 263: "stifled by the terrible rush" to "without ever maturing": JS to William Mock, Oct. 24, 1948, Dartmouth College Library.

p. 263: "Alas, alas": JS to Edward Joseph Chay, July 3, 1948, JS Collection, U. of Co.

p. 264: at least not to his friends: Frank Parker interview with author, Nov. 23, 1990.

p. 264: At a later stage: Hamilton, *Robert Lowell,* p. 155.

p. 265: "Cal is in a sanitarium": JS to Paul and Dorothy Thompson, Apr. 25, 1949, courtesy of the Thompsons.

p. 265: "It is an awful irony" to "that poor boy": JS to Mary Lee Frichtel, postmarked Apr. 12, 1949, JS Collection, U. of Co.

p. 265: *Les Maudits*: from "For John Berryman," Robert Lowell, *Day by Day,* p. 27.

p. 265: "Is it wrong": JS to John Berryman, May 17, 1948, John Berryman Papers, University of Minnesota Libraries, Minneapolis.

p. 265: "analysands all": "The Lightning," John Berryman, in *The Dispossessed* (New York: William Sloane Associates, 1948).

p. 265: "There's a strange fact" to "book of the age": Robert Lowell to Theodore Roethke, July 10, 1963, quoted in Hamilton, *Robert Lowell,* p. 337.

p. 266: "It is not news": JS to Paul and Dorothy Thompson, Feb. 13, 1947, courtesy of the Thompsons.

pp. 267–269: "is impolite" to "memory by writing of it": JS, "Truth and the Novelist," pp. 187–189.

p. 270: "very hard at work": JS to Peter Taylor, Apr. 26, 1949, Vanderbilt University Library.

p. 270: "I feel that I have": JS to Mary Lee Frichtel, June 10, 1949, JS Collection, U. of Co.

p. 270: "hidden pathological tortures" to "writer you'll be": Dr. Mary Jane Sherfey to JS, n.d., JS Collection, U. of Co.

p. 271: Alfred Kazin: Alfred Kazin interview with author, Oct. 1, 1986.

p. 271: "I so terribly want": JS to Peter Taylor, Dec. 6, 1949, Vanderbilt University Library.

p. 271: "When the whole thing": JS to Oliver Jensen, Jan. 19, 1950, JS Collection, U. of Co.

p. 271: "all of life": JS to Oliver Jensen, n.d., JS Collection, U. of Co.

p. 272: "Mr. and Mrs. Oliver Jensen": JS Collection, U. of Co.

p. 273: "it was fitting": JS, "A Modest Proposal," *Collected Stories,* p. 68.

p. 273: "To be quite frank": JS to Cecile Starr, n.d., courtesy of Cecile Starr.

p. 273: "I think Tommy": JS, "Polite Conversation," *Collected Stories,* p. 131.

p. 274: "fascinating and poetic": Katharine White to JS, Oct. 20, 1948, JS Collection, U. of Co.

p. 275: "From every thought": JS, "A Country Love Story," *Collected Stories,* p. 140.

p. 275: "Sometime, he said": JS, *In the Snowfall* miscellaneous, JS Collection, U. of Co.

p. 275: "Jean Stafford's 'The Nemesis'": Granville Hicks, "Selected Stories—Told with Integrity," *The New York Times Book Review,* July 15, 1951, p. 5.

pp. 275–276: "fat to the point" to "arrogant self-possession": JS, "The Echo and the Nemesis," *Collected Stories,* p. 37.

p. 276: "No doubt remains" to "and so of course also one": Dr. Alfred Cohn to JS, Dec. 17, 1950, JS Collection, U. of Co.

p. 276: " 'I am exceptionally ill' " to "Most people do": JS, "The Echo and the Nemesis," *Collected Stories,* p. 52.

p. 276: "Are you afraid": Ibid., p. 53.

p. 276: "with her hands locked": Ibid., p. 145.

p. 277: "As you described": Katharine White to JS, Aug. 4, 1951, JS Collection, U. of Co.

p. 277: "empty ecstasy": JS, *Collected Stories,* p. 105.

p. 277: "a horrible fear": James, *The Varieties of Religious Experience,* p. 135.

p. 277: "In that hideous grin": JS, "Life Is No Abyss," *Collected Stories,* p. 105.

p. 277: "who can't take anything" to "state of grace": Ibid., p. 112.

p. 277: "The fact is": Ibid., p. 418.

p. 278: "I, who never act": Ibid., p. 420.

p. 278: "penetrate at last" to "something to eat": Ibid., p. 422.

p. 279: "I think maybe": JS to Oliver Jensen, Aug. 15, 1951, JS Collection, U. of Co.

p. 279: "I don't want to go": JS to Mary Lee Frichtel, Sept. 23, 1951, JS Collection, U. of Co.

p. 279: "the three big topics": Oliver Jensen letter to author, May 12, 1991.

p. 280: "I feel a desperate fatigue": JS to Oliver Jensen, July 29, 1952, JS Collection, U. of Co.

p. 280: "I cannot give you": JS to Oliver Jensen, Aug. 9, 1951, JS Collection, U. of Co.

p. 280: Her reluctance: Alex and Marie Warner interview with author, Dec. 17, 1986.

p. 280: "concluded at last": JS, "An Etiquette for Writers," p. 2.

p. 281: "the private-made-public life": Ibid., p. 7.

p. 281: "In recent years": Ibid., p. 8.

p. 282: "Writing is a private": Ibid.

p. 283: "I am all": JS to Oliver Jensen, Aug. 9, 1952, JS Collection, U. of Co.

p. 283: "Her pessimism": Oliver Jensen to Mary Lee Frichtel, Nov. 18, 1952, JS Collection, U. of Co.

p. 284: "I will soon be": JS to Robert Lowell, n.d., Houghton Library, Harvard University.

p. 284: "All I ask": JS to Mary Lee Frichtel, Sept. 23, 1952, JS Collection, U. of Co.

p. 284: "Please do not read": JS to Caroline Gordon, n.d., Princeton University Library.

p. 284: "I only refurbished": JS to Oliver Jensen, Mar. 1954, JS Collection, U. of Co.

p. 284: "I don't know what": JS to Robert Lowell, n.d., Houghton Library, Harvard University.

p. 285: "It deals with people" to "kindly and uninhibited": JS, "Truth and the Novelist," p. 189.

p. 286: "was looking right" to "everything written there": JS, *The Catherine Wheel* (New York: Ecco Press, 1981), p. 150.

p. 286: "fuse the two manners" to "leisurely ... embroidered": JS interview with Harvey Breit, "Talk with Jean Stafford," p. 18.

p. 286: "He waited": JS, *The Catherine Wheel,* pp. 15–16.

p. 287: "Once Andrew had": Ibid., p. 27.

p. 287: "These fine long faces": Ibid., pp. 66–67.

p. 288: "in her rarefied world": Ibid., p. 43.

p. 288: "It struck her": Ibid., p. 84.

p. 289: "Man's life is": Ibid., epigraph.

p. 289: it even made it: Roberts, *Jean Stafford,* p. 370.

p. 289: "At other times": "'Parsifal' in Modern Dress," *The New Yorker* 27, (Jan. 12, 1952), p. 78.

p. 289: "Miss Stafford's prose": Irving Howe, "Sensibility Troubles," *Kenyon Review* 14 (Spring 1952), p. 348.

p. 289: "You need to get": JS interview with Harvey Breit, "Talk with Jean Stafford," p. 18.

p. 290: "gifts for language" to "all the paraphernalia": Peter Taylor, jacket blurb, *The Catherine Wheel.*

p. 290: Lowell was struggling: Axelrod, *Robert Lowell: Life and Art,* p. 81.

p. 290: At the end of her life: Robert Giroux, "Hard Years and 'Scary Days,'" p. 29.

p. 291: "I'm very happy": JS to Peter Taylor, Apr. 19, 1954, Vanderbilt University Library.

p. 291: "I see almost no one": JS to Blair and Holly Clark, n.d., courtesy of Blair Clark.

p. 291: "spinsterish, rural life": JS to Paul and Dorothy Thompson, Jan. 13, 1954, courtesy of the Thompsons.

p. 292: "The depression has": Apr. 8, 1953, JS diary, JS Collection, U. of Co.

p. 292: "writing like crazy": JS to Blair and Holly Clark, n.d., courtesy of Blair Clark.

p. 292: "an example of emotion": Mary Louise Aswell, ed., *New Short Novels* (New York: Ballantine Books, 1954), introduction.

p. 293: "I am at peace": JS, "A Winter's Tale," in *New Short Novels,* ed. Mary Louise Aswell, p. 226.

p. 293: "an ascetic Boston Irishman": Ibid., p. 230.

p. 293: "It was not love": Ibid., p. 262.

p. 293: "a lack of talent": Ibid., pp. 259–260.

p. 294: "I haven't any politics" to "best of all": Ibid., pp. 272–273.

p. 294: "There had always been": Ibid., pp. 275–276.

p. 294: "I am exalted": Ibid., p. 276.

p. 295: dispute with Harcourt, Brace: Roberts, *Jean Stafford,* p. 314.

p. 295: "It's mainly indolence": JS to Albert Erskine, n.d., Random House Papers, Rare Book and Manuscript Library, Columbia University.

p. 295: "I'll tell you": Alden Whitman, "Jean Stafford and Her Secretary 'Harvey' Reigning in Hamptons," *The New York Times,* Aug. 26, 1973, p. 104.

p. 296: "I do hope": Katharine White to JS, July 14, 1955, JS Collection, U. of Co.

p. 296: "absolutely on top": JS to Paul and Dorothy Thompson, Dec. 1954, courtesy of the Thompsons.

p. 296: "I'm still no better": JS to Paul and Dorothy Thompson, Jan. 13, 1954, courtesy of the Thompsons.

p. 297: "I have never had": JS to Blair and Holly Clark, n.d., courtesy of Blair Clark.

p. 297: "I dreamed that": JS hospital diary, July 28, 1947, JS Collection, U. of Co.

p. 297: "Jean, why the Sam Hill": John Stafford to JS, Feb. 1, 1955, JS Collection, U. of Co.

p. 297: "But each knew": JS, "Fame Is Sweet to the Foolish Man," childhood MS, JS Collection, U. of Co.

p. 298: "to try to pleasantly remind": Mark Twain, *The Adventures of Tom Sawyer*, ed. Paul Baender (Berkeley and Los Angeles: University of California Press, 1982), preface.

p. 299: "people you thought": Robert E. Kroll, ed., *Weldon Kees and the Midcentury Generation: Letters, 1935–1955* (Lincoln: University of Nebraska Press, 1986), p. 107.

p. 299: "I do not think": JS, "The Healthiest Girl in Town," *Collected Stories*, p. 207.

p. 300: "awful tongue": JS, "Bad Characters," *Collected Stories*, p. 263.

p. 300: "Emily Vanderpool": JS, *Bad Characters* (New York: Farrar, Straus and Cudahy, 1964), pp. vii–viii.

p. 300: "possessed with a passion": JS, "Bad Characters," *Collected Stories*, p. 263.

p. 300: "Tom was like": Twain, *Adventures of Tom Sawyer*, p. 48.

p. 300: "Yes, sir, Emily": JS, "A Reading Problem," *Collected Stories*, p. 343.

p. 301: "I had never heard": JS, "Bad Characters," *Collected Stories*, p. 268.

p. 302: "She felt that she was": JS, "Cops and Robbers, *Collected Stories*, p. 431.

p. 302: "life was essentially": JS, "In the Zoo," *Collected Stories*, p. 286.

p. 302: "How lonely I have been": JS, "The Liberation," *Collected Stories*, p. 322.

p. 303: "bamboozled into muteness": JS, "Maggie Meriwether's Rich Experience," *Collected Stories*, p. 5.

p. 303: "the most sophisticated": Ibid., p. 17.

p. 304: "They were far too young": JS, "Caveat Emptor," *Collected Stories*, p. 79.

p. 305: "When Beatrice": JS, "Beatrice Trueblood's Story," *Collected Stories*, p. 385.

p. 305: "whole menagerie": Ibid., p. 390.

p. 305: "humiliating, disrobing displays": Ibid., p. 401.

p. 305: "She had not bargained": Ibid.

p. 305: "My God": Ibid., p. 403.

p. 305: "I have had two": JS to Ann Honeycutt, n.d., JS Collection, U. of Co.

p. 306: "If one can accept": JS to Nancy Flagg Gibney, quoted in Nancy Flagg, "People to Stay," *Shenandoah* 30, no. 3 (1979), p. 75.

p. 306: *Writer's Newsletter:* Jessyca Russell, quoted in James Oliver Brown to JS, Apr. 18, 1956, James Oliver Brown Papers, Butler Library, Columbia University.

p. 306: "is done in such an interesting style": Katharine White to JS, Oct. 13, 1955, JS Collection, U. of Co.

p. 307: "one of the most beautiful women": JS, "The End of a Career," *Collected Stories*, p. 447.

p. 307: "Perhaps, like an artist": Ibid., p. 451.

p. 307: "There is an aesthetic": Ibid., p. 456.

p. 307: "If [my gift]": JS to Mary Lee Frichtel, June 10, 1949, JS Collection, U. of Co.

p. 308: "If any little detail": Peter Taylor to JS, Dec. 24, 1954, JS Collection, U. of Co.

p. 308: To Nancy Flagg Gibney she admitted: JS to Nancy Flagg Gibney, n.d., courtesy of Eleanor Gibney and Charlotte Margolis Goodman.

p. 308: "I thought the story": JS to Peter Taylor, Mar. 16, 1955, Vanderbilt University Library.

p. 308: "I'm quite sure": JS to Paul and Dorothy Thompson, Feb. 22, 1956, courtesy of the Thompsons.

CHAPTER 12: *Isle of Arran and Samothrace*

p. 309: "Your last letter" to "to please you": Katharine White to JS, July 26, 1956, JS Collection, U. of Co.

p. 309: Despite her health: Goodman, *Jean Stafford: The Savage Heart,* p. 252; and JS letters to Ann Honeycutt, JS Collection, U. of Co.

p. 310: "I have eaten nothing": JS to Ann Honeycutt, June 25, 1956, JS Collection, U. of Co.

p. 310: "After the age": JS to Joan Stillman, June 15, 1956, quoted in Roberts, *Jean Stafford,* p. 318.

p. 311: "is so much": JS to Ann Honeycutt, July 16, 1956, JS Collection, U. of Co.

p. 311: "I have looked on myself": JS to Nancy Flagg Gibney, Sept. 12, 1955, courtesy of Eleanor Gibney and Charlotte Margolis Goodman.

p. 312: "As to the word waif": A. J. Liebling to JS, July 16, 1957, Dept. of Rare Books, Olin Library, Cornell University.

p. 312: "the abrupt lunge": Raymond Sokolov, *Wayward Reporter: The Life of A. J. Liebling* (New York: Harper & Row, 1980), p. 286.

p. 313: "I've been having": JS to James Oliver Brown, Aug. 1956, James Oliver Brown Papers, Rare Book and Manuscript Library, Columbia University.

p. 313: "I seem to have held": A. J. Liebling to JS, Oct. 16, 1956, Dept. of Rare Books, Olin Library, Cornell University.

p. 313: "All through the last 100 pages": A. J. Liebling to JS, Nov. 18, 1956, Dept. of Rare Books, Olin Library, Cornell University.

p. 313: "I began to write": A. J. Liebling to JS, Feb. 10, 1957, Dept. of Rare Books, Olin Library, Cornell University.

p. 314: "Liebling and his set": Wilfrid Sheed, "Miss Jean Stafford," pp. 94–95.

p. 314: "I want you to write": A. J. Liebling to JS, Dec. 13, 1956, Dept. of Rare Books, Olin Library, Cornell University.

p. 315: "The bookstore in the hotel": A. J. Liebling to JS, Feb. 23, 1957, Dept. of Rare Books, Olin Library, Cornell University.

p. 315: "forward to the night": Robert Lowell, *Life Studies and For the Union Dead,* p. 19.

p. 316: "On the joint Mason-Myers bookplate": Ibid., p. 12.

p. 316: "Well, I stand off": Robert Lowell to Peter Taylor, Apr. 11, 1955, quoted in Hamilton, *Robert Lowell,* p. 221.

p. 316: So did Liebling: Sokolov, *Wayward Reporter,* pp. 292–293.

p. 316: "I was moving": JS to Nancy Flagg Gibney, Feb. 1957, courtesy of Eleanor Gibney and Charlotte Margolis Goodman.

p. 317: The project": Sokolov, *Wayward Reporter,* p. 296.

p. 317: "The book's the thing": A. J. Liebling to JS, Spring 1957, Dept. of Rare Books, Olin Library, Cornell University.

p. 317: "It may be all": A. J. Liebling to JS, Mar. 29, 1957, Dept. of Rare Books, Olin Library, Cornell University.

p. 317: "I don't understand": A. J. Liebling to JS, Spring 1957, Dept. of Rare Books, Olin Library, Cornell University.

p. 317: "The New Yorker married us": A. J. Liebling to JS, Aug. 1, 1957, Dept. of Rare Books, Olin Library, Cornell University.

p. 318: "kept getting too busy": Sokolov, *Wayward Reporter,* p. 290.

p. 319: "During our marriage": Ibid., p. 299.

p. 320: She told Blair Clark: Blair Clark interview with author, Jan. 13, 1987.

p. 321: "You will have read": JS to Peter Taylor, Feb. 3, 1958, Vanderbilt University Library.

p. 322: "On a winter night": JS notes, Samothrace folder, JS Collection, U. of Co.

p. 322: "My dreams are" to "work of non-fiction": Ibid.

p. 323: "plain, thrifty": Ibid.

p. 323: "Why shouldn't the island" to "was my husband": Ibid.

p. 323: "As an old student": Karl Lehmann to JS, Samothrace folder, JS Collection, U. of Co.

p. 324: "felt now that I": JS notes, Samothrace folder, JS Collection, U. of Co.

p. 324: "I was at the castle gates" to "I had never heard": Ibid.

p. 324: "The trip was": JS to James Oliver Brown, Sept. 22, 1959, James Oliver Brown Papers, Rare Book and Manuscript Library, Columbia University.

p. 325: "My weekend in the bosom": JS to Nancy Flagg Gibney, n.d., courtesy of Eleanor Gibney and Charlotte Margolis Goodman.

p. 325: "Really, when I come back": JS to James Oliver Brown, James Oliver Brown Papers, Rare Book and Manuscript Library, Columbia University.

p. 325: called the *Griffin:* Roberts, *Jean Stafford,* p. 339.

p. 325: "It's been so long": JS to Peter Taylor, May 2, 1961, Vanderbilt University Library.

p. 326: "for a number of reasons": JS to Albert Erskine, May 31, 1962, Random House Papers, Rare Book and Manuscript Library, Columbia University.

p. 326: Later that spring: Roberts, *Jean Stafford,* p. 344.

p. 326: "Robert [Giroux] is": James Oliver Brown to JS, June 27, 1962, James Oliver Brown Papers, Rare Book and Manuscript Library, Columbia University.

p. 327: "from the spectacle": JS, "The Tea Time of Stouthearted Ladies," *Collected Stories,* p. 227.

p. 327: "For the first time": Sokolov, *Wayward Reporter,* p. 319.

p. 327: "I can show you": A. J. Liebling to JS, May 25, 1963, Dept. of Rare Books, Olin Library, Cornell University.

p. 328: He had in mind a "Wayward Press" column: Sokolov, *Wayward Reporter,* p. 319.

p. 328: "Jean, I am now": John Stafford to JS, Dec. 26, 1963, JS Collection, U. of Co.

p. 328: "Please forgive me": John Stafford to JS, n.d. JS Collection, U. of Co.

p. 329: "You and I might as well": JS to Ann Honeycutt, n.d., JS Collection, U. of Co.

p. 329: JS's symptoms: Dr. Thomas Roberts's files; and Dr. Thomas Roberts to JS, June 1, 1964, courtesy of Dr. Thomas Roberts.

p. 330: "I'm so very glad": James Oliver Brown to JS, Jan. 7, 1964, James Oliver Brown Papers, Rare Book and Manuscript Library, Columbia University.

p. 330: "like a bear": JS to James Robert Hightower, Dec. 14, 1964, JS Collection, U. of Co.

p. 330: "It was interesting": Ibid.

p. 330: "we learn": Robert Lowell, "Jean Stafford, a Letter," in *Day by Day,* p. 29.

p. 331: "In the spring": JS, *Parliament of Women* MS, JS Collection, U. of Co.

p. 331: "My disappointment" to "distressful secret": Ibid.

p. 332: "I tried to recite": Ibid.

p. 333: "I was a sick": JS, *State of Grace* MS, JS Collection, U. of Co.

p. 333: "Within such cul de sacs": Ibid.

p. 334: "This is not bilocation": Ibid.

p. 335: "I wish" to "unfathomable mystery": JS to Mary Lee Frichtel, Aug. 1964, JS Collection, U. of Co.

pp. 335–336: "There's no possible way" to "cherish that": JS to Robert Lowell, May 6, 1964, Houghton Library, Harvard University.

p. 336: "Cal is at work": JS to Peter Taylor, May 26, 1964, Vanderbilt University Library.

p. 336: "All is well": JS to Peter Taylor, July 6, 1964, Vanderbilt University Library.

CHAPTER 13: *Long Island*

p. 337: "I'm well and restless": JS to Robert Lowell, n.d., Houghton Library, Harvard University.

p. 337: "I should be forced": JS to Mary Lee Frichtel, n.d., JS Collection, U. of Co.

p. 338: "not a word": JS to Nancy Flagg Gibney, Aug. 1, 1965, courtesy of Eleanor Gibney and Charlotte Margolis Goodman.

p. 338: "There's something inimical": Helen Dudar, "The Subject Would Not Sit Still," *New York Post,* Mar. 27, 1966, p. 27.

p. 338: "for a magazine": JS to Allen Tate, n.d., Princeton University Library.

p. 339: "Jean Stafford is surely": Gene Baro, "Breaking Out of Isolation," *The New York Times Book Review,* Oct. 11, 1964, p. 4.

p. 340: "While autobiography": JS, "Truth in Fiction," *Library Journal* 91 (Oct. 1, 1966), p. 4560.

p. 340: "Let me change": Ibid., p. 4564.

p. 340: "What I wanted": Ibid.

p. 340: "It seemed to me": Ibid., p. 4565.

p. 341: "I was tired and headachy": JS, *A Mother in History* (New York: Farrar, Straus & Giroux, 1966), p. 30.

p. 341: "I'll write a book": Ibid., p. 12.

p. 341: "Now maybe Lee Harvey Oswald": Ibid.

p. 342: "Perhaps Miss Stafford": Martha Gelhorn, "American Mom," *Books and Bookmen* 12 (Oct. 1966), p. 59.

p. 342: "I had come to Texas": JS, *A Mother in History,* pp. 4–5.

p. 343: "in a winter mope" to "to live this completely alone": JS to Peter Taylor, Jan. 20, 1966, Vanderbilt University Library.

p. 345: "I wear pants": Whitman, "Jean Stafford and Her Secretary 'Harvey' Reigning in the Hamptons," p. 78.

p. 345: "a Westerner" to "keep my company": JS, "East Hampton from the Catbird Seat," *The New York Times,* Dec. 26, 1971, p. 1.

p. 345: "I can be a grasshopper": Ibid., p. 13.

pp. 345–346: "I'm a compulsive housekeeper" to "staring-into-space depressions": Fern Marja Eckman, "Adding a Pulitzer to the Collection," *New York Post,* May 9, 1970.

p. 346: "I give presents": JS, "East Hampton from the Catbird Seat," p. 13.

p. 346: "the cultivation" to "thinness": Henry James, *The Portrait of a Lady* (New York: Penguin Books, 1963), p. xvii.

pp. 346–347: "I know enough" to "in her garments": Ibid., p. 93.

p. 347: "sufficiently outré": JS to Peter Taylor, June 8, 1974, Vanderbilt University Library.

pp. 347–348: "would undergo" to "saints on high": Ann Honeycutt to Henrietta Stackpole, in James Oliver Brown Papers, Rare Book and Manuscript Library, Columbia University.

p. 348: "this so-called 20th Century": Wilfrid Sheed, "Miss Jean Stafford," p. 94.

p. 348: "Things grow grimmer": JS to James Oliver Brown, Jan. 1967, James Oliver Brown Papers, Rare Book and Manuscript Library, Columbia University.

p. 348: "There is a markedly passive" to "severity of her depression": Dr. Jacques M. Quen to Dr. Thomas Roberts, Mar. 8, 1967, Dr. Thomas Roberts's files, courtesy of Dr. Thomas Roberts.

p. 348: "intense, beautiful": "The Second Chance," *Time* 89, no. 22 (June 2, 1967), p. 72.

p. 349: "I was, to tell the truth": JS to Peter Taylor, n.d., Vanderbilt University Library.

p. 349: "It has been a most": JS to James Oliver Brown, Sept. 7, 1967, James Oliver Brown Papers, Rare Book and Manuscript Library, Columbia University.

p. 349: "I am so rustic": JS to Nancy Flagg Gibney, Jan. 3, 1967, courtesy of Eleanor Gibney and Charlotte Margolis Goodman.

p. 349: Edward Dahlberg, who, though not: *The Edward Dahlberg Reader,* ed. Paul Carroll (New York: New Directions, 1967).

p. 350: "I have nothing": JS, "Intimations of Hope," *McCall's* 99 (Dec. 1971), p. 118.

p. 350: "I am out of my element": JS to Peter Taylor, n.d., Vanderbilt University Library.

p. 351: "It is not entirely" to "within a form": JS, "Love Among the Rattlesnakes," *McCall's* 97 (Mar. 1970), pp. 145–146.

pp. 351–352: "The direct appeal": JS to Peter Taylor, n.d., Vanderbilt University Library.

p. 352: "Peter Taylor and I": JS to Frank McShane, Aug. 4, 1968, courtesy of Frank McShane.

p. 353: "I have it in": JS to *East Hampton Star,* Aug. 9, 1968.

p. 353: "public persona achieved": Hamilton, *Robert Lowell,* p. 374.

p. 353: "It is a little hard" to "mythology of the Wuberts": JS to Peter Taylor, Apr. 24, 1968, Vanderbilt University Library.

p. 354: "I doubt that I will": JS, "Why I Don't Get Around Much Anymore," *Esquire* 83 (Mar. 1975), p. 132.

p. 354: "compulsively I accept" to "made me undemocratic": Ibid., p. 134.

p. 354: Cora Savage: Charlotte M. Goodman suggests that in naming her protagonist, perhaps Stafford was recalling Miss Savage from the West in Richard Eberhart's verse play, *The Mad Musician,* about Robert Lowell. She also points out that Lowell linked a character in *The Mills of the Kavanaughs* to Persephone or Core, who is abducted to Hades by Pluto. See p. 295 of *Jean Stafford: The Savage Heart.* Stafford's own work on her Samothrace MS suggests her interest in Core.

p. 355: "Once Cora lost control": JS, "The Philosophy Lesson," *Collected Stories,* pp. 364–365.

p. 355: "A darkness beat her": Ibid., p. 369.

p. 355: "her first": "The Year of the Novel," *Time,* 93, no. 1 (Jan. 3, 1969), p. 66.

p. 355: "Everything that we desire": *The New York Times,* Feb. 14, 1969, p. 56.

p. 356: "an event in our literature": Guy Davenport, *The New York Times Book Review,* Feb. 16, 1969, p. 1.

p. 356: "And if Jean Stafford's": *The New York Times,* May 6, 1970, p. 42.

p. 356: "I find it awfully heartening": Al Cohn, "For Fiction: A Gentle Woman," *Newsday,* May 5, 1970.

p. 356: "For a few days": JS to Mary Lee Frichtel, May 12, 1970, JS Collection, U. of Co.

p. 356: "I'm now getting": JS to Allen Tate, Mar. 18, 1970, Princeton University Library.

p. 356: "None of them": JS, "On Writing," unpublished MS, JS Collection, U. of Co., quoted in Roberts, *Jean Stafford,* p. 372.

p. 356: "I could wish": JS, " the good life is indeed now," *McCall's* 97 (Jan. 1970), p. 30.

p. 357: "For the next two weeks": JS, Barnard Lectures, 1971, unpublished MS, JS Collection, U. of Co.

p. 358: "man embattled" to "in a handbasket": Ibid.

p. 358: "The lectures almost seemed" to "such a pastoral life": Linda Stern, "Jean Stafford on Writing, Language, Women's Lib . . . ," *Barnard Bulletin,* Mar. 10, 1971, p. 7.

p. 358: "I look back upon": JS, Barnard Lectures, "Sense and Sensibility," JS Collection, U. of Co.

p. 358: "all for equal opportunity" to "bad public performance": Stern, "Jean Stafford on Writing, Language, Women's Lib . . . ," *Barnard Bulletin,* Mar. 10, 1971, p. 7.

p. 359: "not opposed by any means": Ibid.

p. 359: "Who will carry on" to "sweetening the pot": JS, "Plight of the American Language," *Saturday Review World* 1 (Dec. 4, 1973), p. 18.

p. 359: "Besides the neologisms": Ibid., p. 14.

p. 360: "I came here in fear": JS, Barnard Lectures, "The Snows of Yesteryear," 1971 unpublished MS, JS Collection, U. of Co.

p. 360: "share-croppers" to "by the next day": Sheed, "Miss Jean Stafford," p. 95.

p. 360: "She was cruelly funny": Ibid., p. 99.

p. 361: "Once again back": JS to Mary Lee Frichtel, June 14, 1971, JS Collection, U. of Co.

p. 361: "real or imagined need of money": Peter Taylor, "A Commemorative Tribute to Jean Stafford," p. 58.

p. 361: "the fustian and the hollering": JS, "Women as Chattels, Men as Chumps," *The New York Times,* May 9, 1970, p. 24.

p. 362: "She wrote numbers": Taylor, "A Commemorative Tribute," p. 58.

p. 362: "The man revealed": JS, "Wolfe Hunting," *The New York Review of Books* 19 (May 9, 1968), p. 20.

p. 362: "He's not above": JS, "Spirits," *The New York Review of Books* 12 (Apr. 24, 1969), p. 28.

p. 363: "Such whims": JS, "Lioness," *The New York Review of Books* 10, (Jan. 18, 1968), p. 22.

p. 363: "Cherish but do not pamper": JS, "Don't Send Me Gladiolus," *Vogue* 161 (Mar. 1973), p. 146.

p. 364: "the Fenwick caper": JS to Nancy Flagg Gibney, May 21, 1975, courtesy of Eleanor Gibney and Charlotte Margolis Goodman.

p. 364: "Christmas has come": JS, "Katharine Graham," *Vogue* 162 (Dec. 1973), p. 221.

p. 365: "the venting of spleen": JS, "Somebody Out There Hates Me," *Esquire* 82 (Aug. 1974), p. 156.

p. 365: "I find that on April 28th": JS to Con Ed, July 20, 1978, courtesy of Joseph Mitchell.

p. 365: "Digression is integral": JS to Shana Alexander, Mar. 1, 1970, James Oliver Brown Papers, Rare Book and Manuscript Library, Columbia University.

p. 366: "I knew they would": JS to James Oliver Brown, Mar. 28, 1972, James Oliver Brown Papers, Rare Book and Manuscript Library, Columbia University.

p. 366: "Writers of books": JS, "Christmas Books for Children," *The New Yorker* 46 (Dec. 5, 1970), p. 200.

p. 367: "Come if you like": JS to Mary Lee Frichtel, May 1, 1972, JS Collection, U. of Co.

p. 368: "I am so unproductive": JS to James Oliver Brown, Jan. 16, 1975, James Oliver Brown Papers, Rare Book and Manuscript Library, Columbia University.

p. 368: "Do you loathe me": JS to Robert Lowell, Sept. 23, Harry Ransom Humanities Research Center, University of Texas, Austin.

p. 368: "One of the principal": JS to Robert Lowell, Oct. 21, Harry Ransom Humanities Research Center, University of Texas, Austin.

p. 369: "Old though she is": JS memo to Dr. Thomas Roberts, n.d., JS Collection, U. of Co.

p. 370: "All of this valetudinarianism" to "I was born": JS to James Robert Hightower, n.d., JS Collection, U. of Co.

p. 370: "peevishness, . . . irascibility": JS to Louis Auchincloss, Mar. 18, 1975, JS Collection, U. of Co.

p. 371: "Since my speech": JS to Mary Lee Frichtel, May 9, 1977, JS Collection, U. of Co.

p. 371: "The last time": Flagg, "People to Stay," p. 76.

p. 372: "This is the last review": JS, "Mrs. Hemingway Remembers," *Esquire* 86 (Oct. 1976), p. 30.

p. 372: "passive hostility" to "linguistic grasp": May 1977 report to Dr. Thomas Roberts from the County of Suffolk Department of Health Services, Sonia Keahon, speech pathologist, Dr. Thomas Roberts's files.

p. 372: "1940. Remember Chimes Street": Robert Lowell to JS, postmarked Sept. 6, 1976, JS Collection, U. of Co.

p. 373: "I think the ambition": Robert Lowell to Frank Bidart, Sept. 4, 1976, quoted in John Thompson, "Robert Lowell: 1917–1977," *The New York Review of Books* 24 (Oct. 27, 1977), p. 14.

p. 373: "Everything's changed": "The Old Flame," Robert Lowell, in *Life Studies and For the Union Dead,* p. 6.

p. 374: "Men may be superior": Robert Lowell, quoted in Grace Schulman, "Robert Lowell at the 92nd St. Y," record notes for *Robert Lowell: A Reading,* Caedmon Records, 92nd St. Y Poetry Center Archives, New York.

p. 374: "outlines for novels": Robert Lowell, "Jean Stafford, a Letter," *Day by Day,* p. 29.

p. 374: "Tortoise and hare": Ibid.

p. 374: Joseph Mitchell, who had come : Joseph Mitchell interview with author, Jan. 30, 1987.

p. 374: "I who have least reason": JS notes on telephone conversation with Robert Lowell, Jan. 1971, courtesy of Blair Clark.

p. 376: In a reminiscence: Dorothea Straus, "Jean Stafford," *Shenandoah* 30, no. 3 (1979), pp. 85–91.

p. 376: During those same last weeks: Joseph Mitchell interview with author, Jan. 30, 1987.

p. 376: "He saw nothing" to "why I married him": JS notes on *The Mills of the Kavanaughs,* courtesy of Joseph Mitchell.

p. 377: " . . . Here bubbles filled": Robert Lowell, "The Mills of the Kavanaughs," *Lord Weary's Castle and The Mills of the Kavanaughs,* p. 85.

p. 378: "For the time being": JS, *Boston Adventure,* p. 525.

Index

A NOTE ON THE TYPE

*This book was set in Granjon, a type named in compliment
to Robert Granjon, a type cutter and printer active in
Antwerp, Lyons, Rome, and Paris from 1523 to 1590.
Granjon, the boldest and most original designer of his time,
was one of the first to practice the trade of type founder apart
from that of printer. Granjon was designed by George W.
Jones, who based his drawings on a face used by Claude
Garamond (c. 1480–1561) in his beautiful French books.
Granjon more closely resembles Garamond's own type than
do the various modern faces that bear Garamond's name.*

*Composed by Graphic Composition, Inc., Athens, Georgia
Printed and bound by The Courier Companies, Inc.,
Westford, Massachusetts
Designed by Peter A. Andersen*